Convention, Translation, and Understanding

SUNY Series in Logic and Language
John T. Kearns, Editor

Convention, Translation, and Understanding
Philosophical Problems in the Comparative Study of Culture

Robert Feleppa

State University of New York Press

Published by
State University of New York Press, Albany

© 1988 State University of New York

Printed in the United States of America

For information, address State University of New York
Press, State University Plaza, Albany, N.Y., 12246

Library of Congress Cataloging in Publication Data

Feleppa, Robert, 1946–
    Convention, translation, and understanding.

    (SUNY series in logic and language)
    Bibliography: p.
    Includes index.
    1. Ethnology—Philosophy. 2. Ethnology—Methodology.
3. Culture—Semiotic models. 4. Quine, W. V. (Willard
Van Orman) 5. Semantics—Philosophy.   6. Intercultural
communication. I. Title. II. Series.
GN345.F   1988   306.4   87-12176
ISBN 0-88706-673-9
ISBN 0-88706-674-7 (pbk.)

10 9 8 7 6 5 4 3 2 1

To the Memory of Richard Rudner

Contents

Acknowledgments

I would like to thank Anthony C. Genova, Roger F. Gibson, and especially Deborah H. Soles for helpful comments and criticisms on various sections of manuscript drafts. I am also indebted to David Dean and Karen Lucas for their assistance in preparing the manuscript. Work on the manuscript was partly supported by research and sabbatical grants from The Wichita State University.

Chapter 1

Meaning and Understanding

Meaning, Metaphysics and Translation

The mark of a sensible utterance or inscription is said to be its possession of a meaning, and understanding such expressions is said to involve the grasping or apprehending of their meanings. On some accounts meanings are viewed as abstract, platonic objects, on others as concrete mental, behavioral, or neurophysiological items. In the latter case, the mind makes contact with meanings in much the way that it apprehends physical objects and the like. In the former case, the mind, in grasping meanings of expressions, grasps universals that exist in a realm, or on a level, distinct from that of the concrete particulars of experience and that cannot be apprehended through normal sense experience. (Thus, notes Morton White, "a deal is struck" between the metaphysician in search of extraexperiential contact with universals and the epistemologist in search of something extralinguistic to grasp in understanding symbolic expressions.[1]) On either account, meanings serve the more modest task of explaining certain equivalence relations presumed to hold among the expressions of one or more languages: Expressions are thus equivalent, or synonymous, in virtue of possessing a shared meaning. As successful communication involves the *transmission* of these meanings from speaker to hearer, interlinguistic translation becomes a matter of matching the meanings of expressions in the source (translated) and receptor (translation) languages; that is, it becomes a matter of insuring that a translation manual will transmit the correct meanings to its users.

Thus, to account for successful communication, a separate realm from that of the intersubjectively perceivable universe may come to be posited and filled with objects of a special sort. Yet even in the platonic type of theory, whose realm of significance is distinct both from the physical and the privately mental, its universals are not independent of the realm of sense experience: For recognition of universals is considered impossible without sense experience; and, more importantly, sense experience is incoherent without mediation by universals. What one makes of the world critically depends on the conceptual scheme one brings to bear on it. This holds equally well for those views that construe conceptual schemes as comprised of private mental structures (a 'concept' may be construed as either a platonic or a concretely psychological entity).[2] If world-view is so dependent on conceptual scheme, then adequate translation is a *sine qua non* not only for the understanding of meanings of expressions but also for understanding how speakers of some source language experience and conceptualize the "objective" world around them. Their responses to particular features of most, or perhaps all, incoming stimuli, and not to other features, are largely channeled by linguistic and broader cultural conditioning.

So long as communication and translation occur within or among social groups that are closely related historically and culturally, there may seem little reason to shake our faith in a shared likeness of sensory, mental, or extrasensory universes. However, the gradually increasing contact of anthropologists with radically different cultures during the nineteenth and twentieth centuries gave birth to a number of deep and perplexing problems concerning criteria of adequacy of translation, again where adequacy is viewed as demanding a matching of meanings or concepts interculturally. It became increasingly clear that the categories that were satisfactory for systematically accounting for the significance of languages and other symbolic phenomena in the Indo-European community were poorly suited to the translation and understanding of radically foreign cultures and that the conceptual resources of the ethnographer needed qualitative enrichment in order to meet these new tasks.[3] However, the fact that experience itself is alleged to be filtered by one's socially conditioned set of universals raised serious methodological problems. How could one's observations be sufficiently objective to determine what a radically different scheme might be like? If the linguist's only means of access to a native language is, at least initially, through associating observed subject verbal behavior with associated nonverbal stimulation, and if the linguist's own selectivity of salient stimulation reflects cultural conditioning, then there seems to be little, if anything, the linguist can presume, without begging crucial questions, to share with the subject. And if one shares the grasp of a common attribute only if one applies a *receptor* expression that is applied to experience discriminated in the same way as that to which the putatively synonymous *source* expression applies, how can radically foreign universals or concepts ever be determined? Coming to share a conceptual scheme seems to depend critically on successful translation, which latter depends on having similar perceptions of the world. Yet having such similar perceptions depends on sharing a conceptual scheme (a condition characterized by Dilthey and others as the "hermeneutic circle"). These difficulties, as many anthropologists realized, made it all too easy for an ethnographer to "impose" familiar, western grammatical and ontological categories upon subjects, rather than determining theirs.

Many anthropologists have used these problems to call for a variety of emendations in anthropological methodology, so as to ensure the eventual capturing of meaning in translation and ethnography. However, W. V. Quine, in investigations in the philosophy of language with pivotal relevance to these anthropological problems, sees these very same problems as indications of further difficulties for the already infirm notions of meaning involved. Whatever initial plausibility the projection of such abstract or mental realms might seem to have, their hypothesized (or hypostasized) objects fail to fulfill what are minimal and necessary criteria, in Quine's view, for tenable "posits"—namely, clear identification and individuation. Moreover, aside from these (destructive) problems, no one has as yet, constructively, come up with a generally satisfactory account of meaning in all the long history of the problem. What Quine sees in the situations he calls "radical translation" are telling considerations against the very coherence or intelligibility of the notion of natural synonymy, whose accounting constitutes the purpose for positing shared meaning. According to the arguments he presents in *Word and Object* and elsewhere, the fact (recognized generally by anthropologists) that linguists can develop divergent but empirically adequate translation manuals for source languages carries the consequence (*not* generally recognized by anthropologists) that translational hypotheses are not fully legitimate hypotheses, and that it makes no sense to speak of the objective existence of meanings or even of natural synonymy relations holding between source- and receptor-language expressions.[4] Essential to Quine's argument are two more points generally acknowledged by anthropologists: (1) The vast majority of translations depend critically on the imposition of linguistic *categorizations* with which translators and receptor-language speakers are familiar. (2) Translation does not seem possible without the prior assumption that source- and receptor-language speakers share *beliefs*.[5]

Unfortunately, while Quine's radical indeterminacy thesis provides, as is well and indisputably recognized, valuable and deep insights into the nature of meaningfulness and into various problems of semantics and translation, it seems to have completely "devalued" a number of important insights by anthropologists. Among these are such relatively recent classic contributors as Franz Boas, Edward Sapir, and Benjamin Lee Whorf—all of whom worried about the same or very similar problems concerning imposition and all of whom argued that a necessary condition of good ethnography was taking very seriously the source culture's conceptual scheme and world view. Quine's arguments, however, raise these same points in an effort to challenge criteria of objectivity of translation and ethnography that are based on realistic attitudes regarding meaning. However, this seeming consequence has, in turn, devalued certain of Quine's own important insights in the eyes of some anthropologists, linguists, and philosophers. It might appear, although this is not Quine's intent, that there are no such tenable criteria at all.[6]

Whatever the cogency of Quine's arguments, the points in the mentalist position upon which Quine and other philosophers (and similarly critical anthropologists) focus seem to be symptomatic of deep afflictions for some still quite common semantic assumptions. Similarly afflicted are a number of assumptions made in the very characterizations of "culture" that define the fundamental objects of anthropological inquiry. Hence, I believe the anthropological context from which much of Quine's indeterminacy thesis is derived, as well as the constructive contributions of anthropologists, warrants closer examination. There is, I believe, an important and special indeterminacy of translation, as Quine contends, and I believe it results primarily from those factors upon which Quine focuses attention. However, I think the mediating arguments bear reconsideration and reconstruction, both to enhance their plausibility and anthropological relevance and to reveal certain more constructive consequences for cultural anthropology. I view indeterminacy problems as calling for a reconsideration of the character of the translational enterprise and its criteria of success and objectivity. There is, I shall argue, an important difference between the task of an inquirer explaining the significance of symbolic behavior and that of one engaged in noninterpretive explanation. The difference concerns, in part, the *rule*-governed nature of symbolic behavior, as opposed to the merely *law*-governed nature of the phenomena studied, say, by a physicist. In particular, translation itself turns out in my view not to be a matter of hypothesis formation or acceptance (as Quine and most anthropologists hold),[7] but rather the prescriptive task of codifying rules of translation. This distinction hearkens to one central to the views of Ludwig Wittgenstein and Peter Winch, but differs on a number of major points; notably, my position does not entail Winch's view (and similar views expressed by philosophers and social scientists) that the methodological character of social inquiry is fundamentally different from that of the natural sciences.[8]

I shall develop my inquiry as follows: The first three chapters are devoted to setting the anthropological and philosophical contexts of the indeterminacy thesis by an examination of problems of meaning recovery salient in, and shared by, each discipline. (Evidently I shall be concerned with aspects of general linguistic theory as well, but these shall generally be viewed in the context of anthropological application.) In these early chapters, I shall also examine the genesis of the "radical translation" problems in Quine's thought and in that of other twentieth-century philosophers, comparing them to parallel developments in the work of certain "landmark" figures in anthropology and their present-day descendants. My anthropological survey will give particular attention to evident tensions between the importation of anthropological and linguistic constructs to the study of culture on the one hand, and the revelation of cultural specificity and social reality on the other. This central worry in the evolution of anthropological theory lies also at the heart of Quine's critique of translation. I shall also attend to an important and controversial distinction Quine tries to draw between underdetermination of physical theory by evidence and indeterminacy of translation. For it is this distinction that I contend is better seen in terms of a contrast between description and codification. In the fourth chapter, I shall try to overcome some of the difficulties in Quine's formulations by explicating that difference in terms of a contrast between rules and laws, appealing in the process to David K. Lewis' game-theoretic analysis of "convention." I shall conclude by tying this reconstruction to a number of pragmatic trends in recent anthropology and by developing some constructive implications for recent problems in that field.

One of my main concerns in Chapter 5 will be to try to find reasons for supporting various "language and culture" or "Boasian" methodologies without appealing to the metaphysical and semantic theses that I think Quine and others correctly challenge. However, I will do no more by way of "taking sides" on some of the bitterly controversial issues I shall discuss. I certainly will not argue that anthropology *must* be done on a linguistic, or cognitive, or symbolic, or any other particular kind of basis. My attitude is a pragmatic, pluralistic one that encourages any paradigm that delivers, or at least promises, fruitful yield.

Some Approaches to a Theory of Meaning

Many philosophers—not the least Quine himself—have noted the very general significance of Quine's attacks on the determinacy of meaning in translation. Accordingly (and no doubt justifiably), they have taken his use of a widely discussed, extended anthropological example in his *Word and Object* as a convenient device for developing these pervasive philosophical results—a continuing development of Quine's own earlier enunciated positions in philosophy of language—for virtually every major area in philosophy. However, my aim here is to take quite seriously the application of Quine's considerations to anthropology. I want to show both how some of these considerations are adumbrated with surprising fullness by a number of classic and recent anthropologists and also that confining our attention, at least initially, rather narrowly to the immediate anthropological consequences of Quine's arguments allows a substantial gain on recalcitrant problems in that field—this without the initial burden of meeting some stronger and perhaps even more recalcitrant conditions in its widely generalized application.

I shall begin by looking briefly in this chapter at a number of major theories of meaning developed by philosophers and linguists, elements of which have been adopted, and problems of which have thus been inherited, by anthropologists. In the latter part of the chapter, I shall discuss a number of general criticisms made by Quine and others of some of the basic assumptions. It is important to emphasize that my intention in presenting this survey is simply to highlight those aspects of these theories that are particularly relevant in view of their susceptibility to Quine's critique and their influence upon anthropology. I shall also emphasize those problems in connection with these theories that are especially reminiscent of Quine's concerns. Many of these same problems turn out also to have motivated several major theoretical developments in anthropology. In so doing, I shall direct my attention mainly to a number of earlier (perhaps by now "classic") contributions to the theory of meaning that provide the setting for Quine's work. Although I will look at a number of more recently developed theories, I will not mention a number of recent and important approaches developed in semantics, linguistics, and the philosophy of language. The aspects of the earlier theories that Quine attacks are so fundamental that—as I think shall be quite evident—the more recent theories, for all their greater sophistication on various points, are also susceptible.

Theories of meaning may be differentiated according to a variety of criteria.[9] Here I shall distinguish *entificational* from *non-entificational* theories. Entificational theories take the meanings of expressions to be some sort of individuatable entity grasped by the competent user of those expressions. These theories may be further differentiated into those that take meaning entities as either or both (a) *platonic* entities (i.e., abstract, nonspatio-temporally bounded entities) that exist independently of knowers and believers; (b) concrete *psychological* entities, temporally and perhaps spatially bounded, existing in the minds of knowers and believers. Notable among such *ideational* accounts are those that take meanings to be transformational-generative structures or components. Finally, I shall consider non-ideational, entificational approaches that take meanings to be (c) *stimulus and/or response* complexes associated with linguistic expressions through prior conditioning of the user.[10]

Nonentificational theories endeavor to explain synonymy without making any theoretical commitment to meanings as entities "shared" or "matched" by synonymous expressions. Under this heading I shall consider *meaning-as-use* theories and the closely related meaning-as-linguistic-act theories (though some versions of these theories have entificational elements). These theories explain the significance of expressions in terms of their function in linguistic and related nonlinguistic contexts.

Ideational Theories and Their Place in Semantics and Epistemology

Ideational theories bear the closest similarities to the dominant theories of the modern period, which typically follow Locke in taking meaningful expressions to be signs of "ideas before the mind," and thus equate meanings with these ideas. Some ideational theorists posit propositions and concepts as objects of the so-called "propositional attitudes" of belief, doubt, knowledge, and so on, that is, as the "intentional" objects of mental acts. A philosophical-psychological thesis of "intentionality" complements a number of philosophical programs that give *epistemological* concerns high priority, insofar as it provides a partial answer to questions as to what and how we know. Its fundamental point is that mental phenomena are essentially different in kind from physical phenomena in that the former, and not the latter, are always directed toward intentional (or "inexistent") objects.[11] The objects in question (either the propositions believed or the concepts manifested in them) are not reducible to designated physical objects, relations, or states of affairs, owing, among other things, to the possibility of false belief. Rather, they are regarded either as psychological or as platonic entities. Along this line, the intentionality thesis may be put in linguistic terms (as it was by its author, Franz Brentano) without reference to peculiar sorts of mental objects. Briefly, statements expressing beliefs or desires are intentional insofar as their truth value does not depend on the actual dispositions of the actual designata of the expressions contained in the sentence that states the proposition believed or known. For example, the nullity of the reference class of 'lions in Antartica' may have no bearing on the belief one has in the presence of lions there; or the common reference of 'the ringed planet' and 'the sixth planet' may have no bearing on the parallelism among one's beliefs with respect to each. These logical characteristics of belief-contexts led Brentano to argue for a distinct science of the symbolically meaningful.[12]

Other philosophers whose attention is directed more to *semantic* concerns with the relationships between symbolic systems (formal and natural) and the world, posit propositions and concepts as the "inten*s*ions" of expressions. Propositions here are typically platonic entities posited to account for translational equivalence among expressions, to be the bearers of truth and falsity of sentences, and so forth. Problems analogous to those that motivate Brentano's intentionality thesis arise in contexts of concern to semanticists. For example, the truth of 'the ringed planet is necessarily ringed' is not preserved when its subject term is replaced by the coreferential 'the sixth planet'.

(The similarity of 'intension(al)' and 'intention(al)' is an obvious potential source of confusion, especially given the close relationships between these two notions.[13] The problem is compounded by the fact that 'intention' as Brentano and others use it is a sort of mental object, and not the speaker's purpose in uttering some remark—although, again, these two notions of intention are intimately related to one another. This second sense of 'intention' figures, however, in some other theories that I shall examine below, such as Searle's.)

Often the cogency and applicability of theories of meaning have been threatened by excessive stress of semantic and platonic aspects over epistemological and concrete-psychological ones. Indeed, given the primacy of semantic concerns in much twentieth-century philosophy of language, psychological and epistemological aspects are often neglected by theorists of meaning. The resultant ready availability of discussions are partial theoretical solutions of problems in semantically oriented theories is partly responsible, I think, for a parallel tendency to stress platonic aspects of meaning in (general and anthropological) linguistics, psycholinguistics, ethnography, and ethnology; this despite the emphasis on human cognition that many thinkers in these areas espouse. 'Platonism' has thus been a common subject of criticism in these areas.

This platonic bias is reflected in Frege's broadly influential nineteenth-century investigations into the foundations of mathematics and semantics. Indeed, the theory of meaning he offers contains (if in rough form) most of the salient features of ideational (and other) types of theories that figure in the philosophical and anthropological problem areas of concern here, and is thus a good starting point despite its relatively early origin. An aim of his philosophical program was the clear determination and systematic treatment of meaning through the sort of regimentation of ordinary language that is involved in spelling out and reconstructing its logical form. By suitably translating normal, imprecise discourse into a logically rigorous "concept script," Frege hoped to facilitate a clearer linguistic embodiment of the meanings of vaguer, ordinary language expressions. Regimentation identifies the "single thought" expressed by a sentence and seemingly can serve to identify thoughts cross-culturally, insofar as all humans share a "common stock of thoughts" despite interlinguistic diversity.[14] The platonic bias of Frege's theory of meaning stemmed from objections to Locke's and Mill's psychologistic treatment of mathematical significance. By rooting it in mind-dependent entities existing *in* the mind, Frege argued, these theories made explanation of mathematical discovery impossible. He preferred to see mathematical and other statements as deriving their significance and truth value from abstract objects apprehended *by* the mind, but existing apart from it.

Frege established a fundamental distinction between the *sense*, or linguistic meaning, of expressions and their *reference*: a distinction that is reflected in many subsequent theories. The sense, or as it is often called, the *intension* is what must be known by a speaker simply in virtue of his knowledge of the language in question, perhaps without any awareness of or acquaintance with the objects or properties designated by the expression. Briefly, the intension of a sentence is the *proposition* it expresses, while the intension of a term is the *concept* it expresses. However, knowledge of these dimensions of meaning is generally insufficient, evidently, to determine truth or falsity. This requires knowledge not only of sense, but of reference, or *extension*. The notion of extension is clearest with respect to what are called "categorematic" expressions, which apply to classes of objects: Nouns such as 'planet' or predicates such as 'is a planet' have certain classes of objects constituting their extensions, and at least partial knowledge of this extension is required to know the truth of sentences such as 'The sixth planet is ringed'. Sentences are often regarded as having their own extensions—sometimes these are the "states of affairs" described; sometimes these are abstract objects called "truth values."

In either case intension, which Frege construes platonically, is typically said to "determine" extension.[15] By this it is meant that a measure of our grasp of the intension or concept of a term such as 'planet' lies in our ability to apply it correctly to the things in its extension. Or, more simply, grasp of intension issues in correctness of reference. Now precisely characterizing intension is not easy—indeed, this is the substance of many of the central problems in theories of meaning that shall concern us here. However, as Frege argued, it seems clear that intension cannot simply be extension—despite the fact that knowledge of the latter is so essential to knowledge of the former, and despite the fact that the evident primary function of categorematic terms like 'planet' is to pick out the objects that are planets. For owing to the coextensionality of many intensionally distinct expressions (such as 'the ringed planet' and 'the sixth planet from the sun') intension cannot be equated with the class of observable objects that comprise the extension of many commonly used terms. Or, put less technically, in such cases intension varies while extension does not, thus, intension and extension cannot be the same. While this problem is similar to one I cited earlier in connection with belief contexts, and for which I employed a similar example, it is distinct: Belief can vary with respect to intensionally as well as extensionally identical expressions if the subject is not aware of relevant synonymies. Briefly—and I shall give this more attention below—the mark of intensional sameness or difference has more to do with whether a sentence relating two expressions is *necessarily* true or not. The intensional identity of 'the sixth planet' and 'the planet following the fifth planet' is shown by the fact that 'The sixth planet is the planet following the fifth planet' is necessarily true. (Note that necessity goes hand in hand with factual uninformativeness.) Meanwhile, the fact that 'the ringed planet' is only coextensional, not cointensional, with the first of these expressions is shown by the fact that 'The ringed planet is the sixth planet', though true, is not necessarily so. (Also, unlike the previous claim, it offers astronomical information.) The intension-extension distinction is reflected in all the major ideational theories, as well as in other types of theory, and is embodied in the distinction contemporary linguists make between the speaker's "dictionary" and "encyclopedia."

Russell's general program, similar in many key aspects to Frege's, aimed to overcome an epistemological gap perceived in the absence of an adequate explanation of how a speaker can come to associate meanings with expressions or to grasp them in communication. His early logical atomist theory laid the groundwork for a method of contextually defining all ordinary-language expressions in terms of only logical quantifiers and predicates describing immediately perceivable sensory elements. Epistemic primacy was thus given to "basic propositions" that are atomic in logical form and constituted by these sensory elements (knowable "by acquaintance"), with all other claims deriving their meaning by virtue of being "logical constructions" out of basic propositions.[16] He thus hoped both to achieve Frege's aims of regimenting ordinary discourse to reveal meaning and providing an analysis of mathematics free from Mill's psychologistic assumptions, as well as to answer the neglected epistemological questions. He hoped to effect a rigorous empirical reductionism that would fulfill the classic empiricist programs of grounding knowledge in sense experience and providing an empirical criterion for dividing genuinely informative utterances from vacuous, "metaphysical" ones.

Russell's work, particularly given his emphasis on the psychological-epistemic component of meaning, is especially significant in the present context both because of his support of an attitude (now widely held) that theories of meaning must connect into psychological accounts of understanding,[17] language acquisition, and so on and because of its profound influence (along with much parallel work by Wittgenstein) on the thought of the logical positivists. The views of C.I. Lewis and Rudolf Carnap—both primary targets of Quine's critique—particularly reflect the Fregean dualism of linguistic and factual meaning as well as the Russellian variety of empirical reductionism: elements that Quine views as both essential to, and ultimately destructive of, the theories they propound. The well-known positivist doctrine of verificationism, according to which meaning or meaningfulness is construed as definability in terms of implied sets of phenomenalistic or physicalistic observation-sentences, also evolved from Russell's atomism. However, most positivists came to eschew reference to psychic contents or immediately observable states of affairs in accounting for the empirical basis of knowledge. Thus, while hardly ignoring epistemological questions, they somewhat distanced their theories of meaning from psychological accounts of understanding.

Positivist epistemology came to emphasize "rational reconstructions" of science, that is, normative clarifications and codifications of proper scientific practice. This gave rise to a number of extensively discussed problems concerning the possibility of showing equivalence, reducibility, or translatability of theories to sets of observation sentences that provide (in principle) their empirical confirmation.[18] The more limited goal of determining meaningfulness (as opposed to meaning) was tied intimately to the Fregean linguistic-factual meaning contrast: The realm of significant discourse was divided into *analytic* (or counteranalytic) statements, true (or false) in virtue of logical form or meaning, and *synthetic* statements, whose truth or falsity depend at least in part on the truth or falsity of implied observational consequences, and not entirely on linguistic meaning. (Indeed, the explication of intensional versus extensional identity just given in terms of necessary truth can be done also in terms of this distinction: 'The sixth planet is the planet following the fifth planet' is analytic as well as necessary. 'The ringed planet is the sixth planet' is synthetic. Terms that are cointensional can be replaced in analytic sentences and thereby preserve their analyticity. If merely coextensional terms are exchanged, the sentence ceases to be analytic and is instead only a synthetic truth.)

The verifiability criterion was applied to synthetic statements: Any of these that admitted of no empirical verification procedure were meaningless. In this connection, the positivists often turned their attention to prior philosophies (including those of earlier empiricists) that, the positivists maintained, often foundered on "pseudo-problems" stemming, among other things, from misguided efforts to apply *a priori* modes of inquiry to questions whose answers were synthetic and factual in nature. So, for instance, the traditional mind-body problem, seen as a philosophical dispute about the substance or substances that constitute reality, was rejected and transformed into either factual issues to be resolved by scientific inquiry, or philosophical ones concerning the linguistic framework of, say, psychology. (Here the dualism-materialism controversy could be couched as a genuinely philosophical dispute about the need for mentalistic terminology not definable entirely in material or physical terms.)

The analytic-synthetic distinction still has wide currency. On the other hand, the various empirical reductionist programs that sought to articulate various verifiability or testability criteria, or to provide the empirical component of the meaning of synthetic statements, are generally regarded now as having failed.

Frege's and Russell's theories provide most of the essential points necessary as background to the critiques I wish subsequently to examine. However, a brief examination of Lewis' theory will clarify some important points. Lewis analyzes linguistic meaning into four "modes": *extension, comprehension, signification*, and *intension*. The first two comprise the referential aspect of meaning, with extension being actual reference and comprehension being actual and possible reference. More specifically, the extension of nonsentential "terms" (as he calls them), which I shall here regard as predicates, is the class of actual things to which a predicate applies, while comprehension comprises actual and possible denotata. The extension of sentential terms is the actual world for true sentences and is null for false ones, while the comprehension of a sentence is the classification of "consistently thinkable world(s) which would incorporate the state of affairs it signifies." Signification and intension are modes that are often conflated under the heading of 'sense' or 'intension', but are kept carefully distinct by Lewis—with good reason. The signification of predicates is the set of defining characteristics (or properties or attributes) possessed by members of the comprehension of that predicate, while the linguistic intension (or concept or connotation) is the set of expressions describing those attributes, or the "conjunction of all other terms each of which must be applicable to anything to which the given term would be correctly applicable." (This therefore embraces entailment relations among concepts as well as their definitions. The intension of 'bachelor' would be more than just 'unmarried adult male'; it would include 'human', 'animate being' and so forth: compare Katz's "semantic markers" below.) Lewis wants to assure that defining characteristics are kept out of the head of the speaker and are regarded as (abstract, universal) attributes possessed by a predicate's referents (as opposed to, say, treating them as inner mental representations).

Turning finally to sentential expressions, the signification is defined as a state of affairs and the intension is the proposition expressed by a sentence and all those propositions that would be true in any possible world in which that proposition was true (i.e., those propositions that it entails singly or in conjunction with other propositions). States of affairs, like attributes, are abstract entities and not concrete space-time slabs or "pieces" of the actual world. Asserting a proposition amounts to attributing a state of affairs *to* the actual world. Other key semantic notions are defined as follows: Universal extension is the mark of truth and null extension that of falsity; analyticity and necessity are defined as universal comprehension, or truth in all possible worlds; self-contradictory statements are distinguished by their possession of zero comprehension.[19]

Despite its relatively early vintage, Lewis' theory is of interest for a number of reasons. Various of its elements are adopted by current ideational theories, for instance, the various uses of "possible-world analysis." Also, its helpful distinction between intension and signification makes clear that theories of meaning may make commitments to the existence of two kinds of abstract entity, linguistic (or mental) and nonlinguistic (the latter hearkening more to the notions of traditional platonism). However, given their interrelationships and their similar underdetermination by reference, many criticisms of intension apply also to signification, as we shall see.

Lewis' theory is also noteworthy in virtue of a distinction (elided in the previous paragraphs) between *linguistic meaning* and *sense meaning*. The above characterization of intension is, more specifically, of *linguistic* intension. And it, too, is not quite "in the speaker's mind"—rather it is itself an abstract and publicly accessible entity, something the mind grasps. (Such grasp enables discrimination of significations and extensions, which is Lewis' way of saying "sense determines reference.") These abstract objects inhere in language, as opposed to significations, which inhere in the things described. This is not the only feasible way to analyze intension, and arguably not the clearest but it is nonetheless important to avoid conflating the attributes of things with aspects of the speaker's discriminative defining apparatus. Such conflation is bound to cause serious confusion when one is considering the "world-constitutive" character of language, as are many of the figures I shall be discussing below.

To this point, Lewis' remarks are more or less in line with those of semantically oriented treatises in treating intensions as abstract linguistic entities. However, in turning subsequently to epistemological concerns, where the precise nature of "the *criterion in mind* by which it is determined whether the term in question applies or fails to apply in any particular instance" is the central concern, he turns attention to the psychological aspect of meaning. This aspect of intension, what he terms "sense meaning," must be carefully differentiated, he maintains, from its linguistic aspects.[20] With Russell, and the classical empiricists, Lewis thought it essential to show that "all knowledge has an eventual empirical significance in that all which is knowable or even significantly thinkable must have reference to meanings which are sense-representable."[21] Thus, the inclusion of sense meanings, which are comprised of "mental images" (the image being a "schema" or "rule or prescribed routine and imagined result of it which will determine applicability of the expression in question"), is vital to a coherent theory of language.[22] In distinct contrast to behaviorist approaches, Lewis is most insistent that the analysis of meaning go deeper than the social conditions of communication to account for the acquisition of intension, the recognition of attributes and extensions, and so forth. The epistemic aspects of a theory of meaning and the mentalistic elements of communication and language acquisition, Lewis contends, cannot be ignored:

> It is the social situation principally which language reflects, and our dependence, for survival and for satisfactions achieved, upon cooperation of others. But however fundamental this need to communicate, the need to entertain fixed meanings goes deeper still and must characterize the mentality of any creature capable of consciously affecting its own relation to the environment, even if that creature should live without fellows and find no use for language.[23]

Knowledge of sense meaning is evidenced by a person's ability to use correctly an expression in the appropriate circumstances, while knowledge of linguistic meaning is evidenced by one's ability to give proper definition of the expression.[24] Intensional meaning (as well as extensional) is dependent upon sense experience: The only way one knows the intensional meanings of one's own language or that of another culture, is through knowing "test-schemata" and their anticipated results.[25] If language does not make contact with the world through extension, language becomes an entirely self-contained system in which meanings of expressions are given only in terms of other expressions. So, while Lewis holds that the statements that determine the structure of a conceptual scheme (i.e., which "assert some relation of meanings amongst themselves") are analytic, those statements or that structure must be conditioned by experience. It is the character of this "conditioning" that the distinction between linguistic and sense meaning is intended to clarify.[26]

Thus, we see most clearly in Lewis the foundational worries concerning the relationships between abstract meaning-structures and the concrete psychological and epistemic contexts in which they must also function. His remarks are also of importance insofar as they typify the major theses of mentalistic, linguistic approaches from his time to the present, and insofar as they particularly typify the concerns of the mentalistic tradition in anthropology influenced by the work of Goodenough. It is also important to see his positive and negative influence on Quine, who takes to heart Lewis' empiricist insistence that linguistic meaning must have a basis in sense meaning and, hence, that recovery of linguistic meaning in translation must have its basis in recovery of sense meaning. But, as I intimated above, Quine departs from Lewis quite radically in denying that sense meaning can support the propositional edifice constructed upon it.

Carnap's theory is similar to Lewis' in various essential respects—the most significant difference in detail being its greater degree of logical rigor—and in virtue of its influence on Morris. Carnap does not give quite the attention to epistemological questions that Lewis does, being generally more concerned with formal semantics. However, Carnap was fully aware of the importance of certain questions in natural semantics for his work and was particularly concerned to respond to the criticisms of Quine and others by trying to give empirically legitimate construals of intension and other related notions. This endeavor, which I shall examine below, is of central relevance to my later concerns. Meanwhile, I shall forgo discussion of the details of his theory.[27]

The desire for empirically respectable notions of meaning, analyticity, and so on, also motivates a more recent major innovation in ideational theories: the transformational-generative approach. (I shall settle for a compressed account of it here, giving more attention to its application to anthropology in Chapter 2.) This approach picks up the various concerns of Frege, Russell, and Lewis and endeavors to develop a fully testable linguistic, and, eventually, psycholinguistic, account. The transformationalists' concern for empirical respectability applies not only to the identifiability of intension on an empirical basis but also to enhancing the explanatory power of these notions. J. J. Katz' and J. Fodor's early applications of Chomsky's transformational apparatus to semantics are quite explicitly aimed at continuing the Fregean program of revealing meaning through rigorous linguistic reformulation.[28] Further, Katz and Fodor give much attention to the development of the notion of a "semantic marker" to serve the function of Lewis' "intension" and which may be integrated into the grammatical apparatus developed by Chomsky. It is used to explicate the various notions of analyticity, synonymy, and so forth. Its main difference with prior ideational theories is that the mentalistic rules and structures governing these markers are, in virtue of their placement in generative structures, only unconsciously grasped by the native speaker.[29] Thus, the theory has affinities with anthropological approaches that stress the unconscious character of linguistic and other cultural rules. It has thus been adopted, as we shall see, by mentalistically oriented anthropologists who endeavor to solve theoretical problems by shifting focus to unconscious, and presumably more universal, levels of meaning (much as do structuralist approaches such as Levi-Strauss').[30] They are also motivated by a belief that thus moving to the level of unconscious transformational elements and structures will achieve linguistic results that have a greater degree of "psychological reality," another key desideratum of mentalistic linguistic and ethnographic approaches.[31]

Entificational Theories: Behavioral

The various problems with mentalistic notions of meaning have motivated some theorists to develop behaviorally explicable notions. Such efforts also stem from rejection of a problematic Cartesian philosophy of mind, viewed as inadequate to the explanation of meaning, cognition, and action, owing, among other things, to the privacy of mental states.[32] Bloomfield's pioneering theory identified the meaning of a linguistic form with "the situation in which the speaker utters it and the response it calls forth from the hearer," with the situations or stimulations that give rise to the speaker's utterance being the element that is usually used to define the meanings of terms. Owing to the great variation in total stimulation from instance to instance, *distinctive features* of the stimulus situation are viewed as comprising the meanings of terms.[33]

Certain difficulties with this understandably flawed early account are overcome in B. F. Skinner's work, which isolates such features by virtue of their increasing the probability of occurrence of the expressions they define.[34] Skinner's more ramified account is also beset with problems, perhaps the most central and serious of which are presented in Chomsky's influential review of *Verbal Behavior*. Of importance to the present context is Chomsky's charge that these sorts of theories tend to treat stimuli as psychic contents or, in some other way, "driven back into the organism," thus simply disguising "a complete retreat to mentalistic psychology."[35] However this might apply to what Skinner himself actually says, this danger besets anthropological methodologies that are designed to "behaviorize" mentalistic approaches such as componential analysis. For the behaviorist's "distinctive features" are just the defining attributes (signification, "components," etc.) whose designating expressions are comprised (along with generically higher-order category labels) in the intension of an expression in question in mentalistic theories patterned on Lewis'. And it is the decidedly mentalistic character of the latter's kind of intension (which functions both as a linguistic meaning and a sense meaning) that allows Lewis to use it to explain the competent speaker's ability to discriminate signification and, in turn, extension. While a behavioral approach might easily avoid treating intensions as mental entities, it might nonetheless give a mentalistic analysis of the speaker's recognition of defining attributes by speaking of incoming stimulations as if they were mental representations of attributes or components. This difficulty, which stems partly from the above-noted ambiguity of expressions such as 'defining criteria'—whether as objective properties of objects in a term's extension or as entities in the speaker's mind (or head)—is carefully avoided by the accounts of Morris and Quine.

Morris' various theories have had a significant influence on twentieth-century anthropology. His general approach differs from that of Bloomfield in that it works from a broader semiotic base—being from the start a theory of signs in general and not simply a theory of linguistic meaning. It is of particular significance here, as I noted above, owing to its close allegiances to the ideational theories of Carnap and Lewis. Morris' *Signs, Language, and Behavior* (1946) grounds its analysis of symbolic behavior in a *sign* relation (closely akin to C. S. Peirce's "process of semiosis"): Interpreters react to a sign in a certain way, called the *interpretant*, to a type of object, the *denotatum*, to which the sign refers. They so react in virtue of the *significatum* or set of defining properties of the denotatum.[36] More specifically, the interpretant is "the disposition in an interpreter to respond, because of a sign, by response-sequences of some behavior family"; the denotatum is "anything that would permit the completion of the response-sequences to which an interpreter is disposed because of a sign"; and the significatum is "the conditions such that whatever meets these conditions is a denotatum of a given sign."

(Signification and denotation together comprise what Morris calls, in other contexts, the designation of a sign.)[37] Thus, grasping the concept knife is manifest in the interpreter reliably exhibiting a disposition to use it correctly, that is, to cut things—this disposition being comprised in the interpretant. Meanwhile, the denotatum, a given knife, permits the appropriate cutting behavior, while the significatum comprises those properties in things (such as being reasonably sharp-edged) that are necessary for their being knives.

It is Morris' stated purpose here to explicate the key semantic notions of Lewis and Carnap behaviorally, and his sign relation is intended to eliminate the need to talk of meanings as things "present to the mind." The key element is the interpretant, which parallels Frege and Lewis' intension. Meanwhile, the significatum corresponds to Lewis' signification and the denotatum is the type of object comprising what Lewis calls extension.

Morris' later *Signification and Significance* (1964), which has also had an impact on twentieth-century anthropology, modifies the sign relation in a number of ways.[38] Here it is construed as a relation involving a sign, interpretant, interpreter, signification, and context, with the last two items representing the major modifications. Significations are construed as "certain describable aspects of complex behavioral processes in the natural world" and comprise here not only the defining properties of denotata but the denotata themselves. Contexts are the stimulus conditions under which the sign is interpreted: Thus, the latter sign relation takes into account both stimulus and response, while the earlier account concerns itself only with response.[39] The interpretant remains as the key behavioral correlate of intension, or that which signs "express." A "meaning" in the rough, intuitive sense is a combination of signification and interpretant, while designation remains as it was in the earlier work (except that it is now roughly equivalent to signification given the changes in the latter).[40]

Yet while commitments to criteria in mind are avoided, objections applicable to intension apply to signification as well.[41] The interpretant is regarded as an individuatable and identifiable entity, yet varying characterizations are compatible with the same extension. There is freedom of choice in assignment of either interpretant or signification. Even if one relies on the "externality" of significations to identify significations of source-language expressions with significations of receptor-language expressions, one has the problem of warranting not only the identification but also, on Quine's view, the receptor assignment itself. Indeterminacy plagues even our own semantic and metaphysical categories.

Nonentificational Theories

Wittgenstein, in his later work, takes the assault on ideational meaning and Cartesian dualism a step further. He sees the very idea that meaning is analyzable in any sort of objectual terms—even behaviorist ones—as a key drawback in mentalist theories that must be rejected if explanations of meaning and understanding are to be successfully anchored in observable behavior. Rather than concern ourselves with "unitary meaning," Wittgenstein directs us to "look at the sentence as an instrument, and at its sense as its employment." Satisfactory definitions, whether ostensive or verbal, are definitions that indicate the proper way to use a word. Communication is achieved through conformity to behaviorally scrutable rules of usage, and accounts of meaning are to concern themselves with these rules of usage rather than with giving verbal embodiment to intensional objects. With Quine, he views such posits as useless (though, indeed, other "meaning-as-use" views diverge from him on this important point by seeking to individuate meanings on the basis of use). Knowing meaning is just the proper following of certain rules or proper adherence to certain conventional ways of acting (some specific governing rule may or may not be formulable in a given case). Agreement on such rules or actions is an agreement not merely, or not at all, in opinion but in "form of life." Such agreements are part of a culture's "natural history," part of a shared cultural experience.[42]

The measure of adequacy of translation, it is fair to infer, is also its enabling a learner of the source language to use words correctly. As with the other behavioral approaches, the recovery of behaviorally scrutable rules of linguistic usage is a far more appealing task for social inquirers worried not only about the empirical confirmation problems of mentalistic accounts but also about the tendency of some approaches to encourage disregard for the social content of utterance and meaning. Not surprisingly, Wittgenstein's views have had a decided impact on social science. Also, there are important affinities between Wittgenstein's account and the position I shall develop below. Thus, I shall defer further discussion of Wittgenstein's and related views until appropriate occasions below.

Following (or paralleling) Wittgenstein's lead, John Austin, William Alston, John Searle, and others have developed a type of use-theory known as speech-act analysis. It has had a growing number of adherents among anthropologists. Austin develops a categorization of language function fundamentally different from the syntactics-semantics-pragmatics distinction developed by Morris. For Austin, utterances—or *locutionary acts*—are classified as *perlocutionary* insofar as they cause certain effects in the hearer, and as *illocutionary* insofar as they serve in the performance of certain kinds of acts, defined by particular rules of social context: for example, promising, requesting a service, and so forth. The individuating criteria of these acts are indicated in sets of rules understood by speaker and hearer and by the given speech community in general. Meanings of sentences are captured in the illocutionary acts they are used to perform (they are, as Wittgenstein argues, instruments) and sentences are synonymous insofar as they are used to perform the same illocutionary acts. Sameness of word usage (word-synonymy) is determined from sentence usage by considering the ways in which substitution of certain words in a given position within a sentence can preserve or modify its "illocutionary act potential." (Thus, the Fregean dependence of word-meaning on sentence-meaning is preserved.)[43]

The identification of illocutionary acts, their correlation with sentences, the equation of the meaning of sets of sentences by determining that they perform the same act, and the equation of parts of those sentences through preservation of the list of acts correlated to the sentences are all features that depend on a broad notion of synonymy in natural language. And it is here that we shall see an important and perhaps even more radical break from mentalism than is exhibited in the idea of meaning as use or linguistic act in Quine's reflections on translation. Quine's divergence from these otherwise sympathetic perspectives on language is particularly highlighted with respect to Searle's theory of speech acts. For in the detailed ramification of his theory (influential in both philosophical and anthropological circles), Searle has found reason to advert to the notion of a proposition as an abstract linguistic entity. Searle defines a proposition as "what is asserted in the act of asserting, what is stated in the act of stating" (illocutionary acts). Thus, Searle's theory reinstates intensional objects, while nonetheless following the nonentificational program in most other essential respects.[44] Indeed, the motive for employing propositions is the provision of a truth vehicle: "An assertion is a (very special kind of) commitment to the truth of a proposition." A proposition is thus (again) the what-is-expressed, but rather than speaking in the traditional (semantic) fashion of the sign or sentence doing the expressing. Searle prefers to speak of propositions as what the speaker expresses in *uttering* a sentence. Acts of expressing propositions never occur in isolation, but always as part of illocutionary acts. Yet Searle's propositions are not themselves acts or even parts of acts (an expression is a part of an act, a behavioral event, in which a proposition is asserted); they are evidently isolable, abstract entities.[45]

In this vein, Searle also endeavors to incorporate generative grammatical devices into his speech act analysis (a synthesis attempted also by J. R. Ross—though sharply opposed by Austin). For example, the applicability of a sentence for declarative speech acts could be specified in the deep structure of a sentence as well as providing the means for identifying indicators of component elements of speech acts that are not present in the surface structure. For example, 'I promise to come' has a surface structure that prohibits distinguishing between indicators of illocutionary force and of propositional content (as would 'I promise' and 'that I will come' in 'I promise that I will come'). But the underlying phrase marker of each contains 'I promise * I will come'.[46]

It is worth emphasizing that Searle's analysis commits linguists to the recovery of speaker-intentions (that is, purposes) and community rules. He rejects H. P. Grice's influential account of "non-natural meaning" (namely, the symbol-referent relationship is noncausal), which grounds meaning in the speaker's intention in speaking and in the intention to convey that original intention. However, he rejects this view only because it overlooks, he contends, the function of linguistic rules in meaning.[47] Otherwise, Searle's view is quite similar to Grice's. Searle maintains the following two points: (1) Sentence meaning is determined by rules specifying both the conditions and the character of the utterance. (2) To utter a sentence and mean it is (a) to intend to get the hearer to recognize that there exist states of affairs dictated by appropriate rules, (b) to intend to effect such recognition by getting the hearer to recognize this intention, and (c) to intend to effect such recognition in virtue of the hearer's knowledge of the rules appropriate to the sentence. Thus, sentences provide "conventional means of achieving the intention to produce a certain illocutionary effect in the hearer." Understanding consists in achieving intentions (a), (b), and (c), and this in turn requires rule-sharing by speaker and hearer (and interpreter).[48]

General Criticisms of Intension

As I noted earlier, the various kinds of propositions, concepts, and attributes accommodated by theories of meaning typically serve to support theories of *apriori* knowledge by providing entities for the intellect to grasp as well as something to imbue certain kinds of statements (analytic, necessarily true) whose truth does not seem to depend on accidental arrangements in the universe. Moreover, in order to perform these tasks, many believe these entities must be abstract.[49] Propositions have also served the epistemological task of accounting for knowledge and belief (true and false), leading philosophers such as Russell to confer on them various psychological or phenomenal features. I shall concern myself here primarily with Quine's criticisms of Lewis' and Carnap's abstract notions of intension and against related notions of attribute or property or, as Lewis and Morris put it, signification. I shall also look at some related objections raised by Wittgenstein.

Quine does not object to the use of expressions such as 'meaning' and 'proposition' per se in ordinary speech or in informal scientific discourse. Instead, his concern is with uses that entail commitment to belief in the existence of distinct intensional entities—a commitment that is determined by examining the logically regimented, or "canonical" versions of sentences. The idea is to avoid quantification over variables that have intensions, and so on, as values and generally to avoid use of expressions associated with the propositional attitudes unless these expressions can be accommodated by the objects and can serve for general scientific discourse. Accordingly, he and other critics such as Nelson Goodman and Morton White eschew methods of logical analysis, such as higher-order logics, that commit one to saying that the designata of predicates exist. The undesirable locutions are those that are, as Quine puts is, "ontically committing" to intensions or properties. The heart of the problem for Quine is not just ontological parsimony (which he has a reputation for emphasizing) but that for various reasons these notions must resist development of the coherent principles of individuation that their entification presupposes. Quine shares Brentano's desire to separate intension from natural science, but it is in order to eliminate it from science's ontology altogether.[50]

The various intensional notions form a set of interdefinable terms, which would be acceptable if any one term was—but, he argues, none is. Two expressions may be said to be synonymous when they express the same intension, or when they can be replaced by one another in analytic statements without altering the analytic character of those statements. Alternatively, one can reverse matters by defining intension or analyticity in terms of synonymy. The intension of an expression can be defined simply as the set of its synonyms, analyticity as a property preserved only by substitution of synonymous expressions. Quine challenges proponents of these notions to break into this "circle of terms" by adequately defining one of them.[51]

Attributes and properties suffer similarly. To cite a well-worn example, the property of being human is supposedly identical with that of being a rational animal, while the supposedly coextensional property of being a featherless (unplucked) biped is not. On the basis of what criteria, then, are these distinguished? The problem is the same as the one involved in justifying the idea that 'Humans are rational animals' is analytic, while 'Humans are featherless bipeds' is not, or in saying 'human' and 'rational animal' are synonymous or have the same intension.

Quine and Goodman are also skeptical of the ultimate cogency of the grander programs of Frege, Russell, and others to systematize and formalize broad stretches of ordinary and scientific discourse. However, they do not minimize formalization as a philosophical tool (as do many philosophers influenced by Wittgenstein's later work). Their view is that regimentation is useful provided the tasks to which it is put are clearly defined beforehand. Quine regards regimentation in logic as not revealing "real" form or an ideally clear embodiment of intension (along the lines of Frege's "concept script") but only as a means of clarifying implication relations—with no particular set of such relations being uniquely correct.[52] Goodman is appreciative of the efforts of positivists such as Carnap to develop observation-languages for the reduction of theories but he rejects the idea of epistemological grounding that guides such programs. His own early work on developing a phenomenal observation-language is aimed instead to accommodate more limited tasks, such as the description of pictorial surfaces or perhaps the implementation of psychological studies of perception.[53]

Quine's criticisms are motivated by a belief that underlying the ideational theories of logical empiricism is a profound misconception of the nature of knowledge and of the place of higher-level philosophical, logical, and mathematical inquiry in our overall "web of belief." He criticizes as "dogmas of empiricism" the idea (1) that we can sensibly talk of some statements as being utterly immune to revision in the light of future empirical contingencies; and (2) that it makes sense to speak of the identifiable empirical content of synthetic statements. The analytic-synthetic distinction and empirical reductionism, he argues, miss an important point emphasized by Pierre Duhem:

> The totality of our so-called knowledge . . .is a man-made fabric which impinges on experience only along the edges. Or, to change the figure, total science is like a field of force whose boundary conditions are experience. A conflict with experience at the periphery occasions readjustments in the interior of the field. Truth values have to be redistributed over some of our statements. Reevaluation of some statements entails reevaluation of others because of their logical interconnections—the logical laws being in turn simply certain further statements of the system, certain further elements of the field. Having reevaluated one statement we must reevaluate some others, which may be statements logically connected with the first or may be the statements of logical connections themselves. But the total field is so under-determined by its boundary conditions, experience, that there is much latitude of choice as to what statements to reevaluate in the light of any single contrary experience. No particular experiences are linked with any particular statements in the interior of the field, except indirectly through considerations of equilibrium affecting the field as a whole.[54]

Another metaphorical but helpful account of Quine's general perspective on language consists in his characterization of the social-behavioral, language-learning process as analogous to the trimming of hedges to matching shapes. Uniformity of usage is the result of social conditioning, the need for external conformity; while with respect to individual learners, the actual history of conditioning, the chain of associations of verbal responses to verbal and nonverbal stimulation, varies interpersonally.[55] Thus, Quine joins those philosophers, linguists, and anthropologists who reject the individual (conscious or unconscious) mind as being the important focal point in linguistic study and emphasize instead the shared social character of symbolic significance—but with the idea that the basic notions of synonymy and intension must be rejected rather than reconstituted.

Before looking at the evolution of the indeterminacy thesis out of this background, it will be useful to look briefly at Wittgenstein's parallel criticisms of "unitary meaning." (1) He stresses the lack of clarity of ordinary language usage (and meaning) that is necessary for its flexibility and adaptability. This underlies his aforementioned qualms about the value of formal rigor and systematization in philosophy. Most concepts are not expressible in terms of an exhaustive list of defining characteristics. He stresses instead that a "family resemblance" among the types of activities embraced in a concept accounts for its applicability to them. (He here cites the now famous example of the term 'game', which seems to resist any effort at exhaustive specification of defining criteria.) (2) Although he emphasizes language as a form of "rule-governed behavior," he denies that linguistic understanding can issue in the formulation of highest-order rules (consciously or unconsciously apprehended by the native speaker). (3) He stresses the superfluity of unitary meaning and its explanatory vacuity, arguing that to posit an image or mental construct as meaning-bearer for a publicly observable symbol only pushes the question of significance back one step. The relationship between image or construct and symbolized item remains as unaccounted for as that between symbol and symbolized.[56]

Before returning to Quine, let me make the following point, which I shall examine in more detail later. The social inquirer's grasping of rules, explicitly or tacitly governing linguistic behavior, would seem to be a necessary condition for successful translation in Wittgenstein's view and followers of his, such as Winch, seem to maintain just this. If so, then Wittgenstein will run afoul of translational indeterminacy. However, Wittgenstein's own position may be less committal in this regard and thus more easily reconcilable with Quine's than first appears.

Intension and Synonymy in Translation

Quine has pursued a number of strategies in attacking intension and related notions. However, the most significant for anthropology is one upon which Quine embarked in a 1951 paper entitled "The Problem of Meaning in Linguistics," in which he began to consider the problems a linguist might encounter in trying to apply such semantic notions to field translation. These reflections provoked a rejoinder by Carnap in which the latter relies on field-translation procedures to define operationally a number of key semantic notions. This, in turn, led to Quine's more fully articulated indeterminacy of translation thesis, the most extensive formulation of which appears in *Word and Object* (1960).[57]

The pivotal concern in these and related works is how the translator is to attain interpretive objectivity given the influences of his own linguistic-cultural background. These enter in various ways in the process of translation—notably, in "The Problem of Meaning in Linguistics," in the translator's reliance on formal criteria, such as simplicity, in constructing a lexicon. Quine argues that even if we accept a very rough and minimal notion of synonymy (for example, one that consists "in an approximate likeness in the situations that evoke the two forms, and an approximate likeness in the effect of either form on the hearer"),[58] deep difficulties remain. If we look just to the component of meaning involved in the evoking situation, Quine maintains, it is necessary to ground the likeness of situations in their similarity in certain *relevant respects*. Now identification of important features of the observational field is a facet of any empirical science, and what features are to count as relevant, for any empirical hypothesis, is going to depend on the application and working of the containing theory. However, in making the observations in normal scientific experimentation, we presume a shared linguistic background is possessed by our fellow scientists and hence that they are isolating just the same relevant features of the observed environment that we are. On the other hand, what features the source-language speakers will find relevant will be determined by a different conceptual scheme, conditioned by a radically different cultural background:

> The relevant features of the situation issuing in a given [source-language] utterance are in large part concealed in the person of the speaker, where they are implanted by his earlier environment. This concealment is partly good, for our purposes, partly bad. It is good in so far as it isolates the subject's narrowly linguistic training. If we could assume that our [source-language] speaker and our English speaker, when observed in like external situations, differed only in how they say things and not in what they say, so to speak, then the methodology of synonymy determinations would be pretty smooth; the narrowly linguistic part of the causal complex, different for the two speakers, would be conveniently out of sight, while all the parts of the causal complex decisive of synonymy or heteronymy were open to observation. But of course the trouble is that not only the narrowly linguistic habits of vocabulary and syntax are imported by each speaker from his unknown past.[59]

This last point echoes a central anthropological concern that I shall emphasize later—indeed, it addresses directly the work of Nelson Pike, whose "etics/emics" distinction will be of pivotal relevance—namely, the interdependence of language and world perception:

> Theoretically the . . .difficulty is that, as Cassirer and Whorf have stressed, there is in principle no separating language from the rest of the world, at least as conceived by the speaker. Basic differences in language are bound up, as likely as not, with differences in the way in which the speakers articulate the world itself into things and properties, time and space, elements, forces, spirits, and so on. It is not clear even in principle that it makes sense to think of words and syntax as varying from language to language while the content stays fixed; yet precisely this fiction is involved in speaking of synonymy, at least as between expressions of radically different languages.[60]

As translation gets further away from reference to observable features:

> the lexicographer comes to depend increasingly on a projection of himself, with his Indo-European *Weltanschauung*, into the sandals of his . . . informant. He comes also to turn increasingly to that last refuge of all scientists, the appeal to internal simplicity of his growing system.[61]

But where, in the case of the empirical scientist, the projection is to expected events, observable in principle and described in a common language of accepted scientific theory, here the projection of predicates (of the form " '....' in the source language means '----' " in the receptor language") is over parts of radically different languages. Here, for the most part, the only justification for so correlating strings is that the translational hypothesis belongs to a set of such hypotheses in the linguist's metalanguage that match up source- and receptor-language expressions in the simplest fashion. Where one cannot rely on shared experience to justify these correlations, Quine argues, there is no way of determining whether the lexicographer is correct or not. Lexical decisions will inevitably depend on the *imposition* of receptor-language syntax and lexicon on the source language. Any "discovery" of the way the source language categorizes physical and social reality depends, then, on how the receptor language does so. But how *do* we then know how subjects categorize? "In the case of the lexicon, pending some definition of synonymy,

we have no statement of the problem; we have nothing for the lexicographer to be right or wrong about.''[62] Where the linguist's
hypotheses are not about what he can directly observe, it is not clear
that they are about anything: there is not, or has not yet been
specified, a realm like the empirical one of the physicist for
hypotheses to live up to. And, Quine argues, we cannot assume, for
the sake of simplicity, that we can posit such a realm, based on the
successful application of translational correlations in discourse: For
the marked differences in cultural conditioning, prevalent everywhere
except where linguistic and experiential conditioning go hand in
hand, may not be overlooked.

Manifest here is a challenge Quine curtly, if metaphorically, states
in the first chapter of *Word and Object*. Ideational theories assume
underlying mental uniformity to explain observable behavioral
uniformity, while he prefers to liken language-learning to the trimming of shrubs to similar shapes. In both cases, underlying diversity
(of conditioning and twig-structure, respectively) exists, despite external uniformity.[63]

Perhaps no philosopher felt the impact of Quine's criticisms more
acutely than Carnap, whose positive influence on Quine was considerable. While the program of early logical positivism had under-
gone considerable revision by the 1950s, Carnap still was sanguine
about the prospects of its main lines of thrust. Yet he realized that
Quine's efforts to show the notion of ''sameness of meaning'' as in-
adequately explicable for natural language cut deeply against the fundamental aims and theses of logical positivism. Without a viable notion of synonymy, the analytic-synthetic distinction and the programs
of empirical reductionism, already suffering from Quine's ''Two
Dogmas'' critique, would seem seriously infirm. And, aside from
threatening the loss of a seemingly potent criterion for sorting out
legitimate scientific and philosophical issues from ''meaningless
metaphysics,'' it raised serious challenges to the relationship between
philosophy and science depicted by positivism. Quine's critique challenged the very idea that philosophy could direct itself, qua
philosophy, to the linguistic framework of science—as contrasted to
science's employment of that framework in the making and testing of
factual assertion.

In an appendix (entitled ''Meaning and Synonymy in Natural
Languages'') to the second edition of his third major work on formal
semantics, *Meaning and Necessity*, Carnap endeavors to define intension operationally, in terms of working field-translation procedures.[64]

Carnap offers a "behavioristic procedure" for meaning-recovery, developed from empirical methods an English-speaking linguist would use to establish the extension and intension of German words—giving particular attention to determining differences in intension where differences in extension do not obtain.[65]

This would be achieved, he argues, by noting the affirming and dissenting responses of informants to certain sentences in the presence or absence of certain objects. Although the uncertainty and possibility of error inherent in any inductive inference is present here, Carnap views it as relatively unproblematic and thinks extension can be settled without much difficulty. The controversial point in his view is the linguist's attempt to assign intensions and to determine the cognitive synonymy of expressions in the source- and receptor-languages. (He chooses German and English, respectively, to play these roles.) His thesis is, in direct contrast to Quine's, that "the assignment of an intension is an empirical hypothesis which, like any other hypothesis in linguistics, can be tested by observations of language behavior."[66]

Carnap proposes that the linguist determine intension by direct querying of the informant, once extension has been determined. For instance, in order to determine whether the German term means (1) 'horse' or (2) 'horse or unicorn', the linguist must query the informant concerning not only actually instantiated animals but also possible cases, either by the employment of questions containing modal source-language expressions corresponding to 'possible cases' or the like or by simply describing cases to the subject that the linguist knows to be possible. Affirmative and negative responses to questions will provide the basis for differentiating between (1) and (2), thus establishing the crucial point that (1) and (2), though about intensions of terms lacking visible extensions, are testable, and testably distinct, empirical hypotheses. It is not to be expected that the informant will always be able clearly or easily to specify the intension. But such "intensional vagueness," Carnap contends, does not preclude identification of intension generally; but emerges only in cases of identification or discrimination that are "of very little practical importance" for the subject.[67]

Carnap's account should have a familiar ring to anthropologists and linguists who contend that these sorts of elicitation procedures are precisely what is required to provide the needed empirical input for the formation and test of hypotheses about intension and synonymy. Indeed, Carnap expects this and cites Arne Naess' influential *Interpretation and Preciseness*, which presents a far more extended account of field methods, and which, Carnap contends, "seems . . .to provide abundant evidence in support of the intensionalist thesis."[68] However, his reliance on an instance of nonradical translation (between two closely related languages), Quine argues, diverts attention from problems that surface more clearly as source-receptor differences become more radical.

In precise terms, 'radical translation' for Quine means the translation of the discourse of a hitherto untouched society, which bears no cultural or linguistic similarity to any other studied society—an idealization by intent, but one that is approximated in anthropological field work. Briefly, Quine's examination of the context of radical translation is intended to discover the *ontological limits* of translational methodology in order to determine what it can, in principle, permit us to say about what anthropological subjects as a matter of *fact* mean when they use language or engage in other forms of symbolic behavior. Having examined translational methodology, Quine finally concludes, in contrast to Carnap, that it cannot ever give us a scientific warrant to say that source-language expressions really mean such and such receptor-language expressions, or to speak, consequently, of the meanings that "naturally synonymous" expressions share. But, then, if attributions employing these notions (and their kin) cannot be confirmed (or disconfirmed), then such claims "make no empirical sense." No maligning of method is intended here. Translators can have a warrant for *right* answers. What they lack, by and large, is a warrant for *uniquely true* ones.

Quine's critique has enlightening, but also potentially confusing, similarities to the critical strategies logical positivists like Carnap spun from verificationism. However, it is worth repeating, Quine's indeterminacy arguments are intended to be compatible with, indeed to bolster, his rejection of that criterion and of empirical reductionism generally. Also, Quine really raises no question about the warrant of translation by behavioral evidence. His concerns, as we shall see, have more to do with the compatibility of rival translations with the same behavioral evidence and, indeed, the same total physical world-states.

Carnap suggests that we ask what the subject would say in certain imagined situations but this presumes that we know what we are asking the subject in translating the expressions we have for conveying those imaginings in his language. The problems of indeterminacy stem ultimately from the fact that imaginable differences in meaning, couchable in the receptor language, can be entirely obscured in translation. Expressions in the receptor language that clearly differ in meaning can be employed as translations of the same string in the source language by manuals of translation that are nonetheless equally adequate on all the pertinent grounds, empirical and formal. This consideration undercuts even the slim hope Quine seems to leave in "The Problem of Meaning in Linguistics" for a more adequate definition of synonymy. For there can be no factual basis for saying that there is an objectively determinate intension or synonymy relation, he contends, if it is impossible in principle to claim unique correctness, on any factual basis, for lexicographical correlations, however successful. And uniqueness cannot be ascertained, he argues, even if one had all *possible* evidence.

That this is the thrust on Quine's thesis I think is generally agreed among philosophers, but how his arguments are to be interpreted is quite controversial—as the massive philosophical literature about the indeterminacy thesis attests. Thus, I think the following cautionary remarks are in order before I proceed further. I intend to highlight those aspects of Quine that are of most relevance to language-and-culture anthropology and, eventually, to reconstruct his thesis. I don't purport to offer a thorough analysis, but hope only to draw out what seem to be its most promising elements. My reconstruction will center on the problem of interpreter imposition, but will try to exploit it in a different way than Quine seems to intend.

Radical Indeterminacy

The procedure of Quine's linguist differs from that of Carnap's in important ways. One, related to Quine's choice of *radical* translation, is that the informants' judgments as to the stimulus meaning of expressions are *not* elicited. Indeed, they cannot be at this initial stage of translation. Only the linguist's judgments are taken into account. Another is that Quine's linguist must work with sentences first, that is, with term-meaning being derivative. Quine's prompting procedure must begin with sentences because only these may be affirmed or denied. (It also reflects his agreement with Frege that sentence-meaning is prior to term-meaning.) Finally, Quine emphasizes the holistic and underdetermined character of translation. Beyond those statements whose translation can be pinned firmly to observed verbal behavior, determination of meaning and reference cannot be done on anything like a sentence-by-sentence basis. Instead, interpretive choices admit of rival alternatives compatible with the same evidence. Thus, these selections are made on the basis of additional assumptions by the linguist, but the nature of these assumptions precludes the warranted recovery of intension.[69]

Quine uses the context of radical translation to reveal two distinct, though related, problems: (1) the *inscrutability of reference*, that is, the field linguist's inability, in principle, to determine objectively what the subject's referential and ontological categories really are; and (2) the *indeterminacy of translation*, which challenges the objectivity of most sentence-to-sentence translations. The latter rubric is often used by Quine and others to characterize the conjunction of these theses, and I shall follow in this practice where feasible.

The first chapter of *Word and Object* lay important groundwork for the radical translation argument. Here Quine develops the implications he has drawn from Duhem and from the failures of generations of philosophers to formulate comprehensive observation languages to serve a variety of epistemological and reductionist tasks. These have included demonstrating the unity of the sciences by formulating a common observation language to express their common evidential grounding, elucidating the fundamental character of raw experience ("the given"), and specifying the means of legitimating scientific discourse about unobservables by translating it into an observational idiom. Given this, and granting Peirce's point that the totality of scientific theories is the highest standard of truth, Quine argues (contrary to Peirce) that "we have no reason to suppose that man's surface irritations even unto eternity admit of any one systematization that is scientifically better or simpler than all possible others."[70] Scientific systematizations are underdetermined in principle by all possible evidence, and no one account accords with empirical data to the exclusion of other nonequivalent formulations that serve equally well. And the same goes for translation: No one translation manual can be seen to be uniquely correct, since translation manuals are similar enough in character to theories of nature to be analogously underdetermined. Further, just as the process of assignment of truth values to sentences makes sense only within the context of some theory (with the exception, perhaps, of sentences that describe the content of "immediate" observations) so the assignment of truth values to translational hypotheses is by and large dependent on a containing manual of translation (with analogous exceptions). However, Quine contends that the nonuniqueness of the containing translation manual makes all these dependent component translations indeterminate—while also claiming that an analogous indeterminacy does not arise in physics.

This contrast, which I shall consider in more detail below, has been cause for considerable concern among Quine's commentators, especially as *Word and Object* and other works evidently make theoretical underdetermination a premise of the indeterminacy thesis; that is, he makes his case by drawing first on similarities between physical theorizing and translation and then by establishing an important difference between them. And although Quine elsewhere offers and expresses preference for an indeterminacy argument that does not rest on underdetermination, his contrasting attitude regarding science and translation remains a conclusion that calls for warrant.

Quine opens the second chapter of *Word and Object* with a number of rough formulations of the indeterminacy thesis. Crudely put, it is that

> two men could be just alike in all their dispositions to verbal behavior under all possible sensory stimulations, and yet the meanings of ideas expressed in their identically triggered and identically stated utterances could diverge radically.[71]

This is immediately followed by another formulation that avoids use of the notions of "meaning" and "idea" that the thesis is attacking:

> the infinite totality of sentences of any given speaker's language can be so permuted or mapped onto itself, that (a) the totality of the speaker's dispositions to verbal behavior remains invariant, and yet (b) the mapping is no mere correlation of sentences with *equivalent* sentences in any plausible sense of equivalence however loose. Sentences without number can diverge drastically from their respective correlates, yet the divergences can systematically so offset one another that the overall pattern of associations of sentences with one another and with nonverbal stimulation is preserved. The firmer the direct links of a sentence with nonverbal stimulation, of course, the less that sentence can diverge from its correlation under any such mapping.[72]

The nonuniqueness of mapping here eliminates, Quine contends, any ostensible hope of clarifying the notion of intension by reference to an extant set of discovery and validational procedures. To make this crucial point clearer he turns to radical translation. The point of this idealized construct is to help illustrate exactly what empirical data can warrant: We are not already inclined to think we know the meaning of the source-language expressions, or to have an antecedent idea of its grammatical structures. For Quine, nonradical translation can induce us to think that there is determinate meaning awaiting our translation. In radical translation, we clearly don't have a clue at first as to what source-language strings mean, save for those that indicate immediately present and observable states of affairs, but hope to reconstruct their meaning through careful analysis and test. The actual yield of our efforts is clearer, and, again, Quine contends that the limitations one discovers here extend to all interpretive contexts. (In what follows, I shall use the term 'radical translation' somewhat more loosely, applying it as well to cases that approximate this ideal.)

Put in terms of radical translation, the thesis, then, is as follows:

> Manuals for translating one language into another can be set up in divergent ways, all compatible with the totality of speech dispositions, yet incompatible with one another. In countless places they will diverge in giving, as their respective translations of a sentence of the one language, sentences of the other language which stand to each other in no plausible sort of equivalence however loose. The firmer the direct links of a sentence with non-verbal stimulation, of course, the less drastically its translations can diverge from one another from manual to manual. It is in this last form, as a principle of indeterminacy of translation, that I shall try to make the point plausible in the course of this chapter.[73]

Quine begins his discussion of indeterminacy by carefully describing the translator's data-gathering and empirical confirmation procedures. Once the linguist has established, to a suitable degree of inductive certainty, the expressions of affirmation and denial in a foreign language, and has determined a workable *modulus* of stimulation (that is, what he takes to be the temporal extension of the stimulus episode), he builds his manual through systematic elicitation. The linguist prompts native affirmative or negative responses to chosen short questions in the native language, in the presence of certain objects that presumably produce similar irradiation patterns in the ocular nerve-endings of the linguist, receptor-language speaker, and informant. The linguist's evidence is comprised in sentences whose meanings are largely determined by associated stimulation and response. When the linguist has observed that a question in the native language such as 'Gavagai' is generally affirmed by the informants when rabbits are present, and generally denied when they are not, the linguist may venture the hypothesis that the sentence 'Gavagai' means something like 'Lo, a rabbit', or simply the one-word sentence 'Rabbit'. It is by such associations of stimulation that the linguist and any other language learner gains access to the language and beliefs of a culture.

What the linguist determines at this stage of translation is sameness of stimulus meaning of source and receptor-language sentences. In order to avoid accounting for variations in individual neural conditioning (which could cause differences in the perceived images had by different observers of identical objects), and to avoid certain epistemological problems, Quine focuses on stimulations as initially received by sensory receptors: "A visual stimulation in perhaps best identified, for present purposes, with the pattern of chromatic irradiation of the eye."[74]

Stimulus meaning is defined in terms of the positive and negative responses to promptings. It is the ordered pair of the *affirmative* and *negative* stimulus meanings of a sentence: the former being the class of types of stimulation patterns that would prompt assent from that speaker at that time, the latter being those that would prompt dissent. Hence, stimulus meaning is relativized to individual speakers at particular times. The stimulus meaning of 'There's a rabbit' for some English speaker is the class of stimulation "pattern-forms" that, presented along with a query such as 'There's a rabbit, right?' would elicit 'Yes' from the speaker, ordered pairwise with the class of stimulation patterns that would prompt 'No' when accompanied by the same query.[75] The linguist's task is to find native sentences whose stimulus meanings are identical to those of certain receptor-language sentences, and initial translational correlations are determined on the basis of these identities. That is, we seek to determine what sentence pairs are *stimulus synonymous*. It is worth noting that Quine's stimulus meaning is of the behavioral-entity type discussed above. However, it is far more limited in application. It is, in Quine's view, the only empirically legitimate one available, but cannot sustain the broad linguistic and philosophical tasks to which intension has typically been put. For sameness of stimulus meaning can serve to equate only a relatively small set of the sentences.

Quine's insistence that some notion of empirical meaning is necessary, though it turns out to be significantly different from that of other empiricists and pragmatists, is strongly reminiscent of C. I. Lewis' emphasis on the need for a notion of sense-meaning, as well as Russell's quest for objects of knowledge by acquaintance. Not all linguistic meaning can be a matter of word usage or definition if language is to have any relationship to experience. The only way one may learn a *theory* or a *language*, and the only way one can test one's scientific or ordinary beliefs, is if some of the sentences in either sort of belief-web are such that some relevant segment of experience fully comprises their meaning:

We were impressed [above] with the interdependence of sentences. We may well have begun then to wonder whether meanings even of whole sentences (let alone shorter expressions) could reasonably be talked of at all, except relative to the other sentences of an inclusive theory. Such relativity would be awkward, since, conversely, the individual component sentences offer the only way into the theory. Now the notion of stimulus meaning partially resolves the predicament. It isolates a sort of net empirical import of each of various single sentences without regard to the containing theory, even though without loss of what the sentences owes to that containing theory. It is a device, as far as it goes, for exploring the fabric of interlocking sentences, a sentence at a time.[76]

Quine delineates a number of rough, crosscutting categories of sentences, based on this method of analysis and on the notion of stimulus meaning. First, he distinguishes *occasion sentences* for which assent may be elicited only when the relevant prompting stimulation is present (hence reprompting requires continuation of recurrence of the nonverbal stimulus) from *standing sentences* for which responses may be elicited without a copresent nonverbal stimulus.[77] A second, and more important, categorization Quine makes is that of *observation sentences*. These are sentences whose meanings are fully, or nearly fully, determinable by reference to possible prompting stimulations: They are sentences for which "their stimulus meanings may without fear of contradiction be said to do full justice to their meanings."[78] Owing to the ineliminable influence of what Quine calls "intrusive collateral information," full equation of stimulus meanings of source and receptor-language sentences is exceedingly rare, if not impossible. Individual variations in stimulus meaning of even observation sentences can result from differences in attentiveness to stimulation or perceptual capacities between linguist and informant, and among informants; but these are "ironed out" over the group as a whole. However, in the case of nonobservational sentences, collateral information will play much more of a determining role in subjects' responses. Here little or no regularity in the stimulation-patterns that prompt assent and dissent will exist. Thus, with sentences such as 'Red' and 'Rabbit', the influence of collateral information may be regarded as minimal; while in the case of a sentence such as 'Bachelor', assent and dissent will be determined, from case to case, by the informant's awareness of the marital status of the individual observed, and this information is not generally given in immediate experience. (More precisely, observationality is a matter of degree, with sentences grading according to the determinability of stimulus meaning.) Standing sentences may also be high in observationality: Any observational occasion sentences can be transformed into what Quine calls "eternal sentences," which never vary with respect to affirmation or denial. Also, we can form "pegged observation sentences" by including specifications of space-time coordinates, or generalized "observation categoricals," such as 'Whenever it rains it pours', that are composed of observation sentences.[79]

Again, there is a close connection between observationality of sentences, determinacy of stimulus meaning, and the primary character of this mode of language-acquisition:

> If a sentence is one that (like 'Red' and 'Rabbit') is inculcated mostly by something like direct ostension, the uniformity will lie at the surface and there will be little variation in stimulus meaning; the sentence will be highly observational. If it is one that (like 'Bachelor') is inculcated through connections with other sentences, linking up thus indirectly with past stimulations of other sorts than those that serve directly to prompt present assent to the sentence, then its stimulus meaning will vary with the speakers' pasts, and the sentence will count as very unobservational. The stimulus meaning of a very unobservational occasion sentence for a speaker is a product of two factors, a fairly standard set of sentence-to-sentence connections and a random personal history; hence the largely random character of the stimulus meaning from speaker to speaker.[80]

Stimulus synonymy can be manifest between, and hence serve as an empirical basis for equating, sentences within the source language that are unobservational, providing comparison of stimulus meaning can be made *intra*subjectively, by a competent source-language speaker (eventually, perhaps, the linguist himself). (However, they cannot be "uniquely" translated, even by a bilingual.)[81]

Determination of the stimulus-synonymy of *terms* (or predicates) is effected, in some cases, by determining the *stimulus-analyticity* of sentences (perhaps of the form 'All and only F's are G's') equating them,[82] that is, by determining that an informant will assent to such sentences, if to anything, following any prompting stimulation that might be given at a particular time.[83] However, although the stimulus analyticity of a sentence can be recognized by the linguist, the inference that native terms equated in a stimulus-analytic sentence are stimulus synonymous requires the additional assumption that the natives cut their discourse up into terms as we do, along with the selection of certain logical-grammatical devices for doing this. Although this is, perhaps, a necessary imposition to make on the native language, it is an imposition nonetheless. However, the real difficulty comes in that *inter*cultural stimulus synonymy of source and receptor-language expressions (however it might be achieved, perhaps by deriving it from the stimulus synonymy of corresponding one-word sentences) falls short of equating or doing full justice to the meaning of terms: For the reference of terms, according to Quine, can vary in ways that cannot be determined by any amount of determination and comparison of stimulus meanings: that is, reference is behaviorally inscrutable.[84]

The first thesis clearly delineated in *Word and Object* concerns the inscrutability of reference. This thesis arises because, although dispositions to assent to or dissent serve to establish the meanings of the sentences 'Gavagai' and 'Rabbit', the corresponding terms 'gavagai' and 'rabbit' divide their reference in ways dependent on the associated individuative apparatus of the language:

> For consider 'gavagai'. Who knows but what the objects to which this term applies are not rabbits after all, but mere stages, or brief temporal segments of rabbits. In either event the stimulus situations that prompt assent to 'Gavagai' would be the same as 'Rabbit'. Or perhaps the objects to which 'gavagai' applies are all sundry undetached parts of rabbits: again the stimulus meaning would register no difference. When from the sameness of stimulus meanings of 'Gavagai' and 'Rabbit' the linguist leaps to the conclusion that a gavagai is a whole enduring rabbit, he is just taking for granted that the native is enough like us to have a brief general term for rabbits and no brief general term for rabbit stages or parts.[85]

Quine adds the further possibility that subjects might treat 'gavagai' as a singular mass term, naming the scattered whole or fusion of rabbits, much as the word 'water' is used. The problem is that the various articles, identity predicates, and so on that might serve to distinguish these different types of reference—such as the appropriate use of indefinite articles and pluralization with count nouns but not mass terms—cannot be "discovered" on the basis of stimulus meaning.

Instead, the linguist looks from the start for components of native discourse that can serve as plural constructions; in doing this he makes the assumption that the natives individuate objects as the referents of terms. But the possibility that the native is doing things differently remains open, as is evidenced by the availability of other translation manuals that construe his reference as being instantiations of universals, temporal time-slices, and so forth. Ostension provides no independent check on this, Quine argues: "Point to a rabbit and you have pointed to a stage of a rabbit, to an integral part of a rabbit, to the rabbit fusion, and to where rabbithood is manifested."[86]

Nor can ostension be supplemented by queries such as 'Is this the same gavagai as that?' or 'Do we have one gavagai here or two?', for another equally good manual of translation could enable us to translate the questions we are putting to the native as 'Is this the same-instance-of-the-gavagai as that?', 'Are these stages of the same animal?', and so on. At the initial stages of radical translation, the linguist is incapable of asking these sorts or questions. And even with a more developed manual, he can lay no claim to objective recovery of reference because he does not objectively determine, but only imposes, the individuative apparatus:

> We cannot even say what native locutions to count as analogues of terms as we know them, much less equate them with ours term for term, except as we have also decided what native devices to view as doing in their devious ways the work of our own various auxiliaries to objective reference: our articles and pronouns, our singular and plural, our copula, our identity predicate. The whole apparatus is interdependent, and the very notion of term is as provincial to our culture as are those associated devices. The native may achieve the same net effects through linguistic structures so different that any eventual construing of our devices in the native language and vice versa can prove unnatural and largely arbitrary.[87]

Elsewhere Quine gives a less fanciful example of inscrutability that bears out the point that the interpretation of term-reference can vary, with no visible difference in community dispositions to assent or dissent. In Japanese there are particles known as numerical classifiers that operate in contexts in which numerical quantities of things are given. (There are a large number of these, varying with particular context: there are over fifty taxonomy-specific classifiers, plus classifiers for processes, shapes, and so on.)[88] Since Japanese does not have elements that can be identified as definite or indefinite articles and plural endings, such particles can be viewed either as modifying the number itself, changing its style to suit the modified object, or as modifying the term referring to the object and not "varying the meaning" of the number at all. Hence, a native sentence stimulus synonymous with (A) 'There are five steers' could be regarded as one in which the classifier functioned to decline the number five in the animal gender. But, alternatively, it could be regarded as one that operated on the term referring to the animal, by itself a mass term rather than a general term, transforming it into a composite individuative term such as 'head of cattle'. Given the latter interpretation, one could offer (B) 'There are five head of cattle' as the translation of the Japanese string. But as the native sentence and the two proposed receptor translations (A) and (B) are all stimulus synonymous (and likewise any other sets of sentences in which the translator has this choice to make), there can be no way of empirically determining the superiority of one translation over the other. Yet reference evidently differs.[89]

Stimulus meaning does provide semantic criteria for recovery of the native truth-functional logical apparatus. For instance, negation would be effected by any class of expressions that, when added to larger expressions, would turn affirmations of the original expressions into denials. A principle of "fair translation" or "charity" bids the linguist make every effort to find source-language analogues of receptor-language logical constructions and eliminates any problems of underdetermination stemming from the linguist's freedom to attribute an "inferior" or inconsistent logical apparatus to them. Attributions of "prelogical" mentality to subjects are to be counted as the result of poor translation only. More generally, the maxim applies to any case in which we might be tempted to construe someone as believing a clear falsehood; for example, if by a literal reading, or what Quine calls "homophonic" translation, of their remarks they seem to contradict themselves, we ought to reinterpret their words:

> The maxim of translation underlying all this is that assertions startlingly false on the face of them are likely to turn on hidden differences of language. This maxim is strong enough in all of us to swerve us even from the homophonic method that is so fundamental to the very acquisition of one's mother tongue.[90]

However, the more powerful apparatus of quantificational and polyadic logics are not accessible in radical translation—a point already implied by the inscrutability of the referential apparatus. Where, as in the case of truth-functional logic, there are no other translational options, there is no indeterminacy. Stimulus meaning serves to fix the truth-functional connectives. In the latter case, however, options are available.[91]

The linguist's methods for determining stimulus meaning enable him to translate observation sentences and truth functions, to identify stimulus-analytic sentences, and to determine intrasubjective stimulus synonymy of sentences *within* the source language. (although this does not permit their translation). Stimulus meaning is insufficient to determine any further translational correlations. All further translation is held by Quine to *depend ineliminably* on the linguist's chosen correlations, his *analytical hypotheses*.[92] In the above-noted cases, assertions of equivalence or difference of meaning, observational experience provides an independent check on the linguist's hypotheses, a measure of their correctness or incorrectness. When it comes to reference, individuation, and so on, the linguist's choice of analytical hypotheses (for example, 'Expression *a* is a native *term*'; '*a* refers to chairs'; *b* means 'is identical with') are determined by the *linguist's* choices among alternatives constrained presumably by such factors as the overall systematic import of a given choice for the end product. Wherever the dispositions of a receptor-language speaker to affirm or deny sentences is not determined primarily by reference to immediate experience, employment of those sentences as translations of native strings will depend on the linguist's analytical hypotheses and not solely on determination of stimulus meaning or synonymy. And just as the scientific theorist can manipulate the nonobservational reaches of a theory to make sure it is testable, observational implications match up with experience so the linguist has some freedom to juggle and vary analytic hypotheses and the translations they yield, while preserving stimulus synonymy of the source- and receptor-language observation sentences. However, this freedom calls the translator's standards into question:[93]

> The linguist's finished jungle-to-English manual has as its net yield an infinite *semantic correlation* of sentences: the implicit specification of an English sentence, for every one of the infinitely many possible jungle sentences. Most of the semantic correlation is supported only by analytical hypotheses, in their extension beyond the zone where independent evidence for translation is possible. That those unverifiable translations proceed without mishap must not be taken as pragmatic evidence of good lexicography, for mishap is impossible.[94]

Initial appearances notwithstanding, Quine does not think that grammatical analysis cannot be empirically warranted. His "The Problem of Meaning in Linguistics" makes clear that he views determinations of grammaticality as warranted by behavioral evidence and subject only to normal empirical underdetermination. Grammatical analysis suffers no indeterminacy because it is clear what behavioral responses are being explained and are serving as evidence (for example, subjects' "bizarreness reactions" upon hearing grammatically incoherent expressions). The problem arises in connection with *lexicography*, which goes beyond the grammatical task of explaining *significance* or *meaningfulness* and involves itself with *sameness of meaning* and attendant notions. Indeterminacy is *not* just the result, for him, of some kind of underdetermination of linguistic analysis. It arises where there is difficulty in seeing what behavioral fact is being explained or is serving as evidence. In lexicography, the linguist has only such things as charity and familiarity to rely on in getting a fix on belief-attributions sufficient to get translation beyond what stimulus meaning can help ascertain: Nothing in the behavior-stream itself helps us adjudicate between meaning and belief. From all we can observe, we can choose translations that make beliefs more or less bizarre, or we can choose to attribute beliefs that make translation more or less smooth. As a result, we have no reason to suppose that successful translation warrants the claim that the chosen set of receptor-language characterizations of source-language term-intensions and term-extensions is in fact uniquely attributable to source-language speakers. (And, again, this is only a means to establish the more general thesis that synonymy relations, save for those he allows, are not objective, natural relations.) So even though the underdetermination of grammatical apparatus is a premise in the inscrutability of reference argument, the choice of grammatical apparatus is determinate, though underdetermined, but the attribution of some particular referential scheme is indeterminate.[95]

As I noted earlier, the inscrutability of reference is but one of two problems Quine discusses. It counts against the determinacy of extension and, given the relation of intension to extension, against the determinacy of *term*-intension. Quine supplements these considerations with additional arguments designed to make clear that all translations are indeterminate that are not stimulus-meaning determinate; this would include translations of sentences as well as terms. Another consequence of the freedom of choice that one has in manipulating and choosing theories (in light of his holism and underdetermination theses) is that the linguist has similar freedom in employing those sentences as translations of native strings. The result is that rival scientific theories couched in the receptor language may radically diverge from one another in their theoretical reaches, and yet square equally well with the supporting evidence. Hence, the alternative manuals available in principle to the linguist may likewise diverge in the translations they yield in the receptor language; that is, they are in no sense equivalent, yet no behavioral evidence can serve to distinguish one as the uniquely best one. Such indeterminacy pervades the translation of all sentences that are not stimulus-meaning determinate or high in observationality:

> One has only to reflect on the nature of possible data and methods to appreciate the indeterminacy. Sentences translatable outright, translatable by independent evidence of stimulatory occasions are sparse and must woefully underdetermine the analytical hypotheses on which the translation of all further sentences depends. To project such hypotheses beyond the independently translatable sentences at all is in effect to impute our sense of linguistic analogy unverifiably to the native mind. Nor would the dicates even of our own sense of analogy tend to any intrinsic uniqueness; using what first comes to mind engenders an air of determinacy though freedom reign.[96]

Full indeterminacy, as distinct from inscrutability, emerges in the last sentence of the section:

> There can be no doubt that rival systems of analytical hypotheses can fit the totality of behavior to perfection, and can fit the totality of dispositions to speech behavior as well, and still specify mutually incompatible translations of countless sentences insusceptible of independent control.[97]

The point is restated subsequently and contrasted with the generally accepted point that one cannot expect uniqueness of translation:

> The indeterminacy that I mean is more radical. It is that rival systems of analytical hypotheses can conform to all speech dispositions within each of the languages concerned and yet dictate, in countless cases, utterly disparate translations: not mere mutual paraphrases, but translations each of which would be excluded by the other system of translation. Two such translations might even be patently contrary in truth value, provided there is no stimulation that would encourage assent to either.[98]

Quine warns that actual examples of full-blown indeterminacy are not easily accessible:

There is an obstacle to offering an actual example of two such rival systems of analytical hypotheses. Known languages are known through unique systems of analytical hypotheses established in tradition or painfully arrived at by unique skilled linguists. To devise a contrasting system would require an entire duplicate enterprise of translation, unaided even by the usual hints from interpreters.[99]

But while he does not expect to find instances of fully developed alternatives to existing manuals, he believes this presents no major impediment to our perception of the indeterminacy of translation.

Again, indeterminacy of translation and inscrutability of reference, though closely related, are distinct theses that could be viewed as concerning a similar embarrassment of riches: Behavioral evidence leaves us, in each case, with a multiplicity of divergent but correct answers. Inscrutability results because of reliance on familiarity in choosing a referential scheme for the source language. But as translation is thus "directed away" from the source culture, the linguist's methodology provides no rational grounds for asserting that a given grammar is that of the source culture. The result is that the linguist cannot "objectively" decide on the extension (or intension) of terms. Sentence-indeterminacy, on the other hand, can be seen as resulting from the fact that translation manuals, like scientific theories, are underdetermined in the sense that rival systems of assertions are empirically equivalent, and the linguist has no criteria for determining which of the available, mutually incompatible sets of translations is uniquely correct. We have reason to say that the translation of individual sentences is indeterminate. Unless the connection of a source-language sentence to the receptor-language sentence that "gives its meaning" is secured by firm correspondence in stimulus meaning, the meaning of the source-language sentence is a function of the relations of its receptor-language correlate to other receptor strings. But these relations can vary ad infinitum, yet compatibly with the same behavioral evidence.

These accounts of inscrutability and indeterminacy of sentence-translation seems clearly to be operative in *Word and Object* and are presented in clearer form in a subsequent article, "On the Reasons for Indeterminacy of Translation" (1970). This article also clarifies the difference between the two critiques by pointing out that the inscrutability of reference of the source term 'gavagai' with respect to the alternative receptor translations 'rabbit' and 'rabbit stage' does not also indicate the indeterminacy of translation of the sentence 'Gavagai' either as 'Rabbit' or 'Rabbit stage'; there is a clear criterion of sameness of meaning operative in the case of these sentences—namely, sameness of stimulus meaning. Since stimulus meaning "does full justice to their meaning," there is a firm empirical basis for saying they are synonymous.[100]

This article's formulation of the relationship between underdetermination of theory and indeterminacy of translation runs as follows: Imagining a case in which we are translating a theory that seems the equal of our own (an assumption that is intended only for clarification), Quine argues:

> As always in radical translation, the starting point is the equating of observation sentences of the two languages by an inductive equating of stimulus meanings. In order afterward to construe the foreigner's theoretical sentences we have to project analytical hypotheses, whose ultimate justification is substantially just that the implied observation sentences match up. But now the same old empirical slack, the old indeterminacy between physical theories recurs in second intension. Insofar as the truth of a physical theory is underdetermined by observables, the translation of the foreigner's physical theory is underdetermined by translation of his observation sentences. If our physical theory can vary though all possible observations be fixed, then our translation of his physical theory can vary though our translations of all possible observation reports on his part be fixed. Our translation of his physical theory than our own possible observations fix our own physical theory.[101]

It is worth mentioning that another line of argument to the indeterminacy thesis is presented elsewhere in Quine and, indeed, seems now to be his preferred one. This does not isolate underdetermination of theory as a distinct premise (perhaps a good thing in light of some modifications Quine has had to make in that theses and which I shall discuss below). However, it still hinges on the idea that there is a multiplicity of right answers in translation. But it generates the multiplicity directly from Duhemian holism (which is not the same as, and does not entail, underdetermination of theory).[102] In "Epistemology Naturalized," Quine argues:

> If the English sentences of a theory have their meaning only together as a body, then we can justify their translation into Arunta only together as a body. There will be no justification for pairing off the component English sentences with component Arunta sentences, except as these correlations make the translation of the theory as a whole come out right. Any translations of the English sentences into

Arunta sentences will be as correct as any other, so long as the net empirical implications of the theory as a whole are preserved in translation. But it is to be expected that many different ways of translating the component sentences, essentially different individually, would deliver the same empirical implications for the theory as a whole; deviations in the translation of one component sentence could be compensated for in the translation of another component sentence. Insofar, there can be no ground for saying which of two glaringly unlike translations of individual sentences is right.[103]

The key difference in this latter line is that we are not asked to accept the idea that wholesale changes in theories and manuals are possible, only that any given hypothesis or translational correlation can be varied provided compensatory adjustments are made elsewhere. And this is adequate to establish the key difference Quine envisions between rival translation manuals: one offers receptor translations that diverge from those offered by the other. Subsequent to these remarks, Quine makes evident his departure from logical positivism and shows it to be in the classic empiricist style of showing previous empiricists to be guilty of the very dogmas they reject:

For an uncritical mentalist, no such indeterminacy threatens. Every term and every sentence is a label attached to an idea, simple or complex, which is stored in the mind. When on the other hand we take a verification theory of meaning seriously, the indeterminacy would appear to be inescapable. The Vienna Circle espoused a verification theory of meaning but did not take it seriously enough. If we recognize with Peirce that the meaning of a sentence turns purely on what would count as evidence for its truth, and if we recognize with Duhem that theoretical sentences have their evidence not as single sentences but only as larger blocks of theory, then the indeterminacy of translation of theoretical sentences is the natural conclusion. And most sentences, apart from observation sentences, are theoretical. This conclusion, conversely, once it is embraced, seals the fate of any general notion of propositional meaning or, for that matter, state of affairs.[104]

However, either account of indeterminacy provokes the challenge as to why translation generally does not issue in facts, while physics does; the contrast between underdetermined fact (in physics) as opposed to indeterminate nonfact (in translation) evidently remains as a consequence of Quine's views regardless of the line of argument one chooses. (And holism applies to science and translation equally as well.) I shall give more attention to this later on. For now I hope the thrust, if not the cogency, of Quine's theses is sufficiently clear for the purposes of preparing the way for my subsequent examination of his theses' relationships to, and import for, anthropology. For now let me simply note the following: There is critical dependence on a pragmatic notion of scientific truth here, one Quine draws largely from Peirce. Physics is a kind of ultimate source of facts. It provides final justifications to any purportedly warranted claim about factual states, events, and processes. If we can settle our physics but not, in the process, settle our translations, then translation (insofar as it depends on charity and familiarity to supplement behavioral evidence) must then depend on choices not based on physical fact. But, for Quine, what cannot correlate with physical fact is not a fact of any sort. (Note that unlike in the earlier "Problem of Meaning in Linguistics" Quine no longer focuses on simplicity.)[105]

To summarize, all the confirming evidence that a theorist could hope for would still leave room for (that is, be compatible with) equally adequate alternative theories, nonequivalent to, indeed incompatible with, his chosen theory. Applying these points to radical translation reveals, for Quine, the dependence of most translational hypotheses on the containing body of hypotheses, the manual of translation, rather than a dependence on shared stimulation and dispositions to assent or dissent, as well as a dependence of grammatical and ontological determinations on the linguist's imposition of certain initial analytical hypotheses. Moreover, these points further indicate the linguist's inability in principle to have a factual basis for selecting one manual to the exclusion of *incompatible* (but equally evidenced) alternatives. The set of *ideally* good manuals is such that choice of any one member excludes the others. Yet to claim that there is no uniquely correct translation manual (save for those parts comprising correlations that may, perhaps, be determined on the basis of stimulus meaning) is to claim that no individual translational hypotheses may rightly or wrongly express a fact of the matter (save for those that are stimulus-meaning determinate); for their factual correctness depends on that of the containing manuals, and this, Quine argues, cannot be ascertained.

Again, this is not to say there are no coherent criteria of correctness; rather, his point is that we cannot factually warrant belief in natural synonymy from translation that meets the appropriate criteria. Also, it is worth reiterating that Quine's critique, unlike Wittgenstein's, is not simply aimed at intensional objects; It is aimed at natural synonymy itself. Indeed, if we recall Quine's remarks about the "circle of terms" such as 'synonymous', 'intension', 'analytic', 'necessary', and so on, all of these—including 'intension'—are acceptable if any one of them is. Indeed, Quine remarks in a more recent essay:

> If in general I could make satisfactory sense of declaring two expressions to be synonymous, I would be more than pleased to recognize an abstract object as their common meaning. The method is familiar: I would define the meaning of an expression as the set of its synonyms. Where the trouble lies, rather, is in the two-place predicate of synonymy itself; it is too desperately wanting in clarity and perspicuity.[106]

Of course Quine is not here contemplating allowing the *epistemologically* inert objects that seem Wittgenstein's main concern. Nonetheless, by attacking synonymy Quine seems to cut against any efforts, including Wittgenstein's, to explicate it.

The key problem for Quine, again, is that he cannot see what translation is "right or wrong about," what behavioral facts serve as standards of correctness (beyond what is stimulus-meaning determinate). Let us return for a moment to the contrast between grammar and lexicography: We know what grammatical analysis is about; and knowing this is also knowing what its factual basis is. We have a set of grammatical or significant strings determinable on grounds independent of the particular grammar applied; that is, whatever behavioral reactions are indicative of significance or non-significance. The grammarian is explaining, providing a means for producing, this output. It is what the grammar is right or wrong about and it is the grammar's factual basis. The lexicographer has no parallel, independently identifiable output—thus Carnap's motivation to rely on translation method and theory itself in answering this question. If he succeeds, then the question "What is translation right or wrong about?" is answered as follows: If behavioral evidence warrants one correct lexicographical mapping on application of empirical translation procedures, then it warrants our reliance on the mapping to justify our belief that all along there was, indeed, a "fact of the matter" guiding our translational efforts. It justifies, on a factual basis, the belief that there is a way that subjects interpret, a set of somethings which they mean, which it is then the legitimate scientific task of translation to reveal. (Although there is some circularity in this, it is not vicious—at least not according to the "internal realism" Quine espouses and which I shall discuss in Chapter 3.) However, translation actually produces conflicting answers from the same body of evidence, and only appeal to familiarity and charity can narrow options. This shows, Quine believes, the failure of Carnap's operational ploy. We are left with no clear understanding of what we are explicating or what facts warrant claims of success or failure in describing intension or synonymy in natural languages.

Chapter 2

Methodological Problems in the Study of Alien Culture

Boasian Themes in Twentieth-Century Anthropology

In Chapter 1, I discussed a number of trends in theoretical development away from the consciously apprehended Lockean idea and Fregean proposition. Although Frege-Lewis type theories still abound, many thinkers have been motivated by a variety of problems with these approaches to move the locus of significance either to the unconscious level (Katz and Fodor) or to the social-behavioral level (Morris, Wittgenstein, and Searle). However, I have also noted that Quine's various criticisms pertain to all these types of theory. Also, we saw the initial development of Quine's radical indeterminacy thesis from his perception of deep philosophical import in problems familiar to anthropologists—particularly those concerning the imposition of concepts and beliefs on the discourse and thought of ethnographic subjects.

In this chapter I shall take a closer look at twentieth-century anthropology to get a clearer picture of the role of translational indeterminacy problems in the genesis of anthropological theory. I shall give particular attention to those linguistic, ethnographic, ethnologic, and sociolinguistic approaches that have evolved in what has been called the "language and culture" tradition—including ethnoscience, the new ethnography, cognitive anthropology, sociolinguistics, structuralism, and symbolic anthropology. This survey is intended to develop the following points: First, I wish to indicate the intimate, complex, and often deeply antagonistic relationships between Quine's reflections on the indeterminacy of translation and various aspects of theoretical developments in the the language-and-culture methodologies. The antagonistic thrust of his arguments will be clear in part due to the evident mentalistic commitments of many of these approaches. (It will also be clearer still in certain cases wherein the influence of Morris, Chomsky, and Searle on anthropological theorists and field workers is direct and explicit.) Quine raises particular worries for those approaches (both mentalistic and social-behavioral), which, as we shall see, insist that anthropologists operate from an "emic" perspective, that is, revealing, even adopting in one way or another the ethnographic subjects' points of view. Related problems with aims to attain "psychological reality" or "cognitive validity" of ethnographic results will also be examined. I shall note significant detractors from these various views, several of whom perceive problems similar to those emphasized by Quine. Yet even their remarks may not adequately encompass the full import of translational indeterminacy. However, despite evident antagonisms, the commonality of philosophic concerns between the philosophers and anthropologists I consider will finally provide the makings of a constructive solution to these problems. This solution will be in line with pragmatic trends in recent literature in such areas as cognitive anthropology and structuralism.

As I have indicated and as shall become increasingly evident below, if Quine's indeterminacy thesis is correct, we have cause to worry that something is seriously wrong with language-and-culture and other major branches of anthropological metatheory. And it may have to do with the foundationl anthropological concern with recovering *culturally specific* elements. This concern may be founded on mistaken semantic and cognitive assumptions. Indeed, given the close and important interrelationships between Quine's critical theses and these theoretical concerns, and given the enormous impact Quine's work has had on recent philosophy, it is puzzling that he has had relatively little impact on anthropology, a social science that is usually sensitive to developments in relevant areas in philosophy. Part of the reason for this is that Quine's indeterminacy arguments, on first glance, might seem *so* extremely skeptical as not to warrant any more serious concern than, say, those of Sextus Empiricus. However, Quine is not advocating a simple semantic analog of skepticism: It is a different line of argument that rests, intriguingly, in part on a physicalist thesis that also figures in his rejection of traditional skepticism about the natural world. Also, it is worth repeating that his arguments do not make translation an irrational procedure. Translators have criteria for *correct* translations; what is not clear is whether they have criteria for *true* translations.

Before proceeding further, let me emphasize that my intention here is to give only a brief outline of certain general methodological trends in anthropology that reflect a common ancestry of problems and concerns with philosophy of language. This account is by no means intended to be exhaustive of past or current views on meaning in anthropology, or even fully to accommodate all those significant contributions to the problem areas of central interest to this book. Nor will I try fully to explain the views I have chosen to discuss (and will rely in places on extensive quotation). Rather, I intend only to indicate that the problems and consequences of Quinean indeterminacy are significant for anthropology, to reveal what shall turn out to be precedents for the view of translation I shall later develop, and to provide some concrete cases for its application.

Let me begin with a few foundational figures. As cultural anthropology developed in the late nineteenth and early twentieth centuries, theoreticians and field workers became increasingly sensitive to problems plaguing their attempts to attain what many regarded as their central objective: the determination of the beliefs and world views of alien cultures. Eschewal of ethnocentrism became a widely accepted admonition of principle. However, the difficulties in avoiding the imposition of western-oriented conceptual schemes and values were considerable, especially in light of the fact that determination of the nature of foreign perspectives was crucially dependent on accurate field translation. While these problems were well known by his time, it is Franz Boas who is generally regarded as the first to perceive how fundamental recovery of language is to ethnography and ethnology. His classic work, *The Handbook of American Indian Languages*, espouses respect for the native subject's, not the field linguist's, categorizations of experience, a point that demanded mastery of the subject's language.[1] He further argued that language study is essential not only in facilitating ethnography but itself constitutes a central theoretical area of ethnology; the ethnographer, qua ethnographer, is a linguist, and the linguist's area of inquiry comprises, ultimately, "the mental": "If ethnology is understood as the science dealing with the mental phenomena of the life of the peoples of the world," he contended, then "human language, one of the most important manifestations of mental life, would seem to belong naturally to the field of work of ethnology. . ."[2]

This concern to recover elements comprised in the mental lives of field subjects, and the belief that linguistic method is suitable to the task, developed into a widespread interest in applying linguistic *models* to ethnographic and ethnological tasks. The influential sociolinguist Dell Hymes remarks:

It is in the twentieth century that linguistics comes to be a recurrent methodological model for anthropologists. The beginning is with Boas, just before the First World War. Boas did not put the issue in its full form, but present understanding of it is the outcome of a development that stems from him. He and his students shaped modern professional anthropology in the United States, and shaped also its conception of the relationship between study of language and study of culture.[3]

In addition, Boas stressed the prior character of linguistic study (independent of cultural context), owing to what he viewed as the *unconscious* nature of the laws governing speech behavior in primitive societies—this in contrast to the generally conscious nature of other ethnographic phenomena.[4] Because of this, Boas' thought is manifest also in methodological trends in which concern was expressed for studying not only linguistics, and through it the consciously mental, but also the unconscious. This point is taken up by many, including current proponents of generative grammatical approaches in anthropological linguistics and ethnography, and broadly expanded by structural anthropologists.

For the purposes of this inquiry at least, the most significant of Boas' advances is his recognition of language study as being more than an instrument for fieldwork but also a means for reaching to deeper, more tacit levels of thought—something of whose significance Boas himself was fully aware. The extension of linguistic method to other areas of ethnography and ethnology for which Hymes credits him is only implicit in Boas' stress of linguistics as intrinsic to anthropological inquiry. As linguistics became a standard part of anthropological training, an environment conducive to the extension of linguistic methods was nurtured.[5]

Hymes subdivides the minimal instrumental application of language study into the following types: *facilitating*, or using language for gaining access to a community, surviving, and establishing rapport; *generating*, or using language for the production of data (for example, eliciting responses to gain further linguistic and ethnographic data); and *validating*, or eliciting native responses as to the correctness of tentative findings. The dependence upon correct translation is already quite evident here, even before one considers the more ambitious projects concerning what Hymes further classifies as the *penetrating* use of linguistic inquiry in delving to more tacit mental or social levels. In all four of these functions, problematic meaning elements are manifest, and insofar as language study serves as a source of new methodological approaches in other areas of ethnography, which Hymes characterizes as its *foundational* use, the consequences of these criticisms extend that much more widely.[6]

Edward Sapir and Benjamin Lee Whorf shared Boas' concern of avoiding ethnocentrism and like Boas saw the key to penetration of foreign culture in careful *grammatical* analysis. The relative fixity of grammatical patterns as compared with more superficial linguistic phenomena suggested to them a certain structural isomorphism between grammar and the more fixed conceptual structures constitutive of world views. Though this world-constitutive character is typically associated with Sapir and Whorf, Hymes notes a direct continuity in this regard with the central elements of Boas' thought:

> It is easy to see how the linking [of grammar and world view] might arise and persist in western thought. Grammar has seemed to occupy a special place, central or basic to the linguistic scheme of things, because it is relatively more stable, both through time and across dialects, than vocabulary and phonology often are; because it contain features that are relatively more general and fundamental, since, unlike individual words and sounds, they "must be expressing" [quoting Boas]; and because the concepts associated with general grammatical features often pertain to general categories that find a place in metaphysics—space, time, act, person, thing. Join this to views of language and thought, or of language and logic, as interdependent, perhaps two sides of the same coin; confront it with the dramatic diversity in grammar that is apparent in the languages of the world; and it is understandable how grammar might seem to go to the heart of the problem of interpreting other ways of life or thought in relation to our own.[7]

Another important development of Sapir's was to stress the *unconscious* character of world-formative grammatical patterns to such a degree that language takes on the causally prior role to typically conscious phenomena that comprise other areas of culture. "In effect," Hymes notes, Sapir takes the Boasian view of the value of language because of "the unconscious and unrationalized nature of linguistic structure . . . and runs away with it, leaving culture to shift for itself."[8] However, Sapir also welcomed the possibility that the methodology of linguistic inquiry to the cultural depths of language and culture might be applicable to the study of other cultural phenomena, which might be seen to be rooted in underlying "innate-forms":

> If it can be shown that culture has an innate-form, a series of contours, quite apart from the subject-matter of any description what-

soever, we have a something in culture that may serve as a term of comparison with and possibly a means of relating it to language.[9]

Although he did not pursue this line of development, and although his most well-known works emphasized the value of linguistic inquiry per se in anthropology, Sapir (in the above passage and elsewhere) encouraged foundational progress that culminated in the development of a number of linguistic *models* in ethnography (which I shall discuss shortly).

Sapir's stress on the world-constitutive character of linguistic categories also made him particularly sensitive to the pervasive problems of imposition and cross-cultural diversity that threatened the objective penetration of radically foreign cultures. In order to reveal these underlying (linguistic and other) patterns of culture, one had to scrutinize one's subjects and data carefully, and, as Sapir often stressed, one had to go about radical ethnography as if one knew nothing about the society in question and was learning about their culture only through painstaking observation of day-to-day relationships. What particularly motivates this emphasis is his belief that the formative processes of language "are to explained, if explained at all, as due to the more minute action of psychological factors beyond the control of will or reflection."[10] Particularly, one had to rely on the penetrating function of linguistic inquiry, precisely because this provided the access to underlying categories and, derivatively, access to the different worlds in which one's subjects lived. One's prior observations of the world were, you might say, too "culture laden":

> It is quite an illusion to imagine that one adjusts to reality essentially without the use of language and that language is merely an incidental means of solving specific problems of communication or reflection. The fact of the matter is that the "real world" is to a large extent unconsciously built up on the language habits of the group. No two languages are ever sufficiently similar to be considered as representing the same social reality. The worlds in which different societies live are distinct worlds, not merely the same world with different labels attached.[11]

Whorf's influential studies of the Hopi bore results that fortify these points of Sapir's, and, like Sapir, he viewed the linguist's translation problem (and the ethnographer's problem generally) as one of "calibrating" radically different conceptual schemes of reference.[12] A profound form of ethnocentrism would be manifest in linguistic and ethnographic study that sought to liken the foreigner's conceptual scheme (roughly, his system of coordinates) to the linguist's or to that of the receptor-language community.[13] One had to be wary, Sapir warned, of a conceptual (and derivatively ontological) relativity "generally hidden from us by our native acceptance of fixed habits of speech as guides to an objective understanding of the nature of experience."[14] Such calibration appears, in Sapir's view, as the only means of transcending the influence of one's own language and conceptual scheme on one's perception of the language and scheme of another culture. The environing world he likened to the "world of points" delineated under different geometrical frames of reference:

> The formal method of approach to the expressed item of experience, as to the given point of space, is so different that the resulting feeling of orientation can be the same neither in the two languages nor in the two frames of reference. Entirely distinct, or at least measurably distinct, formal adjustments have to be made and these differences have their psychological correlations.[15]

Language, he argued, had to make contact with this environing world in order to be applicable and learnable. But once more fully elaborated it becomes "a self-contained conceptual system which previsages all possible experience in accordance with certain accepted formal limitations."[16]

This point, reminiscent of Kant, and, more pertinently to the present context, of C. I. Lewis, comes to have extremely important bearing on Quine's indeterminacy thesis. The problem is just how the needed calibration is to be made, and the intractability (and in part, perhaps, the insolubility) of this problem was quite evident to Sapir:

> Such categories as number, gender, case, tense, mode, voice, "aspect" and a host of others, many of which are not recognized systematically in our Indo-European languages, are, of course, derivative of experience in the last analysis, but, once abstracted from experience, they are systematically elaborated in language and are not so much discovered in experience as imposed upon it because of the tyrannical hold that linguistic form has upon our orientation in the world. Inasmuch as languages differ very widely in their systematization of fundamental concepts, they tend to be only loosely equivalent to each other as symbolic devices and are, as a matter of fact, incommensurable in the sense in which two systems of points in a plane are, on the whole, incommensurable to each other if they are plotted out with reference to differing systems of coordinates. The point of view urged in this paper be-

comes entirely clear only when one compares languages of extremely different structures, as in the case of our Indo-European languages, native American Indian languages, and native languages of Africa.[17]

In light of the possibility of such extreme contrasts, one wonders how much of what linguists and ethnographers in this tradition set out to do can feasibly be accomplished. Whorf's "calibration" of the Hopi and Western schemes is curtly criticized, for instance, by William Bright, who contends that Whorf "tends to assume, rather than to demonstrate, that the Hopi actually hold such a view of the world."[18] The pressing question to be asked of Sapir and Whorf, as well as of their critics, is what criteria of adequacy are to be appealed to in putative demonstrations that the Hopi do or do not "actually hold such a view of the world"?

The hope of developing a general method for the analysis of non-linguistic, as well as linguistic, symbolic forms was envisioned by DeSaussure and Cassirer,[19] but neither of them seems to have influenced language-and-culture anthropologists directly (save for Levi-Strauss).[20] Even though mentalism prevails in subsequent language-and-culture methodologies, the more limited behaviorist semiotics of Morris have direct (that is, acknowledged) influence on a number of major figures in anthropology, including F. G. Lounsbury, Ward Goodenough, and Joseph Greenberg.[21] Greenberg's influential article "Linguistics and Ethnology" cites Morris' *Signs, Language, and Behavior* and Carnap's *Introduction to Semantics* for semantic-theoretical constructions that he believed could be brought to bear on radical translation and the reconstruction of radically different social realities. The designation (in Morris' sense) of morphemes, insofar as they are "objects in the cultural universe of the speakers," must be provided to the linguist by supplementary ethnographic analysis (done by him or someone else). Though the recovery of such cultural objects is more difficult as cultural differences increase, such recovery is possible in principle and is of value not only to the linguist but to the ethnographer as well, since "the semantics of the language of the people in whom he is interested . . .presents him with a practically exhaustive classification of the objects in the cultural universe of the speakers." In addition, Greenberg views the semiotics of Morris as particularly useful in cases where designata "are not sensually perceivable events in the space-time of the investigator."[22]

This incorporation of Morris' notion of designation, evident still in more recent fieldwork,[23] makes clear the methodological commitment to "recovery" of a facet of symbolic meaning, along with bolder objectives regarding the discovery of ontology and underlying grammar or subconscious linguistic structure of the source language. These make the consequences of Quine's reflections on these same problems particularly evident—even for a behaviorist approach that would seem, initially, compatible with the behaviorism often espoused by Quine himself.

These same problems are reflected and magnified in the contrasting mentalistic-cognitive tradition that follows the work of Goodenough, whose methodological views shall receive detailed attention in subsequent sections. At this point I would like to rehearse some of the general themes of this section and subsequent ones by examining a number of methodological points made in Goodenough's "Cultural Anthropology and Linguistics" (1957).[24]

Goodenough premises his methodological views here and elsewhere on a basic view of culture and an intentionally parallel view of language as consisting in "whatever one has to know or believe in order to operate in a manner acceptable to [or in order to communicate with] its members, and do so in any role that they accept for any one of themselves."[25] This initially nonmentalistic-sounding definition (which I shall exploit in later chapters under a nonmentalistic interpretation) is immediately interpreted by Goodenough as entailing the penetration by the social inquirer of his subjects' mental realm. Roughly, culture is viewed by him as a set of rules determined by judgments and intuitions of propriety, aptness, and so on of persons within the cultural community. The goal of ethnography, Goodenough argues, is to allow outsiders to *get along* with members of that community; and getting along, Goodenough contends, requires participation to a degree sufficient to internalize the society's rules:

> By this definition [of culture], we should note that culture is not a material phenomenon; it does not consist of things, people, behavior, or emotions. It is rather an organization of these things. It is the forms of things that people have in mind, their models for perceiving, relating, and otherwise interpreting them. . . . To one who knows their culture, these things and events are also signs signifying the cultural forms or models of which they are material representations.[26]

This task of penetration he views as difficult and poorly understood, but one whose success is guaranteed by our obvious ability to understand and communicate with one another:

The great problem for a science of man is how to get from the objective world of materiality, with its infinite variability, to the subjective world of form as it exists in what, for lack of a better term, we must call the minds of our fellow men. We all of us succeed in doing so, somehow, or we couldn't learn to understand each other. That language exists at all is evidence enough of this. But the processes by which we do it have eluded our grasp.[27]

Goodenough shares Greenberg's confidence in Morris' semiotics as a method for penetrating to the important realm of significance (though he is more broadly mentalistic), and he shares Bloomfield's conviction that descriptive semantics is not only a linguistic task but comprises a major aspect of ethnography: "We learn much of a culture," he contends, "when we learn the system of meanings for which its linguistic forms stand. Much descriptive ethnography is inescapably an exercise in descriptive semantics."[28] He views Morris' distinction of iconic from noniconic signs (the latter being those signs "which themselves lack the properties delimiting the classes of phenomena they signify") as of central importance to ethnography.[29] Failure to determine the "conceptual forms" that noniconic forms designate—difficult as this is—Goodenough views as a central failing of approaches that eschew meaning altogether.

Contrasts with a position such as Quine's, which most avowedly eschews meaning-recovery, are no doubt already evident. However, the following passage makes the contrasts even more perplexing and startling. For Goodenough is quite well aware of the fact that empirical data (roughly, one's success in "getting along") underdetermine cultural hypotheses and that the linguist and ethnographer must be guided in large part by formal considerations:

> Given such a definition, it is obviously impossible to describe a culture properly simply by describing behavior or social, economic, and ceremonial events and arrangements as observed material phenomena. What is required is to construct a theory of the conceptual models which they represent and of which they are artifacts. We test the adequacy of such a theory by our ability to interpret and predict what goes on in a community as measured by how its members, our informants, do so. A further test is our ability ourselves to behave in ways which lead to the kind of responses from the community's members which our theory would lead us to expect. Thus tested, the theory is a valid statement of what you have to know in order to operate as a member of the society and is, as such, a valid description of its culture. Its acceptability beyond this depends largely on the esthetic criteria to which

scientists and mathematicians customarily refer by the term "elegance."[30]

Thus, for Goodenough the most empirically adequate theory of a culture (measured by the correctness of the ethnographer's predictions and by its ability to enable a user to coordinate activities with that culture), which is also the most formally elegant one developed, is necessarily a theory about the conceptual models of the members of that culture. The theory's theoretical predicates refer to members' theoretical (in a broadened sense) constructs. Roughly, it is a theory of their theory of nature, a theory of the nonobservational, theoretical constructs of their theory. However, elegance involves the full range of "western-scientific" criteria of adequacy—simplicity, familiarity, and charity—that, we have seen, threaten to bring about just the pervasive sort of imposition that Goodenough is seeking to avoid—or thus it is as Quine sees it. In the process of developing an ethnography that is readable by anthropologists and other outsiders and that contains elements incorporable into general anthropological theory (though many anthropologists eschew cross-cultural comparison, as we shall see below), one builds into one's ethnography, from the very start, "foreign" elements and structures that might have little or nothing to do with what goes on "in the natives' head."

Now this commitment to determinate cognitive recovery is not one universally shared by anthropologists, indeed, not even by all who employ Goodenough's methodology (as I shall point out below). Motivated partly by concerns about the pervasiveness of the imposition problem, as well as related problems stemming from a general mistrust of mentalism, other anthropologists have sought empirical respectability through reinterpretation of anthropological ends and through the employment of other semantic-linguistic theories and ethnographic approaches modeled on these. Of course, despite their divergence in these regards, they remain in an important way under Goodenough's (and derivatively Boas', Sapir's, and Whorf's) influence insofar as they continue to value the role of linguistic theory, though they might prefer different theories, both as a part of ethnographic inquiry and as a necessary base for other forms of ethnographic inquiry.

However, the implications of the Quinean syndrome of problems go beyond their mere reflection in the background and foreground of the work of the foundational figures discussed above. It is significant that they are found there, given their acknowledged influence on current anthropology—particularly within the language-and-culture tradition—but these problems can be tied more directly to certain

more recent, and more sophisticated, methodologies. In this vein I
shall turn now to examine recent developments within the Boasian
tradition: first to a number of mentalistic approaches that both use
and model ethnographic inquiry on particular linguistic theories
(including further discussion of Goodenough), and then to more integrated approaches such as sociolinguistics and structuralism.[31] In
the process of doing this I shall bring to light a number of central
methodological controversies in which opinion has been divided in
ways that manifest the problems underlying the translational indeterminacy thesis.

Etics, Emics, and Componential Analysis

The etic/emic distinction was coined by Kenneth Pike and is an
adaptation or analogue of the familiar phonetic-phonemic distinction
in phonology. Roughly, phonetics concerns the mechanically
measurable features of human speech, while phonemics concerns the
phonetic differences that language users discriminate as making a difference in meaning. Phonemic contrasts are often notably different
from those evident to the Western ear (particularly in radical
translation), and phonemic inquiry must involve querying of informants with regard to phonemic contrast. Such querying essentially
involves determining *complementarity* and *contrast* by introducing
phonetic variations into some expression to determine which variations make a difference in meaning and which do not. Phonemics and
phonetics are not independent of each other, because the description
of phonemic contrast requires a phonetic metalanguage. The
etic/emic method of *semantic* analysis is modeled from this approach. Subjects are queried to determine defining features of things
by determining *complementarity* and *contrast*. A defining feature will
be identified if its removal from an object will induce an informant to
change the categorization of that object. Thus, emic concepts, that is,
those specific or familiar to the subject, are revealed; and, as in
phonology, this requires use of concepts imported by the inquirer,
that is, etic ones—thus, the concatenated "etic/emic" label. These
are intended as complementary notions.

Pike insisted that "the emic analysis of the emic units of human
behavior must analyze that behavior in reference to the manner in
which native participants in that behavior react to their own behavior
and to the behavior of their colleagues." Appropriate elicitation was
needed in order that the etic behavior stream, viewed as "waves of

activity" initially by the observer, could be properly broken up into emic "particles of activity," which comprise the "discrete behavioral entities" the subjects perceive in that stream.[32] (Thus, Pike was more of a behaviorist than many of those who have adapted his distinction and might thus appear to be less prone to the earlier-noted objections of Quine. However, Quine's critique, as I have noted, counts against behavioral meaning entities as much as against mentalistic ones.)

A key motivation behind this method is to overcome interpreter imposition. Charles Frake remarks: "The distinctive situations, or eliciting frames, or stimuli which evoke and define a set of contrasting responses are cultural data to be discovered, not prescribed, by the ethnographer." Paul Kay adds: "The very provenience of the emic / etic distinction, namely phonology, should make clear that the guiding spirit of an emic approach is to rid oneself of *pre*conceptions about universal structures so that the data may be analyzed objectively to reveal the true universal structures.[33] However, the close kinship that these remarks elucidate of the etic / emic distinction to key Boasian concerns regarding the very nature of anthropological inquiry makes it unsurprising that the terms *etic* and *emic* have been incorporated into broader methodological discussions and controversies. They have thus come to have notoriously loose and varying usages in the anthropological literature: 'Etic' has come to characterize *methods* that describe or explain, or *phenomena* that are described or explained, without reference to the particular conceptions that subjects have of that behavior. Correspondingly, etic *concepts* are characterized in terms of their being cross-culturally valid or familiar to the inquirer. One needs only to make reference to cross-culturally valid hypotheses of physics, biology, psychology, and other conceptions shared by the community of scientific inquirers in order to account for such phenomena. 'Emic', on the other hand, applies to methods (or phenomena) in which concepts are used that are significant to the members of the society under study. Emic phenomena are not adequately accounted for unless the inquirer understands the significance they have for the subjects. An emic concept is defined as being culturally specific, meaning familiar to members of the subject society, or perhaps understood only by them. As applied to the phenomena themselves, the term 'emic' is equatable under certain usages with 'untranslatable'. (These rough and controversial definitions will be discussed further below.)

An important consequence of the broadening of these notions is that their interdependence is no longer obvious. Indeed, they have often been treated as characterizing sharply opposed methodologies: Etic ones emphasizing use of cross-culturally valid notions; emic ones emphasizing recovery and / or use of subject conceptions. Underlying this contrast is, among other things, a long-standing controversy between comparativists, who view etic description as essential to the formulation of universally valid theories of culture, and descriptivists, who view such theory-building as inhibiting or preventing the revelation of cultural particularities. However, the dominant attitude is Weberian in spirit: Emics and etics should complement each other, since the point of cultural anthropology is to unify emic perspectives into a comparative theory of culture. Proponents of this view cite the evident complementarity of emics and etics in the earlier model.[34]

In order to sort through the extremely complex methodological, theoretical, and philosophical issues involved here, I shall return to the work of Goodenough. He is one of the earliest exponents of the method of *componential analysis*, easily the most widely used method to evolve initially from the etic / emic approach. He is also a dominant figure in the development of the related, broader theoretical paradigms (ethnoscience, and so on) that have subsequently evolved in the language-and-culture tradition and which I shall discuss below. Thus, his work has been the focal point of much criticism and controversy and will provide a good point of departure—this in addition to the aforementioned point that aspects of his views of culture and language are compatible with the position I shall articulate later.

While the etic / emic approaches are subject to varying epistemological interpretation, componential analysis as developed by Goodenough, Frake, and others typically manifests a variety of mentalistic commitments. Its mentalist character results from deliberate efforts to replace behavioral and materialistic approaches with one in which, in the words of one reviewer, "the conceptual frame of culture becomes the object of study" and in which "the semantics of natural languages gains paramount importance."[35] Natural-language semantics gains this stature because semantics is regarded as a bridge between linguistics and anthropology insofar as cultural categories such as kinship groupings (the most frequent subject of componential analysis) are always represented linguistically. Further, the classification of natural phenomena by societies, Floyd Lounsbury and others contend, seems rather to be structured by their linguistic rules rather than according to any evident natural ordering (presumably determined by reference to, say, physical theory). This view echoes Sapir's central contention.[36]

Under componential analysis, relevant aspects of culture are analyzed as the *semantic dimensions* and *semantic components* of linguistic phenomena. It is this restriction in domain that sets componential analysis apart from other emic contrastive methods. A semantic dimension is a selected set of attributes (relative to some ethnographic theory) by which semantic categories or classes are differentiated. For instance, difference along the dimension *sex of a relative* will constitute the essential difference between the kin classes labeled 'uncle' and 'aunt' (which are not distinguishable along the semantic dimensions *membership in the same or different generations* or *lineal versus collateral relationships*). Differentiation within semantic dimensions is determined by the semantic components that classes of individuals share or fail to share. (Components are the variables of these dimensions.) So possession of the semantic component (or attribute) *is a member of the male sex* will distinguish 'uncle' from 'aunt', while two classes that share this component, say 'uncle' and 'nephew', will differ insofar as the latter possesses the component *membership in a generation one degree descendant to that of Ego* (or simply *-1 generation*). The most typical application to componential analysis is in kinship studies, and a set of cross-culturally applicable criteria are delineated, the "classic" list (developed by Alfred Kroeber and George Murdock) being consanguinity/affinity, generation, sex, collaterality, bifurcation, relative age, descedence, and genealogical distance.[37] This list varies, and we shall see significant differences of opinion on what seems to be a paradoxical tension between the concern to recover one's informants' criteria in mind and the use of such technical concepts cross-culturally (which might have no evident analogue among the receptor-translations of informant discourse). This is particularly significant in light of the demand by Goodenough (and others) to reveal subjects' criteria in mind, or to attain results that have so-called "cognitive" or "psychological" validity.[38]

Goodenough's influential "Componential Analysis and the Study of Meaning" (1956) clearly shows the influence of Morris, as is evidenced not only in an early footnote in which he indicates that he is using Morris' (*Foundation of the Theory of Signs*) notions of significatum and denotatum throughout,[39] but also in an introductory paragraph in which he sets down semantic guidelines strongly reminiscent of Morris (and, indeed, more so C. I. Lewis):

> The aspect of meaning to be dealt with is signification as distinct from connotation. . . . [T]he significatum of a linguistic form is com-

posed of those abstracted contextual elements with which it is in perfect association, without which it cannot properly occur. Its connotata are the contextual elements with which it is frequently but less than perfectly associated. Significata are prerequisites while connotata are probabilities and possibilities. Only the former have definitive value.[40]

Morris' influence on anthropology, in particular kinship semantics, is noted more recently in a review of the field by Harold Scheffler (1972), in which Morris' more recent *Signs, Language, and Behavior* is cited. There is a significant modification here, one of a species of such revisions of componential and other forms of semantic analysis, as we shall see, in that Scheffler suggests that nondistinctive, connotative features be given greater attention.[41]

Also, Goodenough's recent *Description and Comparison in Cultural Anthropology* cites Morris' earlier *Foundations* again, while giving a mentalistic interpretation that, in effect, replaces some mentalistic elements from Lewis' theory that Morris sought to eliminate:

> In the usage of Morris (1938), a linguistic expression may be said to *designate* a class of concepts or images. It may be said to *denote* a specific image or subclass of images within the class on any one occasion of its use. And it may be said to *signify* the criteria by which specific images or concepts are to be included or excluded from the class of images or concepts that the expression designates. What is signified consists of the definitive attributes of the class, the ideational components from which the class is conceptually formed. Componential analysis is a method for forming and testing hypotheses about what words signify.[42]

Thus, Goodenough evidently intends to incorporate both the concretely and abstractly ideational aspects of components. Scheffler concurs in identifying defining or distinctive features as the signification of the class of items in the designation of a sign ("they are the necessary and sufficient conditions for membership of the class and for designation by its linguistic sign") and also takes Morris' iconicity as a working notion.[43] Indeed, Scheffler (whose recent work I discuss below) credits Morris himself with the important insight that (kinship and other) terms "refer to relationships 'known' to or posited by the people who use the terms. The components of all significata are cultural constituents; and similarly for the components of their connotative meanings."[44]

Goodenough's remarks to this point seem to embody only a commitment to the *recovery* of subject conceptions. However, elsewhere in his early and more recent work he exhibits a related commitment to the *use* of subject conceptions by the inquirer. Componential analysis is aimed at describing the culturally specific in etic terms. (Goodenough defines emic concepts as those specific *only* to the culture under study; thus the components of kinship, being cross-culturally applicable, are etic for him.[45] However, in his studies of the Trukese he advocates the incorporation of the fundamental "emic primitive" of the *corporation* into the descriptive ethnographic language itself. This concept, as he initially discovered it, combined elements of property ownership and kinship in ways that no other studied culture did, and he used it as a fundamental organizing notion for his ethnography. Later, when the concept was successfully applied to a related culture, the concept became, by Goodenough's lights, a cross-culturally valid *etic* one. Citing the complementarity of the original notions of etics and emics, he maintains that the recovery of an emic primitive introduces that notion into ethnographers' "etic kit" of notions potentially applicable to the study of other cultures. Upon becoming elsewhere applicable, it becomes etic.[46]

However one terms these conceptions (and we shall see substantial disagreement by Marvin Harris on this and other points shortly), it is clear that the use of subject conceptions puts a special burden on translational determinacy. To give an erroneous or insufficiently warranted account of a fundamental concept that lies at the heart of the organizing principles of an ethnography is to compromise it seriously. Exactly what the concept-sharing Goodenough demands here amounts to is not entirely clear, as some of his formulations of his aims have less of a mentalistic ring than others (something I shall exploit later on); for instance, he speaks at one point of defining "in terms of whatever criteria enabled me to distinguish among the entitlements and transactions in a manner *consistent* with the distinctions the people of Truk *seemed* to be making" (my emphasis).[47]

Similar commitments to the identification of defining characteristics or attributes are manifest in Frake's influential "The Ethnographic Study of Cognitive Systems" (1962). However, as with Goodenough's definitions of culture and language and the qualification just noted, recovery of criteria-in-mind is not always explicitly implied by what Frake says. Consider, for example, the following curt summary of the ethnographer's task:

> To define 'hamburger' one must know, not just what objects it includes, but with what it contrasts. In this way we learn that a slice of cheese makes a difference, whereas a slice of tomato does not. In the

context of different cultures the task is to state what one must know in order to categorize correctly.[48]

However, other passages emphasize categorizing according to the criteria that one's subjects employ—though one might only ask that the resulting *reference* classes of source-language predicate and its translating target-language predicate be identical. If one notes Frake's definition of 'object' as "anything construed as a member of category . . . whether perceptible or not," this task amounts simply to that of categorizing anything correctly, including abstract notions.[49] Also, Frake views his method of determining complementarity and contrast as broadly applicable, "whether aimed directly at perceptual qualities of phenomena or at informants' descriptions of phenomena or at informants' descriptions of pertinent attributes."[50] Thus, despite his limitation to generally less problematic examples such as color and animal types, his approach ranges over extensions of abstract objects and is meant to apply to the recovery of observable and unobservable attributes.

Frake's remarks is this early paper thus seem to buy into the semantic platonism Quine and others criticize. Thus, it is of interest that in later work his desire to employ eliciting frames that are to be "discovered, not prescribed, by the ethnographer" connects to deep dissatisfaction with what he and other critics term "platonistic" rigor and structure in the ethnoscientific approaches that have evolved from componential analysis. Indeed, the term has much the pejorative ring for these anthropologists as it has for Quine, Goodman, and White.[51] I shall consider this problem in more detail below.

Componential Analysis and Psychological Reality

These concerns expressed by Frake and Goodenough to discover "eliciting frames" and "criteria-in-mind" (or in the head) connect to a broader theoretical difficulty in the context of validation; namely, that of showing the "psychological reality" (or "cognitive validity") of the cognitive structures one recovers. Contrary to this, Robbins Burling has argued in a widely discussed article, "Cognition and Componential Analysis: God's Truth or Hocus-Pocus?", that if only predictive success (in "getting along," categorizing correctly, and so on) may corroborate hypotheses to the effect that the native is *following a certain rule* or using *certain criteria of discrimination*, then, as there is no way of determining a *uniquely* adequate conceptual framework, he argues, "psychological reality" seems a criterion of adequacy that cannot be met:

> Any of hundreds of thousands of logically alternative solutions might predict which term can be used [in some situation], but the success of that prediction does not demonstrate that the speaker of the language uses the same scheme, or indicate whether or not all speakers use the same one.[52]

Burling's article deserves emphasis at this juncture, as his concerns are closest in character to Quine's and as he champions a fictionalist attitude toward componential analysis that is generalizable to other approaches and well-adaptable to my later reconstruction of Quine.

Burling argues that nagging problems of "indeterminacy" make determination of the specific psychological actualities problematic. Citing an attempt by Harold Conklin to determine a botanical taxonomy and constructing a hypothetical taxonomy of his own,[53] he argues:

> It is my feeling that the analysis of terms into hierarchical taxonomies that have lately been discussed have rather glossed over the problems of indeterminacy. In fact, in my example I also glossed over some difficult problems of this sort . . . What about "cedars"? Are they "needled trees"? Not really of course, but they are not "leafy trees" either. Should "balsam," "hemlock," and "spruce" be classed together as "short needled trees" (Christmas trees) as opposed to "pines"? Or should they all have equivalent taxonomic status? What is the essential "cognitive" difference between hemlock and spruce? Is it gross size, type of needle, form of bark, or what? I do not know how to answer these questions, but they are the types of questions which must be answered before any single semantic analysis can claim to represent the cognitive organization of the people, or even claim to be much more than an exercise of the analyst's imagination.[54]

Burling then compares this taxonomy, with its problems of indeterminacy, to a proposed taxonomy of diseases in Subanun (a language of Mindanao) given by Frake:[55]

> Analyses of terms in exotic languages may obscure the range of possible alternatives. For instance, Frake discusses some disease terms in Subanun. . , and he makes appealing suggestions for their analysis: yet, I cannot help wondering if he does not convey an unjustified certainty in the particular analysis he offers. Frake gives a diagram . . . of

the same form as my diagram of English plant terms. . . , in which certain skin diseases are assigned to various taxonomic categories and subcategories. Not knowing the language, the reader can hardly question the data, and yet he may still wonder if this diagram is less subject to question than my diagram of plant terms.[56]

He isolates Frake's particular difficulty as one of insufficient data and argues that until a suitable method and sufficient data are offered by some application of componential analysis, the plausibility of assertions of psychological reality remains, for him, highly questionable:

> Students who claim that componential analysis or comparable methods of semantic analysis can provide a means for "discovering how people construe their world" must explain how to eliminate the great majority of logical possibilities and narrow the choice to the one of the few that are "psychologically real." I will not be convinced that there are not dozens or hundreds of possible analyses of Subanun disease terms until Frake presents us with the entire system fully analyzed and faces squarely the problem of how he chooses his particular analysis. In the meantime, I will doubt whether any single analysis tells us much about people's cognitive structure, even if it enables us to use terms as a native does.[57]

Burling's main contention is that linguists maintain a "hocus-pocus" attitude toward their structural-semantic and related ethnographic results—while nonetheless preserving the theoretical apparatus, and attendant semantic notions, of componential analysis.[58]

However, for many anthropologists, Burling's antirealism involves concession of much too critical an objective for anthropological inquiry. This would seem particularly so for Boasians, whose motivation for doing etic / emic or componential analysis has much to do with aims to attain objective recovery of subject points of view. Burling would seem to be conceding the very point of doing emic anthropology.

Burling's emphasis on insufficient data suggests lines of counterargument based on the acquisition of more data of appropriate types. In an influential response to Burling, "Cognitive Aspects of English Kin Terms," A.K. Romney and R.G. D'Andrade contend that "slight differences in the operation or the definition and number of components imply different pictures of psychological reality" and argue that "the solution of this problem lies in further behavioral measures of individual cognitive operations."[59] The wider evidential base to which they appeal contains such items as semantic differential measurements, observations of frequencies of term pairings (called "triad" analysis), and determinations of salience in memory. In triad analysis, for instance, the idea is that greater frequency with which subjects pair terms, for example, 'father'-'son' as opposed to 'father'-'uncle', will indicate degrees of semantic "proximity." Romney and D'Andrade contend that these tests show "that people respond to kinship terms as if each term contained a bundle of distinct meanings." And the tests they devise are aimed at constructing the topography of the semantic realms of their subjects. These sorts of tests, and many others developed in recent cognitive anthropology and psycholinguistics, are aimed at providing determinate results regarding the cognitive aspects of components (and other semantic and grammatical structures).[60]

Romney and D'Andrade contend that semantic components function as discriminative stimuli of objects and that such stimuli are associated in the minds of persons with words for those objects—thus making these stimuli the meanings of words. In the process they stress the similarity of linguistic analysis and native language acquisition (something stressed by a number of anthropologists as well as by Quine):

> A discriminative stimulus is most efficiently learned when a subject is repeatedly presented with events which differ or contrast in one particular feature and in which the subject's responses to the contrastive stimuli are differentially reinforced. What both the individuals who use the native system and the analyst do is learn the set of contrasts which signal a difference (although the reinforcement for the analyst may be only a neat system while the reinforcement for the individual in the system are approval and understanding).[61]

Cecil Brown, whose views shall receive more attention later, cites this passage in the course of crediting Romney and D'Andrade with making an important attempt "to explain the manner in which the *meanings* of words are learned." However, he acknowledges telling mentalistic commitments: "Semantic components as the meanings of words become fixed in the mind permitting appropriate responses to the words with which they are associated on some future occasion of encountering them."[62] Brown rejects this mentalistic view of components on the Wittgensteinian grounds noted in Chapter 1:

> Semantic components are not directly treated but are nonetheless implied in [Wittgenstein's] broad criticism of the three types of unitary

meaning. Thus, if objects are not the meanings of words, neither are the stimuli (discriminative or otherwise) empirically associated with them; if images are not meanings, neither are images of such stimuli; or if feelings or mental experiences are not meanings, neither are feelings about or experiences involving stimuli.[63]

Brown similarly rejects mentalistic commitments manifest even in a later paper by D'Andrade, which attempts to modify componential analysis (and ethnoscience generally) in line with the acknowledged need to take account of use. D'Andrade here expresses a willingness to incorporate analyses of language use *in addition* to standard techniques of componential analysis (thereby qualifying Goodenough's insistence that the signification of expressions is all that is worth inquiry and admitting the value of taking "connotata" into account). However, D'Andrade is insistent that assignment of labels to things must precede learning the use of expressions, and that this point (overlooked, he contends, by Wittgensteinian analysis) leads to a two-stage analysis of meaning for the field linguist: First, the linguist must decide on the assignment of native labels to objects through standard componential techniques. Second, the linguist must discern the agreed-upon patterns of word-usage of his informants. For example, it is important to realize the import of a native's applying the term for a cousin to a nonrelative (say, as an expression of honor or intimacy), but understanding this rule of usage is impossible without first understanding the (emic) labeling rule that assigns that expression literally to certain kin.[64]

Thus, we see here not only the sort of revision of traditional componential analysis suggested by Scheffler, namely, the incorporation of accidental along with essential characteristics, but also an endeavor to incorporate elements of more behavioristically oriented theories. D'Andrade insists that an "emic" understanding of subject intentions or defining characteristics is presupposed by the (thus) supplementary behavioral analysis (compare Searle's use of intensional and generative concepts). But, as Brown notes, the revision does not go to the heart of the matter. Indeed, as we shall see, Wittgenstein's later reflections on language are typically perceived (as they are no doubt intended) as calling for deeper methodological revision.

And of course such modifications will not satisfy Quine. He views the conditioning to isolate distinctive features as so vastly different, in the native's case as opposed to the linguist's, as to raise serious questions about the linguistic objectives here. Also, it is important to keep in mind that the "empirical slack" Quine perceives comprises all *possible* data and thus does not evidently leave the door open to attain psychological reality by gathering more data:

The metaphor of the black box, often so useful, can be misleading. . . . The problem is not one of hidden facts, such as might be uncovered by learning more about the brain physiology of thought processes. To expect a distinctive physical mechanism behind every genuinely distinct mental state is one thing; to expect a distinctive mechanism for every purported distinction that can be phrased in traditional mentalistic language is another. The question whether. . .the foreigner *really* believes [theory] *A* or believes rather [empirically equivalent rival] *B* is a question whose very significance I would put in doubt. This is what I am getting at in arguing the indeterminacy of translation.[65]

Also, while Burling's challenge to the notion of psychological reality is much akin to Quine's critique of meaning and synonymy, it may not go clearly to the heart of the matter. The deeper concerns surface not so much in Burling's explicit criticisms of Frake but rather in his own self-doubts. He asks for the "cognitive" difference (the scare-quotes are his) between *hemlock* and *spruce*. One could easily read that remark as challenging whether such questions can be answered at all: It is precisely these more radical sorts of objections that philosophers such as Quine and Wittgenstein raise, and their objections may demand more serious changes than Burling envisages. (I will look at more radical Wittgensteinian critiques below.) Indeed, Quine's indeterminacy argument ultimately attacks the clarity and scientific usefulness of intension, rather than its sheer ontological excess. If it does so successfully, it is not clear how simply adopting an antirealist attitude, while keeping intensional constructs, will be of any help.

Descent to the Unconscious

Earlier I noted Boas', and more so Sapir's, recognition that significant elements of analysis might not be objects of ethnographic subjects' conscious awareness. Many have taken this, as well as aforementioned problems in determining psychological reality, as signaling a need for far greater emphasis on deeper, cross-culturally and psychologically valid, unconscious structures rather than on superficial intension of the Frege-Lewis variety.[66] This is particularly evident in the language-and-culture approaches that incorporate Chomskian transformational-generative devices and psychological / psychoanalytic categories, as well as those influenced by Levi-

Strauss' structuralism. These represent a significant shift in emphasis from Boas, despite his acknowledgment of the need to go beyond subjects' conscious awareness—Boas did not foresee going nearly as *far* beyond it. Correspondingly, they represent also deep and controversial points of contrast to other approaches evolving in the "Boasian" tradition that continue to emphasize culturally specific items within, or closer to, subjects' conscious awareness. I shall look briefly here at transformational and structuralist approaches, citing some problems that arise particularly in connection with them. In the next section, I shall turn to broader range of recent developments and problems in the various cognitive approaches.

Transformational-Generative Theories

The transformational linguist John Lyons credits C. F. Hockett's *A Course in Modern Linguistics* (1958) with specifically calling attention to "deeper connections" between sentences that "cut across surface grammar", this in contrast to, say, Sapir's stress of the often unconscious character of surface grammar.[67] It was Hockett's view that such deep connections were pivotal in the structure and acquisition of language, yet up to that time they had been largely unexplored. With the impact and increasing influence of Chomsky's work in the 1960s, it grew into one of the dominant linguistic theories in language-and-culture anthropology. And, as with the approaches previously discussed, it has been modeled in ethnographic theory—notably in the work of Noel Schutz.[68]

In brief, these approaches endeavor to take linguistic—mainly grammatical—analysis beyond the taxonomic classifications of surface grammar yielded by earlier structural-linguistic models. Instead (and here I refer to the later theory developed by Chomsky in *Aspects of the Theory of Syntax* and ramified in various places by Katz and Fodor), surface grammar, meaning, and phonological representation result from the workings of a subsurface complex of components that create and transform underlying strings in accordance with patterns and rules that differ markedly from those evident from examination of the linguistic surface. The *syntactic component* consists of a set of phrase structure rules, which give the constitution of sentences in terms of various grammatical categories; transformational rules, which indicate the ways in which sentences can be restructured while preserving their meaning (for example, for transforming active to equivalent passive constructions); and lexicon insertion rules, which indicate which words from the lexicon of a language may be inserted

for some generated category in order to produce a surface or
"terminal" string. The full representation of the generation of a sentence via phrase structure and lexicon insertion rules is said to be the
representation of its "deep structure" or its "underlying phrase
marker," while transformational rules operate on the underlying
marker to produce "derived" and finally "superficial" structures.
The phrase markers thus produced by the syntactic component are in
turn "operated upon" by two other components, the *semantic* and
the *phonological*. The former, which is of main interest here,
provides the intension of the lexical items by assigning semantic interpretations to deep syntactic structures in keeping with the
"projection rules" that make these assignments in accordance with
the "semantic markers" for these lexical items. These markers, as I
noted earlier, correspond to Lewis' intension; that is, they give the
hierarchy of semantic categories to which the item belongs (for example, *bachelor*: object; physical; human; adult; male; not
married).[69]

Hymes notes the fit of this approach into the Boasian tradition:

> The logic here is essentially the same as that used by Sapir (1925) to
> show that an implicit level of phonology exists behind the observed
> level of phonetics: differing sets of sounds may have the same under-
> lying patterns, and the same sets of sounds may have differing under-
> lying patterns. Recognition of this logic brought to the fore a new func-
> tional relation. CONTRASTIVE RELEVANCE could warrant the
> status, and disclose something of the organization of elements;
> TRANSFORMATIONS (or operations of equivalent role) were re-
> quired to give an adequate account of their organization.[70]

What was viewed as desirable about this new form of analysis,
Hymes contends, was that it accounted better and more simply for
systematic relations between sentences by specific principles that
operated not simply on surface patterns but also on the underlying
structural relationships themselves.[71] As such, he notes, its generative goals are but a special case of the goals of ethnography set down
by Goodenough and followed, notably, by Frake, Sturtevant, and
Conklin.[72] Also, it embodies a shift in attitude toward the role of
semantics in anthropological linguistics. Whereas, as Schutz notes,
Goodenough's work "invited the suggestion that the ethnographic
approach to meaning and the linguistic approach to language might
provide complementary approaches to language—with ethnography
providing input into linguistic description," more recently semantic
theory "has come to be an integral portion of the organization of lin-

guistic description; indeed, some linguists have come to regard semantics as the most basic part of linguistic description.''[73]

In addition to Schutz' ethnographic model, more limited models have been employed by a number of influential theorists. Lounsbury has incorporated three generative rules and their corollaries into the componential analysis of Crow-Omaha kinship, systematizing eighty-two kin types into twenty-six kin categories.[74] Similar "reduction rules" are employed elsewhere: Mridula Durbin views these rules as designed "to establish an equivalence among multiple denotata of one term by selecting one denotatum as primary reference (e.g., sister's son) and by converting the rest of the denotata (i.e., secondary ones such as father's sister's son) into the primary denotatum through a set of rules."[75] These aims are in addition to those shared with general linguistics, such as accounting for competence and intuitions of meaningfulness, detecting ambiguity, and so forth.[76]

The influential anthropologist Oswald Werner has also placed emphasis on the value of transformational analysis. In a 1970 article he and coauthor Joan Fenton contend that the "ideational orderings" sought by Goodenough are best achieved by a "loose integration" of componential methods with generative grammar. The formal structures embodied in culture, they claim, have the character of "cognitive maps" (a concept they derive from Michael Polanyi), with a cultural system being the overlap of individual maps or "individual competences." Their universe of discourse consists of classes of components and attributes.[77]

Many transformational linguists are keenly concerned with the psycholinguistic aspects of their work, especially accounting for the child's language acquisition. This motivates them to place special demands on the adequacy of their grammatical (and semantic) analyses; that is, in Chomsky's terms, *descriptive* adequacy for grammatical analysis does not delineate the full task: the ultimate objective is *explanatory* adequacy. Briefly, descriptive adequacy characterizes the demand that generative grammar yield strings that are grammatical, account for amphiboly, and so forth. (This level is said to characterize the ideal speaker-hearer's "linguistic competence" or tacit knowledge of the language.) Explanatory adequacy adds additional demands that the grammar that produces those strings have maximal systematic simplicity and that one uniquely correct grammar be specified, within the constraints of empirical underdetermination. Explanatory adequacy also entails that the linguist's constructions can be related to hypotheses about the child, viewed as a "language acquisition model" (AM) or "language acquisition device" (LAD).

Some linguists demand only two things of grammatical analysis: (1) it should recover deep structures; (2) it should provide a more dynamic account of language from the corpus of utterances from that language (and other pertinent data): that is, a mechanical procedure for classifying and sorting the parts of sentences according to the surface-structure categories. Katz advocates (following a suggestion by Chomsky) a more demanding "rationalist" strategy that attributes an "evaluation procedure" to the child (or a discovery procedure that involves an evaluation procedure):

> The particular form that the rationalist theory of learning takes in the case of language acquisition is that of an *evaluation procedure*, *viz.*, a criterion for making an empirically justified choice among a set of equally simple grammars, each compatible with the available evidence and each in the form prescribed by linguistic theory. Like a discovery procedure, an evaluation procedure can serve either as a methodological apparatus for the field linguist or as a hypothesis about the internal nature of [the AM]. In the latter capacity, the procedure constitutes a nativist theory of how the child learns. The child makes essentially the same choices as the linguist; each chooses a new grammar or reaffirms his previous choice whenever his corpus of available data increases. On the rationalist theory, the child chooses an optimal grammar from among a set of possible grammars determined by innate principles about the form of human language, the choice itself being governed by the requirement that the grammar selected be the simplest among the possible grammars that best predict the data available at the point of choice.[78]

The evaluation procedure allows the child to order possible grammars (the class of which is constructed *a priori* by the child) according to their relative complexity and to "test" them in attempting to form grammatically correct strings on their basis. Thus, again, comparisons of linguist and child language acquisition processes are viewed as enlightening: the hope here being for a linguistic theory that will produce not only grammars but accounts of how linguist and child acquire them. Indeed, the linguist's evaluation procedure is said to incorporate an "evaluation measure," or an empirical hypothesis about the structure of the AM and about the degrees to which the resultant grammar reflects these elements. This further involves claims concerning the universal characteristics of human languages and the relationship of these to certain universal properties of the human mind.[79] Explanatory adequacy is integral to the broader notion of "psychological reality" for the AM, which is viewed as essential to broader psycholinguistic aims such as explaining language acquisition.[80]

Although deep structures reflect the rules that competent speakers of a language follow, speakers are typically not consciously aware of these structures, nor are the deep structures evident in the surface structures, as I have noted. The unconscious nature of deep structures places special burdens on the field linguist, who cannot simply ask informants to produce meaningful utterances. An efficient means of testing informant intuitions is required, and one interesting approach employed, apparently with some success, by I.F.H. Wong (in Korea) and Kenneth Hale (in Papago) involves actually teaching informants some transformational linguistics.[81]

However, while transformationalists operate in the spirit of Romney and D'Andrade in seeking a richer data-base and more complex theoretical devices, their concern with still less behaviorally scrutable levels of language may tend to magnify Boasian worries. The particular approach suggested by Wong and Hale seems especially problematic in view of qualms about importing Western viewpoints to the informants. Indeed, thus training one's informants seems to run the risk of "westernizing" the informant—one of the very problems that motivated Boas' emphasis on learning the source-language instead of relying on bilinguals.[82]

In addition to these particular problems in the field application of transformational theory, there are a number of problems plaguing the general linguistic theory that are worth mentioning here. One major problem in the present context stems from the conscious attempt, noted in Chapter 1, to present a sophisticated and empirically fruitful Fregean theory of meaning, in whose terms the various notions of intension, analyticity, and so on could be redefined and thus empirically legitimated. The aims of Katz and Chomsky bring Quine's concerns with the "black-box" viewpoint and translational objectivity clearly to the surface.

Now how closely Chomsky's position comes to Katz's with regard to its commitment to the existence of meanings is not entirely clear. A lot depends on how one views the deep structures upon which the semantic component operates, and the semantic component itself. If one views them as purely hypothetical constructions for reproducing grammatical strings, such that other constructions might do as well—that is, if one adopts a "hocus-pocus" attitude towards them—one may dodge some of Quine's and Wittgenstein's concerns. Moreover, Chomsky and other transformationalists are not as concerned with the semantic component as are Katz and Fodor (although

Chomsky includes as "syntactic features" categories that parallel Katz's semantic markers), thus making their commitments with regard to *intension* somewhat unclear. And, as I noted in Chapter 1, to the degree that Chomsky's concerns can be limited to accounting for grammaticality, indeterminacy may present little cause for concern, except for the broader commitments made in connection with explanatory adequacy and psychological reality. However, if instead transformational theory aims at accounting for natural synonymy, even a fictionalist attitude toward intension may not escape indeterminacy. As I noted in connection with Burling, Quine's indeterminacy arguments are aimed primarily at the clarity of semantic notions and these concerns seem in turn rooted in doubts about the very amenability of "natural synonymy" to systematic analysis. Unlike grammatical analysis of "significant strings," semantic analysis, he argues, lacks something to be "right or wrong about."

Chomsky certainly seems to perceive a negative import of Quinean indeterminacy for his and similar programs. And, as we shall see, Chomsky sees much hinging on the assessment of the import of empirical underdetermination for translation and linguistics.

However, the abstractness of the transformationalist's various constructs (of deep and surface structure) motivates antiplatonist objections from anthropologists and psycholinguists, reminiscent of those voiced by Quine and other philosophers. These concerns are reflected in work by psycholinguists concerned with psychological reality. Recent discussions of "competence models" have shown concern that overemphasis of *idealizations* such as competence, as opposed to the dynamics of actual output (performance), social factors, and the like, has rendered the accountability of these latter types of phenomena, as well as the potential range of determinable, psychologically real cognitive elements, highly problematic. Despite the greater theoretical sophistication involved, the problem here seems much the same as one perceived by Russell and Lewis in earlier ideational theories—namely, the inadequacy of theories dominated by the rigor and platonism of formal semantics to apply to important psychological and epistemological objectives.

For example, W. J. M. Levelt notes that the idealized character of LAD acquisition has promoted an attitude among linguists that minimizes the importance of linguistic input.[83] It is simply assumed, he contends, that a corpus of utterances is received by the child, and the child's ability to absorb this corpus is treated as presupposing the nativist assumption that "the child could not possibly learn the syntax of his language unless he was endowed with some innate, language-specific mechanism for just that purpose."[84] However, Levelt argues, the consequently felt need to "protect the idea of spontaneous emergence of language" has led to a problem of what he calls "dogmatism" that is importantly analogous to the imposition-problems I have discussed. His concern is with linguists' excessive reliance on the creative expansion of hypotheses (or assumptions?) about the inner character of the LAD at the expense of widening their range of observations, a choice he charges Chomsky as giving "the appearance of a logical necessity."[85] The worry, hardly new to rationalism in its various forms, is that the data will be selected in a question-begging way to fit the chosen theory.

In addition, Levelt is concerned that "the tacit assumption that language development could be satisfactorily explained *in vitro*" will have the consequence of cutting off research on competence, and other facets of transformational theory, from research on the early learning of sentences—thus inhibiting application of the theory to developmental issues. These problems for psycholinguistics have their analogues in anthropology (for example, Geertz' critique of the "hermetical" effect of transformational inquiry, which I shall discuss below), both for the reasons given by Levelt—many anthropologists being understandably interested in the prospects of relating their work to pertinent areas in psycholinguistics and cognitive psychology—and for reasons more specific to anthropology.

V. J. Cook expresses similar worries in another recent critique: Insofar as the AM is related to competence, Cook contends, it must be regarded as similarly ideal, platonic, or timeless.[86] Language acquisition must be falsely (though intentionally) assumed to be instantaneous—an idealizing assumption that he sees as having the result that "the instantaneous model has in effect cut itself off from evidence about the child."[87] Also, the fact that evidence for the AM is evaluated according to an evaluation measure that, itself, commits one to certain views concerning the internal structure of the model produces an undesirable circularity (compare Levelt's charge of "dogmatism"). Cook sees this as further hindering the explanation of psychological reality.[88]

Structural Anthropology

Structural anthropology, classically embodied in the work of Claude Levi-Strauss, is similar to generative grammar in delineating an unconscious (and universal) locus of symbolic meaning. Its main difference lies, perhaps, in its being from the outset an integrated anthropological approach to both linguistic *and* nonlinguistic symbolic phenomena and in its not modeling these structures along the lines of an already developed linguistic theory. Levi-Strauss gives significant credit for its origins to Boas, as well as to the Russian formalist Trubetskoy.[89] He gives little attention to the conscious cognitive level of significance wherein, by contrast, C. I. Lewis locates "sense meaning" and intension.

In any case, a central tenet of the structuralist approach is that the essential features of cultures and cultural systems that should be studied are patterns and structures that remain invariant under historical transformations. Structuralists view cultures, in the words of one reviewer, "as logical mechanisms for reducing the randomness of history"—that is, for integrating the novel and unexpected. Though particular solutions vary cross-culturally, the *underlying* mechanisms, being "essential and universal features of mankind," remain invariant.[90]

Owing to the integrated nature of this approach, it is difficult to distinguish linguistic from nonlinguistic underlying structures (hence, there is greater divergence from Sapir here than is exhibited by linguistics-based approaches); similarly it is difficult to distinguish linguistic theory or model from ethnographic theory or model. The underlying rules and structures are such that yield all types of cultural phenomena at the surface. For Levi-Strauss, the *myth* occupies a methodological position analogous to Chomsky's deep structure, insofar as it underlies *langue* (analogously, competence), which in turn underlies *parole* (analogously, performance). In the terms of a recent review:

> In this view, myth is defined as a . . . cognitive character. It delineates the parameters within which they are lost. . . . They also, by virtue of this, teach which associations are permitted and which ones are not, within specific parameters.[91]

Underlying structures are viewed as being quite rigorously formal in nature, having the character of rigorous logical systems and possessing combinatorial features "similar to an anthropological Mendeleev's table." (Similar remarks are made by Katz with respect to semantic markers.)[92] These highly abstract structures are seen to underlie a wide range of phenomena and to be broadly pancultural. Ideally, underlying structures conform to topological patterns, which, once revealed by anthropologists, will serve to interrelate structures, indicate likely transformations through time, show underlying unities of principle, and so forth.[93] Typically, folk myths are studied cross-culturally with attention paid to recurring story patterns, parallel use of animal symbols, the function of these myths in preserving societal belief-structures, and so forth.

Levi-Strauss sketches his approach as follows:

> Starting with a myth chosen not so much arbitrarily as through an intuitive feeling that it was both rich and rewarding, and then, after analyzing it in accordance with rules laid down in previous works . . . , I establish the group of transformations for each sequence, either within the myth itself, or by elucidation of the isomorphic links between sequences derived from several myths originating in the same community. This itself takes us beyond the study of individual myths to the consideration of certain guiding patterns situated along a single axis. At each point on the axis where there is such a pattern or schema, we then draw, as it were, a vertical line representing another axis established by the same operation but carried out this time not by means of apparently different myths originating from a single community, but by myths that present certain analogies with the first, although they derive from neighboring communities. As a result, the guiding patterns are simplified, made more complex or transformed.[94]

New "axes" branch out from the original ones, embracing a wider range of myths, including some originally neglected because they seemed insignificant or uninterpretable. Thus, this structural system expands into a increasingly comprehensive "multi-dimensional body, whose central parts disclose a structure, while uncertainty and confusion continue to prevail along its periphery."[95]

Of course the visible structures of myth serve more than the metaphorical, heuristic function evident here. Structuralists employ topological principles and generative formulae when possible to indicate likely developments or interrelationships among mythic structures not at first perceived. A typical kind of transformation is the repetition in reverse of a pattern in series (a "reflection"), represented spatially as a series of rotations and reflections that can generate a number of figures or myths.[96] The meaning of mythic elements, Levi-Strauss argues, "is entirely in the dynamic relation which simultaneously creates several myths, or parts of myths, acquire a rational existence and achieve fulfillment together as opposable pairs of one and the same set of transformations."[97] This has little to do with conscious thought:

> Mythological analysis has not, and cannot have, as its aim to show how men think. . . . I therefore claim to show, not how men think in

myths, but how myths operate in men's minds without their being aware of the fact. . . . It would perhaps be better to go still further and, disregarding the thinking subject completely, proceed as if the thinking process were taking place in the myths, in their reflection upon themselves and their interrelation.[98]

Indeed, his interest is not so much in the myths, or what underlies them, particularly, but rather "to clarify . . . the system of axioms and postulates defining the best possible code, capable of conferring a common significance on unconscious formulations which are the work of minds, societies, and civilizations."[99]

The ultimate aims of structuralism extend beyond the determination of structures underlying the social phenomena of a single group or culture, or related groups of cultures: the deepest underlying structures are universal, as they depend on the structure of the human brain. One must, it is argued, see every element and every level of culture as an interconnected web, with surface meaning fully dependent for its proper determination on accurate reproduction of the entire system. Linguistic and all other social phenomena are "the projection, on the level of conscious and socialized thought, of universal laws which regulate the unconscious activities of mind." Further, "the 'natural basis' of the phonemic system" is "the structure of the brain."[100]

Given its relative lack of concern for producing hypotheses that explain or generate intension, the potential conflict of structuralism with the indeterminacy thesis is not as clearly drawn. However, structuralists seem wedded nonetheless to the "black-box" idea. Also, broader Boasian criticisms concerning the neglect for emics seem pertinent. There seems no reason to deny that a variety of alternative structures might equally serve to account for the mythic and cultural "surface"—or at least for those elements "intuitively felt" by the inquirer to be manifesting deeper significance. Particularly alarming for the methodologist who worries about whether the "underlying structures" he "finds" are the native's, or simply his own, or simply certain conventional structures arising in the scientific inquiry that have no analogous pattern in anybody's head, is Levi-Strauss' above-noted remark that he chooses his mythic starting points "not so much arbitrarily as through an intuitive feeling that it is both rich and rewarding."[101]

As might be expected, there have been concerns expressed in more recent structuralist literature concerning the cognitive aspects of code recovery, especially in light of "multiplicity" problems that spawn the critical reflections of Burling and Quine. Two recent reviewers, David Kronenfeld and Henry W. Decker interpret Levi-Strauss as confronting this problem in a different way—namely, by accepting multiplicity and contending that *all* the "reasonably parsimonious" analyses are correct:

> In stating that "it is in the last resort immaterial whether in this book the thought processes of the South American Indians take shape through the medium of my thought, or whether mine takes place through the medium of theirs" . . . , Levi-Strauss appears to be asserting that many codes can lie behind any one message, and that any code which one human mind can find in a message is there for any other mind to find. . . . This seems to be a reasonable claim. In kinship studies where a claim such as this has been rigorously explored, it does not appear that the search for a single "psychologically real" analysis has been misguided. It appears that any reasonably parsimonious analysis of any part of English kinship terminology that any anthropologist has been able to come up with will actually be used at one time or another by any native speaker of English. . . .[102] In other words, any *conceivable* analysis is a true one—at least within some broad limits. If this is true, then the analyst of a native folktale deals with whichever codes she or he finds most approachable.[103]

Thus, Levi-Strauss seems to sidestep the conflict of imposition and the objective determinacy of his structural yield. He gets to the truth of the matter—or, rather, to the many truths of the matter. However, the claim that structures or codes are there "for any mind to find" seems to be carrying a lot of weight here—being all that seems to block the challenges of Burling and Quine.[104] It seems to rest, if anything, on an assumption of psychic unity about which Quine expresses deep skepticism.

However, in interesting contrast to the "God's truth" spirit of these remarks, there is the following passage in *The Savage Mind*:

> It is of course only for purposes of exposition and because they form the subject of this book that I am apparently giving priority to ideology and superstructures. I do not at all mean to suggest that ideological transformations give rise to social ones. Only the reverse is in fact true. Men's conception of the relations between nature and culture is a function of modifications of their social relations. But, since my aim here is to outline a theory of superstructures, reasons of method require that they should be singled out for attention and that major phenomena which have no place in this program should seem to be left

in brackets or given second place. We are however merely studying the shadows on the wall of the Cave without forgetting that it is only the attention we give them which lends them a semblance of reality.[105]

This passage can easily be viewed as giving reason to believe that Levi-Strauss is more sympathetic to the "hocus-pocus" view, at least as pertains to the fundamental character of the structures he seeks to reveal.[106] But then, on the other hand, he might well contend that the interpreted structures are, despite their ephemeral character, nonetheless *isomorphic* to universal brain structures—functioning, in the terms of the adapted platonic metaphor, as their "shadows" in the light of interpretation.

There are also interesting parallels between structuralist analysis and the ideal-language programs of Russell, the early Wittgenstein, and others, programs that we have seen bear much of the brunt of Quine's and Wittgenstein's criticisms. Levi-Strauss evidently views the underlying structures and generative principles of myth as being rigorously explicable in formal systems viewed as offering an ideal embodiment of those structures and principles. This connection has been noted by Lee Drummond:

> Despite obvious differences in subject area, *Mythologiques*, the *Principia* and the *Tractatus* are brilliant examples of the metalinguistic, or ideal language, approach which seeks to dispel the inherent ambiguity of natural (ordinary) languages by creating a set of non-ambiguous, "ideal" propositions based entirely on logical relations and operations. Hence the "transformations" and "binary operators" of *Mythologiques*, the "elementary propositions" of the *Principia*, and the notion of proposition as "what is the case" in *Tractatus*. The ideal language approach conceives *meaning* as a logical property contained in ordinary language but obscured by its unsystematic nature, so that the meaning of utterances in ordinary language can be determined only by translating, or reformulating, them in a logical and precise *code* about language, or a metalanguage. The problem of meaning is then solved in ideal language philosophy by identifying the unit of meaning—the minimal requirement necessary for an utterance or expression to have meaning—as the *relation*. . . . The postulate of reformulation rests on the identification of meaning as relation, and in turn forms the basis for the semantic edifices of *Mythologiques*.[107]

Drummond sees structuralists as too neglectful of factors at the sociocultural surface (where Levi-Strauss sees only "uncertainty and confusion to prevail"). Drummond advocates incorporating into

studies of the oral narrative of myth some means for analyzing surface meaning. In this connection he finds Wittgensteinian meaning-
as-use views accommodating:

> The important feature of Wittgenstein's philosophy is its transition
> from the Russellian conception of the proposition as a logical form to
> the "meaning-as-use" theory of the utterance as an unfolding process,
> embedded in a context of other utterances (a "family of relations"),
> and involving an act of intentionality (or someone meaning
> something).[108]

He advocates shifting attention from the state of affairs that makes a
statement true to the speaker's *affirmation* that some state of affairs
exists, and the relevant questions about the speaker's meaning become 'In what does his affirmation, his intention, consist?' and
'What is involved in meaning something if that differs from recom-
bining elements in propositions?' Drummond continues:

> In contrast to the structuralist approach, which identifies the unit of
> meaning with the *relation* between propositional elements,
> Wittgenstein's later views on the subject are strongly processual: a rela-
> tion has meaning in the process of being affirmed by a narrator. Struc-
> turalist analysis sees relations as generated by logical operators, or
> *transformations*, while the "meaning-as-use" theory locates the
> generative principle of meaning-something in the intention of the
> speaker and the *context* of the speech-act. Opposing the concept of
> transformation to those of intention and context permits us to see that
> the epistemological basis of structuralism, what I have called the pos-
> tulate of reformulation, has the effect in myth studies of severing the
> connection between the *structure* of myth and the *process* of its nar-
> ration and exegetical interpretation.[109]

Thus, again, we see the perceived tension between analytic construct and social reality motivating a modification of a formal
approach—and one primarily concerned with unconscious cognition.
Moreover, there is the suggestion of an underlying relationship between problems of formal linguistic analyses in philosophical and
anthropological contexts. Drummond suggests methodological revision in light of these problems and ties his remarks in with a similar
movement in the philosophy of language, that is, away from formal
system toward ordinary-language analysis. Worth noting is another
response that suggests itself if one considers Drummond's objections
in light of the previously cited passage from Levi-Strauss. If one acknowledges, as Levi-Strauss seems to, that inquirer interest has a fun-

damental constitutive effect on theoretical results and if one can fashion a satisfactory *pragmatic* notion of objectivity that takes this into account, one might shift attention entirely to the question of theoretical productivity. If structuralism need lay no claim to psychological reality and if "external" cognitive perspectives are allowed in the study of culture, then a feasible attitude might be that structuralists offer, in Nelson Goodman's terms, but one "world-version," one of the many ways the world is. However, fashioning the appropriate notion of objectivity, particularly in light of the varied problems of imposition that concern us here, is easier said than done.

Cognitive Anthropology: Recent Developments and Problems

Now that we have seen some of the views that have prevailed in several major language-and-culture paradigms—particularly those responsible for the mentalistic flavor of much research—I would like to look at some other approaches and some more recent discussions and trends. What I want to show is how the aforementioned problems continue to prevail and how they have motivated theorists, whom I group here under the rough label 'cognitive anthropology',[110] to move in conflicting directions. Some have continued to emphasize unconscious psychological structures and their effect on cognitive or cultural development. Others, however, have perceived this emphasis as antagonistic to fundamental Boasian concerns with revealing or adopting the subjects' points of view. Some of the latter have tried to restore concern, in various ways, with symbolic structures (albeit still mental ones) more directly tied to behavior. Others have sought to retreat from conscious or unconscious mentalism by relocating the focal point of significance in social-behavioral elements. Others still, understandably, have chosen to avoid the paradoxical tensions of emic analysis by generally avoiding concerns with either cognition or subject viewpoints. In this section I shall discuss representative views that remain within the ethnoscientific and cognitive paradigms. In subsequent sections I shall look at more comprehensive methodological transformations.

Oswald Werner is a strong proponent of continued emphasis on transformational analysis. This is evident in the aforementioned article (with coauthor Fenton) favoring grounding componential analyses in transformational ones for the sake of developing a universal theory of knowledge. It is also borne out in a recent article by Werner and Donald Campbell that makes a strong commitment to explanatory adequacy and relates it intimately to the fundamental emic task of ethnoscience: They demand that linguistic inquiry begin with "decentered" translation, aimed at reflecting their subjects' surface and subsurface linguistic categorizations, rather than "centered" translation, aimed at the smoothest translation of source-language discourse in the target language. Successful, decentered translation, they contend, involves the recovery of linguistic deep structure, semantic interpretations, and semantic structure, in addition to the recovery of more superficial elements; moreover, they hinge the very possibility of decentered translation on the existence of these empirically determinate (and at the deepest levels universal) generative elements. These points are also emphasized in a later piece in which Werner and Lawrence Fisher advocate defining 'emic' so as not to limit it to what subjects say or consciously think.[111]

However, others have favored returning to something more like Goodenough's idea of discerning rules of behavior. For example, Stephen Tyler rejects the idea that anthropology must strive for the explanation or specification of developmental processes. Instead, he views its proper concern as being with determining "only . . .what is expected and appropriate." And, with Goodenough, he further contends that the "cultural anthropologist is only concerned with those events which are expressions of underlying thoughts." His aim is to penetrate beyond mere material representation to the logical nexus of underlying concepts. As with Goodenough, he emphasizes the derivation of formal systems, platonically mentalistic (and public) in character, while generally ignoring individual psychology.[112] Implicit here is the allegiance of platonistic meaning-analysis with emphasis on publicly shared significance.

Partly following Tyler's lead, others have developed sophisticated models of native decision making and information processing. Perhaps the most prolific of recent contributors in this area is William H. Geoghegan, who has applied a fairly extensive information processing model to ethnography. He joins Geertz, Cook, and others in rejecting the insular platonism of formal analyses, contending that these provide the main stumbling block to the attainment of ethnographic results with demonstrable psychological validity; something he contends cannot be done while competence is stressed at the expense of examining the "performance routines" of the native actor.[113]

These concerns echo those just noted in connection with the formal constructs of transformational linguistics and structuralism. However, while Geoghegan avoids some of the drawbacks, he remains committed to the recovery of other abstract mentalistic items such as native "modes of thought," "models in the head," "decision rules," and "cognitive processes." So while he may temper the universalistic fervor of transformationalists (and, indeed, of their counterparts in cognitive psychology) with a greater sensitivity to intercultural variation, mentalistic commitments and problems remain.

The concern that important elements are overlooked if contextual variation is ignored in the quest for formal structure has been seen in several methodological contexts above, and continues to be a prevalent concern. Tyler, for instance, worries that "typological analysis or formal analysis based on genealogical criteria alone is apt to obscure important data."[114] Cecil Brown's (and R. G. D'Andrade's) criticisms of "unitary theories" in anthropological application, as we have seen, are similarly motivated by a concern with contextual variability of meaning. Brown has elaborated these concerns more constructively in a recent monograph that applies Wittgenstein's views on meaning to the development of a theory that strikes a compromise between the strongly behavioral theories of structural linguistics and, as Brown puts it, the "excessively detailed . . .wiring model" of Chomsky.[115] Brown attempts to achieve this by analyzing "socially real" and public linguistic *functions* of expressions within (perhaps, in some cases, universal) language games. I shall discuss this in more detail in my concluding chapter.[116]

In a similar vein, Johannes Fabian tries to modify idealized competence models in folk classification by emphasizing their function in historical accounts of cultural development within the society in question. His view is that an unfortunate consequence of the great interest in formalization is the neglect of the *evolving* character of these systems and their *causal* role in cultural-historical processes. Thus, placing categorizations is historical context, he contends, serves to eliminate the arbitrariness and relativity manifest in the selection of formal categorizations; that is, the question of cognitive, or social, reality is met by endeavoring to fit the recovered scheme into a sensible, historical account. In a fashion similar to symbolic anthropologists such as Mary Douglas, he contends that these categorizations are only temporarily fixed in the constant fluid flow of cultural change and thus that their essential "open-endedness" must be reflected in ethnographic analysis.[117]

Concern with folk classification has been prominent in ethnoscience since its inception, since it is a natural consequence of Frake's and Goodenough's belief in the fundamentally semantic character of culture. (This, as I noted above, also provided the philosophical underpinning for the various extensions of linguistic method in ethnography that I have examined.) However, folk classification studies have diverged from those following the lead of, say, Romney and D'Andrade in that the former have not become actively concerned with psychological testing. Yet, as noted in a recent review by the Rockerfeller Laboratory of Human Cognition, it nonetheless preserves the psychological concerns of earlier work:

> This tradition strays far from the ethnographic base from which it emerged in order to make broader claims about the human mind and its evolution, a diversion which causes considerable problems in the interpretation of the taxonomic data it has to work with, as they are not constrained owing to their cross-domain and cross-cultural interests by their normal contexts of occurrence in a natural community.[118]

The more ambitious workers in this area seek universal principles of arrangement, viewed as actually existing cross-culturally or as coming into existence through evolutionary progression, with the most significant study being that of Brent Berlin and Paul Kay on basic color terms (one of the main targets of Fabian's critique).[119] The Laboratory notes a range of theses, from claims about mental structure to "the less powerful claim that the folk taxonomies represent only the categories available to people if and when they do some thinking about the domains in question."[120]

However, the Laboratory expresses extreme skepticism about the validity of inferences to such cognitive structures from interview data. Indeed, it seems clear that even the less powerful claim by folk taxonomists has a fundamentally emic thrust—the qualification there reflecting, I think, only the concern that ethnographers not impose more systematization of language and culture than is already "there":

> In view of their data-gathering techniques, students of folk classification are well advised to avoid psychological claims. Formal interviews on the similarities and differences in named objects or colors, and dictionary forays with the same ends in mind, cannot give strong data on how people are processing the information in question. In the terms of this paper, the task is ill defined from the points of view of either analysts or natives. When the distinctions the people make fall into a pattern, something interesting must be going on, but it is hard to know about it in any detail.[121]

These reviewers make a compelling appeal, in this regard, to the work of the cognitive anthropologist Eleanor Rosch, whose work on cognition and semantics has influenced anthropologists interested in cognitive processes.[122] Despite her interest in cognitive structure (shared by her anthropological following), the Laboratory notes a recent cautionary caveat of hers regarding inferences to underlying cognitive structure:

> Although her work has often been interpreted as defining a competence model for the kinds of conceptual structuring systems people have in their heads, Rosch has recently stated that: "the issues in categorization with which we are primarily concerned have to do with explaining the categories found in a culture and coded by the language of that culture.". . .She specifically rejects the idea that her research is designed to specify how the categories are processed. Before more detailed psychological statements can be made, the objects specified in the classifications would have to be detailed in terms of their use "in the events of everyday life.". . .If it is the case that "events stand at the interface between an analysis of social structure and culture and analysis of individual psychology,". . .then her future work will be of special interest to anthropologists.[123]

Thus, we see here, again, evidence of the increasing concern for the "context-sensitivity" of semantic and other formal and structural analyses, as well as the widely held belief that such sensitivity will significantly minimize the indeterminacy of inferences from linguistic and nonlinguistic behavioral data to cognitive structure. However, the commitment to translational determinacy remains, and thus these problems may not, if Quine is right, be adequately met.[124]

In light of this perceived tension between aims to reveal the subject's point of view and to study cognition, one could well wonder if cognitive studies should be regarded as "emic" in any sense. Fisher and Werner seem to express a general willingness to regard studies of unconscious as constituting emic inquiry. In interesting contrast, Lawrence Watson in a recent article expresses an attitude that such categorizations—specifically those of psychoanalysis—be regarded as etic. What's more, he views such etic categories as inhibiting the appreciation of subject perspectives and consequently inhibiting the acquisition of valuable anthropological insights. In a recent study of Guajiro Indian adaptation to city life in Maracaibo, he compares etic-psychoanalytic models he himself employed in earlier work with more recently applied emic ones. His etic model, he argues, depicted the Guajiro as "helpless or incompetent,'' passively and "automatically" reacting to conditions defined in etic terms alien to them. Rohrschach and TAT tests showed subjects to have unconscious feelings of "vulnerability and dependency" stemming in part from their marginal economic status. This perspective made salient the negative effects of their traditional tribal background, which in various ways seemed to play a role in parents inducing dependency in their children.[125] His emic model, which analyzes "spontaneously recalled personal data" provided in answers to "open-ended questions" geared to "the subject's immediate and authentic interests and orientation," provided quite distinct results. These showed, he argues, that his earlier assessment of their seemingly poor understanding of the city reflected instead his own misunderstanding of their different frames of reference, whose key units of orientation were Guajiro neighborhoods. Also, he came to change earlier negative evaluations of the influence of the tribal background, which were constrained by predefined etic parameters of adaptive versus maladaptive behavior. The emic model permitted more positive evaluation of the background's importance in promoting individual self-respect.[126] Generally the etic model

> deflects attention away from what the Guajiros are to themselves, to what they ought to be , judged by external standards. . . .We emphasize a wider (and to them incomprehensible) sphere of activity. Our understandings focus on processes of which—almost by definition—they are not aware.[127]

Concern with how the ethnographer's data are to be shown to be psychologically real and, more generally, how this input is to be used in inferences concerning cognitive structures and processes are still prevalent in the ethnoscientific literature. Thus, the general philosophical and methodological problems raised by anthropologists and philosophers concerning inferences from behavioral input to cognitive process are of paramount significance. Many inquirers, I suspect, are unsatisfied with Burling's "hocus-pocus" attitude, not so much because they expect more of anthropological inquiry itself than Burling (and for that matter Tyler) thinks it can achieve but because Burling's relativization of criteria of adequacy to anthropological concerns makes problematic the future synthesis of ethnographic and anthropological linguistic results with work in cognitive and developmental psychology, psycholinguistics, and so forth. And, evidently, this dissatisfaction would extend to Quine's indeterminacy results.

Ethnoscientists are by no means unaware of the problems that Burling sees with trying to get warranted psychological reality, or that Rosch and the Laboratory of Human Cognition see with trying to make further inferences about cognitive processes. These concerns and conflicts are reflected also in the literature on native decision making. Geoghehan's influential work, as I have noted, is explicitly aimed at the determinate recovery of cognitive processes. In closely related work, Christina Gladwin endeavors to recreate a model of choice procedures that, she contends, her informant "mentally goes through." She claims that her subjects, fish sellers, calculate the likelihood of a day's market being good based on its condition on the previous day. However, the subjects, she admits, never talk of such calculations, and the choice-model is validated on the basis of its successful prediction of when fish sellers actually go to market.[128] Thus, despite her concern with cognitive processes, she contrasts with, say, Tyler in stressing her ability to predict behavior as the measure of success, and she contrasts with many of the figures we have seen in not feeling constrained by her subjects' discourses and verbal reports in her ascription to them of certain thought processes. However, without appeal to verbal reports to substantiate claims about mental processes, the underdetermination of her resultant hypotheses by data seems particularly acute, and this seems especially to invite imposition of her own reconstructions of thought processes on her subjects. The omission of substantiating verbal reports is the focal point of subsequent criticisms by Naomi Quinn (who criticizes Hugh Gladwin's work on similar grounds), who argues, on the basis of a study of another group of fish sellers in the same region, that Gladwin's account of decision making under uncertainty makes a "cognitively unrealistic assumption" that subjects calculate probability distributions in assessing the riskiness of their possible choices—unrealistic precisely because of the absence of corroborating verbal reports.[129]

Also relevant is a related controversy between Hugh Gladwin and David Lewis concerning the capability of micronesian navigators to engage in abstract thinking and planning brings these points to the surface.[130] Lewis criticizes Gladwin's work for lacking sufficient evidence to support his view that the navigators cannot engage in this sort of thinking—Lewis' contrary results being derived from observations of the subjects under more extreme and exceptional circumstances than considered by Gladwin, as well as from closer attention to verbal reports.[131]

Thus, we see emerging again something of the difficulties implicit in Sapir's contention that linguistic habits may in large part be outside the conscious awareness of ethnographic subjects. And, again, it is evident that the pervasive Quinean skepticism that turns on some of the very points at issue here cuts across both contrasting views: For, on Quine's view, it seems, verbal reports do little to minimize indeterminacy and bring one any closer to "cognitive reality."

As in its discussion of Rosch and cognitive anthropology, the Laboratory of Human Cognition points out that obscurity regarding the character of inferences from behavior (verbal or not) to thought processes confuses the basic points at issue and makes resolution, at present, impossible.[132] It also brings another variety of imposition-problem into the already clouded picture of current cognitive anthropology, namely, the concern with "imposing Western rationality" itself in too quickly assuming that the subjects' basic cognitive tasks are what they at first evidently seem to be to the Western eye. This problem connects, of course, into a number of long-standing controversies in anthropology and philosophy of social science centering on the classic contributions of Levy-Bruhl and J. G. Frazer and the more recent work of E. E. Evans-Pritchard (particularly, *Nuer Religion*), to which I shall give more attention later. The Laboratory contends that identification of "task environment" is the solution to this particular problem: "much of the argument concerning statements said to reflect primitive mentality . . . [is] rooted in disagreement about the definition of what tasks people are working on when they say such a thing [as] . . . 'Twins are birds'."[133]

This solution is perfectly in keeping with Wittgensteinian trends the Laboratory sees in more recent language-and-culture anthropology, and which I shall consider further below. Indeed, in addition to his criticisms of traditional mentalistic theories, Wittgenstein's later work is seasoned with criticisms to the effect that it is all too easy to attribute the wrong practice or language-game to one's ethnographic subjects, thus missing the significance of what they say and do. In particular, his more recently published *Remarks on Frazer's Golden Bough* takes Frazer's scientistic imposition in the analysis of primitive religion severely to task. He thus adds significant philosophical weight to criticisms of the "natural" working assumption of figures in what is called the "intellectualist" tradition in anthropology that native religious beliefs are to be treated as a kind of theory-formation, susceptible to empirical error and open to improvement (as measured by Western scientific standards of hypothesis acceptance) in light of this error.[134]

Ascent to Social-Behavioral Context

Concern for context-sensitivity, as we have seen in previous sections, has grown steadily in the anthropological literature. However, the remedies considered thus far generally amount more to emendations of existing methodologies. I would like now to consider more radical methodological breaks. Here I shall consider the views of people working still within the Boasian tradition. Subsequently, in Chapter 3, I shall look at Marvin Harris' broad critique of what he terms "idealist" anthropology, in support of a fully contrasting, and non-Boasian "cultural materialism."

I think it most appropriate to begin this discussion of methodological divergence from ethnoscience by considering the recent skepticism of one of its founding fathers, Frake. In "Plying Frames Can Be Dangerous," Frake takes on not only the transformational approaches (suggested in his title's pun on Chomsky) but a whole range of ethnoscientific approaches that introduce what he regards as excessive and distorting rigor in their reliance on "eliciting frames." He views these often elaborately ramified question sets as blinding inquirers to the social context. Understanding this context, he argues, is absolutely essential to understanding the significance of the questions one puts to subjects and the answers one receives (compare my discussion of Watson above). He favors a more flexible dramaturgical form of analysis that shifts emphasis to the prior delineation of "query-rich settings." These settings generate emically significant question sets and units of context specification.[135]

Very similar concerns motivate major recent methodological developments, which have issued in approaches falling under the rough rubrics of "sociolinguistics" and "symbolic anthropology." In the case of sociolinguistics, the aims of this broad area of inquiry involve ascertaining the function of utterances in social contexts, which, in turn, involve more than verbal communication. "The central concept of the whole of semantics considered in this way," notes J.R. Firth, "is the context situation. In that context are the human participant or participants, what they say, and what is going on."[136] Among its general aims is the determination of the actions performed, roles played, social stratification and customs expressed, and so on, in verbal and nonverbal behavior.

Some, such as Hymes who has developed a sociolinguistic approach known as "the ethnography of speaking," view it as an integrated approach to language and culture, in contrast to those that give linguistic theories and models methodological priority. Hymes also contrasts it with linguistically based approaches, as well as with the integrated structuralist approach, in terms of sociolinguistics' self-conscious eschewal of the mentalism and abstractness of these approaches, although there are many sociolinguists who incorporate transformational and structural features in their work.[137] One particular perceived shortcoming of these other methodologies that motivates the shift to sociolinguistics involves the correlation of distinctly different linguistic and ethnographic theories. Hymes questions the division of labor involved, for instance, in approaches that distinguish studies of surface grammar, construed as comprising abstract, self-contained codes, and studies of ethnography, which are supposed to provide social interpretation and content. (This concern obviously extends to the transformational and structuralist approaches that place far less emphasis on the ethnographic side of the division.)[138]

However, though it eschews mentalism, of central importance to this approach is the determination of the source-language society's social and sociolinguistic categorizations and rules of appropriate behavior through accurate translation. In a 1972 review, Werner notes this, while also remarking on the believed empirical possibility of this goal:

> Many problems in the social uses of language can be conceived as answers to questions: e.g. "What does one do when a stranger approaches camp?" "How does one behave in the presence of the president?" or "When is it proper for a young man to speak?" These are questions appropriate to an ethnography of speaking but also clearly questions that have possible answers. They are formulated in the native's language to reduce ethnocentric translation bias and, equally importantly, to avoid imposing one's own categories. Quite likely not all socially significant contexts are explicitly open to description by native speakers. They do misjudge situations on occasion or are unable to state the precise contextual rule. However, since verbalizable contexts are by no means rare or small in numbers there is no reason to exclude them from semantics. . . . Contextual attributes can be listed with other attributes.[139]

Moreover, context is treated as semantic, and it is added to other semantic notions whose recovery is also thus an object of inquiry. Werner's remarks on these additional elements indicate that extension and certain ideational elements (attributes and mental images) are included:

Features of context in a lexical semantic field are not separate from other semantic facts. An occasional sentence containing the referent "red" (in the literal sense) requires some red object to be present. Similarly, it implies that certain listeners are involved, or that these correlate to each other in some way, or what mode they use to communicate, or their style of delivery and the topic of discourse. .depend on the presence of these factors. That these are modifiers analogous to "red" can be seen from the observation that the speaker and listener(s) must have past experiences against which to judge these external clues. Such internal representations are probably identical with attributes. It is not necessary that attributes be simple, especially since the elicitation of contexts may be derived from the elicitation of long texts.[140]

The intension of such "occasional sentences" (parallel in character to what Quine calls "occasion sentences") is not problematic in Quine's view, although the extension of their terms is. However, problems arise as soon as one extends the method, as it is obviously intended to be, to remarks about less observable matters.

While Werner's view of sociolinguistics may be more mentalistic than that of others, commitments to intension and translational determinacy are pervasive. For instance, Hymes' influential theory provides an analytic framework coded mnemonically on the word 'speaking': *s*etting or scene; *p*articipants or personnel; *e*nds (goals, purposes, and outcomes); *a*ct (characteristics) (described by sociolinguists Richard Bauman and Joel Sherzer as "both the form and content of what is said"); *k*ey (the tone, manner, or spirit in which an act is performed); *i*nstrumentalities (channel and code); *n*orms of interaction and of interpretation; *g*enres (type of speech act or event).[141] Aside from general indeterminacy problems involved in identifying speaker goals, purposes, norms, speech acts or events, specific Quinean implications intrude in the category of *speech act*, whose study is evidently susceptible to the analytic techniques of Austin and Searle. These philosophers are cited in a number of ground-breaking methodological essays as well as field studies. For instance, Bauman and Sherzer note that:

> the members of a community may conceptualize speech activity in terms of acts rather than genres. Speech acts and genres are, of course, analytically distinct, the former having to do with speech behavior, the latter with the verbal products of that behavior. A speech act is an utterance looked at from a functional point of view, a way of doing something with words, to paraphrase J. L. Austin. . . .It is in this sense

that a community's range of speech acts constitute means for the conduct of speaking—they represent conventionalized ways of doing things with words, ready-organized building blocks with which to construct discourse.[142]

These reviewers further cite Michael K. Foster's "When Words Become Deeds: An Analysis of Three Iroquois Longhouse Speech Events,"[143] which endeavors to show the underlying pattern relating to a variety of Longhouse Iroquois ritual speeches for beseeching a hierarchy of spirit forces for benefits. It initially employs Austin's theory in identifying a key performative utterance in these speeches that distinguishes beseeching from thanking. Foster values Austin's analysis for its taking into account circumstances, implicit understandings of actors, and other related nonverbal behavior in the identification of speech acts:

> What is the relationship between the performance utterances and the other statements of speeches? For this we turn to Austin, who has suggested that while the uttering of certain words may often be the crucial part of an act, this is seldom the only requirement: "speaking generally, it is always necessary that the *circumstances appropriate*, and it is very commonly necessary that either the speaker himself or other persons should *also* perform certain *other* actions." (Austin, *How to Do Things With Words*, p. 8)[144]

Indeed, as much of the content of these Iroquois speeches is concerned with specifying the conditions of proper performance, they comprise an Iroquois theory of their ritual speech acts parallel to Austin's and Searle's for ordinary English discourse: the Iroquois theory is deemed recoverable, over and above the speech acts themselves.[145]

It it clear that Foster, among others, views alien speech acts as identifiable by foreign observers, although he cautions that they attend to differences in meaning of component expressions used in performing acts. A key Iroquoian word root appears in *both* greeting and thanking contexts, making it easy for interpreters to confuse the two and hence misidentify speech acts; also there are differences in the preparatory conditions for greeting/thanking in Iroquois and English.[146]

In keeping with Hymes' above-noted remarks concerning the integrational aspects of sociolinguistics, Foster stresses the value of integrating the social and situational level with the psychological, so as to give attention to both and so as not to stress one at the expense of the other. Foster quotes a passage from Austin that he takes to "make clear the relevance of performative analysis to the ethnography of speaking":

> [In order for a performative to succeed] there must exist an accepted conventional procedure having a certain conventional effect, that procedure to include the uttering of certain words by certain persons in certain circumstances. . . . Where, as often, the procedure is designed for use by persons having certain thoughts or feelings . . . then a person participating in and so invoking the procedure must in fact have those thoughts and feelings.[147]

As I noted earlier, the development of sociolinguistics is but one manifestation of a trend in anthropological linguistics and language-and-culture studies that parallel the shift in many philosophical circles to the meaning-as-use approaches and their various offspring. Other anthropologists have employed it as a means of supplementing ethnoscientific methodology (which still lays primary stress on conscious semantic criteria). Still others, who have sought cognitive structures at deeper levels in reaction to perceived shortcomings of earlier emic and componential approaches, have also incorporated elements of these behavioral theories. But what I want to reemphasize is that these notions do not meet the deeper imposition problems that underlie Quine's skeptical reflections on semantics (see my discussion of Harris, Brown, and Romney in this chapter and my discussion of Searle in the previous one). There is something, to be sure, in the pragmatic objections sociolinguists and others (for example, Cook) have to the stultifying over-concern with grammar manifest in these earlier approaches. But simply claiming that meaning in one form or another is *just implicit* in word-usage, social action contexts, and so on (that is, as opposed to being in addition a sort of underlying "beetle in a box") is insufficient to forestall imposition problems entirely, if at all. There seems to be some sense in saying we thus "minimize translation bias" by not focusing so exclusively on mentalistic structures that may have little to do with subjects' conscious categories, structures, rules, or interpretations. However, those who fully import Searle also import a commitment to recovering propositions (as the abstract "what is expressed" in speech acts) as well as speaker intentions. And even those who make sparser commitments must show, in light of Quine's reflections on the very imposition and psychological reality problems that motivate these methodological transformations, how they can warrantably assert that the *subject}* is performing such and such an act, taking on such and such a role, and so on—where some cultural specificity is claimed for the identification.[148]

Such problems are further multiplied where sociolinguists incorporate Morris' semiotic notions and elements of transformational theory (which Searle himself does). For instance, Judith Irvine accounts for the subtle expressions of rank and mood of interaction among the Wolof (of Senegal) in dyadic greeting exchange by reference to transformational rules that effect this manipulation of the standard exchange procedure by operating on the phrase structure rules that determine the latter.[149]

Irvine's study of the Wolof also exemplifies the persistence of imposition problems in field practice (as well as in Quinean reflections on field practice). Citing Frake's insistence that ethnographer's impressions must be related to rules of "socially appropriate construction and interpretation of messages," and stressing with Frake the need to use her subject's sociolinguistic categories in her analysis, she remarks, in an evidently self-critical vein, on the necessity of using her own "internalization" to overcome empirical determination both during and after her field work:

> I have been obliged . . .to use my own internalization of how greeting works rather more than I wished, for two reasons. First, I suspect greetings carried on by others in my presence to have been somewhat skewed toward 'polite' forms and so not to represent a complete range of what I know from my own efforts can be done. It proved difficult to persuade informants to act out hypothetical greeting situations for my benefit, and difficult ever to record greetings on tape. . . .Second, I became aware of many aspects of greeting behavior only after I had left the field.[150]

The first reason offered bespeaks an imposition problem that can be dealt with, while the second is indicative of the more pervasive and intractable sort that I shall try to confront in later chapters.

The various meaning-problems noted above figure importantly in the recent development of another approach (or, better, broad category of approaches) in the language-and-culture tradition known as symbolic anthropology. Its proponents view the failures of earlier methodologies as calling for a more radical reorientation than the modifications envisioned above. One of its major spokesmen, Victor Turner, categorically denies that emic approaches can achieve their (typically) primary objective of deriving "native systems of 'implicit' thought" from "'native' premises"—because of fundamentally mistaken presuppositions concerning the nature of symbolic meaning.[151]

Motivated, in some cases, by Wittgenstein's rejection of mentalistic semantics and, in a more constructive vein, by symbolic inter-actionisms (such as Erving Goffman's) and sociological sociolinguistic studies (such as Basil Bernstein's), these anthropologists contend that symbols must not be construed as signs designating static (concretely or abstractly) mental structures, but rather, as Turner puts it, "as instrumentalities of various forces—physical, moral, economic, political, and so on—operating in isolable, changing fields of social relationships." They view the existence of symbols in abstract systems as dependent on the relative rates of social change; Turner remarks that symbols "can be detached from abstract systems of symbols . . .with which they have been previously connected, and 'hooked in' to new *ad hoc* combinations of symbols to constitute, legitimate, or undermine programs and protocols for collective action."[152]

It is difficult to characterize the work that falls under this rather loose rubric in any precise way. Rather, 'symbolic anthropology' is better viewed as designating a group of theories that stress the manipulability, situational variability, and flexibility of symbols rather than their function in fixed systems (of, say, competence).[153] Typically, they categorically reject the transhistorical and transcultural fixity of generative and structuralist deep patterns, and their work also differs from these and the earlier structural-linguistic approaches insofar as broader functions of symbols (than their formal arrangements) are emphasized. They differ from sociolinguists (though, indeed, this approach could be viewed as a branch of symbolic anthropology) in that symbolic anthropologists generally draw on a wider methodological background and do not give central attention to speech-act analysis.[154] Mary Douglas, a major contributor to symbolic anthropology, characterizes their typical concerns as follows:

> Nature must be expressed in symbols; nature is know through symbols which are themselves a construction upon experience, a product of mind, an artifice or conventional product, therefore the reverse of natural. A symbol only has meaning from its relation to other symbols in pattern. The pattern gives the meaning. Therefore no one item in the pattern can carry meaning by itself isolated from the rest. Therefore even the human physiology which we all share in common does not afford symbols which we can all understand. A cross-cultural, pan-human pattern of symbols must be an impossibility. For one thing, each symbolic system develops autonomously according to its own

rules. For another, the cultural environments add their differences. For another, the social structures add a further range of variation.[155]

The significant Wittgensteinian trends of recent anthropology surface clearly here, and Douglas' philosophical motivations are similar to those that have led to the other modifications and transformations noted above within the language-and-culture tradition. For instance, in crediting Bernstein for providing her main methodological orientation, Douglas notes Bernstein's and her own philosophical reaction to Whorf's key remark that people who speak different languages live in different worlds as sharply critical of "Whorf and others who have treated language as an autonomous cultural agent and failed to relate its formal patterns to the structure of social relations."[156] She thus shares with structuralists and sociolinguists the belief that it is a fundamental mistake to treat linguistic analysis in the methodologically prior manner (both as theory and model) of other language-and-culture methodologies. Her own solution to the methodological challenge implicit in Whorf's remark is, briefly, to analyze symbolic systems as oppositional and cooperative interactions between individual systems (or "grids") and social ones (an account patterned on Bernstein's distinctions between restricted and elaborated codes).[157]

Her concerns and criticisms are generally shared by another influential symbolic anthropologist, Clifford Geertz. In stressing the central role of anthropological "interpretation" in ethnography (that is, the "constructing a reading of what happens" in the social milieu), Geertz warns against the undesirable "hermetical" effect that structuralist, generative-grammatical, and emic approaches engender. By this he means the sealing off of cultural analysis "from its proper object, the informal logic of actual life." Instead, Geertz argues (and Turner concurs) that "it is through the flow of behavior—or more precisely, social action—that cultural forms find articulation."[158] Geertz is also quite explicit in his rejection, for their similarly hermetical effects, of generative grammarians' tendencies inordinately to stress competence—a timeless idealization—at the expense of the anthropologist's ability to "construct a reading" of ongoing social processes (compare Levelt's and Cook's criticisms of Chomsky).[159] Thus, as with Douglas and Turner, Geertz views Whorf's challenge as demanding avoidance of fixed semantic rules, structures, and components—to a degree far greater than envisaged by Whorf and many other language-and-culture anthropologists.

Similar trends are manifest in British social anthropology, which I have neglected to this point in light of its dominance by eticly oriented functionalism. Malcolm Crick, while aiming his main criticisms at functionalism, draws on Wittgenstein in passing criticism of the American ethnoscientists. In a vein similar to Frake, Crick worries that ethnoscientists too easily assume that categories such as "myth," "religion," "poetry," and so on will have direct analogues in the source-language conceptual apparatus. He offers Wittgensteinian grounds for challenging any *assumption* that religious and scientific language games will have parallel identities and parallel interrelationships in other societies. To do so may be to "violate some crucial cultural distinctions" and effectively to abandon the whole point of emic analysis: "There is little point in stressing 'emic' units," he remarks, "if domains themselves are unthinkingly thrust on other cultures."[160] He also expresses agreement with Hymes' cautions against regarding linguistic analysis as a distinct form of analysis to be incorporated as a foundation for ethnography, citing both the nonlinguistic articulation of concepts and the fact that emphasizing the "standard" language of a society may overlook alternative symbolic forms of expression employed by less dominant groups, such as women.[161] His own methodology hearkens to Geertz's (as well as E.E. Evans-Pritchard's and Peter Winch's) in emphasizing the importance of articulating different conceptual categories, with central attention given to *person* categories. In this connection he criticizes the effect of Western philosophy of mind in encouraging the imposition of categories of mind, body, person, and so on that interfere with field work and that have come under fire by philosophers such as Wittgenstein and Ryle and, it is important to add, Quine.[162]

However, despite their rejection of much of the substance of "emic" approaches, many symbolic anthropologists still lay fundamental stress on the recovery of cognitively or socially real products. Their objections to their predecessors center more on the abstraction of their formal systems and, in Geertz's case at least, with the vain attempts of ethnoscientists to achieve some sort of psychological closeness or empathy with their subjects.[163] Beyond this, however, Geertz (whose own work reflects the self-proclaimed influence of Wilhelm Dilthey) has advocated the objective determination of his subjects' concepts of self and their *use* by the ethnographer in the analysis of the culture with which that self symbolically interacts. He thus makes a commitment similar to that manifest in Goodenough's efforts to use emic primitives.[164] (However, as we shall see, his recently expressed sympathy for Nelson Goodman's "irrealism" suggests that he, like Goodenough, may be less com-

mitted to translational determinacy than first appears.) Similarly, the
"grids" that Douglas seeks to analyze are regarded as objectively
determinate and psychologically and socially real.[165] Thus, keeping
in mind Quine's own skeptical reflections on the very remarks of
Whorf that motivate not only the earlier linguistic and structuralist
approaches, but also their rejection and replacement by symbolist
paradigms, we must expect the more *pervasive* Quinean skepticism to
present difficulties for symbolic anthropologists as well. For it seems
that these symbolic anthropologists have not said enough about how
translations of source-language concepts can be determinate enough
to provide an objective base for their broader claims at interpretation.

Indeed, I think the centrality of the "imposition-problem" in
Quine's skepticism should be particularly felt among symbolic
anthropologists insofar as this particular problem is especially salient
in their arguments for the rejection of other more traditional approaches; that is—though, as we have seen, they are not the only
ones who have made this point—many symbolic anthropologists take
seriously a more extreme (and, if coherent, more pervasive) worry
about the imposition of the familiar implicit in the very attempt to
"rationalize" ethnographic subjects' behavior in the process of explaining it. They fear a broad and particularly unobtrusive (and hence
particularly pernicious) imposition of "western rationality." Briefly,
their point is (and here they go beyond even Quine)[166] that the
anthropologist must be wary of viewing native belief systems as organized around the same sorts of broadly *theoretical* aims as those of
people in technologically oriented Western societies—that is, as involved in truth-telling, prediction and control of nature, and so on.
Many symbolic anthropologists contend that "primitive" ideologies
are or may be so fundamentally different in character from those of
the Western inquirer, that it is best only to approach them, as Kaplan
and Manners put it, "in largely symbolic and expressive terms rather
than in cognitive or intellectualist terms."[167]

This sort of attitude is brought out in a recent essay by Douglas
(1975) in a way that connects it, interestingly, with the Humean considerations noted in her previously quoted remarks—considerations
that are central to Quine's philosophical perspective as well (and that
of Nelson Goodman and David K. Lewis, who also figure centrally
below). Citing Hume's contention that causal necessity is the result
of the mind's habitual construction upon past experience, she
remarks as follows:

As anthropologists our work has been precisely to study this habit which constructs for each society its special universe of efficacious principles. . . . From the sheer variety of these constructed worlds, the anthropologist is led to agree, but only guardedly with Hume. Other people's causal theories are put into two sets: those which accord with our own and need no special explanation, and those with are magical and based on subjective associations as Frazer believed, or on affective rather than cognitive facilities as Levy-Bruhl said . . . when he tried to distinguish the mystical from the scientific mind. But Hume claimed that all causal theories whatever and without exception arise from what he called the sensitive rather than the cognitive part of our nature. Whether we reserve our own causal theories from sceptical philosophy, our gut response proves him utterly right. But it is almost impossible not to make this reservation.[168]

What Douglas offers to overcome this gut response is "a more formal mode of discussion in which we can hope to compare causal systems, including our own," contending that "without that shift our only recourse as anthropologists is to translate from other cultures into our own."[169] Otherwise, she fears, each step in the direction of translational success is a step *away* from the ultimate "emic" objective:

> The better the translation, the more successfully has our provincial logic been imposed on the native thought. So the consequence of good translation is to prevent any confrontation between alien thought systems. We are left as we were at the outset, with our own familiar world divided by its established categories and activated by the principles we know. This world remains our stable point of reference for judging all other worlds as peculiar and other knowledge as faulty. Translation flourishes where experience overlaps. But where there is no overlap, the attempt to translate fails.[170]

Thus, in this presentation of the newest of the language-and-culture approaches, we come full circle upon the imposition problem again, and thus is exemplified not only its pervasiveness in the continuing anthropological literature but also the increasing awareness of anthropologists of the potential depth of the problem.

However, the problem runs deeper than even Douglas claims here. For, again, Quine views the necessity of imposition as challenging the very sensibility of the question Douglas is asking here. Yet the problem should be particularly significant to Douglas in light of her expressed general sympathy with Quine's views on a number of other matters: particularly his critiques in *Word and Object* of mentalistic semantics and of Levy-Bruhl's attribution of prerationality to members of "primitive" society.[171] Indeed, while these critiques do bolster the criticisms that symbolic anthropologists make of their predecessors, their full implications cut against symbolic anthropology as well. (It is important to keep in mind that Quine stops short of criticizing the "imposition of western rationality" where this is just another way of saying "adherence to standard validational procedures." Indeed, indeterminacy depends on his belief that it is incoherent to ask us *not* to follow these procedures. Since imposition is thus unavoidable, it is indeterminacy, and not some other methodological essay at objectivity, that is the consequence.[172] I shall discuss this point in more detail in the next two chapters.)

The indeterminacy problem also surfaces in a number of criticisms she makes of Quine and in her own brief account of her constructive solution to the problem. She sees two shortcomings in Quine, the resolution of which, she contends, opens the way to a solution of the problem of emerging from the Whorfian circle:

> For one [Quine's account] leaves the intuition of sameness [of meaning] on the wrong side of rationality: guts are guts and reason is reason, there is a gap in the account of how the two relate. For another, it leaves us with an empty cultural relativism: each universe is divided up differently, period. From here there is nothing more to say about the comparison of universes, since we are always forced to speak within the categories of our own language. But I dare to hope that I can show a path which will lead out of that particular circle, towards generalization about kinds of universes.[173]

Briefly, her solution involves extending Quine's and Strawson's socio-behavioral characterizations of such notions as "self-evidence," "analyticity," and so on in terms of community-wide assent to, and individual "bewilderment" at ostensive denials of, what is deemed self-evident:

> Avoiding bewilderment and experiencing bewilderment are the two extremes at which it is easy to see how logic bites into the emotional life. In between the extremes, the emotions are channelled down the familiar grooves cut by social relations and their requirements of consistency, clarity, and reliability of expectations. I feel we should try to insert between the psychology of the individual and the public use of language, a dimension of social behavior. In this dimension logical relations also apply. This is the nub of my contribution to how intuitions of self-evidence are formed.[174]

However, Douglas' remarks do not acknowledge the full thrust of Quine's critique of intension. For she seems to envision the possibility of a broadly systematic account of sameness of meaning, analyticity, and so on and takes these socio-behavioral characterizations (along with supplementary input) to be suitable to this task. Also, her attribution of a cultural relativism to Quine is not fully accurate. For as I shall point out in more detail below, Quine takes the problem of cultural relativism, that is of various cultures "cutting up the world differently," seriously only to a point. He aims to show that a basic premise in typical reflections on the problem—that is, that there exist *underlying* conceptual schemes that do this "cutting" in thought or perception—is in error. Indeed, as we shall see, he leaves open the question of intercultural comparison, insisting only that it be answered, if it can be, in empirically testable ways. The intransigence of anthropology's objectivity problems is a symptom of mistaken philosophical assumptions that flaw the full range of interpretive inquiry.

Chapter 3

Pragmatism, Physicalism, and Indeterminacy

In this chapter, I would like to tie Quine's indeterminacy thesis more firmly into the anthropological controversies just discussed. In the process, I shall bring out and more closely examine features of Quine's thesis that have puzzled me and other commentators and whose resolution is necessary for understanding indeterminacy's import for anthropology.

Of central concern will be what no doubt has been the single most widely discussed question provoked by Quine's thesis: namely, how underdetermination of physical theory is distinguished from indeterminacy of translation; why physics is factual and translation is not. In the course of this chapter, I shall run through a number of plausible readings of Quine's thesis, several of which will turn out clearly to be misinterpretations. My hope is that this dialectical procedure will help readers not particularly familiar with Quine's work to avoid some typical misconstruals that have sidetracked philosophers (including myself) in the past. However, I will also look at more recent discussions that I hope will be enlightening to readers more familiar with Quine's work.

In the latter part of the chapter, I shall focus attention on what seem to be two types of indeterminacy complaint, corresponding to what Quine terms the "epistemological" and "ontological" nodes of his general position. I shall look at each separately in an effort to see if either succeeds in establishing translational indeterminacy but will conclude, finally, that they do not and thus that both the substance and anthropological import of indeterminacy remain unclear to me. Although I shall offer brief suggestions as to Quine's probable manner of resolving matters, my main objective in this chapter is to prepare the way for my own account.

Etics and Emics Revisited:
Cultural Idealism versus Cultural Materialism

Let me review some of the conflicts that have emerged in the
Boasian tradition. In trying to build a systematic theory of culture,
Boas and others seemed to be making two perfectly compatible—almost identical—points in advocating the study of language
and the recovery of culturally specific conceptions. However, important linguistic and cultural phenomena seem clearly unconscious, or
at least not clearly articulated by subjects. This, in addition to a
desire for theoretical clarity and generality, motivates efforts to import established psychological theories and to develop special ethnoscientific theories. But these efforts, in the minds of critics, have
produced at least two drawbacks: (1) They impose formal, unrealistic, "platonistic" rigor that organizes social behavior according to
the wrong criteria. (2) They lead to excessive concerns with unconscious cognition or psychological development—of interest in their
own right to be sure, but drawing attention away from concerns that,
it is argued, define cultural anthropology. In either case inquirers
lose touch with the social-cultural reality of their subjects. Additionally, some sociolinguists and symbolic anthropologists argue that
even genuine efforts at linguistic analysis may be too narrow in scope
to encompass the full range of symbolic expression.

We have seen representatives of these and other divergent trends
within the Boasian tradition. What we now must consider is whether
these foundational worries are symptomatic of deeper ills that call for
rejection of emic or cognitive perspectives, or at least consideration
of non-Boasian alternatives. While there are many critics of this
tradition and many proponents of such alternatives, I believe Marvin
Harris' work, though highly controversial, will best serve to draw out
the aspects of these inner tensions of most significance to me. For
one, Harris' "cultural materialist" perspective approximates Quine's
in important ways. For another, in extensively criticizing what he
terms "cultural idealism"—a label that embraces *all* the aforementioned paradigms—Harris makes clear the potential incompatibility
between essential pragmatic aspects of culture theory and emic objectives.

Let us recall some aspects of emic anthropology. Pike and others
stress emics so as to heed Boas' warning against the inadvertent imposition of Western categorizations upon radically foreign belief
structures. Frake argues that "an ethnographer should strive to define
[the subjects' abstract and concrete] objects according to the concep-

tual system of the people he is studying.'' Kay, as we saw, insists that ''the guiding spirit of an emic approach is to rid oneself of *pre*conceptions about universal structures so that the data may be analyzed objectively to reveal the true universal structures.''[1] However, emic methodologists realize that the concepts they seek to discover are difficult to get at because of their culturally specific nature (for some this means their privately mentalistic nature), and the results are special difficulties for field translation. Indeed some follow Harry Triandis in regarding emic phenomena as *untranslatable* and even *unexplicatable*:

> By definition, it is impossible to translate perfectly an emic concept. One can discuss the context in which the concept might be used, its antecedents and consequences . . . , its synonyms and antonyms, if any, but exact translation is extremely difficult, if not impossible. Even native speakers have difficulties giving good definitions of emic concepts.[2]

The existence of such usage signals a number of the deeper problems concerning these notions, as well as the very aims of cultural anthropology itself. Evidently, if an emic phenomenon is untranslatable, then it is hard to see how an inquirer will ever state an emic concept in receptor or metalanguage terms—and the absence of adequate source-language definitions doesn't seem to help matters. This would seem to obstruct validation by appeal to bilinguals, among other things.

Now it should be clear from foregoing discussions that this usage and these corresponding attitudes are not universally shared. Those who insist on recovering, perhaps adopting, the subjects' points of view maintain instead that the adequacy of a translation manual in the long run is going to depend upon recovery, or at least more accurate approximations, of culturally specific concepts that their methods enable. Kay's just noted remark shows a clear commitment to revealing cultural universals. However, he insists that getting ''true universal structures'' presupposes an adequate qualitative analysis (whether one subsequently pursues rigorous or ''quantitative'' analysis or not):

> One has to isolate comparable units before one can engage in reasonable comparison. Hence the emphasis in ethnoscience on emics, so called, the analysis of a cultural system or subsystem in its own terms as a precondition to the comparison of different systems.[3]

However, how is one to assure comparability here? If the ethnographer's account succeeds in stating emic concepts in receptor or metalanguage terms, then the road seems clear for successful comparison. But warranting such comparability is another matter if, to put the point in Wittgensteinian terms, the language games or forms of life involved are widely divergent. If emic concepts, stated in the source language or somehow implicit in source-community symbolism or behavior, are not recovered, this aim is not achieved and it is this sort of worry that underlies the criticisms discussed in the previous section.

However, there is another problem. Forgetting for the moment the problem of recovery, if we look just at the ethnographer's formulation of these notions and if we find reason to apply them only to one or several related cultures (whether we formulate the conceptions correctly or not), how will these units aid us in making comparisons to cultures that are "emically distinct"? It would seem that a unit of comparison should be uniform throughout our field of comparison. If our basic units are not uniform, how will a systematic theory of culture ever attain anything approaching universal scope? Worse still, we might not be fully aware of the differences between the units of analysis employed by different anthropologists. What begins to emerge here are not concerns about ethnographic adequacy, but about theoretical productivity and coherence, and it is these that mainly underlie Harris' criticisms.

Harris does not ignore emics, but he minimizes its role, arguing that etic conceptions are and must be the basis for theory-building. While Harris' idealist opponents (save for extreme descriptivists) agree that etic components figure essentially in the cross-cultural validity of their product, Harris and other cultural materialists believe that emic analysis, unless sharply circumscribed, will work against—rather than complement—etic analysis.[4]

These differences in theoretical emphasis emerge in a number of ways, perhaps the most potentially confusing being in the divergence in usage regarding the terms 'etic' and 'emic'. (As Kuhn warns us, such interparadigmatic controversies are likely to issue in this sort of problem.) Already we have seen disputes as to whether 'emic' should be limited to the consciously mental or not, whether it should be tied to predominant concerns with deeply underlying cognitive structures or development, and whether it should issue in emphasis on linguistic analysis as opposed to broader symbolic development. Some also warn of the intrusion of mentalism into what was initially, as I noted earlier, a behavioristic notion.[5]

Harris' usage willfully diverges from all of these:

> The question of whether a construct is emic or etic depends on whether it describes events, entities, or relationships whose physical locus is in the heads of social actors or in the stream of behavior. In turn, the question of whether or not an entity is inside or outside some social actor's head depends on the operations employed to get at it.[6]

That is, if "eliciting operations," queries put to the informant regarding his own thoughts and feelings, are necessary to determine the truth of some hypotheses about, say, the purpose of some activity, the purpose is an emic item. He argues, contrary to Fisher, that a receptor- or metalanguage expression can be emic only if it has explicit source-language correlates. Also, even if the term turns out to have equivalents in other languages, it is still emic—something that Goodenough's earlier definition precludes. For example, Goodenough, as we saw, regards the basic components of kinship as etic because they are not exclusively culturally specific. Harris regards them as emic, if understood (in some appropriate source-language terms) by the subjects. He questions the coherence of Goodenough's claim that emic concepts are subsumed into an etic kit.

Moreover, I think there is reason to worry here. By Goodenough's lights, if an emic concept is even *translated*, then, on the stronger mentalistic readings of Goodenough, source- and receptor-language speakers ipso facto share the concept. But then translatability makes the concept etic, and it is hard to see how, for example, the Trukese concept of a "corporation" is emic. It seems translatable as such if and only if it isn't emic! That is, despite his evident commitment to emic analysis as a means for recovering the subject's point of view, his notion of emics seems easily to slip into the "untranslatable" reading. When this problem is added to the concerns raised by Glynn Cochrane (which I shall discuss later) concerning Goodenough's distortion of Trukese and *Western* usage in his application of 'corporation', the waters become murky indeed.[7]

Harris takes serious issue with the predominant mentalism of language-and-culture approaches. In his view, what Pike sought to do was to take account of subject actors' descriptions of their own *behavior*. Emic events are not to be located in the mental realm but rather in the "behavior stream," and Pike's great contribution, Harris contends, was to "emicize" descriptions of that stream. Pike's distinction is not simply tantamount to one between the mental and behavioral (which, if so, would make his distinction redundant):

both actors and observers are capable of describing events in the behavior stream. Pike's unique contribution among idealists was precisely his attempt to emicize the description of the behavior stream (as distinct from more fashionable attempts to elicit grammars, folk taxonomies, symbol systems, values, and moral codes). That is, for Pike, descriptions of behavior which do not involve phenomenal distinctions . . .that are significant and meaningful to the actors are unacceptable. But behavior stream events seen through actor's categories remain, in one sense at least, behavioral events, just as behavior stream events seen through observer's categories might in another sense be called mental events, because they are what the observers think them to be.[8]

The price idealists pay, he argues, is in terms of theoretical productivity. And here he places a heavy reliance on pragmatic bases for theory-construction:

The test of the adequacy of etic accounts is simply their ability to generate scientifically productive theories about the causes of sociocultural differences and similarities. Rather than employ concepts that are necessarily real, meaningful, and appropriate from the native point of view, the observer is free to use alien categories and rules derived from the data language of science.[9]

In keeping with this pragmatic spirit, he criticizes idealist emics for what he argues are innate atheoretic and antitheoretic tendencies. He contends that idealists introduce inflexibility by limiting the analyst's fund of basic organizing principles; that their research tends toward relatively trivial cultural items, those best amenable to their existing analytic constructs and strategies; and that they are inclined to be too ingenuous regarding the veracity of their informants. In contrast to Kay's insistence that emic qualitative analysis is amenable to successful quantitative analysis (Kay cites the aforementioned work by Geoghegan on residence decision rules as a case in point), Harris argues that it is essential to use etic units in such studies because their typical units of analysis, such as community organization, family organization, marital residence, and so on are particularly prone to emic / etic confusions.[10]

This last criticism is given particularly poignant, recent formulation by another cultural materialist, Ron Marano. He argues that a long discussion of the so-called Windigo (or Witiko) psychosis—a seemingly inexplicable craving by members of certain Algonkian tribes for human flesh—suffers from the confusion of etic, psychological categories such as "obsessive cannibalistic compulsion" with the actual, emic Windigo concept. He sounds similar charges concerning neglect of data and literal acceptance of Windigo stories, which he believes are often used to conceal such things as infanticides necessitated by extreme deprivation. Generally, in applying psychoanalytic (and structuralist) concepts, he believes we may "overpower a very poorly known Witiko phenomenon with our own intellectual creations." He follows Harris—and contrasts directly with Watson—in seeing such problems as bolstering a shift to an etic orientation.[11]

Harris sees himself as operating in a different paradigm, which finds culture within the behavior stream:

> I see emics and etics from the perspective of a research strategy that is radically different from Goodenough's. I see Pike's emic/etic distinction as providing the key epistemological opening for a materialist approach to the behavior stream. Goodenough "sees" emics and etics from an idealist perspective in which the entire field of study— culture—is off limits to the materialist strategies. That is, for Goodenough and other cultural idealists, culture designates an orderly realm of pure idea while the behavior stream is a structureless emanation of that realm.[12]

Harris' cultural materialism emphasizes economic and biological factors that cut across cultures. He relies minimally on emic data, generally relegating it to use in determining the gap between subject belief and factual reality—or "mystification" in roughly Marx's sense.[13]

Harris' worries are of course reminiscent of those motivating the social-behavioral trends manifest in the work of Wittgenstein, Austin, and Searle. Yet it remains sharply opposed to the ethnoscientific, sociolinguistic, and symbolic-anthropological trends that share similar motivation. (For instance, he is sharply critical of Hymes, though both employ speech-act analysis, for his "apodictic restriction of the ethnography of speech to emic meanings.")[14] Harris' critique also shares significant features of Quine's position: in addition to its materialist orientation, the recognition that formal theoretical criteria of adequacy may put systematicity and comparability at odds with emic recovery. Harris' divergence from idealism is also most reminiscent of Quine's divergence from Brentano in seeing the peculiarities of meaning-analysis as calling for its delimitation, as opposed to its elevation to a separate science. There is also a parallel emphasis on pragmatism as a guide to theoretical structure and strategy.

However, even Harris' (and Marano's) criticisms may not cut as deeply as Quine's. Indeed, the latter seem to threaten even Harris' limited use of emics. Quine allows the recovery of stimulus-meaning-determinate sentences, but this falls far short of Harris' claims to be able to translate subject discourse. Harris views as expressing an emic concept any receptor-language term (subsumed, perhaps, into the metalanguage) that correctly translates a source-language term. And he seems committed to the idea that such translations express facts of the matter. Moreover, not only does he claim to know what the informants' categories *are*—in claiming to reveal degrees of mystification—but he also make a quite evident commitment to Searle's speech-act notion of meaning in presenting details of his own view about how to reconstruct the emicized stream of behavior. Arguing that some notion of meaning must be utilized, "since language is a primary mode of human communication and since it is a function of language to convey meanings," he proceeds to develop two notions of meaning: (1) an etic one, comprising "surface" speech acts apprehended by the observer; and (2) the underlying, emic intentions that may be obscured by the surface meanings. Hence, frequent but unenforced requests for quiet by a mother of her children might indicate an implicit intention to express disapproval. Eliciting operations will often be required, he contends, to uncover such emic meaning, thus making evident the dependence upon *accurate translation* of the responses to questions:

> To disambiguate these meanings one must employ eliciting operations, and these alone are the hallmark of emic events. The emic meanings, however, remain the same, regardless of the ultimate result of the elicitation process (which incidentally need not result in speaker or hearer meaning the same emic things). Emic meanings are inside the heads of the actors. But etic meanings are inside the message in the speech act viewed as a behavior stream event.[15]

Harris himself believes that the evident possibility of cross-cultural translation and understanding (by translation manual user and bilingual) guarantees the cross-cultural identifiability of speech acts:

> This line of reasoning can easily be extended to include foreign speech acts, if we grant the proposition that all human languages are mutually translatable. This means that for every utterance in a foreign language, there is an analogue in one's own. While it is true that suc-

cessful translation of a foreign speech act is facilitated by the collabora-
tion of a native informant, the locus of the cognitive reality of the
translation remains inside the observers' heads. That is, what the observers intend to find out is which linguistic structures inside their own
heads have more or less the same meaning as the utterances in the behavior stream of the foreign actors. Thus the translation amounts to the
imposition of the observers' semantic categories on the foreign speech
acts, and . . . the use of native informants is perfectly compatible with
etic descriptions. Of course in any competent translation we again assume that there is a close correspondence between the observers' surface meaning and the native speaker's surface meaning. But once this
correspondence has been established, the observers have in effect enlarged their competence to include both languages, and hence they can
proceed to identify the surface meanings of foreign speech acts as
freely as native speakers of English are able to identify [their own]
speech acts.[16]

The emic/etic distinction comes finally, for Harris, to "the difference between the first level surface meaning of a human utterance
[the speech act it performs] and its total psychological significance
for speaker and hearer respectively."[17] This is intended to acknowledge the necessity of imposition by inquirers on subjects. Yet the
deeper contrasts with Quine remain, as is made particularly clear by
the fact that Harris still shares with his idealist opponents and Frege a
belief that a universal fund of concepts is presupposed by the possibility of translational success, the acknowledgment of imposition
notwithstanding.

Emics and Pragmatism

Harris views emicly oriented paradigms as being fundamentally at
odds with theoretical productivity. However, his critics have shown
concern with the foundational emphasis he gives etics, which Fisher
and Werner view as tantamount to the "emics of scientific
observers." There seems a significant tension between efforts to
predict in terms of observer categories and desires to reveal *cultural*
content. Fisher and Werner (and others) themselves stress theoretical
productivity in criticizing Harris, but it is important to see that they
measure productivity partly in terms of *cognitive* yield. Harris, they
believe, is too concerned with prediction of *behavior*, and they maintain that even his own study of the function of subject ideologies and

their degrees of mystification are thus compromised. In their view Harris' materialist strategy must overlook an important cognitive locus of cultural reality.[18]

However, if the imposition implicit in Harris' pragmatic appeals is the problem, it is not one that idealists easily escape. Although some may view emic analysis (given its presupposition of accurate translation) as free of interpreter imposition, the basis for this faith is unclear, especially if it presumes that it is possible to mirror the semantic-cultural substratum. Fisher and Werner open a section of an essay that is particularly critical of Harris' neglect of the mental with the following quotation:

> All scientific knowing is indirect, presumptive, obliquely and in-completely corroborated at best. The language of science is subjective, provincial, approximative, and metaphoric, never the language of reality itself.[19]

However, a questionable notion of "objectivity" may be operative here. In particular, this citation is reminiscent of what Richard Rudner calls the "reproductive fallacy" of assuming that "the function of science is to reproduce reality"—a fallacy presupposed, he contends, by thinkers (he here criticizes Peter Winch) who see intrinsic shortcomings in the fact "that science distorts through abstraction from physical reality." Rudner characterizes Winch's view, in terms that make clear its kinship to some of the views I have discussed, as "that the only way in which such a social science investigation can achieve understanding is via the adoption by the social scientist of the teleology of the observed." However, he argues, this is to *insist* that social inquiry give "a *reproduction* of the condition it investigates." Citing Einstein (from a similar context) to the effect that a soup recipe need not taste like soup, he argues that Winch places social inquirers in an untenable position analogous to that of a meteorologist whose accounts of tornados must actually reproduce them. Why must *social* descriptions reproduce what they describe, when other types (scientific or otherwise) need not?[20]

Rudner explicitly challenges only the idea that reproductive understanding is *necessary* for adequate social description. If emic description can only be defended on the premise that reproduction must be achieved, this premise cannot stand as an undefended assumption, since it is not at all obvious why social description must differ from other kinds of description in this respect. It would seem wiser to seek a notion of emics that acknowledges the role of observer interests, and, indeed, a number of anthropologists have pursued this line of reasoning; that is, following a traditional pragmatist line of argument against empiricism, they allow that inquirer interests in theoretical productivity, simplicity, generality, and so on have a significant constitutive influence of theorizing and place correspondingly less emphasis on "the data themselves." This is much in line with earlier-noted criticisms of the empirical reductionist programs of twentieth-century logical empiricists.

One such line of argument is afforded by Burling's fictionalism, although it may make a seemingly unacceptable concession to Harris in its abandonment of cognitive validity as a criterion of adequacy. Others have applied pragmatic criteria in redefining, rather than rejecting, cognitivist aims. In a recent discussion of relativism and comparativism in psychological anthropology, Christie Kiefer argues that determinations of similarity and differences in cross-cultural concept identification, as well as criteria of explanatory adequacy, are dependent on observer interests and are not "given" in social phenomena. Similar sentiments emerge in a review of anthropological studies of cognition by Carol Ember, who argues for comparativism over descriptivism on related grounds. These reviewers prefer to replace the metaphysical theses concerning cultural similarity and difference that have supported both viewpoints with theses that seek support in the quality of the final theoretical product.[21]

A similar pragmatism with regard to structuralist analysis is offered by Peter Caws, who contends that inquirers' "explanatory models" need not be identical with those of their subjects, arguing, indeed, that "[i]t is the scientist's representational (i.e., explanatory) model, the theory he constructs to account for the data and their interrelation, that confers objective structure on the system." He highlights "confer," claiming "it would be quite accurate to say that until the explanatory model was constructed the system had no objective structure." Arguing that directional relations such as "north of" are objective matters of fact even though they do not exist until a directional grid is imposed on nature, he contends that similarly the translation of source-language strings as "north of" produces something objectively attributable to subjects—and likewise, generally, for social relations. Similarly, Wallace counsels "that kinship terminologies may only be reckoning devices, like systems of weights and measures, whose utility depends more on internal coherence than on their fit with the social system."[22]

However, there are notable objections to these attitudes. Cecil Brown takes Wallace to task, arguing: "Systems of weights and measures, like all tools, are designed to meet certain requirements extraneous to their own internal logic. One would not . . .weigh letters in fractions of tons, nor concrete blocks in multiples of ounces." He asks how it could be "that kin terminologies in their capacity as linguistic tools do not similarly "fit" the reality they are used to describe."[23]

Related problems for Caws' pragmatic rendering of structuralism are raised by F. A. Hanson who sees the following absurd implications in Caws' view: (1) kinship systems might possess properties, such as a skewing effect in cross-cousin terms, that identical but unanalyzed systems did not; (2) misdescribed systems would possess structures they did not really have; and (3) analytic models would exist prior to the structures they describe. Rather than *confer* structures, inquirers give *formulations of* structures, which have "objective existence in the regularity of usage by native speakers" and which exist prior to ethnographic formulation.[24]

These objections suggest that pragmatic appeal to observer interests may not serve emic-cognitive aims and that Harris may, after all, be correct. However, even he may not go far enough in this regard. Earlier I noted Fisher and Werner's claim that Harris seems to compromise his own aims to study ideology and its distorting effects. Harris does not utterly abandon emics, but believes he can translate subject discourse in such a way as to discover what they in fact mean. Also, as we saw, he believes he can identify speech acts cross-culturally. But Quine would seem to echo Fisher and Werner here: How can these aims be achieved if imposition precludes emic recovery and yet so pervades translation itself?

Underdetermination and Indeterminacy

We have seen Quine's indeterminacy discussions emphasize two points: The first is that translation is underdetermined by all possible evidence. I have spoken of underdetermination both in connection with Quine's inscrutability of reference thesis and his indeterminacy of sentence-translation thesis. Yet, although Quine's "underdetermination" in the strict sense, as concerning systems that are *logically incompatible* though empirically equivalent, is more directly applicable to the latter, I do not think my reliance on the looser usage

up to now, for ease of formulation, is problematic. (I have in places
relied on the equivalent notion of "empirical slack.") Also, it will be
recalled, Quine has offered arguments for indeterminacy that rest on
the full underdetermination of theory and has offered arguments that
rest only on holism. (See my discussion at the end of Chapter 1.) I
have not, as yet, attended to these differences since I believe holism
produces the same translational analogue of underdetermination in
physics: Two manuals of translation can yield mutually incompatible
translations and the key question we must address is why the
analogue amounts to indeterminacy, while physics suffers no such
fate. Also, holism, as well as underdetermination, seems as pervasive
in physics as it is in translation.

The second key point is that this underdetermination of translation
is overcome—that is, translation is validated—by appeal to extra-
empirical criteria, notably familiarity and charity. Evidently these
figure prominently in the broader list of criteria captured under labels
such as "elegance" and "theoretical productivity." Now the existence of underdetermination comes as no surprise to anthropologists.
Fisher and Werner see a significant underdetermination of ethnographic theory by observation, quoting Popper to the effect that
"almost every statement we make transcends experience . . .we *are
theorizing all the time*" (emphasis his). They view this as indicating
a weakness in Harris' emphasis on predictability and as necessitating
efforts to delve into (perhaps unconscious) cognition.[25] Similarly, I
expect, they would acknowledge with Goodenough a similar underdetermination of the anthropologist's theory of the "conceptual
models" of social subjects—which moves Goodenough to remark, as
we saw, that beyond observational strategies one depends largely on
elegance.

To Quine's challenge that such results are underdetermined, the
natural response is to say, "So they are, but then why are we worse
off than any other empirical scientist?" Goodenough emphasizes the
fact that elegance is the recourse of all scientists and quite naturally
believes himself to be one. But then he might begin to worry about
the fact that the appeal to elegance is a concession to imposition,
which seems by his own and other emic anthropologists' lights to be
antithetical to their fundamental aim of recovering cultural reality.
But why should the varieties of imposition that pervade translation be
any more acceptable than others? Emic analysts rest a lot on translation, but can it reliably provide a check against "excessive" appeal
to those interests?

Basically, the worry is that generally *any* quality identifications that depend on translation cannot be legitimate items for emic description, whether formal, quantitative, or otherwise. Emic phenomena *are* generally untranslatable if "translation" must have a factual warrant for the description of objectively existing synonymies. (Again, there is no intended challenge to translation's minimal facilitative aims.) If not definable in terms of stimulus meaning, meanings and natural synonymy relations are not proper objects of scientific study.

These reflections seem to have drastic consequences for emic (and, generally, linguistic-oriented) anthropology: It seems that except for limited cases in which observational criteria serve as a basis for translation, translational claims are "indeterminate" in the sense of being *not warrantedly assertible as true*—however impeccably reasonable the criteria for their selection might be—and this indeterminacy thus compromises the acceptability of any further ethnographic hypotheses that rest on them. (Later I shall return to the matter of whether this is the way 'indeterminacy' must be construed.) And, in a 1970 article, Quine seems quite content to circumscribe anthropology along these lines:

> My position is not that alien cultures are inscrutable. Much can be determined about a culture by leaving language alone and observing non-verbal customs and taboos and artifacts. Much can also be determined, beyond peradventure, with help of language. We can construe observation sentences, after all, on an objective behavioral basis: and we can note, in particular, just which ranges of stimulations are packaged under the shortest observation sentences in a given language. Languages may be expected to differ, in this matter of short observation sentences, in ways that reflect palpable differences in material culture. Also there is . . . a general and undirected measure of remoteness of one language from another in the sheer degree of difficulty of intertranslation, the degree of elaborateness of the interlinguistic manual. Perhaps this rough index of distance can be resolved into dimensional components sometime, and a body of post-Whorf hypotheses worthy of the name of hypothesis may come after. A proper awareness of the purely behavioral nature of meaning, at any rate, is a safeguard against nonsense in this domain and a precondition of responsible theory.[26]

Quine prefaces these remarks with a warning that anthropologists follow Whorf in resisting the temptation "to cast methodological nicety to the winds and to wallow in an unstructured intercultural

impressionism.'' Yet in limiting anthropologists to translations that
are stimulus-meaning determinate, he seems to cast doubt on the
legitimacy of the work of even the most rigorous of language-and-
culture anthropologists. Further, while he holds out hope for post-
Whorfian hypotheses, it is not what post-Whorfians themselves hope
for: For these thinkers, eliciting operations that go well beyond
stimulus-meaning determination are essential not only for understanding linguistic meaning but for understanding properly the "nonverbal
customs, taboos, and artifacts" of which he speaks as well.

Evidently Quine offers a decidedly etic view here, and it is somewhat ironic that Kay opens one of the defenses of idealist emics we
have been considering by quoting Quine as follows: "The familiar
material objects may not be all that is real, but they are admirable
examples.'' Kay sees in Quine's tolerance of the possibility that
other things may exist beside physical objects an opening for the
semantic determinist. Drawing the parallel that "the informant's
most careful statements about the nature of his world may not be all
the ethnographic data, but they are admirable examples,'' Kay articulates that the aim for ethnosemantics is

> to discover some part of the system of meanings by which people
> organize the world. The goal is the raw cognition if you will, but since
> the major realization of this cognition is in the words people speak,
> semantics is considered an integral part of ethnography.[27]

Yet Kay emphasizes here as the basis for ethnoscience a point that
Quine's various attacks on meaning aim to refute: Quine's view is
that there is no underlying semantic fact of the matter to reveal in the
study of "raw cognition.'' Contrary to Kay's assumption of the existence of the "psychic unity of mankind"[28], and to Goodenough's
belief in the existence of subject mental models for organizing experience and behavior, Quine, as we have seen, believes radical interpersonal variability in underlying cognitive structure belies such
uniformity. Goodenough embraces what Quine calls the "museum
myth'' that there is in any sense a subsisting realm of meanings or
ideas that serves to account for the facts of natural synonymy.
Moreover, these very reflections on physics and its objects turn out
to be pivotal to Quine's critique.

To see why this is so, it will help to give some more extended attention to Quine's reflections on underdetermination and to see some
aspects of a central controversy in the past few decades' philosophical literature on indeterminacy. The key question is this: As

Chomsky and Richard Rorty (among others) have asked, why should we view translation's underdetermination as tantamount to indeterminacy yet not so regard the underdetermination of physics?[29]

Quine and Boas on Imposition

Near the beginning of this section I suggested an easy answer to the question of how Quine can distinguish indeterminacy from underdetermination. If anthropologists have good reason to believe that imposition precludes recovery of source-language intension and belief, and if Quine is right in showing how pervasive imposition is, then we do have indeterminacy. The critical difference between physics and anthropology, one might say, is that physics can impose a scheme on physical reality, without concern that its pre-existing scheme is distorted. For it seems quite difficult to make sense of any such notion of a pre-existing scheme. This is not to say that all questions of scientific realism and natural kinds are easily resolvable, but it is hard to defend positions on these issues by asserting that reality already comes conceptualized. However, one might continue, it seems to make evidently good sense to say that the anthropologist does confront a pre-existing scheme, namely that of the source-language speakers. This, one might say, is what gives us reason to worry that a scheme attributed on the basis of familiarity might be the wrong one. However, this answer will not work.

The danger here is that Quine's arguments may be interpreted in such a way as to rest on the very notion of a conceptual scheme that they seek to undercut. If we take as an example the inscrutability thesis (though this problem applies to the general indeterminacy argument as well), we might be tempted to read it as follows: Having all the relevant data, past and future, we can still attribute divergent referential schemes x, y, and z to the subject. We choose x because it employs the most familiar grammatical categories of the three. However, the subject's actual scheme might conform to y; thus, we might be wrong. Therefore, the claim 'the subject really refers in accordance with x' is indeterminate. However, this argument seems clearly to require the premise that there is some referential scheme that the native has in mind, for it is only with that assumption that we have a basis for saying we might be wrong. What else could be the standard by which errors are ascertained under conditions in which no empirical data can provide one? But if the conclusion of this argument is that such a claim, and any other with respect to any empirically equivalent scheme, is not warrantedly assertible, the argument is self-vitiating.

Now one could reinterpret the argument as one that concludes that standard methodology is inadequate to the task of revealing reference. But this is clearly not Quine's intent. Instead, the only other evident way to make Quine out to be concerned with scheme conflict is to construe his thesis as a *reductio* of the assumption that one can warrantably assert that there is some referential scheme (or, more generally, a set of concepts or propositions) to be recovered. The claim that there is some scheme would be shown, then, to lead to the claim that no such claim could ever be warranted. Thus, the reason for concern about possible error comes from this assumption, but the argument no longer is self-vitiating.

However, even if this point is kept clear, how does the *reductio* work against anything but the idea of an *underlying* conceptual scheme, whose platonic and/or concrete components "condition" one's perception in the ways that have been seen to generate the Sapir-Whorf syndrome of problems? Has anything been said to rule out the possibility of reconstruing the notion of a conceptual scheme in ways that avoid these problems? Why not simply equate it with a language, for example? Is it impossible for a proponent of a behavioristic (perhaps sociolinguistic) theory of meaning, to believe in "conceptual schemes," suitably redefined? *If* we think there is an underlying scheme that can so "condition" our experience, the worry remains real—that is, if our central aim is to "capture" (or even, I think, to "approximate") that scheme. But, now, why must someone who doesn't wish to talk of underlying schemes or propositions, but rather insists that any interpretive construct admit of determinability by empirical inquiry, continue to have this worry? Why is it, in Wittgenstein's terms, a basis for *serious* doubt? And if it is not a basis for such doubt, on what can Quine base his distinction between physics and translation as thus construed?

Another reason one might think that all notions of referential and conceptual schemes and the like are suspect is that Quine's arguments are, as I have pointed out, intended to undercut the very notion of natural synonymy that all seem to presuppose and seek to explain. However, until a coherent distinction between underdetermination and indeterminacy (or inscrutability) is made, this general thesis will not stand up. From what Quine says here, nothing seems to follow concerning the various attempts by Wittgenstein, Austin, Searle, and a number of anthropologists to make "the very idea of a conceptual scheme" more empirically palatable (much less does it seem to carry any weight against approaches like Donald Davidson's, to which I allude here.)[30]

Ultimately I think there is a way of making sense of indeterminacy in hermeneutic terms of the conflict of cultural background. For now I only want to say that an important transcendental basis for indeterminacy is still wanting. Here I have asked why we "might be wrong" in making certain choices of translation. But really, what this basis must provide is a reason to deny an objective, factual basis to translations—perhaps even to deny them truth value (that is, to those that are not stimulus-meaning determinate). Presently I am mainly concerned with sounding a warning that we must be wary of implicitly adopting as our standard of correctness the very inscrutable scheme we argue is illusory. This danger also threatens if we too easily grant Quine that imposition of the familiar *ipso facto* precludes warranted assertibility as true; anthropologists may take this step more casually if, indeed, they agree with Boas and Sapir that there is a real scheme to be recovered. But Quine cannot be (and wouldn't want to be) supported in this fashion: a point easily obscured by the commonality of heritage and concern that he shares with the language and culture tradition. It should be emphasized, though, that this problem is potentially critical since it concerns the basis for distinguishing indeterminacy from underdetermination.

Theoretical Underdetermination

Before proceeding further, it will help to get a better idea of exactly what Quine takes theoretical underdetermination to entail. In the strict sense, again, it is that two theories can be empirically equivalent, in light of all imaginable data, yet logically incompatible.

In a 1970 paper, Quine states the underdetermination thesis in the terms in which I have been employing it (which is reflected in his earlier *Word and Object* discussions):

> [Physical] theories can be at odds with each other and yet compatible with all possible data even in the broadest sense. In a word, they can be logically incompatible and empirically equivalent. . . . [S]ome will acknowledge such slack only in the highest and most speculative reaches of physical theory, while others [e.g., Quine] see it as extending even to [descriptions of] common sense traits of macroscopic bodies.[31]

It is important to keep in mind that this is a particularly *strong* sense of underdetermination that is at issue here. The underdetermination of theory by *actual* data, which any natural or social scientist would easily grant, will not carry the burden of the various "impossibility in principle" arguments Quine is putting forth. This strong thesis, plus the "imposition-problem," is needed to show that the linguist's problem is a special one.

Underdetermination of theory results from the adoption or application of expressions, called "theoretical expressions," that make reference to entities and characteristics that are not "directly observable." It is not simply that the choice of terms such as 'electron' is fairly arbitrary; rather, it has to do with the logical relations of many statements containing such expressions to statements more "directly testable"—or, in Quine's terms, more highly "observational." So much seems the result of manipulation on the theoretician's part—in relative independence from empirical findings. So great is the distance of these concepts from the experiential periphery of theory that it seems easily imaginable that, given slightly different historical circumstances, different expressions, bearing markedly different logical relations to the general theoretic structure, would now be part of our accepted theory of nature. Underdetermination is the extreme consequence of this "empirical slack"; the imaginable alternatives can forever conflict with the original:

> If all observable events can be accounted for in one comprehensive scientific theory—one system of the world, to echo Duhem's echo of Newton—then we may expect that they can all be accounted for equally in another, conflicting system of the world. We may expect this because of how scientists work. For they do not rest with mere inductive generalizations of their observations: mere extrapolation to observable events from similar observed events. Scientists invent hypotheses that talk of things beyond the reach of observation. The hypotheses are related to observation only by a kind of one-way implication; namely, the events we observe are what a belief in the hypotheses would have led us to expect. These observable consequences of the hypotheses do not, conversely, imply the hypotheses. Surely there are alternative hypothetical substructures that would surface in the same observable ways.[32]

The existence of this slack has motivated many empiricist thinkers to question the naive or unquestioned acceptance of the referents of such expressions into our ontology. Following Russell and Carnap, some have sought to show ways in which theoretical expressions might be explicitly definable in terms of observables, or partially definable or "functionally eliminable", and so on. Generally the motive is to show that theoretical expressions are convenient "fictions" by the application of which scientists may successfully organize data. If these expressions cannot be so fictionalized by the successful replacement, at least in principle, of the working theory with a formulation that contains no theoretical terms but which can imply all the observation statements that the original does, then we must accept the slack and its consequence, alarming to some, that the best imaginable theory of nature can only be regarded as true relative to some "purely conventional" choices on our part.

A 1975 paper by Quine makes some important clarifications and modifications of this thesis. First, Quine reconsiders his definitions of the key terms 'theory' and 'observation sentence'. Quine redefines the latter (as I noted in passing earlier) as a "pegged observation sentence." This is a standing sentence produced by adding specifications of space-time coordinates to observational occasion sentences. A theory, then, implies "observational conditionals," which are material conditionals whose antecedents are pegged observation sentences describing initial observations, and whose consequents are statements (typically predictions of observable states of affairs) that are inferrable from the antecedent statements and pertinent theoretical laws. (For example, thermodynamics implies 'If the water in beaker A is heated so that at t a local thermometer reads 100° C, then the water in A boils at t', rather than simply 'The water in A boils at t'.)[33]

Second, what implies these observational conditionals are "theory formulations," comprising the higher level theoretical hypotheses or wider generalizations (often called the "axioms" of the theory), plus the various bridge laws that serve to relate theoretical and observational predicates (although Quine does not explicitly mention this latter set).[34] "Theories" are individuated in the following way: theory formulations express the same theory if: (1) they imply the same observational conditionals; that is, they are "empirically equivalent"; and (2) they are either patently logically compatible or can be made so by a systematic reconstrual of predicates. (For example, if our empirically equivalent but conflicting theories were the standard physical theory and a theory that differed from it only in that it had 'electron' in every place that the other had 'molecule', although these would be initially logically incompatible, they could be made to be identical by reconstruing all occurrences of 'electron' as 'molecule' and vice versa.) Theories themselves are the equivalence relation determined by (1) and (2). (Formulations, being sets of sentences, are explicable, in a fashion developed elsewhere by Quine, ultimately in terms of mathematical sequences of sets of actual inscriptions of letters.)[35] Further, the only sorts of theories that are of genuine interest for the underdetermination thesis are those that are self-consistent and whose observational consequences are infinite and cannot be expressed by a finite number of universally quantified conditionals.[36]

The original thesis is restated as follows:

> For any one theory formulation there is another that is empirically equivalent to it but logically incompatible with it, and cannot be rendered logically equivalent to it by any reconstrual of predicates.[37]

The reasons for underdetermination, if the thesis is cogent, must spring from the "slack" inherent in the application of theoretical expressions, which arises owing to the need for a finite theory formulation that implies an infinite and varied set of observation conditionals. Were there some way independently to check the truth value of each conditional, theory could be dispensed with, but clearly physical theory covers too broad and complex a range for this:

> Underdetermination lurks where there are two irreconcilable formulations each of which implies exactly the desired set of observational conditionals plus extraneous theoretical matter, and where no formulation affords a tighter fit.[38]

A more recent paper defines the empirical content of a theory in terms of "observation categoricals," which, as I noted earlier, are eternal sentences phrased so as not to presume any space-time coordinate system and thus achieve a higher level of generality.[39] However, this revision is not important here. Critical for the underdetermination thesis is that "we can encompass more of these true observation conditionals [or categoricals] in loose formulation than in any tight one," where "tightness" is being "without theoretical foreign matter." Hence, this thesis is tied to a series of efforts to develop ways of "eliminating" or "logically reconstructing" theoretical expressions in terms of observational ones. The original Russellian approach has been criticized by R. B. Braithwaite on the grounds that any attempt to explicitly define theoretical expressions in terms of observables makes the theory unextendable to new kinds of data. Although this line of reasoning is unconvincing to some (notably Carl Hempel), explicit definability encounters other difficulties: For instance, there is the classic problem, noted by Carnap, in definitional schemata that equate a theoretical or dispositional predicate to a material conditional containing observational predicates (the theoretical predicate being instantiated whenever the conditional's antecedent is simply false). Further, attempts to construct syntactical metalanguages, comprising only observational (or generally acceptable) predicates that are then used to transform theoretical strings whose theoretical predicates are construed initially as uninterpreted, have not as yet met with success.[40]

Frank Ramsey devised a method by which a theory could be translated into a single sentence—a "Ramsey sentence"—in which all theoretical predicates are transformed into predicate variables.[41] But there are a number of important objections to this procedure: In addition to its importation of the higher predicate calculus that Quine eschews, it seems to eliminate theoretical predicates "in name only" (as Hempel wittily argues in "The Theoretician's Dilemma"). Also, it seems to preserve, along with the logical structure of the theory, the very incompatibility manifest in underdetermination and hence can't provide a means to undercut it. (Quine suggests in fact that theory formulations, belonging to the equivalence relation determined by (1) and (2) above, may be construed alternatively as those formulations expressible by the same Ramsey sentence.) Also, there is a problem noted by Scheffler of the failure of certain important inductive relationships manifest in the original formulation to be preserved in the Ramsey equivalent.[42]

However, a more recent attempt at providing a logical apparatus for providing a "theory-equivalent" that has only observational expressions has made a more decided impact on Quine. William Craig's "Replacement Theorem" provides a mechanical method for replacing any proof of a given observational conditional from elements of an original theory-formulation by a derivation of that conditional from a complex set of observational conditionals. Now the "Craig equivalent" of a theory involves computations that are far too lengthy to do in practice, and that equivalent lacks the axiomatic systematicity of the original formulation (and hence lacks the economy, simplicity, explanatory power, and heuristic suggestiveness of the original)—features that undermine its significance in the eyes of some critics. However, its availability convinces Quine that his strong underdetermination thesis cannot be maintained in its original form. What is important about the Craig-equivalent of a given theory is that, in addition to being couched entirely in observational terms, it can be specified by a set procedure (a recursive one) that amounts to more than simply listing the observational conditionals themselves. For now Quine can no longer claim that *any* manageable formulation of a system that must provide "mass coverage" of the sort demanded of physical theory (and one would think that translation manuals fit into the category of systems of this sort) must have the theoretical looseness that makes for underdetermination. At best he could claim this only for nonrecursive systematizations, with the result that his thesis would at best only mark a relatively minor contrast between types of systematization.[43]

The modified thesis that results from these considerations is this:

> We, humanly, are capable of encompassing more true observation conditionals in a loose theory formulation than in any tight system that we might discover and formulate independently of any such loose formulation. And then the thesis would go on to say, as before, that for each such formulation there will be others, empirically equivalent but logically incompatible with it and incapable of being rendered logically equivalent to it by any reconstrual of predicates.[44]

Further, Quine finds it necessary to make still another important qualification of the thesis: Having isolated the importance of non-reconstruability for the thesis, he admits that there is no evident way of proving this for any case at hand. Having failed to imagine an observational test that could decide between two theories, we might turn to consider possible reconstruals of predicates that could logically reconcile the two finite formulations. Failing the latter, we can only *tentatively* conclude that their incompatibility is irreconcilable:

> There still could be a reconciling reconstrual of predicates, subtle and complex and forever undiscovered. The thesis of underdetermination, even in my latest tempered version, asserts that our system of the world is bound to have empirically equivalent alternatives that are not reconcilable by a reconstrual of predicates however devious. This, for me, is an open question.[45]

So the underdetermination thesis finally comes to this: . . .our system of the world is bound to have empirically equivalent alternatives that, if we were to discover them, we would see no way of reconciling by reconstrual of predicates.[46]

However, even this modified view, Quine argues, has its consequences for one's overall view of science. We must grant that we can always systematically describe the world in a way significantly different from the one we now successfully employ, and the differences will be far more difficult (perhaps impossible) to reconcile than to imagine. Yet while this modified underdetermination thesis might leave Quine's position regarding scientific truth and method intact, it would seem to cast serious doubt on the indeterminacy thesis.

And yet Quine does not see these modifications as at all mitigating the indeterminacy thesis, despite the integral role it ostensibly plays in that thesis. Earlier in the paper under consideration he offers two examples of underdetermination that he rejects as trivial. One involves generating rival theories by taking our standard theory of nature and producing a rival by systematically exchanging the terms 'electron' and 'molecule'. Yet while admitting that is not an interesting case of underdetermination, he argues nonetheless that it is sufficient to make indeterminacy stick:

> Having disqualified these permutations as cases of under-determination, we might in passing consider how they stand as cases of indeterminacy of translation. If in the light of verbal behavior we translate two foreign words as 'molecule' and 'electron', what behavioral evidence could have obstructed the opposite choice? None, surely, except as we invoke what Neil Wilson called the principle of charity: maximize the agreement between the native and ourselves on questions of truth and falsity, other things being equal. Translation is not the recapturing of some determinate entity, a meaning, but only a balancing of various values. An observation sentence and its translation should command assent under similar situations; here is one value. Wide concomitance of assent to standing sentences is also a value. Good translation strikes some optimum combination of values, insofar as they can be compared.[47]

The themes in this passage are by now no doubt familiar. What seems to back up the claim that translation is *only* a "balancing of values" is the fact that the necessity of "maximizing agreement" is a form of imposition that precludes the linguist's "recapturing of some determinate entity." Again, we see charity playing a key role in the argument (much as familiarity of grammatical categorization functions in the inscrutability of reference argument). Now it might be initially puzzling that Quine's first mention of charity in *Word and Object*, and in my exposition in Chapter one, is to defend the *translatability* of the basic truth functions. But there the point seemed to be that there were no alternatives among which to choose. However, in the translation of terms (and thus of predicate logic) and in the translation of most sentences, we have imaginable divergent alternatives compatible with our evidence. When charity (or familiarity) functions to narrow choices, we have indeterminacy. However, we confront again the question, why does *this* make a difference? Why does reliance on extra-empirical criteria preclude truth in translation but not physics?[48]

At the end of Chapter 1, and in the previous section, I noted that Quine has expressed preference for an indeterminacy thesis that requires only a holism thesis—to the effect that any nonobservational (physical or translational) hypothesis can be maintained if suitable adjustments are made elsewhere in the containing system (theory or translation manual). It now seems clear that genuine theoretical underdetermination will not do the trick. And if the *ersatz* possibility just considered seems unsatisfactory, then perhaps we now have all the reason we need to follow Quine in favoring the holism argument. But, as I noted earlier, this is not to answer the question about Quine's contrasting attitudes regarding translation and physics. The translational analogue of underdetermination seems easy enough to explain, even if theoretical underdetermination is not. But it has always been Quine's contention that even if we were to produce an argument for theoretical underdetermination, it would still not make physics indeterminate. Moreover, the holism upon which Quine prefers to rest indeterminacy applies equally to physics. The question remains as to how this contrast in attitude is warranted.

Quine on Ontology and Epistemology

Subsequent commentary has revealed two general and interrelated thesis types in Quine's philosophy, which he characterizes as "ontological" and "epistemological." And one can see evidence for two corresponding attacks on translation: (1) an ontological challenge concerning the ability of linguists to describe objective matters of fact in attributing conceptual schemes (at whatever level); (2) an epistemological challenge focusing on the evidential warrant for translation and linguistics. While Quine clearly favors the ontological reading, I shall give attention to both readings here.

Quine's distinction between ontological and epistemological theses is clarified by Roger Gibson in a recent paper:

> Ontology and epistemology are concerned with different issues. Ontology focuses on the issue of what there is; and what there is is a question of *truth*. Epistemology focuses on the issues of how we know what

there is; and how we know what there is is a question of *method* and *evidence*. And evidence is for Quine sensory evidence, so epistemology is for Quine empiricism. It follows that empiricism is not a theory of truth but a theory of evidence (i.e., of warranted belief . . .). It does not purport to tell us what there is, but only what evidence there is for what there is.[49]

Though different, the two bear a relationship of "reciprocal containment" to one another. Ontology "contains" epistemology (1) in that the latter assumes the existence of an external world; (2) in that the ontological theory implies the key empiricist tenets of his epistemology (the grounding of science and semantics in sensory evidence); and (3) in that the ontological (not the epistemological) theory provides the account of epistemology's basic sensory contact points: sensory receptors (physical objects). This bears out key notions of what Quine calls a "naturalized epistemology"—one that does not seek to move from indubitable sensory or intuitive starting points. It is viewed as a *component* of science, rather than the latter's *a priori* justification. Ontology directly concerns questions of truth and factuality, and, as truth-ascertainment is mainly the task of science, it comprises scientific theories (that meet certain standards). Epistemology, in turn, "contains" ontology in that it provides an account of the evidential bases of the sciences. There is a pervasive circularity in this, but Quine does not view it as vicious; instead, it is an intended consequence of his rejection of a prioristic First Philosophy.[50]

Both epistemological and ontological concerns are suggested in Quine's summary remarks concerning indeterminacy in *Word and Object*.

The ontological challenge.

Thus the analytical hypotheses, and the grand synthetic one that they add up to, are only in an incomplete sense hypotheses. Contrast the case of translation of the occasion sentence 'Gavagai' by similarity of stimulus meaning. This is a genuine hypothesis from sample observations, though possibly wrong. . . . On the other hand no such sense is made of the typical analytical hypothesis. The point is not that we cannot be sure whether the analytical hypothesis is right, but that there is not even, as there was in the case of 'Gavagai', an objective matter to be right or wrong about.[51]

The epistemological challenge.

One has only to reflect on the nature of possible data and methods to appreciate the indeterminacy. Sentences translatable outright, translatable by independent evidence of stimulatory occasions, are sparse and must woefully under-determine the analytical hypotheses on which the translation of all further sentences depends. To project such hypotheses beyond the independently translatable sentences at all is in effect to impute our sense of linguistic analogy unverifiably to the native mind. . . . There can be no doubt that rival systems of analytical hypotheses can fit the totality of speech behavior to perfection, and fit the totality of dispositions to speech behavior as well, and still specify mutually incompatible translations of countless sentences insusceptible of independent control.[52]

Also, a passage I cited in Chapter 1 in clarifying Quine's intent to attack intension by attacking synonymy seems to suggest an epistemological challenge:

If in general I could make satisfactory sense of declaring two expressions to be synonymous, I would be more than pleased to recognize an abstract object as their common meaning. The method is familiar: I would define the meaning of an expression as the set of its synonyms. Where the trouble lies, rather, is in the two-place predicate of synonymy itself; it is too desperately wanting in clarity and perspicuity.[53]

Quine clearly wants us to construe indeterminacy as an ontological thesis.[54] Yet both readings seem to bear out his concerns. If theory in linguistics and theory, ethnography, and ethnology in linguistically oriented anthropology are not adequately tied to empirical evidence—if there is too much "creative freedom" to impose conceptually—then objectivity would seem to suffer seriously. (Again, there is no challenge intended to the facilitative task of translation or ethnography.) We must wonder as to how we can warrant our belief that cultural description really describes culture. On the other hand, if such theories and descriptions have no objective facts to be right or wrong about, then we have the same worry. Put another way, if we construe the indeterminacy of translation as that translations are not warrantedly assertible as true and thus are wanting as scientific hypotheses, both epistemological and ontological considerations seem to support this. If the empirical data do not adequately ground our efforts to find a translation manual that is true, we certainly must worry as to whether its "hypotheses" are *warrantedly assertible* as true. But it would also seem relevant to examine Quine's scientific theory of ontology. If it successfully delimits "facts" in such a way that indeterminate translations cannot express them, this would also seem to bear on one's efforts to say that they are warrantedly assertible *as true*.

Epistemology and Meaning

If the indeterminacy of translation is construed just as an epistemological thesis, does it imply any significant methodological consequences? One key point in this line of argument seems to be that translation does not yield *uniquely* correct translations. In a recent interpretive work that Quine himself heralds for its accuracy, Gibson characterizes indeterminacy as follows:

> Consistent with all possible dispositions to behavior on the parts of all concerned, different systems of analytical hypotheses can be formulated which render different English translations of the same use of a [source-language] . . . expression which, on intuitive grounds, differ in "meaning"; and there is no sense to the question of any one translation being the uniquely correct one.[55]

However, it is not clear what the force of denying unique correctness is. Considering the inscrutability of the term 'gavagai', I doubt any linguist would hesitate at all in telling us what the uniquely correct answer is: 'rabbit'. What reasons would be given for this claim? Obviously, empirical adequacy is one thing but not the only one. No doubt one would add elegance, simplicity, familiarity, and charity. And in adding the last two items, as we have seen Quine argue, the linguist gets into trouble. (Recall that though reliance on simplicity is Quine's central worry in "The Problem of Meaning in Linguistics," his later work does not echo this concern—except insofar as the vague notion of simplicity may comprise familiarity and charity.)

The inscrutability of reference thesis places emphasis on the familiarity principle. But the force of this concern is not clear. Familiarity plays a fundamental role in physical theory. Quine himself is a strong advocate of applying a criterion of *familiarity of principle* or *methodological conservatism* in warranting physical hypotheses, that is, "a favoring of the inherited conceptual scheme of one's own previous work."[56] This would seem to break all ties left over after application of other criteria. Given different historical circumstances, our physical theory could have been such as to countenance a widely different range of theoretical entities, yet for Quine it nonetheless fully legislates what is "real." What then is the difference?

A similar question arises when Quine targets reliance on the charity principle. Why, exactly, is it that we have to acknowledge that "translation is not the recapturing of some determinate entity, a meaning" owing to the fact that charity must be relied on in fixing translation? Conservatism, as Quine and Ullian remark in *The Web of Belief*, dictates that the "less rejection of prior beliefs required, the more plausible the hypothesis—other things being equal."[57] Charity would seem to be a corollary to this principle, since it dictates that one approach an alien culture with a predisposition to effect agreement on certain "obvious" beliefs, all other things being equal. Unnecessary attributions of bizarre beliefs to particular subjects conflict with general attitudes that no one holds such beliefs.

Yet Quine seems to acknowledge all this in warning us, in a discussion of indeterminacy in the concluding pages of *Word and Object*, that indeterminacy means more than that practical constraints govern translation:

> May we conclude that translational synonymy at its worst is no worse off than truth in physics? To be thus reassured is to misjudge the parallel. In being able to speak of the truth of a sentence only within a more inclusive theory, one is not much hampered; for one is always working within some comfortably inclusive theory, however tentative . . . . In short, the parameters of truth stay conveniently fixed most of the time. Not so the analytical hypotheses that constitute the parameters of translation. We are always ready to wonder about the meaning of a foreigner's remark without reference to any one set of analytical hypotheses, indeed even in the absence of any; yet two sets of analytical hypotheses can give contrary answers, unless the remark is of one of the limited sorts that can be translated without recourse to analytical hypotheses.[58]

That the manuals may be incompatible is emphasized here, as well as in the other sample I have offered of Quine's epistemological charge. Also, the easy availability of rival translations, or of divergent grounds to formulate them, is emphasized. But the mere availability of rival translations, even though they might be mutually exclusive, does not seem to carry the needed force. As Rorty puts the point, either make both science and interpretation indeterminate, or make them both determinate.

Chomsky, as I have noted, joins Rorty in seeing no evident breakdown in this parallel. He embraces one of the options Rorty leaves available in arguing that linguists have at most an *additional* under-determination to that of physics. In rejoinder, Quine remarks:

> Theory in physics is an ultimate parameter. There is no legitimate first philosophy, higher or firmer than physics, to which to appeal over physicists' heads. Even our appreciation of the partial arbitrariness or under-determination of our overall theory of nature is not a higher-level intuition; it is integral to our under-determined theory of nature itself, and of ourselves as natural objects. . . . The point about indeterminacy of translation is that it withstands even all this truth, the whole truth about nature. This is what I mean by saying that, where indeterminacy of translation applies, there is no real question of right choice; there is no fact of the matter even to *within* the acknowledged under-determination of a theory of nature.[59]

However, this remark seems to turn us in the direction of Quine's *ontological* thesis. Indeed, Quine notes at several points in his reply to Chomsky that beyond this, there is not much disagreement between them. He even remarks that he intends to create no crisis in linguistics by his remarks. Perhaps this is also intended to apply to anthropology, but this is hard to square with the above-noted remarks that seem to circumscribe that discipline's linguistic data.

Indeed, Gibson remarks:

> From the point of view of *epistemology*, under-determination of physical theory and indeterminacy of translation are on a par: Just as alternative *ontologies* can be erected on the same observational basis, so alternative *translations* of a native expression can be erected on the same observational basis. All are equally warranted by the evidence, let us suppose.

Again, the difference, for Gibson and Quine, is a matter for the *ontological* component to ascertain.[60]

If indeterminacy of translation is just taken to be an epistemological thesis, then perhaps Chomsky's challenge against Quine's methodological charges goes unanswered—unless it is supplemented with the now, seemingly, distinct ontological thesis that no fact of the matter is expressed. But can we find reason—not having to do with factuality—why translation, and any linguistic or anthropological theory that rests much on it, is at hazard? This possibility is explored in a recent paper by Alexander George, "Whence and Whither the Debate between Quine and Chomsky?" It mainly concerns itself with challenges largely pertinent to the Chomskian program, but I think it suggests possible lines of an epistemological attack based on Quinean considerations. I maintain this despite the fact that, as I noted earlier, Quine has still more recently advised (partly in response to George) that he does not take Chomsky's concerns with syntax to suffer indeterminacy problems, even though syntax is underdetermined. For it seems to me that Quine still takes issue with many key points of the general transformational program, points that have had an impact on anthropology. There is Chomsky's concern with explanatory adequacy and psychological reality, for one, and Quine's behaviorism gives grounds to challenge these stronger objectives even where only syntax is at issue. Also, there is Chomsky's employment of a semantic component for the explanation of things such as ambiguity. I am not sure whether a general account of difference of meaning suffers from Quine's challenge to the notion of sameness of meaning; however, the broader semantic goals of generative linguists such as Katz (noted earlier) to employ generative devices for the explication of the full range of semantic notions would seem clearly to suffer from Quinean indeterminacy. In addition, I think it worth the effort to see more clearly how Quine's considerations square with the clearly epistemological worries expressed by Cook and Levelt. These concerns with transformational theory's "dogmatic" self-validation, in suspicious independence of behavioral fact, have an unmistakably Quinean ring. Finally, let us recall that the key complaint against lexicography, but not against grammatical analysis, in "The Problem of Meaning in Linguistics" concerns whether there is a behavioral fact of the matter to explain in the first place. The clarification of this distinction may hinge on one's giving an ontological reading to the thesis, and may not be as easy to perceive by those enamored of an epistemological one.

There is, as George notes, much similarity between Quine and Chomsky. Both are concerned with grounding explanation of linguistic behavior ultimately in neurophysiological structure. Both are willing to posit innate structure. Quine notes that even a radical behaviorist must acknowledge innate abilities for "qualitative spacing": If an organism lacks an innate ability to ascertain stimulus similarity, conditioning is impossible.[61] (However, there is considerable variation in the nature and extent of the structure posited.) Further, for all the acknowledged abstractness of Chomsky's grammars, he explicitly holds out hope for later specification in terms denoting neurophysiological items—thus manifesting an "in principle" agreement with Quine on this ontological point.[62]

The differences, George claims, emerge in just what theoretical matter intervenes between neurophysiology and linguistic output. To be sure, grammar functions as part of a characterization of competence, and its connection to performance is indirect. Also, there is little by way of direct implication for behavior in determinations of competence until a mechanism connecting cognitive state and behavior has been revealed. However, George views Quine's deeper concern as not "the theory's distance from the data" but "its (perceived) independence from them."[63]

In this connection, George sees disagreement arising over the choice between empirically equivalent grammars (G and G') of the one "an individual *really* knows":

> Evidential support for G over G' would then have to be theoretical—though not for that reason any less empirical, Chomsky would urge. For example, a theory of language acquisition might lead to choice of one grammar over another "extensionally equivalent" one on the ground that the first accords with a schematism that makes available fewer grammars to the language learner. Or a theory of Universal Grammar that leads to well-confirmed grammars in a wide range of cases might select G over G' on a basis of available evidence (Chomsky's example). Thus even though a supplemented competence theory may have behavioral consequences, no such data by themselves need lead to choice of that theory over some "extensionally equivalent" system.[64]

George sees Quine's main complaint about this not in the distancing of competence from performance (though recall Cook's and Levelt's concerns about aspects of idealized competence models for research about performance) but in the fact that competence theories are distanced from data "from below," in "fail[ing] to be warranted only by facts about behavior":

> Quine insists that such distancing from below diminishes linguistic theory's explanatory content. "What matters," according to him, "is just the insistence upon couching all criteria in observation terms . . . [that is,] terms that are or can be taught by ostension, and whose application in each particular case can therefore be checked intersubjectively". Since in this case "observation terms" are just those which comprise descriptions of a speaker's behavior, Quine finds

obscure the question which of two "extensionally equivalent" grammars is really the speaker's. According to him, "If it is to make any sense to say that a native was implicitly guided by one system of rules and not by another extensionally equivalent system, this sense must link up somehow with the native's dispositions to behave in observable ways in observable circumstances". In the case of "extensionally equivalent" grammars, such dispositions "must go beyond the mere attesting to the well-formedness of strings, since extensionally equivalent rules are indistinguishable on that score. It could be a question of dispositions to make or accept certain transformations and not others; or certain inferences and not others". But it must be a matter of some set or other of behavioral dispositions.[65]

As we saw before, Quine's central complaint with intension is that "the two-place predicate of synonymy itself . . .is too desperately wanting in clarity and perspicuity." George brings his discussion directly to bear on this:

> Conjectures about linguistic competence *tout court* do not yield behavioral consequences and do not lead to conclusions about the hardware whose functioning such abstractly described states characterize. Additionally and crucially, even if a characterization of competence were supplemented by an account of a mechanism that, given stimulus and cognitive state, yielded behavior, Quine would remain skeptical. In his view unless there is a difference in the dispositions to behavior predicted by an account incorporating competence theory T and an account differing only through incorporation of competence theory T', there is no sense in asking which account is correct. For such an [sic] one as Quine, there is a "crying need" in linguistics "for explicitness of criteria". To whatever extent that "need" is not met, linguistic theory will be undesirable, since it would contain a component employing terms whose conditions of correct application are very far, if not totally, removed from observation of behavioral phenomena, which could not easily be taught by ostension, and thus terms whose applications are not guaranteed to be intersubjectively checkable.[66]

How does this square against Quine's remarks that he has no problem with Chomsky the grammarian? Well, for one, if one reads George's query about the grammar an individual "*really* knows" as signaling Chomsky's concerns with explanatory adequacy and psychological reality, then I think George is still correct in seeing an important difference of opinion. But, as I remarked above, I think the Quinean challenges George articulates carry more weight against the bolder semantic objectives of Katz and others. For Quine sees no indeterminacy involved in theoretical explanation of grammaticality—where he sees a clear behavioral base. It is in efforts to characterize synonymy for natural languages that Quine sees the problem and where he intends his reflections on the elusiveness of behavioral evidence for translation and theory to carry weight. Semantics is also where I wish to place my own emphasis, and thus I shall take George's remarks, though aimed at contrasting Chomsky and Quine, as elucidating differences between Quine and transformational theories with broader semantic aims. (This is not to say that I fully grasp Quine's reasons for diminishing his differences with Chomsky.)

The key problem that we can draw from George lies in the two-stage structure of transformational explanations of linguistic behavior. Linguistic theory—from the earlier structural varieties to generative grammar—applies concepts that Quine suspects cannot be clearly delineated: The general problems I noted in Chapter 1 concerning the inability to specify clear criteria of identity and differentiation for intensions, semantic markers, and the like seem to be bothering Quine here. He seems to share Harris' belief (whether for the same reasons or not) that "idealism" will inhibit research: He argues that we "shortcut the mental bit" in transformational and other mentalistic theories—despite the public, abstract (not private, concrete) nature of their constructs and despite whatever willingness exists to acknowledge in-principle incorporability in later neurophysiological accounts. Quine wants us to attend more closely to neurophysiology now.[67]

A recent comment by Quine on Wilfrid Sellars (which George cites) bears this point out clearly. Sellars has suggested allowing mentalistic predicates as "hidden variables," whose irreducibility to behavioral criteria is to be expected. In response Quine suggests two criteria for evaluating such variables:

> Among hidden variables . . . there are better and worse. There is a premium on any links to observation, however partial and indirect; the less partial the better, and the more direct the better. The importance of behaviorism is its insistence on shoring up mentalistic terms, where possible, by forging substantial links with observation. For a deep causal explanation of mental states and events, on the other hand, we must look not just to behavior but to neurology. For this reason there is a premium not only on substantial connections between our hidden

variables and observation, but also on the amenability of these hidden variables to explanatory hypotheses in neurology. Their value lies in fostering causal explanations.[68]

From remarks Quine makes in this essay and elsewhere it is clear that mentalistic hidden variables, such as Katz's semantic markers, do not meet these criteria. They are neither sufficiently tied to observation nor amenable to neurophysiological causal explanation—the only kind of causal explanation Quine allows here.[69]

Yet exactly what has Quine offered to make us believe that mentalistic semantics must lead us astray? It is possible that the differences are not as sharp as one might suppose. George supplements his earlier remarks concerning the potential compatibility of transformational linguistics with remarks on Quine's views, such as that Quine is simply expressing a preference for an "isolate-the-dispositions-then-find-the-mechanisms approach" and does "not see white or black, but shades of gray" in his evaluation of various kinds of hidden linguistic variables.[70] (But then he also remarks, as we saw, that "unless there is a difference in the dispositions to behavior predicted by an account incorporating competence theory T and an account differing only through incorporation of competence theory T', there is no sense in asking which account is correct.") And of course there is the matter of Quine's recent protestations that he has no qualms, generally, about grammatical analysis. From all this, one might form the impression that Quine is only arguing against a separate science of intension, since, as George puts it (evidently in ontological terms), Quine "believes it is the job only of natural science and its heirs to tell us what is really real."[71] And one can see Quine as arguing only against this or more exclusionary separatist attitudes towards the study of symbolic behavior. The thrust of his thesis, read this way, would simply be that the "museum myth" should not make us think that meanings *must* be posited to explain communication, and so on, and to ask why, as we have seen, even less mentalistic theories such as Morris' and Searle's find it necessary to posit intension.[72]

But there are a number of problems with this interpretation. For one, as we have seen, Quine's remarks seem evidently to have a much sharper antimentalistic bite. And though it is possible that some of his positions have softened in this connection, his attitude toward mentalistic linguistics seems still pretty much what it always has been. Also, it seems to me that Quine's stronger anti-intensionalist claims are significantly vitiated by these concessions.

Also, even if the position is so weakened, it is still not clearly warranted. What reason have we to think Quine's methodological divergence from mentalism is anything more than a matter of taste? The point to Quine's preoccupation with the need to apply criteria of familiarity and charity is now unclear (though their role in the ontological thesis that translation expresses no fact of the matter is clear enough, as we shall see). Emphasis now seems to be on very generally stated concerns about theoretical criteria, replacing behavioral ones in the selection of grammars, or about "freedom" of theory from data; but no great weight of specific problems is brought to bear out Quine's skepticism. Also, the restriction to behavioral data could be challenged as being no more than a refusal to allow transformationalists engaged in semantic analysis to overcome linguistic underdetermination by positing theoretical entities of their choice. Moreover, even the challenge to Chomsky's aims of explanatory adequacy and psychological reality seems obscured. Even if one grants that field translation itself is ultimately supported only by reports of observed behavior with respect to observation sentences, and that certain higher reaches of linguistics presuppose translation, how does this justifiably preclude later confirmation for transformational hypotheses from other, say, psycholinguistic, sources?

There is, to be sure, a nagging worry that the generative program feeds illicitly on itself in relying on deep theoretical rather than behavioral resources for its confirmation (compare, again, Levelt and Cook). This worry also applies to structuralism. Both paradigms may induce their proponents to make theories immune to empirical refutation by being too swayed by theory in the process of validating it—perhaps by giving theory too much say as to what data are "significant" and what are to be ignored. This worry is perhaps magnified by the realization that it is relatively easy to pose and answer questions concerning meaning in accordance with divergent sets of analytical hypotheses. Quine suspects the evident degree of potential freedom of movement here in providing the "theoretical matter" of linguistics. But the full force of this concern is not as yet clearly spelled out. It seems quite easy to think of theories of nature underdetermined in the trivial fashion of the electron-molecule-switch case earlier. So why, exactly, is there greater freedom? And even if this can be shown in the case of linguistic choice, why does freedom entail methodological trouble, especially if this freedom is not exercised because it is often irrational and counterproductive to do so?[73] Finally, turning to the broader range of criticisms leveled against anthropological "idealism," whatever undesirable psychological predispositions (to circular reasoning, ignoring evidence) a paradigm may encourage, there seem many potential correctives that fall short of paradigm abandonment.

Evident here is a tension, which critics have often noted, between Quine's critique of intension and his open-ended empiricism. (A parallel contrast will emerge in his ontological reflections.) I believe these tensions can be somewhat resolved, and the more liberal Quinean attitude supported by casting the "interpreter-imposition" problem in a somewhat different light. However, let us look at Quine's ontological critique before considering revisions. We must not lose sight of the fact that the questions I have raised here concern an epistemological reading that Quine himself disavows.

Ontology and Meaning

An important basis for Quine's views is Peirce's idea that our ultimate standard of truth is provided by scientific theory: There is no independent, perceived or intuited standard—a world as it "really is"—to which the theory may be compared. A theory is not, in Rorty's terms, a "mirror of nature." Whether purported hypotheses express facts is not a matter of comparing them to the *world* as a catalog of facts: physics supplies the catalog (which is not to deny that it does so in virtue of causal connections to material processes). The truth or falsity of any genuine scientific hypotheses turns ultimately on what physicists can in principle tell us about the arrangements of microparticles. (This physicalism is weaker than those that demand definability of legitimate inquiry into a physical vocabulary or subsumption under physical law.) Quine views truth as an "immanent," as opposed to a "transcendant," notion.

Another thesis that coalesces with Quine's views of truth and factuality is a realism with respect to physical posits. According to this thesis, the theoretical predicates of physical scientists are viewed as having factual reference, despite the evident creative contribution of the scientific intellect to the structure and content of physical theory and despite the historical contingency involved in the entrenchment of particular theoretical predicates at particular times. What's more, their entrenchment thus legislates, in part, the viability of later theories, hypotheses,and theoretical concepts in virtue of the latter's familiarity—or conceptual proximity to these entrenched notions.

Quine holds that there "really are" microparticles, with the various properties conferred on them by accepted physical theory. Attribution of these properties to these particles is done by genuine hypotheses, laws, and so on with warrantable truth value. Since physics is an "ultimate parameter," one can have no grounds, beyond inductive uncertainty, to deny reality to the extensions of its predicates or truth to its warranted statements. However, a similar realistic attitude is withheld from many semantic posits and statements.[74]

Quine establishes translation's deficient ontological status as follows: (1) Since divergent theories are compatible with the evidence, divergent translation manuals are as well. As we have seen, the only empirical test of a translation manual, in Quine's view, lies in its implications for verbal behavior. Its receptor-language component gives the subjects' "theory of nature." But if we consider any nonobservational receptor translation of some body, let us say a sentence, of source-language discourse, we can always generate another receptor component that offers a rival receptor string in its place. (This can be premised on either holism or full theoretical underdetermination, with the latter seemingly the more problematic, as we have seen.) The rival manual will be distinct owing to differences (perhaps logical incompatibility) between these receptor strings. But it will be empirically equivalent, owing to other accommodating revisions being made. However, (2) if we look at the additional criteria one would apply, such as familiarity and charity, in justifying our narrowing translational options to, for example, the one that is regarded as correct, we see they are *additional* to whatever went into our selection of our theory of nature. The empirical equivalence of the manuals entails that the choice of translation manuals is not dictated even by a completely established physical theory. If it showed a difference between them, they could not then be empirically equivalent in light of *all possible evidence*. The complete description of physical micro- and macrostates that this theory would offer, and the complete description even an ideal theory (warranted by all possible evidence) would offer, would leave unanswered the question "Which translation manual is correct?" However, given this, (3) then all the physical truth that could conceivably be determined will not bear on these remaining questions and choices. We have exhausted all that can be truly said about "what there really is"; we have exhausted all the "facts of the matter." This means that our question "Which manual is correct?", and in turn the questions "What do the source-language expressions really mean?" and "With what receptor strings are they actually synonymous?'' must resist answer on a factual basis. Thus, the realistic attitude must be withheld with regard to synonymy (beyond stimulus-synonymy) and intension, and any other ''deeper'' posits designed to explicate synonymy.

Quine remarks:

> Since translators do not supplement their behavioral criteria with neurological criteria, much less with telepathy, what excuse could there be for supposing that one manual conformed to any distribution of elementary physical states better than the other manual? What excuse, in short, for supposing there to be a fact of the matter?[75]

The now evidently critical notion of a fact of the matter is defined as follows:

> The intended notion of matter of fact is . . . ontological, a question of reality, and to be taken naturalistically within our scientific theory of the world. Thus suppose, to make things vivid, that we are settling still for a physics of elementary particles and recognizing a dozen or so basic states and relations in which they may stand. Then when I say there is no fact of the matter, as regards, say, the two rival manuals of translation, what I mean is that both manuals are compatible with all the same distributions of states and relations over elementary particles. In a word, they are physically equivalent.[76]

What needs elaboration now is exactly why physicists have, in effect, a license for what Nelson Goodman calls ''worldmaking,'' while interpretive scientists do not. Why is Quine's pragmatism so selective? Quine's attitude toward physics separates him from Goodman's otherwise largely compatible pragmatism. Though no friend of intension, Goodman is skeptical of Quine's efforts to use physics as a criterion of ontological demarcation. In response to Goodman, Quine remarks:

> Why, Goodman asks, this special deference to physical theory? . . . The answer is . . . this: nothing happens in the world, not the flutter of an eyelid, not the flicker of a thought, without some redistribution of microphysical states. It is usually hopeless and pointless to determine just what microphysical states lapsed and what ones supervened in the event, but some reshuffling at that level there had to be; physics can settle for no less. If the physicist suspected there was any event that did not consist in a redistribution of the elementary states allowed for by his physical theory, he would seek a way of supplementing his theory. Full coverage in this sense is the very business of physics and only of physics.[77]

However, pragmatically minded anthropologists could well ask how an avowed empiricist, pragmatist, and *naturalized* epistemologist could tolerate, must less expound theses that judge in advance regarding exclusive privilege to build ontologies. If, as Quine himself claims, "our talk of external things, our very notion of things, is just a conceptual apparatus that helps us to foresee and control the triggering of our sensory receptors in the light of previous triggering of our sensory receptors,"[78] what basis have we for ruling out linguistic contributions? Are we sure they must fail to yield the desired foresight and control? (If, indeed, we are content to limit the aims of social inquiry to these: What precludes our giving a nonpredictive, yet nonetheless factual, account of symbolic meaning?) But this seems not to be a charge Quine wants to make against anthropology.

It seems that in a fully pragmatic and naturalistic spirit we can ask why Quine's physicalist analysis of facts should be adopted: If his rejection of First Philosophy legitimates nonviciously circular efforts at justification, interpretive scientists seem to have the option of presenting a pragmatic case for their own license to build ontologies. If as a consequence of adopting his definition of fact we thus exclude indeterminate translational hypotheses and derivative concepts, hypotheses, and theories, why shouldn't we see this as reason simply to reject the physicalist framework—perhaps on the very ground that accepting it entails the rejection of theoretical approaches that seem to have potential explanatory power (Harris' objections notwithstanding)? Why not simply maintain, on a fully pragmatic basis, that there can be factual differences without physical ones, though the facts will be of a special (perhaps "societal") variety?[79]

A critic might simply grasp the Brentano option—namely, of opting for a separate science of (or, more generally, distinct approaches to the study of) symbolic phenomena by simply rejecting Quine's definition of fact. Rorty, who as we have seen has long been skeptical of Quine's efforts to get an indeterminacy of translation but not of truth, has recently commented on Quine's view of facts as follows:

> Quine . . .thinks there can be no "fact of the matter" about intentional states of affairs because different such states can be attributed without making a difference to the elementary particles. . . . But surely all that such irreducibility shows is that one particular vocabulary . . .is not going to be helpful for doing certain things with certain explananda (e.g., people and cultures).[80]

Rorty, Goodman, and others draw more on the pluralist, Jamesian strains of pragmatism, and thus one might expect from them little sympathy for Quine's sophisticated Peircian-pragmatist account of objectivity. However, there are many who reject the pluralism of Rorty and Goodman (as well as the allied subjectivism of Kuhn) for sailing too close to the idealist wind. The Peircian option gains in attractiveness as against subjectivism, as well as in light of the great difficulties involved in giving some sort of "mirror of nature" account of objectivity (particularly the failures to make the initially intuitively compelling empiricist reduction programs pan out). However, I am not sure that even the followers of Quine and Peirce have been presented with a convincing case against intension.

For one thing, if we reexamine Quine's reply to Goodman concerning the physical character of physical fact, we find Quine specifically referring to *change*: He remarks that there are no changes in nature without changes in microstates, or no happenings without redistributions of physical states. If his thesis is limited to this, a brief rejoinder would seem to be effective: If all Quine means is that nothing *happens* without such changes, one can reply that in the choice procedure that Quine depicts, the question of describing a *change* from one state to another, or an *occurrence* in "semantic space," doesn't really arise. Rather, it is a matter of how an utterance is to be interpreted. The shift from one translation to a divergent one licensed by another physically equivalent translation manual seems only a shift in interpretation by the linguist of what could be viewed as being one physical event.

Imagine, with Quine, that a linguist characterizes a certain bit of behavior as in fact an expression of the native's concept of a rabbit, construed as a physical object. Or, to turn to the more general thesis, the linguist might say that it is (or is not) a fact that some bit of verbal behavior expresses a belief in the special power of witches (presumably involving translations that are not stimulus-meaning determinate). Now the linguist has certain purposes, different from those of the physicist, in so characterizing these behavioral segments, and the attributions the linguist makes depend on the overall virtues of the translation manual. Why should the physicist's privilege to provide an answer to all questions of factual change be of any concern here? Surely if the subject changes some belief, acceptance of Quine's physicalism would entail that some physically determinable change of macro- or microstate accompany this: namely, no change without a physical change. Is it possible that the translator will be able to attribute changes in belief without appealing to anything in subject behavior that correlates with a change in physical state? Of course, if Quine is right, the linguist can change translation manuals and perhaps thus produce a receptor-language string characterizing the belief that is different from the string produced by the first manual (where the difference is such as to justify a claim that the belief or proposition expressed by the rival receptor-language strings is different). But this is not to claim that the *subject* has changed his mind, only that the *translator* has.

But perhaps this is to take Quine too literally. Clearly, he wants to say "no difference without a physical difference," and while the emphasis in the passage recently quoted is on differences that result from processes of change, I think we can construe it as cogently applying to differences in interpretation. Not all of Quine's claims in this regard refer to physical change; for example, the earlier-quoted remark that "there is no fact of the matter as regards . . . two rival manuals" means that "both manuals are compatible with all the same distributions of states and relations over elementary particles."[81]

Here Quine emphasizes the fact that there can be two distinct systems of belief attribution, but only one set of physical facts. Now why is this "difference without a physical difference" a problem? In my understanding, the idea is that the answer one gives to the semantic questions raised earlier is not, and cannot be, uniquely and factually correct because, from the point of view of any one answer, the others are incorrect; but the differences between the answers have no factual correlate. So the *choice* of manual is not fully dictated by the facts, but it is also maintained that manuals express no fact of the matter or have nothing to be right or wrong about, and most importantly here, the latter formulation, whatever else it means, entails compromise of the scientific legitimacy of interpretive hypotheses; indeterminate translations are not genuine hypotheses.

However, I don't see why Quine's exclusionary thesis follows from this. Why emphasize the factual vacuity of choosing manuals in assessing their factual expressiveness? The latter could instead be tied to their empirical adequacy and equivalence. That is, we could grant that manuals are indeed ruled out as incorrect on nonfactual grounds, yet still accord them *factual* correctness and expressiveness. The facts that all express, we could say, are yielded by just the microstate description that is compatible with them all.

In actual practice only one or several of the indefinite number of empirically equivalent manuals will be chosen. Only those will be "correct" for the interpreter community. But I suggest that we nonetheless regard *all* the empirically adequate and equivalent manuals as "factually correct," their factually baseless differences notwithstanding.

This is not to say that all must be listed as part of our theory of nature. No, only those that square with such "nonfactual" criteria as charity and linguistic familiarity will be. But it seems we can say that on the basis of their compatibility with physical theory, all the rival manuals are nonetheless factual. Or, more to the present point, we can say that this relationship to physical fact makes them all *potential* candidates for inclusion in science. It is really a question of just how Quine's physical "ultimate parameter" circumscribes the facts. Does it list only necessary conditions for factuality, or does it contain all the sufficient ones? Let us imagine we are in the position of trying to select among job candidates, and we have narrowed it down to a "short list" of three—all of whom meet all the job requirements, affirmative action criteria, and so on equally well. We are legally and morally bound to check them all carefully against those criteria, but having done so, and having a three-way tie, this does not leave us unable to choose a "winner." We would find some other criterion, additional to those previously mandated, to make the final choice. To be sure we would not have full freedom here (we should not offer it on the basis of who offered the largest bribe), but would law or morality prevent us from using *any* other criteria? This would be unreasonable. We can apply additional criteria (perhaps we would finally flip a coin), and in so doing we do not render the chosen, qualified candidate as *unqualified*. So it is, one could argue, with translation manuals. Squaring with physical fact qualifies them for scientific status, and they remain so after pruning, whether chosen or not. Evidently this is only an analogy, but where does it break down?

Physical Equivalence and Translational Conflict

The passages in Quine I have examined up to now seem aimed at establishing that translation manuals are not factual and that their non-observational hypotheses cannot be warrantedly assertible as true. Also, it seems that the reason for these conclusions has something to do with the fact that translational choice is not fully dictated by physical-theory choice, even idealized physical-theory choice. What's more, it seems important that rival translation manuals conflict with one another, but in ways that are not reflected in differing physical states. This last point would seem to be where my aforementioned analogy may fail. In *Word and Object* Quine warns that we not confuse indeterminacy

. . . with the platitude that uniqueness of translation is absurd. The indeterminacy that I mean is more radical. It is that rival systems of analytical hypotheses can conform to all speech dispositions within each of the languages concerned and yet dictate, in countless cases, utterly disparate translations; not mere mutual paraphrases, but translations each of which would be excluded by the other system of translation. Two such translations might even be patently contrary in truth value provided there is no stimulation that would encourage assent to either.[82]

The key complaint is that one translation manual will accept translations that another will reject. Or, from the point of view of one manual, the other is incorrect, perhaps false. If we accept one manual and thus deny a place to the other in our theory of nature, we would seem to be regarding the first as true, but not the second. What are we to say about the status of the second? Is this not tantamount to saying it is *not true*?

To do so would be intolerable in light of Quine's foregoing remarks about physics and truth: We seem to be judging against the truth of the rejected but empirically and physically equivalent translation manuals, but not on any factual basis. But the physical theory that gives all the substance to our ascriptions of truth and falsity renders them all true, thus how can there be any sense to the claim that they conflict?

However, to ensure scientific legitimacy, we cannot allow the following state of affairs: One manual dictates that source string S means receptor string R; the other manual dictates that S means $R*$, but R and $R*$ differ in meaning such that accepting the first manual entails believing that S *does not mean* $R*$. Under these conditions, accepting the first manual entails regarding the second as false. But, again, our physical truth-parameters render both true. Thus, accepting *all* of the manuals as true would necessarily involve us in using a truth-predicate that violates the constraints of Quine's physicalistic ontology. We would be trafficking in transcendant, not immanent, truth.

However, I believe this inference is blocked by the fact that translation of S into R and S into $R*$ is done relative to two different translation manuals (call them M and $M*$), thus allowing us to describe the conflict between the manuals as follows: S means R in M, S means $R*$ in $M*$. To get an explicit contradiction, we would have to infer that S doesn't mean R *in M* from the second claim. But unless M is a faulty translation manual, this cannot be done. Is there a way to force us to state the two claims from a shared reference point, without relativization to manual? Typically we talk about meaning-difference without reference to any manuals, but it seems Quine's point (and a warranted one) that one can always in principle generate a rival manual to accommodate a rival interpretation at the theoretical level of translation. Indeed, I am not sure a warranted inference of this sort can be made. For the receptor components of M and M^* embed R and R^* and their constituents in fundamentally different linguistic "webs," that is, the divergent receptor theories themselves. (The differences need only be localized to R and R*, though one could view them as embedded in distinct object-receptor languages.) It would seem that belief about meaning based on M logically excludes belief about meaning based on M^*, only if one can infer something about R^* from a belief based on M without changing the meaning of R^* in the process.

Why, then, should the fact that one manual leads us to attribute to a speaker a belief in R and another a belief in R^* entail contradiction? What prevents us from holding that both translations are (or might be) true, or that both attributions to the speaker are (or might be) true?

Though I have provided brief considerations against the commensurability of manuals, it is worth considering the extreme possibility that Quine entertains above that rival manuals might issue in *receptor components* that are logically incompatible. Logical incompatibility would entail that the components containing R and R^* are sufficiently similar semantically to relate R and R^* in the required way. Put in terms of attribution to an ideal speaker, N (who does not hold incompatible beliefs), M leads us to think that N believes R, and M^* leads us to think that N believes R^*. Acceptance of M would then seem to require us to say that it is false that N believes R^*; but lacking any physical contrast to parallel this contrast of truth and falsity, we find ourselves outside Quine's physical parameters for those semantic concepts.

Independent of the sketchy incommensurability remarks just given, I think there is a line of reasoning against the inevitability of logical conflict between receptor components. And it comes from compelling reasons Quine himself has put forth for denying that underdetermination of theory can issue in logically incompatible theories whose logical compatibility is not evidently eliminable by a reconstrual of predicates. Quine has recently come to embrace an option not considered in his earlier discussion of the question in "On Empirically Equivalent Systems of the World". That article pondered, as we have seen, the options of a strong, "in-principle" thesis (maintained in earlier work) that rival theories could be logically incompatible but empirically equivalent and a weaker thesis maintaining only that, given the practical constraints of actual theory formulation, there would be no evident way of showing *logical equivalence* of theories. Quine has more recently come to believe that *logical compatibility* can be nonetheless established between still divergent theories. This arises amidst reflections, which I shall now sketch, on the related and here pivotal notion of factuality.

As I have noted, Quine's advocacy of an immanent as opposed to a transcendant notion of truth lies at the heart of the ontological status he grants physics, despite its acknowledged underdetermination. In his fairly recent "Things and Their Place in Theories," he remarks:

> it is a confusion to suppose that we can stand aloof and recognize all the alternative ontologies as true in their several ways, all the envisaged worlds as real. It is a confusion of truth with evidential support. Truth is immanent, and there is no higher. We must speak from within a theory, albeit any of various.[83]

However, Quine's empiricist leanings lead to a contrasting view on this point in another more recent article, "Empirical Content":

> Suppose, however, two empirically equivalent theory formulations that we see no way of reconciling by such a reinterpretation of terms. We probably would not know that they are empirically equivalent, for the usual way of finding them so would be by hitting upon such a reinterpretation. Still, let us suppose that the two formulations are in fact empirically equivalent even though not known to be; and let us suppose further that all of the implied observation categoricals are in fact true, although, again, not known to be. Nothing more, surely, can be required for the truth of either theory formulation. Are they both true? I say yes.[84]

As Gibson notes, this is incompatible with the passage previously quoted and represents a deep tension between Quine's naturalized notion of ontology and his empiricism. In a reply, Quine attempts a resolution based on an acknowledgment in "Empirical Content" of a point raised by Donald Davidson. It is here that the modification just noted in the underdetermination thesis emerges:

> Being incompatible, the two theory formulations . . . must evaluate some sentence oppositely. Since they are nevertheless empirically

equivalent, that sentence must contain terms that are short on observational criteria. But then we can just as well pick out one of those terms and treat it as if it were two independent words, one in the one theory formulation and another in the other. We can mark this by changing the spelling of the word in one of the two theory formulations.[85]

This "trivial expedient" line (aimed primarily at avoiding relativist implications) establishes logical compatibility, while preserving non-equivalence.

The rival theories *can* all be true, then, and Quine reconciles this with his immanent notion of truth by viewing our theory of nature as

> a single big tandem theory consisting perhaps of two largely independent lobes and a shared logic. Its lobes describe the world in two equally correct ways, and we can simultaneously reckon as factual whatever is asserted in either.[86]

This position, which tolerates the truth of two rival theories, is what Quine terms his "ecumenical" position—as opposed to the "sectarian" position advocated in "Theories and Things." However, the matter is not entirely settled in favor of this empiricist-oriented position. Quine raises a further difficulty, enunciated by Dagfin Follesdal, that speaks finally in favor of the sectarian position. The problem is that there may be "alien terms" in an additional lobe, which cannot be reduced to the idiom of the existing lobe. They can add nothing to the existing lobe and thus represent gratuitous additions, of the sort that are just the prime targets of traditional and contemporary empiricism and no less:

> [The difficult] case . . . is where the alien terms of the annexed lobe are irreducible. The sentences containing them constitute a gratuitous annex to the original theory, since the whole combination is still empirically equivalent to the original. It is as if some scientifically undigested terms of metaphysics or religion, say 'essence' or 'grace' or 'Nirvana', were admitted into science along with all their pertinent doctrine, and tolerated on the ground merely that they contravened no observations. It would be an abandonment of the scientist's quest for economy and of the empiricist's standard of meaningfulness.

The second system, under these conditions, does not make sense in terms of the chosen system: "Our own system is true by our lights, and the other does not even make sense in our terms." Yet Quine endeavors, still, to avoid *ruling out* the second system, even though he now finds he cannot say they are both true:

And what if, even so, we have somehow managed to persuade ourselves that the two are empirically equivalent. Then surely we must
recognize the two as equally *warranted*. Having got the swing of the
alien jargon without benefit of translation, we might even oscillate between the two for the sake of an enriched perspective on nature. But
whichever system we are wording in is the one for us to count at the
time as true, there being no wider frame of reference.[87]

Quine here flirts with the possibility contemplated, we saw, by
Whorf: that two systems might be coherent but impossible to
"calibrate" by translation. (But it does not tread into the aforementioned dangerous waters of presupposing an "underlying scheme."
With Davidson, Quine couches all of this in terms of untranslatability.)

The key question, however, is how this all squares with the
restriction of interpretation in anthropology that seems to follow from
Quine's position? I think it calls it further into question. For in light
of the discussion at the end of the previous section, what reason have
we now for not accepting *all* empirically adequate and equivalent
translation manuals as factually correct and thus capable of issuing in
genuine, though indeterminate, translational hypotheses? They all
seem to have something to be "right or wrong about," namely, the
physical facts that may or may not bear them out. Quine never denies
that they might entail false behavioral (or microstate) descriptions.
Rather, the force of his thesis is that there is some significant form of
"divergence" among the empirically equivalent manuals that goes
beyond normal inductive uncertainty. However, if the divergence between manuals falls short of logical incompatibility, I don't think any
case can be made from Quine's physicalistic standpoint against
translation's scientific legitimacy.

The very same trivial expedient argument employed by Quine in
advocating his ecumenical position can be used to make all the
respective receptor components of each manual compatible, though
still not logically equivalent. It imports a kind of incommensurability
that ensures that we brook no evident *inconsistency* in accepting the
whole set of empirically equivalent manuals as equally correct in
light of the facts. (We needn't, in this connection, consider the possibly irreducible lobes remarked on in the most recent quote from
Quine, as these possibilities would not be warranted by any existing
or potential rival translation manuals; they result from untranslatability.)

It is significant that Davidson, to whom we owe this trivial expedient idea, also maintains that the divergence involved in the indeterminacy of translation is no more harmful than that involved in the varying scales applicable to the measurement of temperature or preference.[88] In both cases we are confronted only with different ways of conceptualizing fact. Again, I allow that the *choice* of manual does not rest entirely on fact. But it rests in large part on it, and this seems to me enough to make translations legitimate hypotheses.

Of course Quine, as we have just seen, finally denies factuality to "lobes" that do not supplement existing ones. Does this give reason to deny that we can embrace all empirically equivalent and adequate manuals as being factual? I do not see how it would. In relying on the trivial expedient to avoid attributing inconsistency, the receptor theories we accommodate do not evidently constitute "danglers" in the theory of nature. Permitting translation manuals and dependent ethnographies in our theory of nature is not to permit the receptor theories themselves into that theory (not even when we translate the radically foreign theory that is the predictive equal of our own). Simplicity is accommodated by the fact that the desire for theoretical fruitfulness would limit choices to useful manuals, and legislate against grossly unfamiliar or uncharitable ones or against embracing pluralities of manuals whose differences go beyond being only "stylistic." Yet while interpreters have reason to limit the number of potential candidate translation manuals actualized as components of our theory of nature, I see no reason why this should compromise the ontological underpinnings of those that make the cut.

Let me try to connect these points, couched in Quine's "ontological mode," more clearly to the methodological issue. Given the connection between "expressing facts" and "being true," the point seems to be that indeterminate premises lack warranted assertibility as true or false in virtue of not being appropriately grounded in fact and, therefore, compromise the warrant for any beliefs that rest on them. The ontological arguments show that they cannot be true or false (in Quine's physicalistic sense), which would seem to imply that they cannot be warrantedly assertible as true or false, thus compromising the soundness of explanations that rest on them. But as yet it is not clear why they cannot all be true when they square with the physical facts, which occurs if and only if they square with the evidence. (This, of course, is not to conceptually equate truth with evidential warrant.) Thus, I see no reason as yet to deny that they are warrantedly assertible as true.

Ontology and Scientific Legitimacy

Impressed with Quine's insistence that indeterminacy is an ontological, not an epistemological, thesis, we have been looking into Quine's reflections on translation and physical fact for reasons for indeterminacy. And I have been construing indeterminacy as meaning that translations are not warrantedly assertible *as true*, and as thus casting doubt on the scientific legitimacy of translation-based anthropology. But I am having difficulty seeing how these pieces fit together this way. Here I want to argue that they indeed cannot.

Typically, when premises in inferences are shown to lack warranted assertibility as true, we regard the inferences as unsound. But it is not clear that something must be or rest on what is "warrantedly assertible *as true*" in order to be warrantedly assertible. We might be able to grant the nonfactuality of translation, its lack of truth value, and yet preserve its scientific legitimacy.

One way to show this might be to allow that *merely* warrantedly assertible claims (that is, not "as true") can be premises in sound explanation. The danger we want to avoid is the reliance on premises about which we are *unsure*, for reasons of potential falsity, lack of clarity, and so on. But do translations, or linguistically oriented ethnographies and ethnologies, intrinsically suffer such problems? If they do, and this has been argued in the anthropological literature, then perhaps there is no clear purpose to these suggested reconstructions. But no telling verdict seems to be in on this as yet. In the next chapter, I shall suggest a slightly different solution that likens translation to the essential prescriptive elements of theories (for example, rules of inference, hypothesis test, credibility ranking) that are not regarded as claims having truth value. We can view translation as performing a similarly prescriptive function—dictating translational behavior (and derivative forms of behavior) that optimizes intercultural discourse and systematic theory-building. Thus, we would deny that translations even function as *descriptive premises* in the reasoning to hypotheses and thereby preserve their scientific legitimacy. To deny their adequacy in a descriptive scientific function is not sufficient to deny their adequacy in any scientific function.

Indeed, it is not clear why all Quine's discussion of the relationship of translation to physical ontology does not work just in the opposite way than is intended. Physics can accommodate rival translations. But then why does this not invalidate Brentano and Quine's thesis of the "irreducibility" of interpretive disciplines to the natural sciences?

As I noted earlier, one sharing my perplexity might be motivated to view translation as resting on special "societal" facts and thereby simply reject Quine's physicalistic characterization of what a fact is. I will not comment on this, except to say that a lot more reflection on the criteria for being a fact is called for here. (I earlier suggested that one could be more of a pluralistic pragmatist appreciative of the explanatory successes of interpretive science and less of a physical naturalist in advocating a position contrary to Quine's in this respect.) More central to my concerns is the scientific legitimacy of interpretive science. And despite the fact that interpretive scientists make choices that go *beyond* what the facts can dictate, despite the fact that these facts may not provide a distinction for every difference in interpretation, I do not see how Quine's methodological consequences are warranted by his physicalistic ontology. There seems no clear reason why supplementing fact should compromise scientific character.

Thus it is still unclear to me why there is no fact of the matter to translation. As things now stand, translational methodology does provide a warrant for believing that a set of determinate synonymy relations guides translation. Divergent characterizations of the underlying "facts of the matter" that translation is "right or wrong about" are available, to be sure; but why is this multiplicity any different from that which attends any scientific description of fact?

The Epistemological Thesis Revisited

Again, I have been considering how we might premise indeterminacy on Quine's restriction of fact to physical fact. I have also been viewing indeterminacy as denying truth value to translational hypotheses (if that is the right way to interpret Quine's stated view that they are "only in an incomplete sense hypotheses"). And I have been tying this, in turn, to seeming exclusionary methodological consequences. To this point, I have made my failures to see how these tie together look like attacks on Quine's intended thesis. But of course this leaves the possibility that I am just misconstruing his intent.

Earlier, I offered the following passage from Quine in support of an epistemological reading of the indeterminacy thesis:

> Among hidden variables . . . .there are better and worse. There is a premium on any links to observation, however partial and indirect; the less partial the better, and the more direct the better. The importance of behaviorism is its insistence on shoring up mentalistic terms, where

possible, by forging substantial links with observation. For a deep causal explanation of mental states and events, on the other hand, we must look not just to behavior but to neurology. For this reason there is a premium not only on substantial connections between our hidden variables and observation, but also on the amenability of these hidden variables to explanatory hypotheses in neurology. Their value lies in fostering causal explanations.

If we look at this passage, instead, in the spirit of the ontological construal just considered, the idea would seem to be that the changes or differences that such variables might explain would be changes unparalleled in physical theory. This exceeding of physical ontology, perceived by examining the relationship of behavioral data to mentalistic variable, could perhaps in turn provide the reason for seeing a failure of such variables to foster explanation in terms of neurological fact. However, in recent discussion and correspondence Quine has offered another reading, which does not *rest* the case against mentalistic variables on their ontological excesses in the way I have in the previous section:

1. How we frame our system of the world depends on the prospective utility of one or another choice of hidden variables, and mentalistic variables show little promise as judged by the criteria emphasized in the above passage. Thus we do not adopt them in framing our system.

2. The resulting system of the world says where there is a fact of the matter and where there is not.

3. This system proves incapable of reconstructing mentalistic semantics from the materials we have accorded it. Consequently it fails to ascribe factuality to some points in mentalistic semantics.

The ring of circularity here is intended and reflects, I think, the aforementioned "reciprocal containment" of ontology and epistemology. And perhaps what should be learned from my failure to see how they work when sharply distinguished is that I have indeed distinguished them *too* sharply. Certainly one direction to take from here is to examine reciprocal containment, which Gibson rightly emphasizes, more closely as it applies to indeterminacy itself. I will not. Instead, I offer the following concluding remarks before pursuing my own lines of thought: However "reciprocal containment" works out, there seems good reason to deny that indeterminacy is an ontological and not an epistemological thesis. It would seem to be *both* (note how reciprocal containment clouds this distinction anyway). It is an ontological thesis insofar as it is *explicated* in ontological terms of failure to express facts. (However, I still do not see that translation suffers this failure: There is no fact of the matter as to why one should be chosen over the other. But I do not see why this means that there is no fact of the matter to the chosen option itself.) But if the nature of the key reasons in support of a thesis are to count in our decision as to how to categorize it, then it is partly epistemological. However, the categorization issue is not nearly as important as the matter of how Quine's first point above is to be supported. The reasons for indeterminacy do seem to concern matters of the relationship between theory and evidence (along the lines of both criteria enunciated in Quine's comments on Sellars). And, as I argued in considering the epistemological line, I am still in the dark as to what these reasons might be. And it would now seem unquestionable that these reasons are pivotal for considering Quine's import for anthropology. It would certainly be interesting to see how exploiting some sort of overlap between epistemological and ontological aspects of the indeterminacy thesis will improve matters when, as it now seems, they are insufficient when taken separately.

As for the other links in my interpretation, it remains clear that translational failures are pivotal to the failure of mentalistic hidden variables (recall the point of the radical translation argument). However, there also remains another possibility of breakdown— namely, in the matter of whether indeterminacy entails that translational hypotheses are not warrantably assertible as true. Clearly they are not, on Quine's view, warrantedly assertible as *uniquely* true, and perhaps one could view this as sufficient to undermine "natural synonymy." I am unsure as to how such a line of argument would work, but the possibility is worth mentioning. Also, there is the matter of what Quine's attitude toward anthropology might be. Clearly, if anthropologists make clear commitments to mentalism (e.g., the full program of Katz), Quine would object. But I have also wondered if any translation-based approach would suffer invalidation because of indeterminacy. In the next chapter, I shall argue that translations can be viewed, coherently, as not warrantedly assertible as true, but that translation-based anthropology does not suffer on that account. My considerations will be clearly "Quinean," but I make no claim to be explicating Quine's position in what follows.

Chapter 4

Translation and Convention

Translation Rules

In this chapter, I shall give an alternative account of the roots and import of indeterminacy. The latter is my main concern, especially as indeterminacy impinges on anthropology, and will receive more detailed attention in Chapter 5. This reconstruction is motivated by two concerns: (1) that Quine has not clearly established that translation is indeterminate, at least not with the clear consequence that translations are not genuine hypotheses; and (2) that he may imply excessively negative consequences for Boasian anthropology. I intend to address both of these points, but am most concerned with the latter: that is, with reconciling indeterminacy with the potential empirical validity of interpretive and cognitive paradigms. (Indeed, the cogency of my reading of indeterminacy's consequences may well be independent of the question of the acceptability of Quine's account of its sources.)

After a preparatory discussion in the present section, I shall raise a number of considerations, general and particular, concerning the setting of radical translation and the logical character and function of translational hypotheses. My aim will be to establish the following thesis as to the proper basis for contrast between translation and natural-scientific theorizing (I shall simply speak, as before, of physical theorizing in speaking of the latter): It lies in the differing compliance relationships that obtain between physical hypotheses (and theories) and their confirming and disconfirming instances on the one hand, and translational "hypotheses" (and manuals of translation) and their compliant or noncompliant instances on the other. The former comprises *law*-governed compliance, the latter *rule*-governed. (The special problems of rule-*following*—for example, whether rules must be consciously apprehended—will not concern me here.) Important differences, I shall argue, between the lawlike and rulelike orien-

tations are manifest not only in the types of regularities that the translator and physicist systematize, but also in the purposes and standards of adequacy of each sort of systematization. The central task of
physical theory is to describe regularities in a way that permits conceptual simplicity, enlightening explanation, and correct prediction.
In translation, although much is required and effected in the way of
explanation of symbolically significant behavior within a culture, and
although successful translation enhances predictability of verbal and
nonverbal behavior, the main burden of translation is to
"coordinate" behavior—behavior involving groups of rational individuals whose behavior, *qua* symbolic behavior, is largely rule-
determinate. (This is not to deny that such behavior might be
nomologically explicable as well.)

I believe that translations, inasmuch as they function in just the
way that rules governing the usage of words do, are not in any literal
sense hypotheses; they are neither true *nor* false. But this follows not
for the reasons Quine offers, but rather because the translator's linguistic correlations are themselves rulelike codifications of rules of
usage, cross-culturally projected from observed source-, receptor-,
and metalanguage behavior. (The notion of codification here is essentially Goodman's, as shall be seen.) Now granting the highly problematic character of convention and the other varieties of confor-
mative behavior, I believe David K. Lewis' analysis, in *Convention:
A Philosophical Study*, is sufficient for present purposes. I shall
employ it to show that linguistic conventions may be adequately construed as arising out of the need to solve coordination problems. As
these conventions are in fact constitutive of complex coordination
equilibria, the analytical "hypotheses" that serve to correlate the linguistic conventions and rules of one language with those of another
themselves represent coordination equilibria and are thus themselves
conventions. In their initial stages of development, their genesis
might seem indiscernible from, or at least intimately parallel to,
those of physical hypotheses. However, the fact that their systematic
interrelationships are patterned by the conventional relationships
among the verbal strings that they serve both to reveal, and especially to codify in a broader intercultural context, makes them
"conventional" in a way that physical hypotheses are not.

The bulk of Lewis' book is devoted to bringing the apparatus of
rational choice theory to bear on the analysis of convention, and it is
this part of his work that most concerns me here. (His subsequent
analysis of *linguistic* conventions in fact diverges quite radically from
Quine's and my own views on a number of key points.) In essence,

the coming to be, continuation, and passing away of conventions is primarily determined, in Lewis' view, by their efficacy in achieving maximal coordination among persons, who are thus motivated to coordinate out of rational self-interest. Hence, the rigor of rational choice theory makes it ideal for my proposed analysis. Lewis defines 'convention' in terms of complex "higher order" expectations that rational (that is, utility maximizing) persons form as a result of the gradual evolution of behavior patterns in which, in Hume's words, "the actions of each of us have a reference to those of the other, and are performed upon the supposition that something is to be performed on the other part."[1] Rational parties form conditional preferences for performing certain types of actions in certain sorts of situation, the condition being that all others perform that action if they do.[2] Performance of that action turns out to be best for all, provided all perform it. Combinations of actions that best yield optimal results for all are coordination "equilibria," that is, solutions to such so-called "coordination problems" in which all parties turn out to be best off in the sense that "no one would have been better off had any one agent alone acted otherwise."[3]

Now all behavior is regular behavior in the precise sense that all behavior is, at least in principle, nomologically explainable, and a central task of Lewis' account is to distinguish conventional behavior from other "regular" behavior. And the main feature to which Lewis appeals (as shall I, even more so) is that conventional behavior is essentially *contravenable*, and thus conventions govern behavior in a way that is different from the way in which scientific laws "govern" behavior. This becomes evident on examination of Lewis' criteria of conventionality, which for present purposes I shall leave in rough form, ignoring a number of subsequent changes made in *Convention* and elsewhere.[4]

The following are necessary conditions for a regularity R in behavior being a convention in a recurrent situation S among the members of a population P in any instance of S:

1. Everyone conforms to R.
2. Everyone expects everyone else to conform to R.
3. Everyone prefers to conform to R on condition that the others do, since S is a coordination problem and uniform conformity to R is a coordination equilibrium in S.

And further (1)–(3) are common knowledge in P.[5] This last feature of "common knowledge," embracing as it does certain notions of "potential," "irremediably nonverbal" knowledge, and knowledge "confined to particular instances,"[6] is perhaps problematic, but I think serviceable for present purposes. Such knowledge can arise from explicit agreement, from the salience of some one type of action (due perhaps to visible similarities borne to previous equilibria), precedent, or perhaps the sheer inertia of past conformity. The process of conformity through time can begin by explicit agreement, but may also arise from "an exchange of manifestations of a propensity to conform to a regularity"—to cite an example Lewis draws from Hume, when two rowers, without verbal communication, gradually coordinate the rhythm of their strokes.[7]

Two emendations to this initial list do bear mention here: The first is that it is necessary only that *nearly* everyone conform to a given regularity in behavior in order for the regularity to be a convention, thus allowing for violations and exceptions. Second, another condition is added to the list, one that demands the possibility of deviation from a given convention, rather than simply permitting it:

4. Everyone (or nearly everyone) would prefer that everyone (or nearly everyone) conform to R', where R' is some possible regularity in the behavior of members of (population) P in some (situation) S, such that no one in any instance of S among members of P could conform both to R' and to R.[8]

That is, another regularity that in a broad sense is incompatible with the first could have served in its place. It is important to note that the preference for R over R' is rationally grounded in the fact that others are expected to perform the former and not the latter. One is nearly always free to perform an action that is not in conformance with the dictates of convention. Such alternatives could be either such as to be conventions in their own right, were they accepted by nearly everyone, or such as to be not viable, for some reason, as conventional alternatives, though performable by individuals in isolated cases. (This is a type of violability not fully accounted for by Lewis, though cited in the analyses of 'rule' offered by Winch, Wittgenstein, and others.) But if we presume a rational preference for maximization of utility among the members of a group, we see that the tendency to coordination equilibria that results selects unique solutions from sets of equally adequate alternatives.

Lewis excludes action out of obligation and sanction from the class of conventions. However, these features are, I believe, proper components of many linguistic conventions, and a suitable definition of a 'rule of usage' can be derived from (1)–(4) by amending (3) and (4) as follows:

3'. Almost everyone prefers that almost everyone conform to R, or be obliged to conform to R, on condition that almost everyone conform to R, or on condition that failure to conform to R will lead to some form of sanction.

4'. Almost everyone would prefer that almost anyone conform to R', or be obliged to conform to R', on condition that almost everyone conform to R', or on condition that failure to conform to R' would lead to some form of sanction, where R' is some possible violable regularity in the behavior of members of P in S, such that no one in any instance of S among members of P could conform both to R' and to R.

A rule of usage, then, will comprise (1), (2), (3'), and (4') as necessary conditions. (Subsequently I shall speak of linguistic rules, rules of usage, and rule-governed linguistic behavior, without considering whether certain of these rules might in fact conform to Lewis' narrower definition.) Evidently these formulations are rough, and they certainly do not exhaust the list of necessary conditions (or comprise sufficient ones) for linguistic rules or conventions. However, enough has been said, I believe, to establish a groundwork for my thesis. Now I turn to some general considerations that have bearing on the prescriptive nature of translation.

The Conventional Character of Translation

The language communities that the linguist confronts can manifest a variety of levels of systematicity in their rules of usage. Conventional (that is, rulelike) regularities might be utterly uncodified, though uniform enough, and "tacitly" followed to a degree sufficient to allow the communication needed to survive. Or the society in question might have gone so far as to have achieved a written language and perhaps so far as to have codified grammatical rules and lexicographical equivalences. Indeed, there might even be a well-established antecedent practice of translation (in the strict, intercul-

tural sense as opposed to Quine's broader usage) among certain
members of the community, for example, merchants. The linguist approaches this community initially in an effort to correlate the uttered
strings of the source language with the receptor language on the basis
(following Quine) of stimulus meaning, something Quine and most
linguists regard as an inductive, descriptive task that is properly
characterized as one of hypothesis-formation.

Yet even here we must note an important difference, namely, that
the regular affirmation of certain sentences in the presence of certain
sorts of stimulations, as well as the other regularities in usage, are
contravenable, rule-governed regularities and not matters of uncon-
travenable, lawlike regularity—the application of an expression to an
object or to other expressions, or its various equivalence and sub-
stitutability relations, are to a large degree the result of conventional
coordination. Coming up with a right answer (that is, a member of
the admittedly nonunit set of right answers) in any simple case of
translation depends on certain coordination equilibria being reached.
For example, a simple coordination problem is manifest in the
linguist's endeavor to prompt affirmative responses to presentations
of stimuli; while a number of promptings will comprise a more complex coordination equilibrium, such as discovering an expression in
the source language that has the same stimulus meaning as some expression in the receptor language. The latter sort of coordination
equilibria—complex ones—would be preferred for their facilitation,
in turn, of equilibria in other coordination problems (for example, to
extend Quine's example, those that might be instanced in rabbit
hunts involving linguist and natives).

In general (for the field translator and for colleagues who may use
the manual), analytical hypotheses comprised in a translation manual
will serve to coordinate action cross-culturally, and such
"hypotheses" will be tested by their ability to effect coordination.
They help accomplish this specifically by helping to map the utterances or inscriptions that reflect rule-governed patterns of verbal
behavior in one language onto utterances or inscriptions reflecting
such verbal patterns in another language. In terms of their
(*inter*lingual) function and the test of their adequacy, then, they seem
quite analogous to the various sorts of codifications of usage that
might be developed *within* either language. *Intra*lingual antecedent
practice would admit of much individual and temporal variation, but
there would be enough consistency of usage and use to permit, and
presumably enough complexity to make rationally preferable, certain
grammatical and lexicographical systematizations (what Quine calls

regimentations) of usage. Once developed, these would come, in turn, to possess a normative force over particular questions of usage, spelling, and so on so that they would, indeed, affect future practice; but they would remain malleable to future variations in usage that were extensive enough. The important point of contrast here is that it is rational preference to conform that primarily underlies whatever fixity codifications have. On the other hand, the evidential grounding of physical theories, for all the codificational aspects of such theorizing, avails them of a basis that is fairly independent of the changing tides of preference. Physical hypotheses themselves are not codificationally justified, though physical definitions and rules of hypothesis acceptance may be.

The notion of "codification" I am employing here is expounded most clearly by Goodman with respect to the problem of justifying inductive procedures in science, and it has more recently been extended to ethical contexts by Rawls.[9] The accepted rules of induction (and, for that matter, deduction) are culled from the antecedent practice of working scientists, that is, from the set of inferences scientists regard as acceptable. The culling and formulation are reconstructions rather than simply descriptions of that practice. By applying these reconstructed, systematized, codified rules in the assessment of the validity of any inductive argument for acceptance of a theory, those arguments that scientists find clearly intuitively acceptable prior to application of the rules should be ruled valid on the basis of the rules. On the other hand, those that are clearly intuitively unacceptable should be determined invalid. The general rules of induction are designed to assess particular inductive inferences. Yet at the same time they are derived from reflection on antecedent inductive practice and are answerable to that practice. If the rule counts as valid an argument that scientists uniformly regard as clearly invalid, the scientists will keep the inference and amend the rule. In this vein, Goodman continues:

> This looks fragrantly circular. I have said that deductive [and inductive] inferences are justified by their conformity to valid general rules, and that general rules are justified by their conformity to valid inferences. But this circle is a virtuous one. The point is that rules and particular inferences alike are justified by being brought into agreement with each other. *A rule is amended if it yields an inference we are unwilling to accept; an inference is rejected if it violates a rule we are unwilling to amend.* The process of justification is the delicate one of making adjustments between rules and accepted inferences; and in the agreement achieved lies the only justification needed for either.[10]

One of the main purposes of this or any other sort of codification is to improve on the uncodified antecedent practice. By explicitly formulating and incorporating into a coherent and generally acceptable set the rules that govern some practice (be they rules of a game, of legal practice, or of right action), a number of advantages are gained. Of particular importance is the enhanced ability to form expectations of what others, known to be following the same rules, will do: this, of course, is the very advantage that convention formation (and convention formulation) manifests on David Lewis' view. The additional insights that Goodman's earlier reflections on codification provide is that the very stability of the codified rules depends on how well they square with the *ongoing* practice they codify (not simply the temporally antecedent practice from which they are derived). That is, one employs the rules to govern the practice and is always willing to modify the rules if they diverge too much from that practice. As long as principles and practice generally coincide, they thus remain in what Rawls calls a state of "reflective equilibrium." However, Rawls further points out:

> This equilibrium is not necessarily stable. It is liable to be upset by further examination of the conditions which should be imposed on the [imagined] contractual situation [by reference to which principles of justice are determined] and by particular cases which may lead us to revise our judgments.[11]

The open possibility of future "disequilibrium" is particularly important to keep in mind in the case of linguistic codifications such as grammars, dictionaries, and translation manuals. For while a dictionary may *indicate* word usage, linguistic practice is of course very much subject to change. (I use 'indicate' in a general sense, such that descriptions and prescriptions are both counted as indicators.) Even though there is good reason (again, the increased likelihood of achievement of more nearly optimal coordination equilibria) for stability of those codifications and for the attendant stability they confer on usage, gradual shifts or consciously prescribed variations (for example, technical languages), may nonetheless occur. And if these are extensive enough, the codifications themselves must be altered.

Moreover, I think it is illuminating to note that these linguistic conventions are prescriptive. They are such as *ought* to be followed within the source society, as well as by outsiders who have dealings with it. (Lewis' account concerns itself more with the genesis than the justification of conventions.) Given that the linguist's main purpose in developing a field manual is to enable speakers of the receptor language, other ethnographers, and so on to communicate successfully with source-language speakers, thereby effecting coordination equilibria in a wide range of contexts, the linguist ought then to endeavor to develop his manual of translation so that its users may conform ideally to rules and conventions of linguistic usage operative within the source society. As, at least, a "partial joiner" of that society, he and any manual user should seek to fulfill the expectations of the members of the source society. The very reasons that justify our saying that manual users ought to conform to the rules of usage of the source society, also justify our saying that manual users ought to conform to the dictates of the manual. For unless they have fully mastered the source language, they can only conform to the former rules by following the manual. Obviously problems can arise regarding the potential conflict between conformity to certain of the source society's conventions when such behavior conflicts with the moral dictates of one's own culture. The difficulties that underlie the well-known debates over ethical and cultural relativism, however, do not I believe significantly affect the present context in any general way. If moral dictates are not violated, and if prudential dictates strongly favor conformance to rules of usage, then one ought to conform to them. I believe the same goes for general problems with the circularity of reflective-equilibrium accounts that have emerged in recent literature.[12]

Now thus far I have argued only that it is cogent to claim that a linguist or manual user *ought* to employ a manual of translation in order to be able to conform when necessary to the source society's linguistic conventions. However, it still remains to be shown that "employing the manual" amounts to adhering to a set of *translation rules*, that is, that the manual is, generally speaking, prescriptive. I have not yet established this latter claim since one could argue that all that has been established in showing that the manual *ought* to be employed for some purpose is that it *should* be employed *as a descriptive theory* for that purpose. In short, we still might want to call the manual entries descriptive hypotheses *about* rule-governed behavior. The patterns of behavior on which these hypotheses would be based would admit of much more "free" variation (for example, momentary or gradual shifts in usage, by individuals or groups), and this would no doubt affect the logical form of the nomological generalizations that might be involved. One would not, for example, demand unfailing deductive predictability of individual, specific affirmative native responses to promptings to rabbit-stimuli, for the usage of a term like 'gavagai' might come to shift in ways requiring "lower valued" statistical generalizations correlating such usage with shifts in the regular application of terms to the animals an English-speaking person would call rabbits. One might think, however, that on the face of it such variability might call only for a "loosening" of the logical relations between hypotheses and prompted responses, in whatever ways such relations are ordinarily obtained among statistical laws and the evidential statements supporting them in any reach of scientific inquiry.

However, I think two more related points will serve to establish that analytical hypotheses are more cogently to be construed as rules and *not* as hypotheses at all, and that, correspondingly, translation manuals are more cogently to be construed as *codifications* of rules and *not* as scientific theories. More importantly, I am claiming that the form of the manual is not the one that Quine appears to be committed to in arguing for the indeterminacy of translation—and that this misperception on his part accounts for some of the difficulties and puzzles that have characterized interpretations of the significance of his results.

The first point to note, then, is that the variability of usage and the fixity of usage are both relative to the interrelated choices and preferences of speakers of a language. Because the rules (unlike laws) can be violated and changed, and because rational preference among alternatives is a key element that may figure in favor of or against such violation or change, rules possess what Lewis and others take as a defining characteristic of having to admit of contravenability, against the choice of which latter course rational preference, presumably, usually dictates. But where preference plays a role in *change* (or constitution) of rules and conventions, it can, of course, play no such role relative to immutable scientific law. No doubt entrenchment, familiarity, and simplicity of predicates play important roles in the formulation of both laws and rules. Still, the logical structure and semantical character (for example, the truth or falsity) of lawlike statements and empirical generalizations, and the logical relationship of hypotheses at various levels of physical theory to these laws and generalizations and to observation statements, are determined by a disparate semantical status that the formulations of theories and hypotheses have—in contrast to the semantical status of rules: Formulations of laws are to fulfill the function of *making claims about what is the case* in contrast to the function of formulations of rules, which is, broadly speaking, to indicate what should be, but which might *not* be the case *without abridging the acceptability of the rule.* So, scientific laws (that is, true lawlike statements) will, of course, not fulfill important criteria of conventionality: First, they will be "conformed to" always and everywhere, even where no one prefers conformity to them; hence they violate the third criterion of conventionality (or rulelikeness) noted above. Second, failure of an observational statement (implied in a scientific theory to hold) cannot be "withstood" by any proposed scientific law. Either the law or the counterinstance must be "rejected"; we cannot accept both (the point applies *mutatis mutandis* for the statistical laws as well). If there exists a state of affairs (including, in the statistical case, ensembles of events) that is regarded as a contravention of a law, the law must be amended, that is, rejected. Precisely such violability (without abridgment) is, however, a defining characteristic of conventions.

Although it is, indeed, partially covered by Lewis' fourth criterion of conventionality, and although it is at least implicit in his qualification of several of the formulations of criteria of conventionality (that is, qualified as to apply to *almost* everyone), the violability criterion is not clearly or rigorously or fully captured by Lewis' definition of convention. In particular, one would want to insist on the inclusion of a condition that unequivocally implies that alternative behavior be possible that would not constitute an alternative convention. There are many alternative actions one could take that would constitute violations of a convention, but that could not constitute alternative conventions. There are many alternative actions one could take that would constitute violations of a convention, but that could not themselves ever become stabilized, conventional behavior patterns among a rationally self-interested group of people.

What Quine calls "analytical hypotheses," on the other hand (and this goes, presumably, for other translational hypotheses as well), may well be construed as meeting the criteria for rules. For the "correctness" of a sentence, " 'gavagai' means (is to be translated as) 'rabbit' " will depend on continuing *rule-governed* regularities, at least among receptor- and source-language users, regarding utterance of certain expressions in the presence of certain animals. This will, in fact, be (in the sense of Lewis' analysis) a matter of choice and preference and coordination of behavior. If, for example, the source-language speakers evolve a second term for gray-haired rabbits, applying the first only to white-haired rabbits, and emendation in some original analytical hypothesis may be required. And, just as any source-language speaker might violate the convention of applying 'gavagai' to rabbits, and just as other conventions of rabbit-naming must be available, so may a manual user choose not to translate an expression according to the manual's dictates, or choose not to use 'gavagai' in a context that calls for indicating the presence of a rabbit, and so must other translational conventions or isolated options be available to the user. Indeed, one very good example of a viable alternative translation rule to "'gavagai' means 'rabbit'" is "'gavagai' means 'rabbithood'" (or "'gavagai' means 'rabbit-stage',", and so forth). Although one could, with suitable emendations throughout one's manual of translation, get along in the source society equally well using either convention, one of them might be preferred over the other in contexts of translating source strings into receptor strings, or in using such translations to determine native beliefs. As it stands, the preference of anthropological translators is (let us say) to use 'rabbit' as the receptor string, but they might well prefer 'rabbithood' if all or almost all other translators did. Hence, alternatives to existing translational correlations are available owing to the potential variability of choice of conventions or rules of usage in three different contexts: that of the source society, that of the receptor society, or that of the linguist's own technical, anthropological society. Further, it might plausibly be argued that as translation manuals are so constructed that users conform to source-language usage if and only if they conform to the translational correlations and to the receptor-language usage, any violation of a source-culture rule, by anyone, is *ipso facto* a violation of some corresponding convention, under a suitable description, for receptor-language speakers and translators dealing with the source-language community; that is, anyone's failing to conform to the convention of ascribing the term 'gavagai' to rabbits (that is, a convention that we are now stipulating to be stated entirely in the source language) is also violating the following convention:

> Persons should apply source term 'gavagai' to animals that comply with the condition of being the referent in conventional English usage of the receptor term 'rabbit'.

Hence, certain translational correlations may be construed as violable simply because source language usage is violable.[13] But any translational correlation is violable, and any is such as to admit of a fully feasible alternative. Indeed, actions in conformance with such alternatives are simply a subset of the class of nonconformists to a convention. As Lewis defines them, alternatives to conventions are such that one cannot conform to both a convention and to any such alternative.

Again, within receptor- and source-language communities, choice, preference, and coordination will underlie the rulelike regularities in behavior from which the linguist develops a manual, and these features will be manifest *in the occasional violations* that the linguist will note in the utterances of informants. The linguist can get the informant to correct them, or can justifiably write them off without advisement as violations once the manual is sufficiently developed. Also, alternative ways of describing things are possible, which are not to be followed unless others follow them; otherwise, communication is likely to fail. However, some alternatives that could become generally acceptable will be seen to emerge as conventions as usage evolves. The character of translation-manual entries will be responsive to these rule-governed regularities within receptor- and source-language communities considered in isolation from one another. And the manual entries will be further dictated by the conventional agreements of translators.

In summary, then, my first point in arguing to the rulelike character of translation is that translation manuals and the "hypotheses" that comprise them fulfill the conditions of *rulelikeness*, generally, in possessing certain key characteristics of violability and of being replaceable by equally viable alternatives (the class of whose compliant behaviors must be different). They also possess that characteristic feature of codifications, namely, of being "responsive" to variations in the antecedent practice of language use by source- and receptor-language speakers, and the antecedent practice of translators themselves, without being *descriptions* of any of those practices. They are in "reflective equilibrium" with the intuitions of proper usage of members of each of those three communities and function as instruments of coordination.

My second point can also be seen to evolve from a reconstruction of certain of Quine's views and requires, in particular, subscription to the broadened notion of "translation" that he employs; that is, on Quine's view, the regularities in usage that a *grammar* (or a dictionary) codifies are in fact regularities in antecedent practices of *translation*: For all interpretation, communication, construal, and so on that goes on within a language community is construable as *intralinguistic* translation. Granting this, then if the source- and receptor-language speakers' respective grammars and lexicons are to be regarded as codifications (and I am arguing that they do meet the requisite criteria), and if these are codifications of antecedent "translational" practice, how can we fail to regard translation manuals as belonging to the same genus they do? Both are codifications of rules rather than descriptive theories. They enable speakers of one natural language to understand and respond to speakers of another language, in just the way that a dictionary might well enable a child to understand and respond to the otherwise unfathomable talk of elders. Further, once adopted and put to extensive use in *inter*cultural communication and interaction, the manuals will in their turn undoubtedly have an influence on the general character of the coordination problems that speakers of each language will face. For instance, they will follow this insofar as they allow cultural interchange and the posing of new sorts of coordination problems to members of each culture. As such changes will, in turn, be bound to have an effect on linguistic usage, the manuals themselves will then play a role in transforming each language. Nor is it entirely unlikely that translation manuals might come to have a normative effect on receptor or source usage, in the way that their respective grammars do.

These considerations lead me to view "analytical hypotheses" (and "translational hypotheses" in general) not as hypotheses at all but as *rules*, in the sense delineated above. Moreover, they are taken to be rules that justifiably possess a normative force, since conformity to them is the "outsider's" means to conformity to source-society linguistic conventions, and conformity to the latter is clearly "dictated by reason," where one's purpose is to "get along" in the source-language community. Thus, formulations of translations are best construed as having the canonical form of *imperatives*, rather than declaratives.[14] Such a form clearly indicates that they are not statements of fact but prescriptive statements, directing manual users to make source-language utterances and inscriptions that will optimally effect coordination of activities involving source-language speakers and themselves. Though typically construed as assertions, sentences such as " 'gavagai' means 'rabbit'," " 'rabbit' is the meaning of 'gavagai'," or " 'rabbit' and 'gavagai' have the same meaning" are to be seen, after reflection on the problems of indeterminacy and the codifying function of these metalinguistic sentences, as best construed as the imperative "Translate 'gavagai' as 'rabbit'." Of course this is not to say that instances of the former types of locution need be abandoned in practice. What is important is that we not be misled by their apparent form into thinking that by using them we are stating facts about what source-language speakers mean, or, for that matter, into thinking that one is ontically committed, by virtue of their use, to the existence of meanings as entities shared or meanings as entities transmitted.[15] No doubt rules must have referring expressions in order to be effective, and this applies to translation rules. However, they only need refer to utterances or inscriptions. The temptation to see them as referring to sublinguistic or mental entities is lessened if we can finally account for the creation of certain linguistic and behavioral patterns in essentially the way that Hume accounts for the patterned movements of his rowers.

In the context of field translation, these rules function in the following way: Through careful study of source-culture linguistic and related nonlinguistic behavior, the linguist compiles a manual of translation that, ideally, will enable all receptor-language speakers who use the manual to communicate successfully. There will be no failures to coordinate activities or to fulfill certain expectations, traceable to faulty translating or misuse of words. Presumably the linguist's field methodology will be such as to test the developing rules of translation as exhaustively as possible. This will insure that these rules will enable a user to employ source-language terms in such a way as to insure that the coordination equilibria that depend on verbal communication will not fail to be achieved on account of linguistic failure. The mark of a good translation manual will be that it will contain rules that, if adhered to by receptor-culture users (who must then also be privy to the linguist's metalanguage to some degree), will enable them to conform to rule-governed regularities of speech behavior operative in the source-language community.

Analytical hypotheses differ, then, in important ways from ordinary scientific hypotheses—and as such are best viewed, I think, as not being hypotheses at all: that is, as neither true nor false nor to be accepted as true or false. But the reason for this is not because they cannot be *right* or *wrong*, acceptable or unacceptable (an untenable view that is often and unjustifiably attributed to Quine), nor simply because of the multiplicity and imposition problems that Quine cites. Rather, it is because they are conventions and/or rules. These two problems are symptomatic of our taking a prescriptive task to be a descriptive one, and they cease to afflict us once the recommended shift of view is made. We should expect there to be a variety of incompatible translation rules or manuals available to us, for such availability is a necessary characteristic of rules. We should expect our resultant systematization to reflect the imposition of elements familiar to the metalinguistic and receptor-language communities. It is a codification that is sensitive to the antecedent linguistic practices of three language communities and which is geared to effect coordination of linguistic and nonlinguistic behavior among members of those three language communities.

Of course I do not here recommend that actual translation manuals or the procedures for their construction be changed to match the idealized manual and entries I have discussed. In arguing for a new *canonical* form, I suggest only a new *construal* of those entries, for the sake of avoiding philosophical muddles. The guiding spirit here is, I think, similar to that which guides Burling's "hocus-pocus" thesis, in that I construe translation manuals, roughly speaking, as sorts of instrumentalities for facilitating intercultural coordination and subsequent theory-building—but as otherwise incapable of fulfilling the various demands for deeper "penetration" into objective semantic subrealms. (However, there are some important differences between my view and Burling's, which I shall elaborate below.)

Whither Translation?

The extreme thesis that translation is simply impossible, though a misconception of Quine's point, is worth further consideration. A proponent of this view might well cite the very feature of what I have been calling the "variability of rules," claiming that it is just this that makes it pointless to speak of *right* answers, when so many mutually incompatible right answers are so easily available (in the form of other translation manuals or alternative construals thought up on the spur of the moment). In this regard they might cite the following pivotal passage from *Word and Object*.

> The parameters of truth stay conveniently fixed most of the time. Not so the analytical hypotheses that constitute the parameters of translation. We are always ready to wonder about the meaning of a foreigner's remark without reference to any one set of analytical hypotheses, indeed even in the absence of any; yet two sets of analytical hypotheses equally compatible with all linguistic behavior can give contrary answers, unless the remark is of one of the limited sorts that can be translated without recourse to analytical hypotheses.[16]

This might be taken to say that we can't hope to develop manuals that in rational practice become standard and in so doing serve to proscribe incompatible construals and manuals. However, this is most implausible. We should expect that great variations in translation at earlier stages of the ethnographic study of some society might gradually be overcome after a more ramified manual of translation has been developed. The rational preference of manual users for accomplishing coordination lends a certain stabilizing influence to their choice of translational schemes. Indeed, in cases where source-language usage is relatively uncodified, successful manuals and enhanced intercultural discourse might serve to stabilize native usage to the point where it may be codified. The mere facts that the individual native can choose at any time to change his usage momentarily or for a longer duration, or that he could well have opted for different conventions, or that a linguist can at any time try an alternative way of translating that might be incompatible with the dictates of his chosen manual, while serving the task of translation equally well, do not themselves imply that linguistic practice cannot become sufficiently stabilized through the very process of translational codification. For such stability, or "fixity," is presumably rationally preferable to its alternatives.

Another more plausible reading of the above passage is that even if we did have an entrenched manual, we still would have no justifiable grounds for such proscription, precisely because of the ready availability in principle of incompatible but equally serviceable alternatives. This is not Quine's point either, as he doesn't mean to challenge translators' abilities to cull and apply standards. Instead, he challenges translation's ability to describe fact. However, he is easily interpretable in this way, and it is an initially plausible sounding objection at any rate. A brief discussion of it will, I think, be enlightening and will provide further elaboration of my view.

This reading is suggested by the following passage in which Quine argues that the seeming objectivity derived from importing our familiar grammatical categorizations to the native language is illusory:

> To project [analytical] hypotheses beyond the independently translatable sentences at all is in effect to impute our sense of linguistic analogy unverifiably to the native mind. Nor would the dictates even of our own sense of analogy tend to any intrinsic uniqueness: using what first comes to mind engenders an air of determinacy though freedom reign. There can be no doubt that rival systems of analytical hypotheses can fit the totality of speech behavior to perfection, and can fit the totality of dispositions to speech behavior as well, and still specify mutually incompatible translations of countless sentences insusceptible of independent control.[17]

However, if we keep in mind the conventional underpinnings of translational "hypotheses," I think a countervailing factor to the mere availability of alternatives becomes immediately apparent.

Indeed, translational correlations, being best construable as rules or conventions in the senses above defined, admit by definition of alternatives. The reason the alternatives are not chosen is that it is known that the given translation rules are accepted and preferred by manual writers and users, and not the equally serviceable alternatives. Meanwhile the alternatives *would* be preferable to individuals if they were believed by each individual to be preferred by everyone else, that is, if the manual comprising them were entrenched. Moreover, although incompatibility among manuals presumably would not affect discourse with the native, it might well produce disagreement or failure to coordinate activities among manual users. Hence, rational preference would dictate elimination of such potential disagreement by conventional agreement on one manual over the other.

Now, as before, it must be shown that linguists should *seek* this sort of coordination. Thus far, I have argued only that the users of some one manual ought to use it in the interest of fulfilling the expectations of members of the source culture, and the linguist's manual should be so constructed as to allow them to do this. But differing groups of speakers of one language could use different manuals from the underdetermined set, S*, to achieve this. Why should they all use some unique manual? The answer lies in the fact that the linguist-ethnographer's penetration into a new culture marks the beginning of a new type of coordination problem, over and above those that pattern his, or manual users', behavior in the field; that is, he is adding another translation manual to the set of previously developed ones, for which certain patterns of selection and of expectation among linguists and manual users have been developed.

For instance, there is (we assume) an established preference among English-speaking linguists for analytical hypotheses that assign utterances to familiar English categories such as 'noun', 'verb', and so on. Indeed, such preferences might eventually be accounted for in a sociological theory of translation, or more generally of conventional behavior (containing *hypotheses* of the form 'Conventions of type A are likely to arise among populations of type B in conditions of type C', where the linguist's situation is covered by categories B and C and his resulting manual by A). Here, then, the community of technical linguists would have very sharply defined expectations of a particular linguist to select a manual fitting category A, or a part of which fits category A, as opposed to another, from S*, which does not. Of course there is no such sociological theory of the behavior of linguists available as yet, but in the case of the accepted "universal" set of grammatical categories, there is a clear set of preferences and expectations that it is reasonable for the linguist to fulfill if possible.

It seems clear that the following "universals of grammar" could not be determined unless field linguists agreed to employ grammatical predicates such as 'is a noun', 'is a verb', 'is a plural construction', and so on, or unless their lexicons reflected these grammatical categories:

(a) Languages with dominant VSO [verb-subject-object] order are always prepositional.

(b) With overwhelmingly greater than chance frequency, languages with normal SOV order are postpositional.

(c) Whenever the verb agrees with a nominal subject or nominal object in gender, it also agrees in number.

(d) If a language has gender categories in the noun, it has gender categories in the pronoun.

(e) If there are any gender distinctions in the plural of the pronoun, there are some gender distinctions in the singular also.[18]

Of course, although conventional choice of basic linguistic predicates is a necessary condition for the formulation of universals such as these, they do not arise *entirely* because of convention. Within the constraints placed by the community on the use of predicates (that is, constraints that dictate employment of entrenched predicates, a feature of any scientific theory), certain conventions concerning word order, modifier agreement, and so on, seem to obtain, whereas others do not, and this constitutes enlightening information. There seems evidently to be nothing to gain and much to lose by a linguist's deciding to opt for translation manuals that serve the local tasks of translation sufficiently, yet that employ widely different grammatical predicates to codify source-language usage.

The reasonableness of the linguist's projections of 'is a noun' over sets of native utterances is enough to mitigate some of these seemingly harsher consequences of Quine's thesis: Such choices are not to be written off as "parochial," for it is perfectly reasonable (that is, part of a rational convention) to avoid violating the expectations of other linguists and manual users and to avoid unnecessary disagreement. Indeed, these seem to be just the rational grounds that underlie Quine's principle (*rule*) of methodological conservatism, which enables us to maintain our current theory of nature as a standard of truth despite its underdetermination. Surely there is as much reason to minimize unnecessary disagreement where *no* theory of conventional behavior or translation is available as when there is, and if the hypothetical case were actualized, methodological conservatism itself would dictate conformity to expected patterns.[19]

The source culture is being drawn into (is being viewed as part of) a larger community of linguists and other speakers of other languages, whose expectations ought to be fulfilled as much as possible, just as the source-language speakers' expectations should be. The technical community's expectations might eventually come to be embodied in a theory of linguists' behavior or a theory of translational conventions. Now I am by no means claiming that there is or must eventually be such a theory. I cite the open possibility of one merely to indicate the similarity of the codifying task of translation manuals within the technical linguistic community, as well as within the source-receptor community. This wider community might eventually come to embrace members of the source culture as manual users, when such persons come to learn the systematization that outsiders use to communicate with them. In such cases those source-language speakers might have emendations and revisions in the manual to suggest, so as to square it with their own grammatical intuitions. Here there is no reason to think that such construals of their grammar in a receptor language—say English—might forever seem unnatural, as Quine seems to think.[20] Of course the lower-order coordination problems that successful translation serves to facilitate could be handled adequately by any manuals belonging to S^*, but the incompatibility of these manuals manifests a failure of coordination among translators, which it is perfectly reasonable to want to eliminate. I conclude, then, that the mere availability of alternatives is not enough to allow us to infer that we have no grounds for selecting one as correct. There seems to be a perfectly legitimate rational principle to which one may appeal in determining the correctness of one alternative and hence the incorrectness of its empirically equivalent rivals. Simply put, it is the principle of avoiding unnecessary disagreement, and it seems just the principle operative in the fixing of underdetermined physical theory.

The main difference between scientific theory and translation on this point is not that a different principle applies, nor in the reason *why* it applies, but rather in the consequences one draws for the "objectivity" of the hypotheses and rules thus determined.

The rational grounds for selecting that manual which best coordinates and codifies the linguistic practices of the three communities involved lies precisely in the fact that it so well serves that function. Indeed, it can only serve that function if everyone (or almost everyone) in either of the communities (receptor and technical linguistic) who might come to use the manual can rightly expect that nearly everyone else uses it. Such rational grounds for regarding the manual as correct are not much different from the grounds for accepting a theory as true. But there is a difference; the linguist does not have, on the basis of the criteria for *correctness-of-manuals*, a basis for claiming that he is describing, or saying, things that are true (or false) of the source culture's "own" grammar, a grammar they alone have or that is manifest in structures in their heads or minds. Nor does he have a basis for saying that his translations "represent" or "capture" their meanings. As I noted above, he is not bound to such claims because his sentences do not describe anything or assert anything about anything (meanings, and so on) and are not descriptions having truth conditions—for in canonical form, they are prescriptive, not descriptive, formulations. But, crucially, this does not imply that there are simply no standards of correctness. For rules may be correct or incorrect, while not being about anything (without being descriptions having truth conditions). And even though there are alternative sets of rules (translation manuals), which are equally correct on all imaginable behavioral and formal grounds with regard to the task of applying them to the source culture (yet which yield mutually incompatible translations), there are perfectly good rational grounds for the community of manual users to treat the actually existing *best* manual as the *right* manual.

Once linguistic predicates have been satisfactorily employed in translation, the linguist has grounds for using them and excluding alternative predicates that could serve in conflicting hypotheses. Once "Translate x as 'rabbit' " has become entrenched through satisfactory projection of translations such as "Translate 'gavagai' as 'rabbit'," conflicting translations such as "Translate 'gavagai' as 'rabbithood' " are ruled out. (This is not to say that 'rabbithood' could not serve as a translation of some other native string.) Of course to one who does not agree with Quine regarding the special indeterminate character of analytical hypotheses as opposed to scientific hypotheses, all of this should be perfectly agreeable (assuming, too, as I have been doing here, that they find Goodman's notion of projectibility sound).[21] My point is that even if we do drive the sort of wedge Quine does between translation and scientific theorizing, suitable criteria for selection still obtain. Goodman's theory is applicable in either case: For the way I am construing translational correlations, they are more closely akin to the metalinguistic rules of inductive acceptance (or rules of projectibility) applied to physical theory, rather than to the object-language hypotheses of any such theory. Indeed, they are most closely akin to the prescriptive codifications of technical usage that function in the construction of any empirical theory (a point to which I shall return later in discussing whether my account makes the social sciences either poorer or somehow exceptional in comparison to their natural cousins).[22]

However, what now of Quine's objections? Again, these concern not our ability to entrench manuals but what claims are thus warranted about meaning and synonymy. In the rest of this chapter I shall answer this question in connection with some general issues in linguistics and the philosophy of language. In Chapter 5 I shall consider its particularly anthropological aspects.

The key point is that any suggestions to the effect that translation cannot adequately "fix" its parameters, or that it is too variable with respect to empirical data, cannot be taken to mean that the reflective equilibrium of translation rules is easily destabilized. For rationality dictates otherwise. This point provides the main substance of my disagreement not only with the extreme thesis just considered but also with Quine. Indeed, we can for various reasons tolerate actually existing incompatible or otherwise nonequivalent manuals of translation, or we can allow individual manuals to give divergent translations of the same source-language discourse. For that matter, there is potential for divergence by existing manuals from the dictates of some manual that translates, for example, Swahili into English, even if there is only one accepted manual designed to correlate those languages. For alternative translation schemes can be generated by translating Swahili first into Urdu, and Urdu in turn into French, and French finally into English. It would be most surprising if all the various translation routes one can take, using only existing manuals of translation, will be compatible with the direct routes. (This sort of situation might well arise in discourse involving United Nations delegates.) If no disagreements arise, or appear likely to arise, because of these divergences, then there is no reason to worry about them. If disagreements do arise, then they are handled as best as possible on a case by case basis. We might simply choose one manual's translation over another, or choose the direct translation over the indirect route, and so forth. As I see it, the situation is quite parallel to that involved in continually ongoing codifications in jurisprudence. Synonymy relations, in a weak sense, are still accounted for by translation manuals, which prescribe not describe them. There is no reason to expect the initial formulation of a manual to close off future revision, nor to provide a definitive response to all interpretive problems that might arise. However, stronger notions of synonymy—that take it to be a natural relation described by translation and accounted for, perhaps, by the positing of meanings shared by synonymous expressions—suffer more from these latter considerations. For it is hard to see how one is going to make sense of this if transitivity of synonymy breaks down, as it would seem to when we consider comparisons of direct translations with indirect ones. If I translate sentence S into sentence R using one manual, but translate S into divergent R' using several manuals, how can the entrenchment of manuals warrant talk of a natural relation between S and R, or of objects shared by S, R, and the corresponding synonyms in the manuals used in the indirect translation of S into R?

Some General Consequences for Linguistic Analysis

Although I have modified Quine's indeterminacy thesis significantly, there is, as I have noted, one important consequence of this thesis that my account seems to preserve: namely, the rejection of the idea that translation is "about" natural synonymy, propositions, conceptual relations, and so on. I achieve this in the strict radical translation case by stressing the violability-in-principle of translation rules, and the point seems to have equal force when one considers systems involving one natural language (although, strictly speaking, even this case involves dividing linguistic tasks between a metalanguage and an object language). Of course my reason for focusing on this case is that I am interested in the anthropological aspects of the indeterminacy problem, and from the outset I have eschewed consideration of nonradical interpretation contexts. However, I think the idea of starting with radical translation in order to clarify the general problem is a good one. Examining the consequences of the multiplicity and imposition problems of (pure or approximate) radical translation succeeds in bearing out what is peculiarly "nonobjective" about home-language construals and systematizations, even though it seems odd to say there is a parallel problem of "imposition" when one is interpreting discourse in one's own native tongue. What the radical case shows is that individual construals and the practices and systematizations that guide them are all rule-governed in the Lewis-Rawlsian sense I have delineated.

I am not sure if the full-blown "indeterminacy-at-home" thesis I would make would require all the strategies Quine employs in establishing this thesis. I have misgivings about treating, without more argument than Quine offers, intralinguistic interpretation as form of translation—typically, "homophonic" translation, especially if imposition is to play such a crucial role in the argument. Of course we do violate homophonic translation on occasion, as Quine points out, in the interest of interpretive charity (for example, when the speaker makes what we view as an obvious verbal slip), but it is not easy to see how this point is enough to show that intralingual interpretation is *generally* pervaded by indeterminacy. The general thesis is intended, I think, to rest more on the plausible idea that each individual speaks a divergent ideolect, the learning of which depends on interpersonally divergent histories of conditioning to social uniformity (recall, again, Quine's bush-metaphor). Moreover, the observation of that uniformity, manifest in the individual or the group, by the interlocutor, grammarian, or translator from some radically foreign society will not of itself provide a basis for giving a warranted descriptive account of the "ideas" that "underlie" such uniformity despite the acknowledged interpersonal divergence in learning-history. If one wants to treat talk of such "ideas" as just another way of talking about how remarks are interpreted or translated—as a "shorthand" of sorts—then I have no quarrel with this (nor does Quine). Linguistic patterns, whether codified or not, arise owing to the need of each such divergently conditioned individual to coordinate a wide range of activities with others. An account of how conformity is achieved (whether by a child learner or a professional ethnographer) is best undertaken on the basis of certain minimal assumptions about persons' rational self-interest and in the full realization that all one should hope to achieve is conformity, even, indeed, if one is a professional linguist. If we have no reason to presuppose such uniformity, especially since a reflective-equilibrium account of the matter seems feasible, then it would seem that a wide variety of linguistic tasks can get by without problematic ontic commitments. Moreover I think it is fair to say, with Quine, that these consequences apply as much to transformational theories as to, say, Frege and C. I. Lewis. Quine's thesis is intended to remove such notions both from the realm of abstract object and from the realm of cause and effect. According to my reconstruction, the reasoning would be that in giving a generative account of semantic relations, we are simply operating at a higher level of generality than when we construct a lexicon. And I see things operating pretty much the same way for grammatical analysis.

Both serve to codify intuitions—of grammaticality, syntactic or semantic ambiguity, and so on, in much the way that Rawls' ethical methodology is designed to systematize and improve on ethical intuitions, in part by the determination of higher-order principles of justice. "Codifying an intuition," again, is just to improve on prior practices of judgment, which may be based on already existing principles, perhaps consciously apprehended and previously codified. If one is inclined to think that the structure revealed in such a theory of justice need not be isomorphic with some underlying moral or conceptual reality, such an attitude should accommodate what I say about transformational structures. And if one is inclined to be critical of Rawls because it is felt that a theory of *justice* needs more for its justification, I do not think such problems carry over to translation. As I argued earlier, the question of why one *ought* to conform to linguistic patterns is more easily answered.

If this parallelism to Rawls' ethical "theory" exists, then we have good reason to mitigate the temptation to treat the structures of linguistic theory as somehow "reflecting" real, underlying psychological structures; that is, if we find no reason to seek such a "deeper" grounding for the structure of this sort of ethical account, but rather see its structure as stemming (as Rawls does) from the rational preference for stability and fulfilled expectations (among other things), then we would have good reason to extend this attitude to translation and other forms of linguistic analysis. We would have, I think, good reason to agree with Quine—though for reasons that differ from his—that these analyses involve "not the recapturing of some determinate entity, a meaning, but only a balancing of various values."[23] The reason that, in adhering to the justificatory canons of translation and linguistic analysis, we are *only* balancing values is that these canons—though parallel in function and, indeed, codificational character to those employed in physics—are facilitating the formulation of lower-level codifications (field translations and the like) rather than the formulation of descriptive theories.

Thus, I do not claim that there is no need for talk of generative grammatical and semantic structures, if all that these are taken to be are linguists' metalinguistic constructions aimed at lending greater systematicity to accounts of grammar, and so forth. By virtue of their success in achieving the tasks of purely linguistic analysis, they needn't lead us to posit structures and entities in speaker's minds or speaker's heads,[24] even though speaker's intuitions provide part of our evidential basis for employing these constructions. Any codification is answerable to intuition, and, contrary to Katz's view, linguistic analysis alone gives us no reason to liken "semantic markers" to the chemical elements. Nor is "explanatory adequacy" going to be an obviously cogent desideratum.

However, my sympathies with Quine on this point only go clearly as far as denying that underlying order—at the level of deep structure—*must* be presupposed and that successful *linguistic* analysis requires this. The reason is that once one goes beyond purely linguistic analysis, say to psycholinguistic tasks such as accounting for language acquisition, we may find that empirical success places certain additional constraints on what, for example, grammatical structures one imputes to speakers. Linguistic uniformity is not necessarily indicative of underlying, psychologically real or cognitively valid subsurface structure. This seems particularly clear in the case of semantic structure and also, indeed, for grammatical structure, especially if the latter is burdened with the strong demands of Chomsky's explanatory adequacy and psychological reality (although there are many in the transformational camp who reject or avoid taking on these burdens). But while I don't see such structures as necessitated, I don't see clear reason to foreclose on transformational psycholinguistic research programs.

Much depends on the motivation for seeking psychological reality, which might be of the questionable mentalistic variety I reject, but which might not. Just as pragmatic attitudes about theory constraints may, as we saw, present less metaphysically problematic defenses of emic and structuralist anthropology (if Quinean indeterminacy can be accommodated), they can also lead to productive redefinition of objectives like psychological reality in generative theories. And expressions of such pragmatism can be found in the literature. For example, the linguist Joan Bresnan argues that the notion of psychological reality should be construed "in the broad sense: it should contribute to the explanation of linguistic behavior and to our larger understanding of the human faculty of language." Indeed, she contends that, given the present state of the art in psycholinguistics, wherein a number of seemingly adequate but divergent theories of grammar exist and no generally accepted criteria for narrowing the field prevail, the "grammatical realization problem" is best pursued without waiting for the resolution of the former, "grammatical characterization problem." She suggests, in fact, that work on the psychological reality problem may help narrow the number of feasible solutions to the characterization problem.[25]

In a similar vein, the Laboratory of Human Cognition counsels against cognitive anthropologists seeking to obtain from cognitive psychologists techniques for determining "what goes on inside people's heads," as the seeming determinateness of psychological accounts of this matter, they contend, is to a great degree the result of ignoring cross-cultural variation. The contribution of cognitive psychology to anthropology, they argue, "should not be sought in presumed privileged access to people's thought processes because it is not to be found there" (compare Geertz's similar remarks to this effect in Chapter 2). "[R]ather," they contend, "the virtue of cognitive psychology is to be found in its procedures for limiting uncontrolled speculation about thinking."[26]

What these inquirers envision is a looser and empirically more flexible view of the relationships between accounts of language and accounts of cognition. (Compare Rosch's and Levi-Strauss' views regarding the "reality" of semantic data and codes—and particularly the latter's acceptance of multiple characterizations—noted in Chapter 2.) The aim of demonstrating psychological reality for some linguistic systematization need not hinge so much on revealing universal cognitive or even neurophysiological causal structure. Instead, what is emphasized is the potential integration of linguistic analyses into other areas such as cognitive anthropology. Success here would seem to be desirable for the resultant pragmatic gains in generality and explanatory power. A wider range of theory would come, then, to enter into theoretical reflections on the meanings of expressions. If this finally issues in no enhancement of neurophysiological explanation, Quine would evidently be dissatisfied. But this does not mean that genuinely scientific gains have not been made, or that 'psychological reality' is not the right term to describe the dimension in which progress has been achieved.

Quine's indeterminacy thesis does, I think, undercut this possibility of inclusion (and thus Chomsky's most recent work on the psychological reality issue, *Rules and Representations*, devotes a good deal of attention to rejecting the indeterminacy thesis, though this is hardly the first place in which he has endeavored to do this).[27] My reconstructed indeterminacy thesis does not have this consequence. Unlike Quine I do not take it that translational correlations function as descriptive hypotheses that are thus "incorporable" into ethnography or whatever as *premises*, and thus I do not conclude that their failing to describe anything undermines any conclusions that rest on these premises. There is no reason to think, at first glance, that translational correlations and related grammatical concepts cannot come to fit into psycholinguistic and cognitive psychological theories. Also, in addition to being compatible with this pragmatic construal of psychological reality, it provides a way to avoid foundering on the multiplicity and imposition problems. The "homeward thrust," to use Quine's expression, of pragmatic considerations need not occasion any theoretical worry about the possibility of misdescribing meaning. I believe I have greatly alleviated the tension I noted at the beginning of Chapter 3 between Quinean indeterminacy and such pragmatic trends in psycholinguistics. (I shall return to this point later in a number of particularly anthropological contexts.)

All in all my account gives both clearer grounds for saying (with Quine) that there are no such things as natural synonymy relations and does not create the impression that there are no empirical standards of *correctness* in translation. Indeed, I provide no basis for regarding even the translations of highly observational occasion sentences as genuine hypotheses, but nothing of great interest hinges, I think, on this additional divergence with Quine. I am sympathetic with Quine's efforts in this regard to provide an important empirical basis (hinging on retinal images rather than sense-data) for the accessibility of language to both a child learner and a speaker of some foreign tongue.[28] With respect to those synonymies that can be adequately accounted for in terms of stimulus *meaning*, I see no problem in acknowledging a descriptive hypothesis corresponding to the translation rule in question. I will say, however, that I see no reason to call the entity in question a stimulus meaning, and am somewhat sympathetic to those who find it hard to accept the idea that the sentences 'Lo, a rabbit' and 'Rabbithood again' share the same meaning, as Quine maintains. Quine's aims to assure some form of what Lewis calls "sense meaning" can, I think, be met without calling Quine's entities "meanings", but I shall not pursue this further here.

Another potential contrast between Quine and me is more serious and deserves mention here. If there is some intended tie—and you will recall I am not sure just what it is—between failure to express facts and exclusion from science, then what I say may produce more methodological tolerance than Quine may want to allow. For if I can restore to legitimate scientific status the indeterminate translation and whatever rests on it, I may restore every methodology, including the mentalistic ones, that would seem to fall before indeterminacy. However, for one thing, I am not sure just what Quine's position on methodologies in social science is. To be sure, he attacks mentalism, but he might agree, for his own reasons perhaps, with my efforts in the next chapter to keep methodologies while dispensing with methodologically inert and confusing commitments to mentalism. For another, if Quine's earlier-noted comments on the restricted scope of anthropology are to be taken as his current view about all anthropology *can* rely on, then I fully intend to oppose him in this regard. However, in a more positive vein, what I have said is potentially supportive of his worries about theories that rely on mentalistic hidden variables. For any codificational structure, say, a set of definitions, must aid a theory in its explanatory tasks. And if I am right in seeing, for example, much of the transformational apparatus as a massive codification of intuition, and not, in itself, a structure that one would expect to have any extensive parallelism to neurophysiological structure, then I provide reason to be wary of the prospects of that apparatus ever promoting causal-neurophysiological explanation. Of course simply being codificational in character does not preclude its contributing to causal explanation, but it seems reasonable to keep an eye on ultimate explanatory prospects as one constructs any such apparatus. And one element in the fears expressed by Quine, as well as by Cook and Levelt, is that this is not being done to their satisfaction.

Finally, there is the matter of Quine's differential attitude concerning grammatical versus lexicographical analysis. The former, as I noted earlier, does not suffer indeterminacy in his view. I have not particularly attended to this difference in the past two sections, as I am not sure if my reconstruction of indeterminacy warrants it. (Recall also my puzzlement expressed in connection with George and the epistemological reading of the indeterminacy thesis in Chapter 3.) However, while this is an important matter, I do not think it is necessary to address it in detail here. Even if Quine's contrast is warranted, I see no great difficulty in restricting the points I have raised about the status grammatical categories to the context of their application in *lexicographical* analysis. Moreover, regardless of how circumscribed Chomsky's own work is, the "Chomskian" influence in language-and-culture anthropology has largely semantic, and not only syntactic, import.

Chapter 5

Translation in Anthropology

Emics Reconstructed

I shall now consider the import of my reconstruction of Quine for a small, though I believe representative and important sample of anthropological doctrine, beginning in this section with a reconsideration of the emics/etics contrast, and developing some points further in discussing componential analysis in the next. Owing to the relevance of his views on language and culture to the positions I have discussed and the account of translation I have developed, Ward Goodenough's work will be given emphasis in this chapter. In the course of my discussion of Goodenough, I shall indicate, where appropriate, consequences for some of the related problem areas discussed in Chapter 2. As for the philosophical literature, while Quine has been my focal point up to now, I will give more emphasis in this chapter to Goodman and Wittgenstein.

As is indicated in my earlier discussions of etics and emics, even a cursory glance at the literature reveals much variation of opinion and confusion concerning the exact nature and consequences of the etic/emic distinction. An emic concept is for some an untranslatable one, for others nearly so. Untranslatability seems entailed by definitions that make emic concepts unique to one culture, and thus cultural specificity in a less exclusive sense is often emphasized. Emic concepts are then simply those familiar to subjects, with such familiarity warranted by various methodologies aimed at yielding, through appropriate elicitation procedures, receptor-language or metalanguage terms that express these concepts. Elicitations are guided according to componential, generative-grammatical, and other concepts, and question-sets are sometimes established according to rigorous, prestructured routines, and sometimes themselves result from a hermeneutic process designed to frame questions organized according to source-culture saliencies.

190

An important feature of emic phenomena is their inaccessibility to simple observation, which only reveals what properties an object or event possesses according to some theory already familiar to the observer, or what properties it symbolically expresses according to some symbol scheme familiar to the observer. Yet neither the theory nor the symbol system need be anything like the subject's, and it is the latter that, it is argued, must be recovered. For some, emic analysis is given a broad foundational role, and, it is argued, theoretical concepts and generalizations depend for their adequacy on their logical relations to emic concepts. Yet inaccessibility to observation is precisely what makes them prone to indeterminacy.

The alleged characteristics of emic analysis that I would like more closely to examine are as follows. It surely involves (1) the demand that the ethnographer develop or learn another symbol system, different from those familiar to anthropologists or to receptor-language speakers. This is required to account for the significance of source-language expressions or of any extralinguistic entities that are construed symbolically by source-language speakers. But it also typically involves more than this. It is usually taken to entail (2) that the symbol systems, meanings, rules, and so on of the source culture thus recovered be "really" those of its members. Further, it is said to entail (3) that these very source-culture notions be somehow used as explanatory constructs by the ethnographer. My view is that (1) is a reasonable demand but that (2) and (3), even though they rest on legitimate concerns for descriptive accuracy, are not. I see no basis for (2), and thus reject (3) since it presupposes (2). While I hold out some hope for notions of psychological reality or psychic unity that might breathe life into (2) and (3), I don't think success here is promised simply because translation and communication succeed. However, to reject (3) is not to reject emic methodologies, even those that place heavy emphasis on emic analysis. I think we can redefine such analyses in less mentalistic, more purely methodological ways: for example, in terms of the use by inquirers of expressions that *correctly translate* source-language expressions. (Of course "correct translation" is to be taken without any of the mentalistic commitments I have followed Quine in rejecting.) I think a similar account can be given of *implicit* emic notions (which lack clear source-language vehicles), but I will not deal with that more complex question here.

The discussion of item (1), which shall be the task of the rest of this section, will involve simply the question of what semantic devices are, in general, necessary for describing another symbol system, without broaching the issue of "whose" system the anthropologist may be said to be describing. Further, the discussion of (1) will supplement the arguments presented in the previous chapter insofar as the nominalistic austerity of the devices I shall suggest avoids questionable ontic commitments that might arise in the ethnographer's choice of a metalinguistic apparatus. I shall use the next section's reexamination of Goodenough to spell out my reconstruction of (3).

It is evident from the foregoing discussion of emics that those who counsel attentiveness to emic phenomena are making at least the minimal demand that one be aware of the fact that there are detectable differences (which might require careful scrutiny to reveal) between, on the one hand, the theories and other symbol systems that source-language speakers bring to bear on the world and on their own behavior and, on the other hand, those systems with which outsiders (nonsophisticates) are familiar. It is strongly insisted that those differences be accounted for by anthropologists rather than ignored or hedged. Now, in order to reveal these differences, the anthropologist must have the theoretical devices needed to describe other symbol schemes (presumably those of the native, but, again, I am not broaching that question right now). What might here shed light on some of these difficulties would be to indicate how the general semantic apparatus developed by Goodman in *Languages of Art* can suit these needs, while also avoiding the various "intension-difficulties" I have been discussing.

In Chapter 2 I briefly noted Goodenough's appeal to Morris' concepts of iconic and noniconic signs, signification, and so forth. Using these notions of Morris', Goodenough and others have sought to discover attributes, "cultural forms," and other items peculiar to the source cultures they study and thus, I have argued, are susceptible to the criticisms of Quine and others.[1] Goodman's apparatus has the advantage of being able to deal with a wider range of symbol systems. It accommodates (1) nonassertive as well as assertive systems, the former instanced by musical scores and maps, the latter by theories; (2) nondiscursive as well as discursive ones, instanced, respectively, by paintings and novels; and (3) nondenotational as well as denotational ones, respectively instanced by abstract and representational art. Despite this power and flexibility, the apparatus is fashioned so as to countenance talking of the symbolic relationships among symbols, labels, and objects, while avoiding ontic commitment to abstract entities such as attributes.[2]

Goodman develops a general notion of *reference* suitable to all the above-mentioned types of systems. It comprises *denotation* (which in some respects is similar to the homonymously indicated notion employed by Morris and Goodenough) as well as to two sorts of *exemplification*. Goodman's predicate 'x denotes y' is like more familiar notions insofar as x denotes y just in case x (a predicate or, somewhat more broadly, a label) is *true of* y (an object, person, another label, etc.), this latter fact determinable by, for example, the implication of this claim by acceptable scientific theory. Conversely, the object or person (a value of the y variable) is said to *comply* with the label that denotes it, or to be within its *compliance-class*, and the object is said to *possess* a property that the label (more platonistically) is associated with.[3] Goodman himself prefers to talk, ontologically more austerely, *not* of individual things and the properties or attributes "they possess" but rather of individuals and the (individual) predicates or labels that "are true of them." He uses 'possession' in these contexts as an eliminable concession to usages with which the probable majority of his readers are familiar. In any case, incorporation of these relations as thus far explicated will confer sufficient richness upon the ethnographer's metalanguage to describe source-language theories and contrast them with receptor-language formulations (once translational success is achieved).[4]

However, for Goodman mere possession of a property does not make an object a symbol, or confer on it a signifying relationship back to some property or label that is true of the object (though the term or label that denotes the object is, of course, thus functioning as a symbol and though the relationship of denotation running from such a term or label to the object is a symbolic relationship). Rather, such a denoted object itself functions as a symbol if there is some "backward" reference to the label true of it. In such cases, Goodman takes a relation he calls the *exemplification relation*, running from object to label, to be satisfied as it is determined by some type of system of rules of correlation. Scientific theories determine possession, that is, what characteristics an entity in fact possesses, but such theories do not of themselves determine exemplification:

> If possession is intrinsic, reference is not; and just which properties of a symbol are exemplified depends upon what particular system of symbolization is in effect.[5]

For example, a tailor's swatch exemplifies a certain fabric color owing to its function in a symbol system understood (usually tacitly) by tailors and customers. In cases of *literal* exemplification such as this, a necessary condition for the swatch's exemplifying a certain color (or more precisely a certain color-label) is that it possess that color. However, possession of certain properties is not sufficient for their exemplification. The sample swatch does not exemplify its shape, weight, or texture properties even though it "possesses" them just as much as it possesses the color properties it does exemplify (relative to the adopted tailor-customer system of symbols: that is, conventions, for samples, of "selective iconicity"). Of course it might exemplify shape, or weight, or texture under other symbol systems. For instance, a school teacher might use the very same swatch as a sample, or a representative, of the class of square things, placing it on his blackboard under an inscription of the exemplified label 'square'.[6]

Goodman also discusses a second type of exemplification, namely, *metaphorical* exemplification, or *expression*. The red swatch might serve to exemplify a label or property not literally but only metaphorically ascribable to it, such as 'simple minded'.[7] Of course the more typical application of the semantic notion "expression" is to works of art. These rarely denote, and interest in them typically involves what such works express more often than what they possess or even literally exemplify.[8]

Exemplificational reference, as Goodman applies this notion to nonassertive symbol systems such as those involved in works of art, is a "two-way" relationship in which a symbol exemplifies the labels that denote it while also "referring back" to those labels non-denotatively. If a depicted face *expresses* sadness (or the label 'sad'), then 'sad' in turn denotes the face. Exemplification of label (by, for example, some art work, which for Goodman is itself a symbol) always entails denotation of symbol by label. Meanwhile, labels may denote many things that are not symbols, which is to say they are not referential at all, and hence lack this "backward" reference from compliant to label.[9]

Again, the obvious advantages of such extended or amplified semantic notions of "reference," "compliance," and so on are that they provide the basis for a metalanguage powerful enough to describe the full range of symbol systems or, alternatively, the kinds of symbolic significance that might be operative in a source culture, in addition to those systems that embody only the natives' assertions about the world. The extended semantics could then be employed along with a translational metalanguage in giving accounts of different nonassertive symbol systems characteristic of foreign cultures, thus meeting desires we have seen expressed by symbolic anthropologists for a broader semiotic base. At the same time, it would preserve the advantages of the type of translational metalanguage I have suggested. For example, it helps keep semantic levels clear and helps avoid commitment to or reification of such abstract entities as propositions or attributes. The ethnographer might thus make the following sorts of claims: "This particular series of dance gestures denotatively refers to a historically famous intertribal war," or "This gesture expresses (exemplificationally refers metaphorically to) 'courage'," or "The gesture denoted by source-language expression *S* denotes or expresses such and such,"[10] or "The gesture denoted by *S* expresses a subtle feeling, to which the source term '-----' is applied and which is roughly translatable into English as 'alienation'," and so forth. It should be noted that in actual field manual entries such accounts of symbolic significance often do not involve either the *use* or the *mention* of source-language expressions, although of course a claim such as "The gesture *g* expresses 'courage'" would no doubt be in part supported by the fact that native ascriptions of a term best translated as 'courage' are held to be true of the gesture in question. One could thus also account for the discriminable differences between an uninitiated Westerner's interpretation of the same dance gesture as expressing 'fear', owing to the typical symbolic function of similar gestures in receptor culture contexts, and the native's quite different interpretation (which is what the ethnographer may here "be after").

Perhaps a more typical sort of application to these technical, semantical devices is to differences in the interpretation of "expressions" in the broader sense: for instance, when that which a Westerner would call a "smile" expresses, in the source society, anger instead of happiness.[11] Goodman's technical notion of "expression" involves metaphoric affection ascriptions and is probably not the suitable regimentation for the presystematic sense of 'express' that is employed in the preceding case. Rather, 'refers' ('denotes' or 'exemplifies') provides a precise and still rich enough interpretation, while further specificity is not required for the present context. Again, the minimal demand of emicists in this sort of case could be met: A good ethnography would contain a sentence such as "Smilelike gestures (which are denoted by source term '-----') refer to (signify, indicate, etc.) what is denoted by source term '.....', and elliptically a term best translated in English as the receptor term 'anger'"; or more simply and elliptically, "Smiles signify for the source speaker what English receptor speakers call 'anger'.'' Again, I am not suggesting that the ethnographer dispense with even more elliptical locutions such as 'Smiles express such and such' in, say, daily field work. What I am suggesting is a canonical form that keeps semantic levels, and theoretical implications, clear.

By making such claims as "The dance gesture expresses 'courage''' or "'-----' means 'ineffable''' or "Smiles signify anger,'' one is certainly making claims that have something to do with what is going on in the source society. The differences between what a symbol-vehicle might express to the sophisticate in contrast to the "outsider,'' or naive observer, requires explanation by recourse to *metalinguistic* descriptions of symbol systems. These systems differ from those familiar to the receptor-language speaker, yet these systems give the best available characterization of the ways in which source-language speakers conceptualize the world and themselves in their own language. The question now is whether one must, or indeed cogently can, additionally show that these "recovered'' systems, theories, and so on are *actually* those of the source culture. (Goodman has some views in this connection as well, and though he shares Quine's mentalistic attitude, we shall see that he offers a rather more explicitly pluralistic notion of "reality''—and by implication "social reality.'')

Componential Analysis: Neither God's Truth nor Hocus-Pocus

As I noted earlier, Goodenough views two features of emic analysis as being of paramount importance: the recovery of the source society's conceptions, and the employment of these as fundamental explanatory constructs. Moreover, in places he clearly avows a C. I. Lewis' style of mentalism. Here I would like to examine these points in more detail. I emphasize Goodenough for a number of reasons: (1) His methodological and theoretical positions have had a major formative impact on ethnoscience and, derivatively, Boasian approaches that have rebelled against it. His work establishes in a particularly clear way both the problems they seek to solve and, indeed, some of the aims they strive to achieve. (2) His general views on language and culture are sympathetic with those I develop here, although his mentalism must be tempered. This I shall try to achieve both by examining the tensions between him and critics such as Burling on the question of psychological reality, and by considering some of Goodenough's own less mentalistically committal remarks.

The task he seems to be setting for the field linguist is one of discovering the platonic attributes that characterize the native's conceptual scheme, and hopes to accomplish this task by reconditioning himself to discriminate stimulation patterns associated with native expressions in the way the native does. Indeed, as he characterizes it in a 1970 work, this task requires traffic in intension and mental imagery:

> Expressions do not denote things but images of things. Things serve as material representations of the images (or of concepts of them constructed in the act of perceiving them) and are *tokens* of the class of such images designated by the expression. The observer makes a record of his images of the material representations of his informants' images.[12]

Once a sizable record of such denotata has been made, the linguist-anthropologist, according to Goodenough, seeks to recover the defining attributes or components of these classes of denotata by determining complementary and contrastive distribution. He tells us that:

> In following the method, we make a record of the specific images or concepts that informants indicate an expression may denote. Our next task is to find a set of definitive attributes that will account for what informants have said may and may not be denoted by the expression and that, by the same token, predict what informants will say may be denoted by the expression in the future. We do this by a combination of two operations. One is to inspect the denotata, as we have recorded them, for common attributes. The other and more crucial operation is to contrast the set of the expression's denotata with sets of denotata of other expressions.[13]

It is worth noting at this point that accounts of the attributes thus determined, aside from being couched in the linguist's metalanguage (typically couched in the same natural language as the receptor language) and are also the result of examining not the native's reports of images or concepts, but the linguist's images.

In essence, componential analysis involves the determination of such denotata of expressions, and the determination of certain defining attributes that serve further to differentiate *sets* of denotata, initially differentiated by a large number of terms. A small set of components (predicates conjointly true of classes of denotata) will individuate the classes denoted by certain source-language expressions or their receptor-language equivalents, thus effecting at least *prima facie* a gain in systematic simplicity and force. (That is, definitions will be available, in the metalanguage of, for example, the various kinship terms, which use a small set of predicates designating components, which indicate just what component-predicates must be true of denotata in order for a kinship term to apply.)

Goodenough explains the function of components with respect to English kinship terms. The *metalinguistic* nature of components is quite clear here, as there is but one *object* language in question:

> The English kinship term *aunt* provides an example. As I use the term I would list for it such denotata as mother's sister, father's sister, mother's or father's half-sister, mother's brother's (or half-brother's) wife, father's brother's (or half-brother's) wife.[14] By performing the two operations indicated, we might arrive at the following componential definition of what *aunt* signifies: any relative by blood or marriage who is simultaneously A: female, B: two degrees of genealogical distance from ego, C: not lineal, D: in a senior generation, and E: not connected by a marital tie in other than the senior generation of the relationship. . . .In this way the several conceptually discrete or disjunctive denotata have been brought together in a conceptually unified or conjunctive set. They form a class or category that can be described as a product of the combination of the several definitive attributes. That they serve as definitive attributes in this case is evident from our observing that to vary any one of them results in a judgment that *aunt* is impermissible as a term of reference. Vary attribute A above (the relative's sex), and *uncle* becomes the appropriate term. *Great aunt* becomes appropriate if we vary B, *grandmother* if we vary C, *niece* if we vary D, and *wife's aunt* or *husband's aunt* if we vary E. In this way we can verify the adequacy of a componential definition.[15]

The evident systematic saving becomes clear when one considers that all other kin terms will be differentiable by reference to the finite set of kinship attributes listed earlier. The reputed ideational nature of these attributes is made clear in a subsequent passage:

> In the case of *aunt, uncle, nephew, niece,* and so on, the respective significata differ as functions of the common set of defining variables. The respective designata, moreover, are mutually exclusive and complementary. We seem to be dealing with some kind of conceptual or ideal space—call it a genealogical one—that has been partitioned into cells by a set of conditioning variables, each cell being represented by a

linguistic label. All the labels designating the complementary cells in a conceptual space (or domain, as it is frequently called) form an ordered array or terminological system, one in which the significatum of each label indicates in what respects its designatum differs from the designata of other labels.[16]

Indeed, the genealogical space thus determined is that of the *user* of these kinship terms, a point that holds equally in cases of radical translation as well. Yet the only test for the adequacy of our interpretation of them is that they yield correct predictions as to the applicability of source-language terms to objects. In fact, it seems that the only motive for this importation of questionable semantic elements is simply to allow others (speakers of the receptor language) to get along successfully in a society. In describing its culture, a linguist or ethnographer is endeavoring to

> formulate for the community he studies a set of standards that, taken
> as a guide for acting and interpreting the acts of others, leads to be-
> havior the community's members perceive as in accord with their ex-
> pectations of one another.[17]

It is this endeavor to allow the user of an ethnography or translation manual (recall Goodenough's parallel definitions of language and culture discussed in Chapter 2) that motivates Goodenough to delineate this special way of "describing" a culture, which is something more than simply "talking about" it:

> A science of culture rests on description. We have known this all
> along, to be sure. But we have tended to think of description as simply
> a matter of presenting the "objective" facts about a society, its or-
> ganization, law, customs, and shared beliefs in terms of the audience's
> culture and the audience's interests, as if that culture and those interests
> were all that are involved in depicting the objective facts about people
> who have different cultures and different interests. We have not been
> seriously concerned to understand what one has to know to behave ac-
> ceptably as a member of an Australian aboriginal tribe any more than
> zoologists have been seriously concerned, until very recently, to know
> how to behave acceptably as an ostrich. We wanted to know *about*
> other societies, not how to be competent in the things their members
> are expected to be competent in. Our best ethnographies were, to be
> sure, coming from people whose interests and circumstances led them
> to want to know how to operate successfully with people in other
> societies on their terms or, at least, to communicate with them com-

petently about their activities and beliefs in their language. . . . But none thought of himself as writing a "how-to-do-it" book.[18]

The evident assumption here is that in order to learn how to get along (act competently) in a society, one must "recover" that society's conceptual scheme. Indeed, recovery of the scheme seems both a necessary and sufficient condition of being able to get along. That it is reasonable or cogent to demand this as a *necessary* condition is of course challenged by the problems, delineated above, of the availability of seemingly equally good alternatives, and divergent answers, generating the problems of determining "cognitive validity," and so on for such schemes. Something more than predictive success and elegance of formulation seems required to assure that the "real" scheme is recovered. Yet these are all the criteria that Goodenough offers, and it is not clear what additional criteria one could demand.

Goodenough's insistence that "emic primitives" be sought and used in explaining a culture seems to embody a somewhat different claim than that concerning the cognitive validity of componential analysis in accurately representing, say, the "genealogical space" of the source culture. Components are not in themselves emic at all, given Goodenough's construal of 'emic' as 'culture-specific', as they are applicable cross-culturally (as is clearly evidenced by the kinship components that Goodenough frequently employs). As such they are *etic* notions, belonging to the ethnographer's metalinguistic apparatus. Goodenough refers to his studies of the Trukese (in 1947-1948) to exemplify his methodological use of emic concepts,[19] and although componential analysis figures as part of this study,[20] the bulk of it, and clearly those sections that Goodenough takes to exemplify the present point, involves a more radical thesis regarding foundational reliance on emic notions.

Goodenough remarks on the divergent conclusions regarding residence rules on Truk obtained by him and another investigator (John Fischer):[21]

> The cause of our differences was our different conceptions of the objects of residential choice as the Trukese perceived them. Our different cultures for Truk led to different pictures of the prevailing social structure. To start with the objects of choice as the Trukese perceived them, as they are defined by the standards of Trukese culture, results in a different structure from one arrived at by projecting on them one's own folk culture, or the categories of one's own professional anthropological culture.[22]

Among these emic notions are certain kinds of titles ("divided ownership," "residual title," "provisional title") that divide the powers, rights, and duties of ownership asymmetrically between the two parties to the title, and the recognition of corporate individuals as eligible parties to such ownership.[23]

As in the case of the linguist learning to make new phonemic discriminations of heard sounds, the linguist and ethnographer must learn new syntactical notions:

> As we learn new principles of syntactic order, we add to the kit of possibilities. The more languages we study, the less we find it necessary to add to the kit. Systematization of its contents, of the many different principles of syntactic order we have encountered in specific languages, lays the foundations for a general theory of syntax.[24]

Further, they must be ready to see new relationships between semantic domains (here, those of kinship and property). The study of kinship on Truk in particular demanded careful attention to certain emic conceptions of property peculiar to the Trukese:[25]

> When I tried to prepare an account of the workings of Truk's social organization . . . , I found that I could not satisfactorily describe kinship terminology without having first described kin-group organization. Membership in kin groups was one of the considerations that made sense of the way Truk's people classified kin relationships. And I could not describe kin-group organization without having first described how property worked. The most important kind of kin group was a property-holding corporation. So my description began with the several property transactions and the resulting forms of entitlement that Truk's rules of the social game allowed. Definition of the descent groups could then be made in terms of these forms of entitlement, and so on. Thus I tried to build up an account of the culture of the social organization of Truk from a set of what seemed to me to be elementary or primitive concepts in Trukese culture.[26]

However, careful attention to emics in Goodenough's view has another advantage from the standpoint of the *anthropological* "culture":

> The concepts I developed for Truk proved helpful to Oliver (1953) in conceptualizing and describing the culture of property relations among the Siuai of Bougainville. The notions of "divided ownership," "residual title," and "provisional title" were now a part of the etic kit of possibilities available to Oliver for describing how things worked among the Siuai.[27]

Insofar as initially emic conceptions become applicable in other cultures, they become etic (recall that cultural specifity is the essential characteristic of the emic for Goodenough). In general, in order to get along or to enable the users of their ethnographies or translation manuals to get along in an increasing range of alien cultures, anthropologists must widen their capacity to conceptualize social structures, semantic fields, grammatical and syntactical possibilities, and so on:

> As others continue to meet new ways of discriminating among transactions and forms of entitlement in other cultures, they will continue to add to our knowledge of possibilities. In time, we shall be able to give order to the ideas we have had to develop to describe the elementary emic forms in a large sample of the world's cultures. In ordering these ideas, we shall isolate the considerations with which human beings tend to organize their property relations and shall lay the foundations for a general theory of property that will account for the variance among cultures in the way they employ these considerations. Such theory, it is now clear, depends on the development of a satisfactory etics of property relations, and this latter development depends on our doing many good emic descriptions of particular property systems.[28]

Now I earlier raised qualms about Goodenough's defining 'emic' as 'unique to a culture'. Once a conception is recovered, it goes into the "etic kit," but seems to remain emic until it is successfully applied somewhere else. However, as I remarked earlier, this seems to equate 'emic' with 'untranslatable'. For successful translation would seem to imply that the concept in question is shared by source- and receptor-language speakers. Even if it is only expressible with a metalanguage homologue of the source-language term, its coherent usage in the metalanguage similarly implies translatability. If not, that is, if it is insisted that the emic concept never receive full articulation, then giving emic concepts foundational roles seems subject to concerns raised by Harris. It introduces conceptual vagueness at a pivotal systematic point.

At any rate, Goodenough's discussions of Trukese emic concepts don't seem to have this feature. Moreover, a second look at his aims suggests an evaporation of this problem along with other symptoms of mentalism. What we finally have to say, I think, is that the emic is more thoroughly imbued with the etic than is captured even by Goodenough's and others' insistence that these are intimately interdependent notions. In light of the indeterminacy problems we have considered, we simply have no warrant for believing that any concept expressed in the receptor language or the metalanguage is emic in the senses typically employed.

Goodenough's main concern is that careful attention be given to radically different cultures so as to reveal behaviorally scrutable differences in these sorts of organizations of verbal and nonverbal behavior. But, again, the only test of the anthropologist's componential analyses is in its effecting maximal coordination of activity among manual users and source-society members. There seems no evident reason why these structures should also be regarded as the "real" ones used by the native. Indeed, Goodenough seems at least partially aware of this in the following passage:

> The combinations of rights that characterize Trukese forms of entitlement are not precisely like those with which an English-speaking audience is familiar. Such English expressions as "fee simple," "sale," "rental," and "ownership" could not serve in their English senses as useful terms for describing property of Truk. To be satisfactory, my account had to exhaust the forms of entitlement and the kinds of transaction that were meaningfully distinct for the people of Truk; and the labels I used for them in my description had to be defined in terms of *whatever criteria enabled me to distinguish among the entitlements and transactions in a manner consistent with the distinctions the people of Truk seemed to be making.* (emphasis mine)[29]

The weakened claim that the components enable one to make distinctions in a manner consistent with those made by the Trukese does not seem to go as far as saying that these "primitives" be those actually used by the Trukese. In order to see this, let us first look more closely at the way in which the aforementioned "emic primitives" are employed by Goodenough in his study of Truk.

According to Goodenough, once one has "isolated and defined the primitive elements [of a culture], one goes on to describe the rest of the culture in terms of them and their relative products," in the hope of "tak[ing] one's audience into the culture of another people and allow[ing] it to experience that culture and to learn something of it from the insider's (the sophisticate's) point of view." In order to achieve these goals with respect to the Trukese (source) and English-speaking (receptor) cultures, this demanded that the "primitive" notions related to property-holding be characterized first. In particular, a proper discussion of the social relationships among kinsmen demanded prior delineation of property relations. Goodenough had first to define, and characterize, the various reciprocal rights, responsibilities, duties, and so on of members of the "corporation," which are "a property-holding group . . . composed fundamentally of [matrilineally related] siblings." An understanding of the variation in affective bonding among kinsmen, or of certain variations in kinship ascriptions, is impossible without recognition that certain important kin groups in certain societies are equally corporate property owners. For example, "a mother's brother is classed as an "older brother" in his position as a senior member of one's corporation, but as an individual kinsman he is classed as a "father."[30]

Also, following this genetic line of explanation enables Goodenough to account for the inheritance of corporate property by children, grouped under a single kin term, 'jefekyr', which does not respect individual parentage because their common "parent" *is* the corporation. They are its "heirs" (and this is the receptor-language term that Goodenough offers as the best translation of 'jefekyr'). Goodenough's explanations of the notion of "heir" as well as certain of the important social relationships of heirs on Truk I think clearly exemplify Goodenough's "employment" of Trukese concepts in ethnographic explanation:

> The jefekyr . . .are the children of the men of a matrilineal corporation, and as such are considered the children of the corporation itself. . . . Perhaps the best translation of the jefekyr is "heir". It will be recalled that when a corporation's membership becomes extinct, it is the jefekyr, the children, of the corporation who are its natural heirs. Thus when a person says he is an Jacaw man and an jefekyr of the Pwereka, he not only says that his mother was Jacaw and his father was Pwereka, but indicates that he is a member of an Jacaw corporation and an heir to a Pwereka corporation should the latter's memberships die out.[31]

'Corporation' could be construed either as a metalinguistic term being used, or a receptor-language term being mentioned (it is not the translation of any Trukese expression, even though there is a Trukese term for the kin group that comprises a corporation, which Goodenough translates as 'lineage').[32] It does not involve the use of a native expression, nor does it require understanding concepts foreign to most English-speaking Westerners. The point is simply that an English-speaking reader of Goodenough's ethnography will have a neat and coherent account of Trukese behavior—will thus better understand that behavior—if he realizes that kin group members on Truk relate to one another not only as kin in ways familiar to the Westerner but also as corporate colleagues. And although he is familiar with both sorts of practice, he is not accustomed to seeing them overlap in this way.

However, does achieving this aim carry the further implication that adequacy to such descriptive tasks requires using or capturing the Trukese concept? From the standpoint of the form of the account itself, there is no need to insist that the ethnographer *use* any source-language terms applicable to any of their concepts, thereby incurring spurious concerns as whether and how their concept, expressed in their language, became transmitted to the receptor-language speaker, enabling its description in the latter's terms. Goodenough only *seems* to be using Trukese terms because he chooses only to underscore, but not to set in mention-quotes, the term 'jefekyr', and he is incorporating it in sentences containing English words; these sentences also obscure the differences between the *ethnographer's metalanguage* (which we might call anthropologese) and the receptor language. He thus creates the impression that Trukese concepts are absorbed, in successful ethnography, into the English language or into the heads of English speakers. Yet his explanations will preserve all their explanatory power and meet all the cogent criteria of adequacy an ethnographer could demand, while being couched in a canonical form that keeps clear the distinctions between the meta- and object-languages and avoids the problems of intension sketched above, as well as difficulties noted within the anthropological community. According to this canonical form, the first sentence of the above-quoted paragraph could read as follows:

> Persons in the compliance class of the source term 'jefekyr' are the children of men of a matrilineal corporation, and are considered the children of the corporation;

and the second sentence could read:

> 'Jefekyr' in the source language is best translated as 'heir' in the receptor language.

These two construals pay minimal attention to differences between the receptor language and the metalanguage, something one can perhaps afford to do when the receptor-language speaker is perfectly capable of understanding the metalanguage, and hence the constructor of the metalanguage can adopt receptor-language expressions at will into the part of that language that refers to the objects to which the expressions it mentions refer. A sparser metalanguage might necessitate a somewhat more complicated construal of the first sentence, such as:

> The persons in the compliance class of the source term 'jefekyr', who bear a relation, best translated as 'child of' to persons who comply with a source term best translated as 'father', also bear that relation to an entity best characterized as 'corporation' because the persons to whom they bear that relation belong to that entity.

The need for such complication might not be evident where meta- and receptor-language are couched in the same natural language, but they need not be. Or there may be evident distinctions between metalinguistic notions (from the "anthropological culture") and receptor-language notions (such as seem manifest with technical terms that describe genealogical components), which the canonical form could reflect. Its application should be as general as necessary. Again, these canonical reformulations are not being offered as replacements of statements in field notes or in published ethnographies, but simply as exemplifications of a translation procedure that can clarify the ontic commitments, theoretical implications, and so on of statements actually employed, as the need for clarification arises.

One case in which this need might arise occurs when an ethnographer begins to worry about how he knows a successful and informative manual of translation and ethnography actually captures the meanings, or the cognitive structures underlying the meaning, of native discourse. The worry might in part be dissipated by showing, through canonical translation, that explanatory statements need never *use* a source-language expression, and hence understanding of such sentences does not require that one "reproduce" any corresponding source-culture concept. Rather, the conceptual apparatus required to understand the apparatus is whatever is required to understand the natural language (including some technical notions) in which the *explanatory metalanguage* is couched (as well as, in many cases, the natural language in which the receptor language is couched, and this might require mastery of a second natural language).[33] What need is there then to worry whether one has grasped a concept or attribute identical to one the source-language speaker grasps?

The argument would be further supported by consideration of the philosophical points that motivate the choice of canonical idiom. After all, if the goal and test of the ethnography or translation manual is simply its enabling receptor-society members initially unfamiliar with the source society to get along efficiently with members of the latter, what need is there to worry about the fact that alternative formulations would equally meet all the cogent criteria of adequacy?

But more to the point, if we consider, as I have argued, the very *purposes* of translation manuals, we see that by their very nature they are in part conditioned by the needs of the receptor-language speakers. But this means that they cannot possibly achieve the task of intercultural coordination, while at the same time giving a warranted account of what is going on "inside" the source culture, in isolation from other cultures. So much of the manual of translation is determined by the explicit codifications of usage among speakers of the receptor language (as well as of "anthropologese"), that it makes no sense to ask that the manual come to capture the native's "inner meanings" as well.[34] All the empirical and formal criteria of adequacy that one could demand of it necessarily involve its successful and maximally efficient employment by "outsiders" to the source culture. It is written by and for them. The ethnographer, *qua* ethnographer, is a collective bargaining agent, out to best coordinate the interests of members of two cultures, in keeping with the established procedures of his own anthropological culture. Of course anyone, including the ethnographer, can use the manual and ethnography as a stepping-stone to becoming a fully participating member of the source culture, perhaps fully abandoning his former life. This is quite possible, but it is not the task of an ethnography to *reproduce* this process; its task is to say useful things to receptor- and metalanguage speakers who have some interest in the source society's doings.[35]

If one agrees with Goodenough that in doing ethnography one is *taking one's* (receptor-culture and anthropological) *audience into the source culture* and telling the members of that audience what they have to know in order to get along in the source culture, then I think one must disagree with him that one is thus also telling the audience what the source-language speakers' concepts really are. What the members of the audience learn about Truk is better expressed as follows: If we interacted with one another as they evidently do and if we divided up the extension of our property terms and kin terms in the ways prescribed by our translation manual, we would have to modify our kinship and property terms by incorporating such terms as 'divided ownership' and 'residual title' into our language. We would have to regard our (mother's) brothers as somewhat more than kin.

This reconstrual of Goodenough, as has been seen, takes seriously certain of his foundational considerations (that is, his views on language and culture) and draws consequences from them that are quite divergent from other theses he has vigorously defended. Thus, despite the important compatibilities between his position and mine, the remaining differences are significant. I have tried to indicate why my prescriptive characterization of translational correlations is more plausible, and I have presented a number of other considerations against Goodenough's related "ethnoscientific" thesis that emic notions like the Trukese "corporation" be *used* by the ethnographer, as his ultimate means of avoiding ethnocentric bias and distortion. However, Goodenough's positions, taken together, produce paradoxical results that have fueled a good deal of criticism, as I have indicated. To the degree that my reconstruction avoids problems and paradoxes, I believe it is correspondingly justified. And the resolution of the paradoxes of Goodenough's earlier position depends, I think, on the selective pruning of a set of assumptions that have turned out, in the long run, to be mutually incompatible. (Also, success in the resolution of paradox speaks, I think, for the adequacy of the metalanguage-object-language distinction to which I have adhered, and which is regarded as problematic in some philosophical circles; in *this* context of application, at least, I think such adherence is helpful.)

The paradoxical tensions in Goodenough's position are brought to the surface in a 1971 critique of his study of Truk by Glynn Cochrane, which I should like to briefly consider here in hopes of resolving some of the issues between them by reference to the reconstrual of Goodenough I have given. Cochrane argues that Goodenough's concept of the Trukese "corporation" introduces the very ethnographic bias that he seeks, by its employment, to avoid. In the process of drawing on certain purported similarities between Anglo-American and Trukese institutions, he argues, certain significant differences between the associated rules and behavior patterns of the respective societies are overlooked:

> The Trukese lineage is not corporate; it is not perpetual, and it has heirs . . . ; it has no individual personality of its own apart from members of a lineage; "its" existence has not been conceptualized by the Trukese as anything other than a group of people. Goodenough's claim that "corporateness" exists in Trukese as well as in western law is not valid; the result of this imposition, having little empirical fit with reality, can only have distorted the nature of Trukese property relations.[36]

Given Goodenough's ethnoscientific theses to the effect that he must get at underlying semantic structures in the process of "learning to get along," and that eliciting operations are so essential to this, and the *source*-language concept must be used (and not simply mentioned) by the ethnographer, these sorts of criticisms are understandable and, to a degree, well-aimed. For if one takes these aims seriously, then the significant differences that Cochrane notes between the Trukese and Anglo-American concepts seem fatal to these aims. Yet if we take seriously Quine's suspicions concerning the possibility of this, in light of the seeming need to impose in order to say anything *intelligible to* an Anglo-American about a Trukese (much less to compare their respective practices), then the force of these objections is diminished. Goodenough's emic conceptions seemed at first, I would say, in fairly stable reflective equilibrium with the combined interpretive and related practices of source, receptor, and anthropological communities. Cochrane's objections served to introduce evident instability by showing deviations from Trukese and Western practices. Cochrane does not show a thorough descriptive failure on Goodenough's part, nor does he invalidate Goodenough's emic methodology (whether this was his intention or not). To take them this strongly is to presuppose an unjustifiable interpretive determinacy.

If I am correct, the "distortion" involved in applying the notion of a "corporation" (indeed, in *using* it in ethnography) is neither surprising nor problematic. It is simply a species of the "distortion" that attends any technical redefinition of a scientific term. One draws on some ordinary-language or scientific "background" usage, striving to keep some minimal similarity between technical and ordinary usage. But given the new context of application, with its differing purposes and demands (say the rigorous clarity a term adapted from ordinary-language usage will typically have to be *given* in application to a scientific context), distortion is to be expected. Thus, we need only demand that there are *some* evident similarities between the respective institutional practices of the two societies in question. "Distortion-free reproduction" is not to be demanded, because it is impossible, and the demand manifests, I have argued, a fundamental misunderstanding of the task of translation.

This is not to say that Goodenough cannot then go wrong in attributing "corporate" practices to the Trukese. Indeed, Cochrane also accuses him of misleading manual users, inhibiting historical research (by leading us to ignore differences in detail), and making full understanding of Trukese ownership difficult (by the use of a concept that makes explanation awkward and that creates conceptual puzzles).[37] These purported pragmatic drawbacks cannot be overlooked. What can be overlooked are the considerations that rest on the purported ability of some other account, such as Cochrane's, to better "reflect" some sort of "emic reality." The fundamental mistake is to think that there is an abstract object—a fixed, emic Anglo-American concept—embodied in some English expression, which is identical to the concept embodied somehow in a Trukese expression or some other behavior (whether the concept be that of the "corporation" or whatever Cochrane would prefer). Cochrane seems to maintain this in charging that Goodenough "ossifies the past" in thus applying this concept. And Goodenough correctly replies that the notion of a "corporation" even in Anglo-American usage is not fixed and that the Trukese social entity need only have certain features in common with the Anglo-American one in order to serve as an enlightening ethnographic notion.[38] This Wittgensteinian stance brings Goodenough's account very much in line with my reconstruction, despite the aforementioned divergences: For the variations between *ordinary* Anglo-American usage and *technical* Anglo-American usage, and variations among the various technical usages, are precisely the result, I argue, of the differing purposes and requirements of these varying contexts of application. Differing purposes and requirements change the conditions of the coordination equilibrium in various ways and call for the development (consciously or unconsciously) of differing linguistic conventions. And what is introduced by Goodenough's study of Truk is yet a *further* technical application of the notion of a "corporation" to a new context in anthropological, rather than Anglo-American legal, practice—a practice with its own demands and its own attendant "distortions" of usage.

I think Goodenough's aims continue to have legitimacy. But I advocate modifying his mentalism, as he suggests we should in saying we must probe "what, for lack of a better term, we must call the minds of our fellow men."[39] It is not that I prefer relocating intensional objects in the public sphere (indeed, this remark doesn't necessarily rule this out), but that I allow, with Quine, continued talk about minds and intensions—but only as a verbal convenience. To take minds and meanings too seriously, that is, objectually, simply invites confusion. And if one is to take such a mentalistic step, it should be taken cautiously and with more to support it than the point that translation and communication proceed successfully.

Evidently, my position approximates more to the "hocus-pocus" account of Burling—one which, as I noted earlier, stems from much the same sorts of concerns as Quine's indeterminacy thesis. And the result of his reflections, as with Quine, is a skepticism about the resolvability of the basic Whorfian puzzle around which so much language-and-culture methodology revolves: "The language patterns were there to be sure," Burling notes in reference to the taxonomic analyses he criticizes, "but how, except through intuition, could one tell whether the patterns corresponded to anything else?" His conclusion, it will be recalled, is that structural semantics provides no additional insight into human cognition, though it is still of value in enabling predictions of term use, in facilitating language-learning, and in enabling effective behavior within the source society by an outsider.[40] Similar sentiments are expressed by Floyd Lounsbury in his 1956 study of Pawnee kinship usage in which he argues that "an anthropologist uses semantic analysis of a society's kinship terminology only as a tool for getting at the structure of non-linguistic behavior within the family and kindred of that society."[41]

However, although my position is far more sympathetic to Burling in these regards than to Goodenough's, there are important differences. I believe I offer a more satisfactory explanation of the special problems of structural semantics than Burling's (or Quine's). Burling, like Quine, treats translational correlations as descriptive hypotheses that are somehow "defective," and this carries with it, if only by rough implication, an attitude that those social science theories that rest in one way or another on interpretation are scientifically deficient, or perhaps methodologically divergent. But if my analysis is correct, neither deficiency nor divergence follows so immediately (not that there might not be *other* pertinent considerations), if translations are viewed as prescriptive formulations, akin to technical definitions, designed to facilitate intercultural communication and interaction as well as anthropological theory-building. Also, I am not quite as convinced as Burling seems to be that psychological reality is an empty notion. As I pointed out in the latter part of Chapter 4, modified, pragmatic attitudes toward this notion are accommodated by my reconstruction.

Recent Pragmatic Trends

Consideration of Burling leads naturally to other pragmatic strains in Boasian anthropology. At the end of Chapter 2, I noted several efforts to reconsider the aims of cognitive approaches in light of pragmatist orientations to science in general. Insofar as these involve redefining key aspects of the notion of scientific objectivity, they differ in essentially the way that I have with Burling's "hocus-pocus" attitude. When I first discussed them, my concern was to reveal the tensions between these attitudes and various emic aims, by way of establishing a setting for Quine's indeterminacy thesis. I like now to reconsider some of these positions, to see how they fare in light of my reconstructive efforts.

One broad range of foundational issues to which pragmatic responses have been given recently are those concerning the comparativist as opposed to the relativist or descriptivist character of anthropological inquiry: that is, as to whether anthropological inquiry should be geared to cross-cultural comparison or to careful culture-by-culture study. Typically the methodological wars of the past over this issue have hinged on competing metaphysical premises to the effect, roughly, that cultures are or are not sufficiently alike to warrant comparative study (if not, then comparative studies are based on illusory comparisons resulting from distorting one's picture of individual cultures). However, a number of recent review articles have approached the question in different ways, that is, replacing these sorts of potentially empirical, question-begging, metaphysical claims with pragmatic considerations. An important goal has been to transform these issues from *a priori* to *a posteriori* ones.

On a related point, Carol Ember criticizes the relativist view in ethnoscience for its resultant inhibition of theory-formation: Insofar as cultural descriptions are framed in ways that prohibit applying descriptive terminology to other cultures, she argues, intercultural comparison and, indeed, theories *of culture* are inhibited. (In this last regard her view is reminiscent of Marvin Harris's critique of "cultural idealism.") She favors the comparative view on the pragmatic grounds that "the finding of differences is thought-provoking and leads to more questions and more research, *even if the interpretations of those differences are faulty.*" (emphasis hers)[42] The value of comparison in anthropology and of the concepts and theories that enable it, she contends, is to be supported in these terms and not on *a priori* metaphysical grounds, as the latter amounts to settling open empirical questions by fiat. Comparativism's pragmatic advantages are evidenced, she argues, in the aforementioned study of color terms by Berlin and Kay:

> The Berlin and Kay . . . formulation of a theory about why different societies encode color in different ways provides a very striking example of how productive the formulation of a theory (with some supportive data) can be. Not only did it generate criticism, it also generated further testing . . . , speculation as to how societal com-

plexity might exert its effect . . . , and an alternative psychophysical hypothesis.[43]

The heuristic value of theoretical hypotheses is certainly not a newly developed desideratum in anthropology. What is significant here is the primacy it is given and particularly its displacement of *a priori* considerations (much in the naturalistic spirit of Quine's philosophy, it would seem). A pragmatic-empiricist attitude is expressed here that is significantly reminiscent of a pragmatist dictum of Goodman that "there are many ways the world is" and that scientific "chatter," encouraged by a plurality of paradigms, is a desirable state of affairs.[44]

In a related review article, Christie Kiefer counsels pragmatism with respect to closely related issues of psychological anthropology. She stresses a point often made by Goodman (and intimately related to his "many worlds" thesis) that similarity and difference are not "givens" in (here, cultural) phenomena but are relative to theoretical purpose:

> The usefulness of the concept [of similarity] is determined by the importance of the differences, which is to say by the interest of an observer in them. Things devoid of differences in moral, aesthetic, or practical values are "are all the same.". . . If we are confronted with, say, the contents of a Mexican *mercado* and asked to group them by similarity, the first question we must ask is "For what?" The same question applies to the classification of human acts. Are a bullfight, Hesiod's Theogony, a Japanese High School exam, and playing the dozens in Harlem variations on a single Oedipal theme, are they microcosmic models of the social organization and values of their inventors, or both or neither? The only conceivable answer to such questions must refer to the *use* of the analysis. It does not help to say that one analysis or the other explains the facts more thoroughly, because the interest of the observer determines what facts are relevant and what constitutes an explanation.[45]

Kiefer cites a number of major philosophical critics (including Wittgenstein) of "the unproductive positivist position that there are truths 'out there' which must be described by a purely logical mind," defending her pragmatic view of things on the further grounds that it opens communication among inquirers, frees lines of research, and has positive effects on teaching.[46]

Earlier I also noted a similar attitude expressed by Peter Caws with respect to structuralism. A review of this, as well as of the objections I noted by F. Allen Hanson, will help to dispel lingering worries that the ''homewardliness'' of pragmatic, inquirer-oriented considerations turn attention too much in the wrong direction.

Operative here is a kind of pragmatic or what Hilary Putnam terms an ''internal'' realism reminiscent of Quine's toward physical posits. What I am considering is the feasibility of combining the following points: (1) I want to follow semantic antirealists like Burling and Quine in shifting the locus of key explanatory constructs—into the inquirer's *metalanguage*, I prefer to say, rather than (with Burling and Harris) the inquirer's *head*. (2) Yet I wish to regard emicly focused ethnographical and ethnological systematizations that result as yielding objectively determinate results; that is, accounts *of the ethnographic subject's system*. (3) However, I wish to do this without making any ontic commitment to the existence of semantic constructs such as components. Quine is what we might term an ''eliminative antirealist'' with respect to semantic posits, though a realist with respect to any posits not affected by translational indeterminacy. My own view is something more of a *constructive* semantic antirealism, diverging from Burling mainly in being more thoroughgoing: The sense of loss connoted by ''hocus-pocus'' is diminished by revising notions integral to interpretive objectivity itself. However, I have sympathies also, as I shall elaborate later, with Goodman's ''irrealism,'' which seeks a middle ground between realism and antirealism. (It is hard to label matters precisely, as semantic varieties of irrealism have not, to my knowledge, been clearly articulated in any literature.) But whatever their exact nature, the various pragmatic theses with which I have expressed sympathy must confront the antithetical thrust of Quine's pragmatism. How can we warrantably or coherently describe aspects of the source culture when notions of similarity and difference are admittedly parochial?[47]

This is a loose formulation of the problem, to be sure, and it embraces a wide range of criticisms (themselves of widely varying clarity and cogency), but I think it adequately indicates their general character. Here I would like to indicate how my thesis pertains to and serves to some degree to resolve them—although more fully satisfying solutions hinge on solutions to deeper and perhaps more intractable problems concerning the realistic interpretation of theoretical entities, and so on, which I cannot deal with fully here. The debate between Caws and Hanson will, I hope, be seen to typify a wider range of related problems in cognitive anthropology.

In "Operational, Representational, and Explanatory Models," Caws criticizes Levi-Strauss and other structural anthropologists for their equation of their explanatory model of native behavior with the native's own—a problem that, as we saw in Chapter 2, is particularly exacerbated by Quine's indeterminacy problem and that has a number of analogues in other areas. Caws draws a tripartite distinction between (1) the "operational" model of the native, that is, that which is implicit in his behavior (and which may or may not be characterized as an unconscious entity exemplified in that behavior); (2) the "representational" model of the native, or that of which he is conscious and which will be expressed verbally (to varying degrees of systematization, depending on the degree of verbal codification within the society); and (3) the anthropologist's own representational, or "explanatory," model.[48] The burden of Caws's arguments is to show that the explanatory model is not identical to either of the native models (the conscious or the unconscious one) and to discuss some of the underlying philosophical perplexities and confusions that induce us to regard them as identical. In the context of discussing these latter points, Caws defends a pragmatic conception of the character of anthropological theoretical structures that shall be my main concern here.

Caws's concerns have notable affinities with Quine's. Caws contends that it is the very "supraempirical" character of these models that is the cause of confusions of one model with another. This character derives from the underdetermination of these models by data and from the fact that the theoretical explanatory model is constructed with intercultural comparison in mind (its power to make such comparisons being, in his view, its main virtue).[49] He challenges the view that this mental structure, which is "in the anthropologist's head," must be in some way identical with what is in subject's unconscious—citing considerations parallel to Quine's *Word and Object* remarks concerning the intensionalist assumption that mental uniformity necessarily underlies linguistic uniformity:

> There is no reason to suppose that any two members of the group [being studied] have identical or even similar mental structure; the ontogeny of the brain, in fact, makes it virtually certain that they will not.[50]

However, his main argument stems from his view of the character of social theory. First, he expresses sentiments reminiscent of Ember and Kiefer in praising Levi-Strauss' work *primarily* for its richness of cross-cultural implications. However, unlike Levi-Strauss and many of his followers, this is not viewed as a secondary desideratum subordinate to the accurate reflection of unconscious cognitive structures. (Caws here parallels Marvin Harris.) Scientific theory in this regard (and in general) "has as one of its chief tasks the 'rectification of experience' and it does this precisely by enlarging the scope of theoretical understanding." Indeed, the very notion of "objectivity," typically—and loosely—construed as a kind of matching of theory to fact, is viewed instead by him in terms of the comprehensiveness of the containing analytic framework.[51]

In keeping with these views, Caws argues that in social science the underlying operational model is *not* recoverable, and certainly not warrantably identifiable with the explanatory model. Rather,

> in the social sciences it is often the case that final authority rests with the representational model which becomes part of the empirical data for the investigator. But as we have seen, that does not yield the objective social structure, which is adequately represented neither by the representational nor by the operational models found in the society under scrutiny. It is in the scientist's representational (i.e., explanatory) model, the theory he constructs to account for the data and their interrelation that confers objective structure on the system. And the use of "confer" is deliberate, since it would be quite accurate to say that until the explanatory model was constructed the system had no objective structure.[52]

This passage, particularly its concluding assertion, is sure to bring contrary intuitions to the surface. Given the way Caws regards theorizing and objectivity, this claim seems clearly to follow. However, the implication drawn in this passage contrasts sharply with the widely accepted premise that imposition of the familiar makes for poor interpretation. And, again, as with the views noted in the previous section (and, indeed, more so) Caws's view goes well beyond the hocus-pocus view insofar as he speaks of actually conferring objective, not fictional, structure.

Aside from this, potential problems of internal incoherence threaten in remarks to the effect that "the explanatory model has to take account not only of the empirical data but of the relations that hold between these and the operational and representational models in those heads, and failure to do this will inevitably result in misunderstanding of the data."[53] The problem here, in essence, is that it is not clear how one can "take account" of the relations that hold among things in the ethnographic subjects' heads given the "homeward thrust" of the inquirer's explanatory model. How can it do anything more than simply "fit the data"? If it is correct to reject the reproductive extreme seemingly advocated at times by Levi-Strauss, how is it that any sort of reproduction or recovery of such relations can be warranted. In other words, why isn't the opposing etic extreme position the correct one here?

Although the full thrust of Caws's view is not clear to me, these passages suggest some commitment to a realist construal of the product of translation. And as I have argued in connection with Goodenough above, I don't think this can be cogently given with regard to many ethnographic products. However, I do think my view gives some sense to the demand that the ethnographer's systematization "take account" of native structures as well as data. And, as has been seen, it is an account that does agree with Caws's contention that the distinguishing mark of the social sciences is their concern with "mind-dependent" entities. But the imposition and multiplicity problems make it problematic whether one can say that for *this* reason the social sciences are different in logical character from the natural sciences, as opposed to the more extreme contention that this difference makes them different in the sense of not being sciences at all (or being "scientific" only some of the time).[54] A critic who would prefer to read "objective" as something like "corresponding to something out there" could well accuse Caws of offering an ersatz objectivity through deliberate misuse of language. These "internal realists" might, to the critical eye, find themselves in the position of the man in the joke that concludes Woody Allen's "Annie Hall": When asked why he won't commit his brother, though the latter insanely believes himself to be a chicken, he replies, "Because I need the eggs.") Now while I cannot attend to all the problems that bolster these sorts of criticisms, I think headway toward their resolution is afforded by my foregoing discussion.

Worries of this type are voiced in Hanson's critical commentary on Caws. I noted these earlier, but let me review them now in Hanson's own terms. He agrees that "the relations studied by social science are mind-dependent"; namely, "while natural relations such as between the moon and the tides exist and operate whether men know about them or not, social or cultural relations can be nothing other than what they are construed by men to be." However, Hanson views Caws's account as distorting the implications of this and, indeed, imputes to his position a number of absurd implications: (1) that "a kinship system described by an anthropologist as Crow or

Omaha objectively has a skewing effect in the terms for cross cousins while an identical system which has never benefited from anthropological description and analysis does not"; (2) that "if a social system were *mis*described by an anthropologist . . .that system [would] then objectively 'have' a structure which is *wrong* for it"; and (3) that if "the objective structures we study depend for their existence upon our models of them . . . , this means that, in such cases, the model would have to exist prior to the structure it stands for."[55]

Hanson contends, to the contrary, that a linguist does not confer structure but rather "constructs a more or less accurate *statement* or *formulation of* the structure," and (contra Levi-Strauss) that the structure does not exist in the unconscious mind but "has its objective existence in the regularity of usage by native speakers." He continues:

> As long as their actions manifest regularities there is structure; a structure which exists regardless of whether anyone has tried to say what it is. In a word, while Caws locates structure only in people's minds, I locate it also in their behavior.[56]

In Chapter 2 I noted a similar complaint made by Cecil Brown that is worth reconsideration here. Brown challenges A. F. C. Wallace's contention "that the insights into kin behavior and social structure in the larger sense which can be achieved by terminological analysis may be limited," because "kinship terminologies may only be reckoning devices, like systems of weights and measures, whose utility depends more on internal coherence than on their fit with the social system." (Compare to Lounsbury's characterization (p. 211 above) of kinship semantics as a tool for analyzing non-linguistic structure.) Brown replies that there must be some coherent "fit" between the kinship terminology "discovered" by the linguist and the antecedent practices of the source-language community:

> Wallace's view can be challenged in terms of his own analogy. Systems of weights and measures, like all tools, are designed to meet certain requirements extraneous to their own internal logic. One would not, for example, weigh letters in fractions of tons, nor concrete blocks in multiples of ounces. As for measures, speed cannot be measured in meters, not a football field in miles per hour. I would be surprised to discover that kin terminologies in their capacity as linguistic tools do not similarly "fit" the reality they are used to describe.[57]

Bracketing the troublesome problem of what structures have to be in people's minds in order for social intercourse and inquiry to be possible, I think my account of translation can partly reconcile these sharp disagreements. I agree—as one reasonably should—that there is an antecedent structure implicit in behavior: conventional patterns codified and uncodified by the ethnographic subjects, which are in turn described by the anthropologist. However, in order to enable the task of description, I contend, the anthropologist must perform certain prescriptive theory tasks—in the process of establishing what Caws calls the "boundary conditions of his work."[58] Many of these boundary conditions are fairly well established, before the particular field work is done, by professional training. However, it is also the case, as Caws puts it, that "inside the boundaries he becomes, as the physical scientist does not, a participant in the determination of the structure he studies." Caws continues:

> And this is because the structure was, in the first place, a product of minds like his own, and will continue in being only if sustained by such minds; by taking it as an object of inquiry he has lent his own being to it; future investigators who seek to understand it can reasonably be expected to take note of his conclusions as an integral part of the data for their own work. A society is, in the last analysis, nothing except what is said and thought about it, by those who observe it as well as by those who compose it.[59]

With all this I agree, and I take it to be sustained by the position I have developed above. Caws does not seem to view translation as I do, but this divergence is not critical. A. F. C. Wallace's position seems closer to mine, though again he does not seem to accord translation explicit codificational status. I claim that the translation manual itself is an instrument of sorts for becoming a part of that society, and one becomes a "part" of the society in a way that is significantly like, and then again significantly unlike, the ways in which the members do when one is building and employing the manual. One is part of the society insofar as one successfully participates in its activities; that is, one consciously follows certain rules in such a way that one's linguistic and nonlinguistic behavior complies with the explicit or implicit rules or patterns of expectation of the society. Indeed, one is capable of "communicating ideas" successfully. However, *qua* translator and manual user, one does not *consciously follow* the same rules the ethnographic subjects do (if *they* are consciously doing so, for that matter). The "foreigner" consciously follows the translation rules (at first at least), or follows rules that could be made explicit, and in so doing conforms properly to linguistic and nonlinguistic conventions of the source community. Thus, the resultant explanatory model or account cannot, simply because it rests on successful translation, be said to succeed or fail in revealing or mirroring cognitive structures. A good deal of the structure of one's explanation can be dictated by "internal" and receptor-community constraints, while still having, in an important way, "something to do" with the source community's behavior patterns. Of course structuralist accounts operate at a generally higher level of cross-cultural generality than most. But for all their supposed neglect of cultural particulars, they make extensive commitments to translational correlation and may well fail to match up in terms of some form of intensional isomorphism. But this is no real failure, and no real shadow is cast on the theoretical richness for which they are valued.

With translational hypotheses, including those which serve to form the structures in question, thus construed, Caws's account can be seen to be compatible with Hanson's claim that the structures of behavior exist prior to translation—though I would prefer to say that it is patterns of practice that precede translational codification—while also squaring with Caws's contention that the structure the anthropologist derives, in perfectly legitimate empirical fashion, is also "conferred." The source of the dispute disappears if one drops the initial, "natural" presupposition that social scientists describe the components and relations of abstract semantic (or social) structures in doing linguistic analyses such as translation, kinship typologies, and so forth. This claim will not be acceptable to some structuralists, I suspect, but Levi-Strauss himself might not be entirely unsympathetic to Caws's or my position. Recall his earlier-noted remark: "We are . . . merely studying the shadows on the wall of the Cave, without forgetting that it is only the attention we give them which lends them a semblance of reality."

Also, the purported absurd consequences of Caws's position disappear, for essentially the reasons he offers in rejoinder to Hanson:

> If a system already described has a given structure, an identical one will of course have the same structure whether it has been independently described or not—*as long as it really is identical* (knowing this would automatically provide a description). A misdescribed system, on the other hand, will not objectively "have" a wrong structure, it will simply turn out not to have the structure we thought it had (to put it

another way: the system that has the structure in question turns out not to exist). My point is that the system may not yet have a total or fully developed structure at all. People do not "have" names unless other people agree that they do. Yet it is possible to call them by the wrong names, or credit them with mistaken dignities.[60]

In my view, "misdescription" is a perfectly coherent and describable empirical possibility, and it can be of either of two general types: Of main concern here are translational errors, and I maintain that error is, strictly speaking, not misdescription but faulty codification—this difference, despite the fact that the procedures for telling this are much the same as apply in the determination of misdescription in other scientific contexts. (Codification and descriptive theorizing are structurally quite similar, and this similarity is exploited in White's *Toward Reunion in Philosophy*.) The difference is in what we can lay claim to having justifiably *said about* the society in question. (Thus, I suspect my reading of Caws's claim that the system can turn out "not to have the structure we thought it had" is not quite the same as his.) The second type is misdescription in the literal sense. Once translational and other prescriptive elements of theorizing are adopted, empirical data can dictate results that are clearly not the logical entailments of prescriptive choices (compare my discussion of linguistic universals above). In either case it makes perfect sense to speak of systems having structures and of there being something there—namely, source-community practices—to coordinate with meta- and receptor-community practices. The native's system can "objectively have" a structure, one that is potentially different from the one conferred on him, or perhaps he can have an uncodified one, or perhaps in certain respects his behavior patterns can be so chang-ing as to lead us to say he has no structured practice at all. What I suggest is that we drop the "natural" presupposition that social scientists describe the components and relations of abstract semantic (or social) structures in doing linguistic analyses such as translation, kinship typologies, and so forth. Even Caws seems to make this as-sumption, but under my reconstruction I believe the force of rejoinder is stronger. It is clearer why the observer's interests have such a "constitutive" effect on the resulting systematization.

However, in arguing these points, I don't see myself as siding against Hanson, at least not on philosophically important grounds. Hanson's position falls roughly in with those views that call for a shift of attention to the "surface" social and linguistic background, in line, for example, with Wittgenstein's later reflections on language. His own work is primarily concerned with revealing *social* reality of a sort, and I would characterize these as squaring with the fundamentally emic thrust of Boas' work. Hanson has difficulties with the mentalistic connotations of much of what is regarded as emic anthropology, to be sure. In a joint 1973 paper with Rex Martin, "The Problem of Other Cultures," many of the quandaries of Boasian anthropology are tied to the ties seen between culture and mental life. (Recall Goodenough's more mentalistic passages.) As the article's title suggests, inherent problems in Cartesian dualism of mind and body create these problems, much as they cause the intractability of the "other minds" problem.[61] However, he himself advocates a form of "internal understanding" that emphasizes public, socio-behavioral aspects of significance.[62] He thus fits with positions I have tied to Wittgenstein's later philosophy, though Hanson himself draws more on Gilbert Ryle's behaviorism. I will thus reserve further discussion of him until a later section devoted to socio-behaviorally oriented paradigms having kinship with British Ordinary Language philosophy. (I will not dwell on the differences between Ryle and Wittgenstein, as these are not relevant to my discussion.) For now I will say this: in employing my reconstruction to support Goodenough in his less mentalistic moments, I think I thereby lessen the contrasts between Hanson and Goodenough, as well as between Hanson and Caws.

Of more immediate concern is another tension in Boasian anthropology that I emphasized in Chapter 2, which surfaces in the critiques of Frake and Watson of the importation of alien conception, structure, and rigor by many "cognitively" oriented anthropologists (especially those concerned with more unconscious levels of cognition). The proper Boasian emphasis, according to many such critics, should be on what is culturally specific and generally in or near the conscious awareness of subjects. That is, they follow Goodenough in seeking the ways that subjects conceptualize reality, but they see the rigor that Goodenough himself has championed as deleterious to these aims.

In effect, we find ourselves considering another species of the problem of the seeming tension between the forms of inquirer-interest that structure social inquiry and its efforts to reveal another conceptual scheme (or, to remind ourselves of the Sapirian elements in this, another reality). This point was certainly emphasized by the descriptivist extremist, whose position I think it useful to dispose of now before proceeding further. In light of the pragmatism advocated with respect to the descriptivism versus comparativism issue by Kiefer, it might seem that the deck is stacked against the descriptivist attitude because "theoretical fruitfulness" would seem to entail generality of anthropological principle and thus a comparative emphasis. However, I see nothing in this that precludes our being able to come up with reasons to emphasize particularities in a culture that make it distinct. The idea that a culture can be entirely distinct from others is a position that no *ethnographer* can hold—to the degree to which any translation of the source-language or any description is achieved; correspondingly, there must be some cultural overlap. It seems inconsistent to claim that a translation or description is warranted, while claiming that no cultural overlap exists. One does not have to formulate explicitly comparative hypotheses in order to be committed to comparison. (This *ad hominem* point suffices for my present purposes, but worth consideration in this connection is Davidson's stronger thesis that translatability is a necessary condition for something's being a language at all.)[63]

The "theoretical" value of cultural particularity is, I think, borne out in the article by Watson I discussed earlier. Watson and Frake desire that the source-society's practices have a structural impact on the ethnographer's discovery and validation procedures, and Watson is quite illuminating about the value of doing this. In light of Quine's reflections on translation, it is evident that imposition cannot be escaped entirely, but granting that it pervades translation, distinctions with respect to *further* impositions of strategy and construct can still be made. We can distinguish between analytic frameworks such as "eliciting frames," guided by psychological theory and incorporating various psychological tests of unconscious motivation—frameworks whose predetermined procedures are highly selective of data types—and the more hermeneutic procedures advocated by Watson. Watson makes prior efforts, based throughout on translation, to determine the kinds of questions he later asks in coming to a broader understanding of the Guajiro (than is manifest in his initial emic efforts). And his results are surely warrantable: We can ourselves check the translations and ask our own questions based on an empirically grounded understanding of what Guajiros consciously think. Watson discovered things that were not simply the logical entailments of his emic choices of strategy and conception. Moreover, the theoretical value of doing this seems clear (on the assumption, of course, that we find no empirically determinate error—whether it be faulty description or faulty codification): We come to an empirically grounded understanding that casts new light on their strategies for adaptation. If this is theoretically interesting to know, and it seems clearly to be so, then we have made a theoretical gain. The gain ultimately is measured by the theoretical interests we bring to bear. (And, indeed, as Evans-Pritchard and others have remarked, there is interest in transforming our understanding of ourselves and our methods of social inquiry by doing anthropology. One could see an advantage here over psychoanalytic or materialist strategies insofar as they resist transformation.)

By the same token, Watson's original etic model is not to be devalued entirely either. Watson does not advocate this, as his concern is rather to lessen its *dominance* in anthropology. There are genuine theoretical interests—genuinely anthropological ones, though they be derived from those of the psychological community—to be served in perceiving such things as the inculcation of potentially harmful dependencies by parents in children. Nor are these partly contrasting emic and etic interests entirely contrasting. In this connection, the Laboratory of Human Cognition views psychology's adaptability to anthropology as harmed by what is perceived as inadequate appreciation in the psychology of cross-cultural cognitive diversity. Correspondingly, as I noted in discussing psychological reality, it also values the potential contribution of psychology in "limiting uncontrolled speculation about thinking," which could well serve the sort of emic orientation Watson advocates.[64]

Watson's emic results are enlightening and seem warranted, and it would be unfortunate if etic currents in the field excluded them. However mine is a pluralistic view that tries to accommodate Watson's etic as well as his emic. For instance, nothing in his later work seems to *conflict* with earlier findings that Guajiro parents induced maladaptive dependencies in their children. Seeing a culture from divergent perspectives, even though they might lead to conflicting evaluations of adaptability, is an enrichment—provided, of course, that no data relevant to either have been ignored. But this last worry, it seems to me, results from nothing intrinsic to the choice of perspective. To accentuate or emphasize certain aspects of behavior is not to prevent the emphasis of others. Indeed, even though the very identification of the "aspects" may hinge on the framework of analysis, to adopt one framework is not to prevent the adoption of another.

I reject the idea that the etic excludes the emic. Moreover, I reject any reversed hegemony of emic over etic—especially insofar as it might be based on the idea that the emic procedure reveals an intensional isomorphism of source and receptor elements. Watson's emic position doesn't require this to be either interesting or compelling.

The arguments of Quine, and more so Rudner, are I think compelling against the arguments typically used to support the claim that what Rudner calls "the teleology of the observed" *must* be adopted by the inquirer. Yet, in a suitably defined sense, such a teleology *can* be adopted and can be theoretically fruitful.

Wittgensteinian Aspects of Ethnography

At various points above I have noted the relevance of Wittgenstein's work to my concerns here: His influence on anthropology seems clearly more widespread than Quine's, as Wittgenstein is often cited as a champion of behavioral, sociolinguistic, and symbolic-anthropological approaches. His critique of mentalism presents deep challenges to all views that rest symbolic significance on intensional objects. Indeed, as we saw, even a number of proponents of these latter sorts of views cite Wittgenstein in the interests of modifying various aspects of their positions. Wittgenstein's influence is also immensely felt in the general philosophy of social science literature, both directly and through adaptations of his work to particularly social-scientific problems by Peter Winch and others. Given this impact, and given various important similarities between his view and those espoused by Quine and me, I would like to make some fairly brief remarks concerning key similarities and contrasts.

At the heart of Wittgenstein's reflections on language and society in the *Philosophical Investigations* and later works (as well as in Winch's work) are his views regarding the rule-governed character of human symbolic behavior: views that, as developed by Winch and others, seem to imply a thesis that success in social inquiry requires justificational procedures that differ from those employed in the natural sciences. Insofar as social scientists are involved in the interpretation of symbolic behavior, it is argued, they must both learn and use the rules of the source-language community in order to explain its behavior; such explanations will contain rule-statements that are, or are derived from, accurate meaning-preserving translations of rules followed by his subjects. The model of explanation will then clearly differ from that used in the natural sciences (since violable rules will appear in the explanation rather than law- or hypothesis-statements) and will bear a closer resemblance to the method of conceptual analysis employed by certain philosophers.[65] Given the obvious similarity of concerns that I share with these two thinkers, I think it is important to say something with regard to the important differences that separate us.

Let us first consider Cecil Brown's position, which was briefly considered earlier. He views Wittgenstein's insight that "meaning is use" as being in conflict with a fundamental and mistaken presupposition of transformational approaches:

> A fundamental distinction between my formulation and transformational grammar pertains to the manner in which each accounts for relations holding among words, phrases, and sentences. Of utmost significance in the former account is the assumption that no relations whatsoever hold among sentences which have dissimilar uses; the only sentences which are in some way related are those belonging to the same language-game. Transformational grammar, on the other hand, fails to distinguish among the multitude of functions which sentences serve. It takes language as a coherent structure and describes it in terms of a set of systematically related rules.[66]

Instead, Brown contends, the linguist should proceed by analyzing the use of expressions, and this requires learning the rules governing such usage:

> to learn the use of a sign we look to ordinary language to discover the function it has, or the purpose it serves there. We in fact look to surface structure to discover the rules behind the ordinary use of signs. Yet can we recognize the use of rules if we do not have a priori knowledge of how they are to be followed? In Wittgenstein's view we cannot.[67]

Citing Wittgenstein's view of the character of mathematical statements, Brown contends that whatever universal categories a transformationalist might discern, these are not the rules actually involved with use (which speakers follow, in some sense) but "may be no more than meta-representations or mere artifacts of the act of using language."[68] That is, just as "the symbols upon which mathematical rules operate acquire categorical status only after the act of application or only after the projected or predicted act of application," so parts of speech and other grammatical categories "are viewed here as metaphenomena of language use."[69] In contrast, Brown prefers to seek "functional universals," that is, the language games operative in any language community (such as commanding, questioning, recounting, and so on), and eschews any attempt to characterize innate abilities to apply linguistic rules in terms of unconscious rules.[70]

His more immediate objective in translation and linguistic analysis is to account for sign-use within the source-language community by using "cover symbols of rules" in his explanations, that is, symbols that are not "forever given" but instead "are given only when selection of rules is made" by source-language speakers.[71]

This brief sketch serves, I hope, to indicate the important "God's-truth" commitments that exist in Brown's Wittgensteinian "descriptive semiotics," commitments that have affinities with Winch's insistence on rule recovery and use by the social inquirer. (Recall also Brown's criticisms of Wallace in the previous section.) As with Hanson above, Brown views the important lesson to be learned from the problems of mentalism to be a shift in objective from the recovery of mentalistic entities to the revelation of something somehow implicit in observable behavior. Indeed, Brown is quite insistent that the linguist and ethnographer have objectively determinate results—ones that have determinate "psychological," "social," and "structural" reality.[72] And his basis for this insistence, as noted in the previous section, involves concerns analogous to those expressed by Hanson: There must be something, he believes, for the linguist's constructs to "fit"—and that is an objective source-language or source-culture reality of some kind.

However, it is not clear that the determinacy that Brown and Winch demand of the linguist's systematizations can be justified by Wittgenstein's own lights. Indeed, even Wittgenstein himself may seek more determinacy than his views concerning meaning, belief, and linguistic practices will allow. As noted earlier, Wittgenstein rejects mental entities as the source of symbolic meaning and argues instead that the meaning of a given society's symbolic behavior is grounded in the linguistic and social background in which that behavior typically takes place: that is, in the "language games," linguistic and social "practices," and, most broadly, the "forms of life" of the society in question. Furthermore, coming to *understand* this meaning and, attendantly, the beliefs of the members of the society (no particular priority is given to the recovery of either) requires becoming a participant in these practices on his view. But despite the "emic ring" to these remarks, ethnographical understanding (not to mention ethnological) may not be possible on this account. For the ethnographer must not only participate in a society's practices, he must also *map* (in various ways) the practices of that society onto the practices of another in keeping with the practices of yet a third "society" of anthropologists. But this then places the original source-language expressions—more exactly the metalinguistic mentions of them—in a new, broader practice or life-form of (perhaps universal) social inquiry, and it is this shift of context that should have an impact on their use and hence their meaning: Why should we expect identity in use between 'jefekyr' as used by the Trukese and ' 'jefekyr' ' in the metalanguage (or, as Goodenough tends to treat it, 'jefekyr' in the receptor language)? One might appeal to some claimed "overlap" between the life-forms in question, but substantiating such an appeal is not easy. Even by Wittgenstein's lights, imposition is a problem to be reckoned with.

This becomes particularly evident in Wittgenstein's later works that apply the theses developed in *On Certainty*, concerning the justification of belief in general, to problems of cross-cultural analysis and comparison of belief. In brief, his general position is that beliefs can only be evaluated within some practice in which a hierarchy of beliefs is used (roughly, combinations of higher-order beliefs being used to infer, and thereby justify, lower order ones), or where actions occur in the context of social activity in which correctness of belief is a matter of performing appropriately, as judged by the social group. This yields the following important consequence: It is wrong-headed to evaluate beliefs from the perspective of a practice that differs significantly from the one in which they are formed and in which they function. In application to anthropological problems, Wittgenstein argues in *Remarks on Frazer's Golden Bough* (compare Chapter 2) that Frazer (and by implication many other anthropologists) is misguided in automatically assuming that the religious beliefs of his subjects are prone to empirical error. To the contrary, he argues that Frazer's subjects are not making (in principle, corrigible) factual claims, but rather are expressing religious sentiments of various sorts. He argues that Frazer's view of his subjects as doing incomplete or "primitive" scientific inquiry is the result of Frazer's own impoverished conceptions of religion.[73]

The fuller import of Wittgenstein for social inquiry, many have felt, lies in Winch. However, Malcolm Crick's *Explorations in Language and Meaning* draw these out more explicitly and concretely for anthropology and is worth some attention here. (Also, as we shall see, Crick finally diverges with Winch on a point of pivotal relevance here.) As I noted earlier, I view Crick's work as fitting under the rubric of "symbolic anthropology." His main concern is to create in British social anthropology, a tradition dominated by functionalism, a greater concern for emic understanding. He aims to formulate a "semantic anthropology," one "rooted in the conception of human beings as meaning-makers." However, like Hanson, he wants to avoid the idea, which one could easily assume from such a remark, that either cognitive or linguistic analysis is the linchpin of anthropology.[74]

In connection with linguistic analysis, Crick, as I noted earlier, views certain important forms of symbolic significance lost if only "the language" of a society is studied—for example, the alternative forms of expression that less dominant groups such as women may exhibit. He also worries that linguistic analysis itself will harm the "semantic" aims he emphasizes insofar as alien linguistic category is imposed and joins sociolinguists and symbolic anthropologists in seeking a broadened theory of symbolic significance and an ethnographically based linguistics. In the latter connection, he speaks favorably of "folk linguistic" studies, advocated by Hymes but generally undervalued by sociolinguists, aimed at revealing other societies' linguistic theories:

> Obviously a culture's view of its own and other languages must have a central place in any ethnographically based linguistics. We must know how a culture discriminates various types of verbal acts, and what classification of oral literature it possesses. Using our own terms like 'myth', 'religious poetry' or 'proverb', for example, may violate some crucial cultural distinctions. A more adequate anthropological study of language therefore has a basic import for the general problem of understanding another culture. We shall never know the size of the loss caused by the fact that the functionalist fieldworkers for the most part did not make the investigation of language in this sense a topic to be written up in their monographs.[75]

Here and elsewhere Crick aligns himself squarely with those who follow Evans-Pritchard in opposing the functionalism dominant in British anthropology. However, this passage reveals a problem that Crick believes even these anthropologists have not adequately resolved. Noting one critic's objection that the widely discussed studies by Evans-Pritchard and his followers of witchcraft remain "mainly sociological,"[76] he remarks as follows:

> One of the reasons for the shortcomings of anthropological discussions of witchcraft is the idea that it is a phenomenon which should be treated as a topic at all. So . . . my suggestion is that our understanding will advance when 'witchcraft' is analytically dissolved into a larger frame of reference.[77]

Underlying this criticism are really two species of the imposition problem: One, similar to that emphasized by Watson and Marano, is that the very definition and saliency of the problem area evidently has more to do with aspects of the history of the ethnographic audience. While Watson and Marano cite concerns particularly relevant to the community of social inquirers, Crick cites the general Western cultural community's concern with tensions between witchcraft, myth, and religion on the one hand and science, rationality, and technology on the other:

> It is important to see that witchcraft may have become a separate topic for anthropology because of its appearance in the history of our own society. This occurrence, by supplying us with a ready-made term, would be sufficient to destroy those cautions we observe in the translation of culture in connection with other problems.[78]

This problem brings with it the more salient imposition problem we have been considering, namely the imposition of alien categorization:

> The gulf between the intellectual structures of seventeenth-century England and Zande society, for instance, is vast. . . .English witchcraft existed in a culture which possessed such categories as 'natural philosophy' and a theological system upon which witchcraft beliefs were partly parasitic. Great violence must be done to the conceptual structures of another culture in speaking of witchcraft if it lacks those environing categories which defined it in our own.[79]

Much as Marano rejects the imposition of psychology in the distortion of a Windigo phenomenon by its characterization as a "psychosis," Crick argues against the imposition of sociology in social anthropology:

> We simply cannot confuse categories like 'caste' and 'hierarchy' with the general sociological notions of stratification and inequality. This 'smug sociocentricity' merely sacrifices the goal of understanding to the convenience of an immediate discourse.[80]

Crick's own analysis is reminiscent of Geertz's (whom Crick favorably cites) in that he emphasizes an analysis of "person categories" of a society, as propadeutic to a revelation of its interconnected action and evaluation categories, or what he terms its "moral space." He joins Wittgenstein, Ryle, Hanson, and others in also criticizing dualistic philosophies of mind for inhibiting this study. He also emphasizes a central thesis of Winch's and

Wittgenstein's that the point of practices must be discerned in order to discern their significance of their component concepts and associated beliefs.[81]

Crick builds his theory of understanding conceptual structures from a cartographic analogy. Much as a map's features denote only salient features of a landscape, in accordance with certain cartographic conventions. With Hanson he favors Wittgenstein's notion of a form of life since it "emphasizes the relation of speaking to non-linguistic action by locating language in its broader cultural context."[82]

This leads him to argue, for example, that psychology must be transformed because (owing to Freud) it draws too much on the mapping principles of physics.

> [Freud] adopts the method of theory construction in natural science. He constructs a map in a new language which obliterates this pre-existing semantic system. This leads not to a rewording of a conceptual structure with which we are all familiar, but to a new discourse formation, an autonomous structure with a new theoretical potential which makes it independent of the conceptual landscape it should realistically chart. The new map disguises some features, destroys others, and generates new ones.[83]

Crick's complaint draws on Wittgenstein's widely discussed reflections on the differing natures of reasons and causes. Mechanistically modeled psychologies define their problem area in terms of seeking *causes* and *effects*. Crick follows Winch and many ordinary-language philosophers in arguing that human agency must use categories more appropriate to action; in turn, since semantic anthropology seeks to concern itself with *moral agents* and their *reasons*, and the *concepts* constitutive of actions, cause and effect must be inappropriate concepts. In a vein most reminiscent of Watson's concerns, he remarks that these problems also explain some of the problems encountered in applying psychology to anthropology:

> This viewpoint helps us to see why the efforts to integrate psychology into the social sciences or anthropology have been so unsatisfactory. It is not simply that psychology is culture-bound, but because it and the social sciences are themselves specialist conceptual structures which fracture that semantic field relating to human thought and action which exists in ordinary language. Psychology and sociology do not refer to different subject matters—the individual versus the collective, for instance—they are both concerned with communication, shared

rules, and meanings. Yet one cannot synthesize the two disciplines, because they are not two differently worded descriptions of the same
landscape, but two systems, the languages of which have partially
created their own terrains. Clearly two different terrains cannot be
coordinated.[84]

Finally, let me consider Hanson's position. As we saw, he raises
deep criticisms for Caws' pragmatic rendering of structuralism, yet
does not include himself as one of the cognitively or mentalistic-
emicly oriented anthropologists against whom Caws reacts. Hanson
is particularly interesting in that he offers a definition of culture that
is highly reminiscent of Goodenough, yet strives vigorously to
"dementalize" it—much as I did in my reconstruction (and as much
as Goodenough's own expressed sympathies with the behaviorist
Morris suggest this, despite the turn to Lewis-style mentalism that
Goodenough makes).

Hanson draws on the work of Gilbert Ryle, a philosopher squarely
in the British Ordinary Language tradition that largely follows the
key elements of Wittgenstein's later philosophy. (As I noted above,
Ryle differs from Wittgenstein on many points, but none of them are
critical for my discussion.) Hanson notes Ryle's relevance as follows:
In contrast to the Cartesian dualism of mind and body (to which
Lewis and Goodenough subscribe)

> Ryle's theory of mind [and Wittgenstein's] holds that most mental
> activities are open to public view: they are overt intelligent perfor-
> mances. If understanding thought in another culture means understand-
> ing sharing native mental activities, in Ryle's terms this would mean
> being able to duplicate native overt intelligent performances. It is much
> the same as when we say that one knows or understands a foreign lan-
> guage when he can use it; in Ryle's terminology, understanding is a
> case of *knowing how*.[85]

"The core of Ryle's theory of understanding," he continues, "is not
communion of private experiences . . .but rather one's ability to do
or use something." He here cites Wittgenstein as "shar[ing] this
concept of understanding" and quotes him as follows: "Let us
remember that there are certain criteria in a man's behaviour for the
fact that he does not understand a word: that it means nothing to him,
that he can do nothing with it."[86]

He notes that Goodenough and Wallace acknowledge that
"different natives themselves operate according to different subconscious rules, so that rules that are psychologically valid for some may

not be so for others," but believes that Ryle and Wittgenstein have revealed a far deeper problem that renders "spurious" the psychological validity problem. Thus, while Hanson is interested in emic, "internal understanding," he holds that "Ryle's notion of 'knowing how' does indeed constitute internal understanding in the only meaningful sense of that term."[87]

Hanson's internal understanding is concerned with what he calls "implicational meaning," which, briefly, concerns the logical relations—of logical implication and presupposition—that hold not only among ideas (in their public sense) but also among customs, institutions, and artifacts.[88] Hanson's efforts to embrace things other than ideas in the logical relations he studies captures a central point emphasized by Wittgenstein and others: that it is one, of many, Cartesian errors to try to study relations among linguistic items in relative abstraction from related behavior and artifacts. Now I am not sure if his talk of "ideas" entails the existence of intensional entities (compare my discussion of Searle's importation of propositions in Chapter 1). However, it is clear that Hanson aims to discover semantic and logical relations, and rules of his subjects:

> The implication for understanding other cultures is clear. Thought and behavior are intelligible only in terms of the *a priori* [but historically and interculturally variable] forms which condition and govern them. Those forms, as collective representations, vary from one society to another. Therefore ideas, beliefs and actions should be understood from within—in terms of the categories of the culture from which they come.[89]

I content myself with a brief account of Hanson's theory, as it is sufficient to recognize his commitment to the recovery of meaning-elements warrantedly ascribable to the source-language community, something I have argued is problematic.

In this connection, consider the following passage:

> The question of rationality of alien beliefs poses no baffling epistemological problem at all. The question actually concerns the meaning of those beliefs, and that is perfectly intelligible to us. We determine it by ascertaining the relations among those beliefs, how they presuppose and imply each other in a logical system. The only set of beliefs which would qualify as non-rational or meaningless by this reasoning would be one in which the component beliefs vary randomly, with no logical connections between them at all. I doubt very seriously that such a 'system' (better, nonsystem) of beliefs could exist for long in a human society.[90]

However, Hanson's position is still at odds with translational indeterminacy, insofar as it makes the sort of "mentalistic" (in Quine's broader sense) commitments that I noted in connection with social-behaviorally oriented and nonentificational theories in Chapter 1. In this connection, Hanson's position has significant similarities with that of Peter Winch (stemming, I think, in large part from their common, acknowledged heritage in Collingwood as well as Wittgenstein).[91] Each draws on elements of ordinary language philosophy, with its emphasis on rule-governed behavior as opposed to intensional object, to establish a position that makes socio-cultural analysis a matter of learning rules. However, I think Hanson's commitment to recovery of source-culture logical and conceptual relations and rules is clear here. (As to its implicit "intellectualism," I shall say more about this later.) However, the parallels I have noted between Hanson and Goodenough, as well as my comments on Wittgenstein and Winch should show, I think, that what I have already said in my extended discussion of Goodenough applies quite directly here. Provided we drop the insistence in Hanson (and Winch) that social inquiry *must* proceed according the the "teleology of the observed," I have no problem with what he says. While I somewhat mitigate the Quinean reasons one might have for rejecting this (reasons that would seem to imply that we should not be forced to adopt these methodological guidelines because we *cannot*), Rudner's "reproductive fallacy" argument is, I have maintained, compelling against such forms of "reverse discrimination."

I have suggested that despite Brown's, Winch's, and Hanson's remarks to the contrary, Wittgenstein presents grounds for doubt about the possibility of rule recovery. This implication is drawn most clearly I think in Crick's *Explorations in Language and Meaning*, whose perspective on translation in anthropology approaches most closely, of all the works I have considered, to my own. For Crick takes full account of the fact that a theory of significance grounded in forms of life must take account of the differences of the forms of life involved in translation and ethnography. The inquirer's forms of life (as a social scientist and a member of some culture(s) and social group(s)) will infuse translation, ethnography, and ethnology with unavoidable forms of imposition, but ones that do not *necessarily* or *intrinsically* defeat the purpose of these activities. Rather, they lead us to steer clear of untenable attitudes about the goals of these activities.

Crick's initial discussion in this connection emphasizes, as we have seen, the Winchian claim that the map is not understood unless its "point" is understood and that a proper, emicly oriented map must reveal the subjects' conventions governing saliency, and so forth.[92] Moreover, he states related Winchian themes concerning the inadequacy of causal models for the explanation of action. However, in later discussion of map making, an important corollary of his views concerning the inappropriateness of scientific mapping principles emerges, namely, that there is a "lack of finality" in interpretation and that this "arises from the very nature of translation."[93] He challenges the idea that natural science mapping principles will always be appropriate and ideally informative (an evident consequence of the belief in their universal applicability). He advises instead that any scheme we choose, even appropriately emic ones, be regarded as forever open to change. This eventually emerges, amidst discussions heavily laced with Winchian considerations, as a significant point of departure from Winch. First, pluralistic consequences emerge:

> [Psychic unity] is the presupposition for anthropological discourse—the fundamental unifier of a semantic structure which explores the diversity of 'ourselves' and 'others'. The pair is thus subsumed, and so the meanings of both terms are interdependent. A change in the value of the 'self' inevitably alters the image of the 'other', and vice versa; and either change alters the nature of the difference which they constitute, and by which they are constituted. Different cultures characterize the diversities and the unifying features differently, and over time the images of what is universal and what separates one culture form another change. An anthropological statement of this situation can only result in yet another announcement of the invariants and diversities, so there can be no final definition of the relation between 'ourselves' and 'others'. The real meaning of the relation is thus all its versions.[94]

Subsequently, the hermeneutic thrust of these remarks is made fully clear:

> The semantic powers of humankind make it a self-constituting species, and anthropology as a manifestation of these powers must itself be regarded as a conceptual system. Anthropological thinking belongs to a 'form of life' and builds yet another map of human significance. There is no freedom even for our discipline from man's semantic abilities—all anthropology can do is construct more maps.

If this picture necessarily involves the abandonment of one view of scientific objectivity, at the same time it reveals what the identity of a semantic is and, indeed, must be. Since there is an irremovable indeterminacy in translation, the lack of finality in semantic investigations should not be surprising. But we can express this situation in more helpful and positive terms by seeing that translation is a form of commentary. Thus, in translating a text we create another. To use the cartographic imagery again, giving the meaning of a map is a complex process, which involves both loss and creation of features of a landscape, and which in effect produces a second map to place beside the first. Our increase in understanding can thus be regarded as the ability to refract one structure through a second.[95]

Finally, Crick makes fully clear his break with Winchian reproduction and the similarity of our aims to transcend the etic / emic contrast:

This manner of presenting the anthropological situation enables us to see why we need not pose the question whether understanding is in 'their' terms or 'ours'. If 'their terms' entails a fideistic grasp or an understanding in no way influenced by the fact that we ourselves belong to a conceptual structure, then anthropology cannot envisage attaining it. . . . In human studies objectivity is a type of disciplined intersubjectivity.[96]

By viewing translation's "very nature" as codificational and thus making the stabilization of the reflective equilibrium of translational correlations as partly dependent on ongoing activities in three communities, I bolster such an attitude. Theoretical concerns can change and thus revise or replace basic analytic constructs and with them translations, or the broader interpretations of source-culture behavior. Or the source-culture's behavior patterns can change, with a similar effect. Also, the emphasis Winch and others place on the presupposition of unreflective by reflective understanding is largely captured here: Codification, as Rawls points out, must spring from a fairly advanced and stabilized, uncodified practice, and one who lacks the skills necessary to the practice cannot master its codification. However, I deny that in social understanding there is as much overlap between inquirers' and subjects' unreflective understandings as Winch seems to demand.[97]

Crick grants that his conclusions are such as "many anthropologists may find somewhat disturbing."[98] And I think he must confront objections of the sort that we have seen Hanson and Brown level against Caws and Wallace. What is not clear to me is how Crick intends to evade objections that one cannot both advocate (1) that we try to get to the subjects' points in doing activities, and yet (2) that our selections of how we "map" a culture in doing an ethnography reflect our own interests and forms of life, and thus have a constitutive influence on our ethnographies. Also, the indeterminacy he cites as the key point behind translation's lack of finality seems largely Quine's. But if so, the Quinean import must be dealt with, and it is not, as I have earlier argued, altogether easy to see how Quine's thesis can be turned to emic, much less methodological, separatist ends. In fact, Quine's arguments seem to have precisely the consequence of making talk of the existence of schemes to be compared, imposed, and so on generally baseless. Yet such "ontic" commitment seems made repeatedly in the questions Crick raises and the answers he offers.[99]

Here I would offer the thesis I have developed in response to such criticisms. One can still make sense of the methodological separatist theses Crick expounds (so long as they are not exclusive of nonseparatists). Consider his view that psychology must be transformed because (owing to Freud) it draws too much on the mapping principles of physics. What Crick really compares, his occasional "reproductive-sounding" remarks notwithstanding, are the analytic concepts themselves and the questions to be answered. Much of the argument can come simply from considering issues about "reasons versus causes" and so forth. (Which is not to say I agree with the Wittgensteinian position here; I am simply trying to reveal potentially fruitful avenues of problem-definition and resolution: I am a pluralist, but I do not claim that available paradigms cannot be pruned.) And even where Crick's arguments hinge on efforts to reveal culturally specific rules, I think we can allow that translation can be an "empirical basis" for doing so, despite the considerations of Quine, and evidently Wittgenstein, that seem to cut against our warrantably doing so. What I have tried to do is transform our attitude toward just what sort of "basis" translation provides.

Is "Rationality" Universal?

In the latter part of Chapter 2, I briefly noted some long-standing problems concerning the question of rationality. I noted there allegiances perceived by the Laboratory of Human Cognition between challenges to the "intellectualist" universal imputation of Western rationality and the later work of Wittgenstein. A proper treatment of this complex, controversial, and centrally important question is well beyond the scope of this (or any single) book. But insofar as I make the problem of imposition my central problem, and insofar as I have just been considering Wittgenstein, some at least brief comments seem appropriate.

We have seen Hanson, for instance, offering what may be a strong "intellectualist" thesis that sees "Western logic" as universally instantiated. This stems from his efforts, manifest in the passage I quoted on the rationality of alien belief, to discern in the institutional practices of other societies relations of *implication* and *presupposition*. But if this is so, then his position is in strong contrast with that of the otherwise largely sympathetic Winch. (It is worth noting here that Winch's term 'logic' often has a broad sense equivalent with what is normally meant by 'system', while Hanson seems to construe 'system' in a narrow sense, equivalent to what is normally meant by 'logic'. I shall use 'logic' in the narrower sense.) My inclination is to follow Winch here, who, initial appearances notwithstanding, largely sides with Quine on the matter of how much logic we must import—namely, relatively little.[100] The reason this is so is that on Quine's account, most of what passes for "Western logic" is not translatable on the basis of stimulus meaning. (Again, I accept Quine's stimulus meaning as a basis for determinate translation, even though I have qualms about calling these stimulus-response complexes "meanings.") This might not seem so at first glance, but all that Quine regards as translatable on the basis of stimulus meaning is *truth-functional* logic. As I remarked earlier, even though it is charity that forces truth-functional logic on the subjects, the result is determinate translation, because the "uncharitable" alternatives are simply not feasible. However, where feasible—though perhaps bizarre or unwieldy—alternatives are available, reliance on the charity principle breeds indeterminacy. This means that "logic" beyond the truth functions (for example, predicate logic) does suffer indeterminacy. The facts do not force attributions of broader reaches of Western rationality to subjects.

I see no problem in simply importing Quine's position here. And it leaves quite open the possibility of feasibly attributing other logics. [101] Charity and behavioral evidence places some constraints on us, but it is possible to find reason to attribute systems, perhaps corresponding to what we call "alternative logics," or perhaps such as to be best not described by the term 'logic' at all. (Thus, again, I prefer the narrower concept to the one Winch employs.) Also, if the intellectualist thesis tries to force translators to confer *inductive* norms accepted in current "Western science," there are the following relevant comments from Quine: "another culture . . .[might] take a radically different line of scientific development, guided by norms that differ sharply from ours but that are justified by their scientific findings as ours are by ours." Indeed, they might "predict as successfully and thrive as well as we."[102] It seems that, by Quine's lights anyway, we cannot warrantably rely on charity to support the idea that broader logical bridgeheads are necessary.[103]

The Function of Translation in Anthropological Theory

I have emphasized a prescriptive canonical form for translation, but more important is the underlying philosophical motivation. In considering Quine's arguments against the factuality of translation, I noted what is for me a crucial gap in the argument. An important distinction between an ontological or (albeit naturalized) thesis and a methodological one is obscured in the characterization of translations as "only in an incomplete sense hypotheses." The ontological claim embodied here is that there is no fact of the matter to translation; the methodological one seems to be that translations, and the claims that rest on them, are not fully scientifically legitimate, that their role in the validation of scientific claims must be sharply limited. I have argued that I don't see the clear connection between the two claims, and I can see no other feasible warrant (say, an epistemological one) for this methodological consequence. But, beyond that, I have tried to say something more positive, by showing what I take the connection between the metaphysical and methodological theses to be. I believe we have reason to believe that translation is not based on a fact of the matter, where 'based' means 'warranted as hypotheses are'. Translations aren't warranted this way, being nondescriptive and warranted more in the fashion of definitions or inductive norms.[104]

As I suggested in Chapter 4, one could make a case against Quine's restriction of fact to physical fact, arguing perhaps that there are many types of fact, based on the many types of frameworks required for the delineation of fact. (One might seek sufficiently deep differences to establish such differences in kind, perhaps remarking on the sorts of conceptual incompatibilities that Winch and Crick cite between causal explanations and action explanations.) Then, by inserting a metaphysical premise equating factual expression and truth telling, one might come away believing that translations are, after all, factual in nature. I prefer a different strategy, since I think more elements of Quine's critique of intension are worth preserving than such an account would allow.

By contrast, one could see translation better accommodated by a Goodmanian attitude, one that allows other kinds of adequacy or, as he terms it, "fit" to have status equal to that of physics, to allow other forms of "rightness" (for example, of artistic rendering) to be on equal footing. This is not because such systems perform the tasks of physics just as well, but because they perform different tasks. A kind of incommensurability precludes any prejudicial ranking of systems, in terms of sharply different systems, and no warrant exists, he argues, for ranking the purposes that motivate the systems—say, practicality over curiosity.[105] As I have already remarked positively on the potentially fruitful applicability of Goodman's semiotic resources for anthropology, I think it will be useful to comment briefly on some related "metaphysical" positions of his (if this is a fair term to use).

Goodman's pragmatism is of a decidedly more pluralistic stripe than Quine's and has led to the development of an intriguing and provocative "irrealist" thesis in recent work. Irrealism, he remarks, "sees the world melting into versions and versions making worlds, finds ontology evanescent, and inquires into what makes a version right or a world well-built."[106] He does not want it viewed as "one more doctrine" among these various ones but "rather an attitude of unconcern with most issues between such doctrines" (thus my guarded use of 'metaphysical' above). He sees as pointless and confused most philosophical concerns about how to characterize the relationship between language or theory and the world. Indeed, in establishing this position, Goodman takes concerns such as Sapir's, that varying cultural accounts constitute different worlds, "not the same world with different labels attached," as having more radical consequences than Sapir perceived. This, of course, reminds us of Quine's efforts to go beyond Sapir in this connection. However, Goodman means to go beyond Quine as well. He perceives far more radical consequences stemming from these problems, contending that the motivations behind Quine's rejection of the analytic-synthetic distinction and attendant critique of semantics makes untenable such basic distinctions as that between conceptual schemes and their contents, or between the world and various theories and other symbolic representations of it—"versions" as he calls them. Briefly, if we cannot delineate sharply the (analytic) statements that simply articulate the conceptual scheme itself, and if we cannot either delineate the (synthetic) statements that have factual content or spell out what that content is (say, through some sort of empirical reduction), then, Goodman maintains, we do best to avoid distinguishing "the real world" from the symbolic schemes that describe or depict it altogether. Thus, he advocates a radical pluralism according to which there are as many worlds as there are adequate versions. Especially, given the failure to identify the factual "input" to a scheme, we must finally admit, Goodman argues, that "the line between convention and content is arbitrary and variable."[107] He thus eschews traditional metaphysical stances such as idealism and realism (including Quine's internal realism), which he believes do not fully acknowledge the merely *conventional* bases we have for choosing a version.[108] He wishes to turn philosophical attention away from all forms of foundationalism towards a pluralism that looks within systems, not outside of them, in evaluating their ultimate adequacy:

> In what non-trivial sense are there, as Cassirer and like-minded pluralists insist, many worlds? Just this, I think: that many different world-versions are of independent interest and importance, without any requirement or presumption of reducibility to a single base. . . .If all right versions could somehow be reduced to one and only one, that might with some semblance of plausibility be regarded as the only truth about the only world. But the evidence for such reducibility is negligible. . . .

> With false hope of a firm foundation gone with the world displaced by worlds that are but versions, with substance dissolved into function, and with the given acknowledged as taken, we face the questions how worlds are made, tested, and known.

> The realist will resist the conclusion that there is no world; the idealist will resist the conclusion that all conflicting versions describe different worlds. As for me I find these views equally delightful and equally deplorable—for after all, the difference between them is purely conventional![109]

This position (as well as Goodman's broad semiotics) has, I think, potentially fruitful affinities with the symbolist position of Crick, and it has met with the express approval of Geertz.[110] Crick's above-quoted remark that "the real meaning of the relation is thus all its versions" is strongly reminiscent of themes, indeed terminology, that dominate Goodman's *Ways of Worldmaking* and other work. Also, I am sympathetic to the idea that certain philosophical worries about the "reality" of theoretical posits, or about the actual "correspondence" of warranted physical theories to the world may hinge on baseless worries about global error existing even though all the extant criteria of adequacy of a theory are met. And, it will be recalled, I have reason to share his puzzlement about Quine's ontology of physical fact. (However, it is worth making clear that Goodman's rejection of scientific hegemony in no way entails a disregard for behavioral evidence. Nor would it lead him to see no value in relating anthropology to physical or psychological or linguistic theory: He would approve of systematic "reductions" of versions to other versions for the resultant pragmatic gains in explanatory power, generality, and so forth.)

What I find most attractive is the key point on which Goodman rests his "irrealism": the inability of either realists or antirealists to formulate coherent complaints concerning version-world relations that would raise doubts about "internal" standards of objectivity. How can one claim that the world either does or does not bear a certain relationship to a theory, Goodman asks (much in the spirit of Berkeley), if the only relata we can coherently put before ourselves are *versions*? And whatever the general strengths or weaknesses of Goodman's irrealism, I think it can be shown to be particularly plausible for ethnography. For here we do not have to take on the matter of whether the "natural world" can be feasibly fragmented into its versions. Instead, all we need to appeal to is the very indeterminacy of translation (which is as much a consequence of his views as it is of Quine's). For it places a severe burden on the sensibility of any worry that "the real scheme" will somehow escape successful translation. Just as concerns about the adequacy of world versions may founder on confused efforts to compare an uninterpreted world to a version; so concerns about social objectivity may founder on misguided efforts to compare the untranslated source-culture scheme to the inquirer's interpretive scheme. Indeterminacy challenges the sensibility of these concerns, since it challenges the warrant for believing that correct translation gives us receptor-language "mirrors" of untranslated source-language meanings.[111]

Let me sum up the present stage of my investigations. What I have argued is that "recovery" of symbol schemes in radical translation is a matter of codification rather than description. (And, with Quine, I would extend the view to all forms of translation, though I have not provided all the necessary argumentation for this broader thesis here.) I have been led to this view by consideration of Quine's indeterminacy thesis, especially its key premise, which seems to rest on an important but complex set of distinctions between scientific theorizing and translation. The nature of these distinctions has not been clearly articulated in Quine's writings, and Quine's vagueness or reticence on these points has had the effect of making it appear to have extreme and disturbing consequences for the anthropologist. I have sought to clarify the basis for these distinctions in such a way as to preserve some of the important consequences of this and other of Quine's theses regarding meaning, while giving some insight into the nature, possible yields, and criteria of adequacy of field translation. A cogent basis for these distinctions, I have argued, is a contrast between the rulelike regularities that the linguist *codifies*, which are themselves constitutive of his own codification, as opposed to the lawlike regularities that the physicist *describes*. In Goodman's terms, again, translational adequacy is a kind of "fit' that deserves a status equal to that of physical truth, but is nonetheless a kind of "rightness" distinct from truth.

It is important to reiterate that what I have *not* argued is that my position with regard to translational "hypotheses" holds as well for *all* anthropological inquiry. The present thesis is not directed at ethnographical or ethnological hypotheses made along with, and perhaps with the aid of, translational codifications. My point is that there are certain aspects of anthropological theory-building activity that are codificational in nature and do not of themselves involve—though they enable—the production of a descriptive theoretical product. For instance, I do not contend that componential analysis cannot be fruitful, or cannot contribute to ethnographic or ethnological theory—indeed, this approach has had extensive success; rather, what concerns me are certain philosophical presuppositions and conclusions made by Goodenough and others, which I believe embody certain confusions. I have sought to clarify the status of componential analysis and to suggest ways of ridding it of ontological commitments and pseudoproblems (for instance, concerning the issue of "cognitive validity," whose cogency has already been challenged by a number of anthropologists, though I have indicated greater sympathy to certain positive views concerning the general question of psychological reality).

The anthropologist's task is not only a matter of codifying, and the important thing is not to confuse, in theoretical reflections, its codificational aspects from its hypothetical-descriptive ones. Once the codificational facets of the anthropologist's work have been settled, some of their generated products may be used in hypothesis formation and theory construction. Field translation is a process of codification that yields receptor-language translations of native remarks, translations that may be used in communication with source-language speakers in order to recover important data concerning, for example, farming practices, procedures in rituals, cultural history, and so on. And a good codification will be such as to yield accurate information regarding these things. Moreover, codification functions also in the background of the anthropologist's metalanguage, used in hypothesis formation. This contains certain technical predicates that arise from a process of codification—that is, the selection and reconstruction (clarification, disambiguation) of antecedent linguistic practice of some natural background language to the metalanguage (in Goodenough's case, English). Terms preserve something of their former usage, while at the same time their usage comes to be governed by more rigorous conventions and rules suited to the anthropologist's tasks. (Again, this is precisely the process Quine calls "regimentation.") This codificational feature is one the anthropologist shares with any other scientist: For the physicist, 'work' has a very precise meaning, which is, nonetheless, not entirely divorced from ordinary English antecedent usage; the anthropologist employs such clarified technical expressions as 'peasant' and 'agriculture', which have also developed through a process of codification, construction, and definition. With this metalanguage thus settled, the anthropologist may formulate and test hypotheses, say, to the effect that past agricultural practices have led to soil depletion and alteration of the means of subsistence, with certain resultant effects on social structure, customs, and so forth. These are fully legitimate hypotheses whose status as such is in no way threatened by what I have said regarding translation.

How well my conclusions and considerations square with all the facets of Quine's position is not easy to tell. He contends that none of the *extremely* disquieting consequences for anthropology that I have indicated follow from his position, and I agree. However, many of his remarks lend themselves to extreme interpretations and I believe my reconstruction makes a gain in clarifying the consequences of indeterminacy and ridding it of the disturbing suggestions that arise from remarks of his to the effect that the "parameters" of translation are not "fixed," or that the linguist has "nothing to be right or wrong about." Also, and most importantly in the present context, I differ from Quine in not wedding the indeterminacy thesis to methodological commitments antagonistic to language-and-culture anthropology: I am simply transporting elements regarded generally as belonging to the descriptive part of theorizing to the prescriptive part (which, in addition, removes the grounds on which such problems might be based that charge that this sort of inquiry is "unscientific"). On the other hand, my view does provide a clearer basis for a distinction of the sort Quine wishes to draw between translation and theory, even if it is not the basis he has in mind. Also, it provides a clearer basis for arguing that successful translational correlations need not involve ontic commitment to intensions and it helps avoid needless worries as to whether or not the subjects' conceptual schemes have been "reproduced."

Notes

1. M. White, *Toward Reunion in Philosophy* (New York: Atheneum, 1963), pp. 5f.

2. These, as well as the other general remarks in this section, will be spelled out in more detail in ensuing chapters.

3. See my discussions of etic-emic and componential analyses below.

4. W. Quine, *Word and Object* (Cambridge, Mass.: M.I.T. Press, 1960). He further argues that this consequence holds for interpretations involving closely related languages, and within single languages. He views interpretation, construal, paraphrase, etc. as forms of "translation."

5. As my purpose in my discussions of translation manuals is (like Quine's) to examine and uncover certain important philosophical consequences of radical translation, I shall be dealing with an idealized notion of a *translation manual*. Yet, although this is an idealization, what I am saying about the nature of field notes is reflected in the work of many anthropologists, including such classic sources as Franz Boas' published field notes, *Kwakiutl Ethnography*, ed. Helen Codere (Chicago: University of Chicago Press, 1966), pp. vii, 20ff., 26ff., 178., 259.; as well as in published ethnographies such as Ward Goodenough, *Property, Kin, and Community on Truk*, Yale University Publications in Anthropology, no. 46 (New Haven, Conn.: Yale University Press, 1951), pp. 81ff., 94ff., 186f.

6. See, for example, Oswald Werner and Donald T. Campbell, "Translating, Working Through Interpreters, and the Problem of Decentering," *A Handbook of Method in Cultural Anthropology*, ed. R. Naroll and R. Cohen (Garden City, N.J.: American Museum of Natural History Press, 1970), p. 398.

7. This despite his basic contention that most translational hypotheses "are only in an incomplete sense hypotheses" (Quine, *Word and Object*, p. 73).

8. Also, while I shall speak of anthropological "theory," "hypothesis" formation, etc., I intend my concerns and remarks to apply also to those approaches viewed as being more humanistic in nature. Even these must be

concerned with giving objective, somehow systematic accounts that are partly grounded in linguistic and behavioral evidence. Such commitments are as much at issue here as in the case of more avowedly scientific approaches.

9. This classification, like the list of theories it categorizes, is not intended either to be exhaustive or uniquely correct; to attempt to do this would beg important questions of what constitutes an adequate theory of meaning, an issue that later chapters shall, in part, concern. Gilbert Harman presents a somewhat different classification of theories of meaning (in "Three Levels of Meaning," *The Journal of Philosophy* 65 (1968): 590–602), which is also fruitfully applicable to anthropological contexts. Harman distinguishes theories according to their primary concern with questions of (1) characterizing the linguistic medium of thought, (2) accounting for communication, and (3) presenting a theory of speech acts. His account is particularly useful in sorting out confusions among these various levels of meaning that are manifest in recent controversies in the literature. My own categorization (drawn in part from William Alston, *Philosophy of Language* (Englewood Cliffs, N.J.: Prentice-Hall, 1964, chaps. 1–2) is chosen for its applicability to recent trends in anthropology as well as to the main underlying currents in Quine's indeterminacy arguments.

10. I shall only mention meaning-as-reference theories in passing here, as they have had little success in the past as systematic theories, though most theories incorporate reference as an aspect of meaning. However, in later sections I shall adapt Nelson Goodman's (context-relative) referential theory.

11. Franz Brentano, "The Distinction Between Mental and Physical Phenomena," *Realism and the Background of Phenomenology*, ed. R. M. Chisholm (New York: The Free Press, 1960), pp. 50–52.

12. See, for example, Roderick M. Chisholm, "Sentences About Believing," Proceedings of the Aristotelian Society 56 (1955–56): 125–48. (The astronomically fastidious will note that it is now known that there is more than one ringed planet. However, common parlance still identifies just Saturn in these terms.)

13. For a helpful discussion of this distinction, as well as of Brentano's and Quine's theses, see Arnold Levison, *Knowledge and Society* (Indianapolis: Bobbs-Merrill, 1974), chaps. 6–8.

14. G. Frege, *"Begriffsschrift*, I. Explanation of the Symbols," reprinted in *Translations from the Writings of Gottlob Frege*, ed. and trans. Peter Geach and Max Black (Oxford: Basil Blackwell, 1966), pp. 1–4. Geach and Black note that by 'thought' (*Gedanke*) Frege means something sharable by many thinkers (p. ixn). The Fregean influence on contemporary linguistic theories is particularly clear in Herbert H. Clark and Eve

V. Clark, *Psychology and Language: An Introduction to Psycholinguistics* (New York: Harcourt Brace Jovanovich, 1977), chap. 11. Also, the book incorporates a good deal of discussion of relevant anthropological research.

15. Frege's particular notion of a "concept" differs from typical construals, but this difference is not critical here. For a helpful discussion of these points see Michael Dummett, "Frege, Gottlob," *The Encyclopedia of Philosophy* 3 (1967): 225–37; and references therein. However fair my account is to Frege's own views, it adequately characterizes, I think, the "Fregean" theories influenced by him and that I discuss below. Also, the reader will, I hope, excuse what I think is harmless impreciseness in my usage of 'expression', 'term', 'designates', etc.

16. See, for example, B. Russell "The Philosophy of Logical Atomism," *The Monist* 28 (1918): 495–527; 29 (1919): 32–63, 190–222, 345–80. Reprinted in *Readings in Twentieth-Century Philosophy*, ed. William P. Alston and George Nakhnikian (New York: The Free Press, 1963), pp. 298–380.

17. Even in Russell's later *An Inquiry into Meaning and Truth* (New York: Norton, 1940) this concern is still manifest, even though many of his earlier objectives have been abandoned.

18. See C. G. Hempel's excellent survey of these problems, "Empiricist Criteria of Cognitive Significance: Problems and Changes," *Aspects of Scientific Explanation* (New York: The Free Press, 1965), pp. 99–122. See also Israel Scheffler, *The Anatomy of Inquiry* (Indianapolis: Bobbs-Merril, 1963), pt. 2. For an overview of logical positivism, see A. J. Ayer, *Language, Truth and Logic* (New York: Dover, 1946).

19. C. I. Lewis, *An Analysis of Knowledge and Valuation* (LaSalle, Ill: Open Court, 1946), pp. 36ff., 48ff. In discussing the signification and intension of sentences, Lewis actually departs somewhat from his prior discussion in distinguishing a sentence from the proposition it asserts and treating the proposition as an abstract object distinct from the sentence (itself an abstract expression-type). The proposition is that which possesses the intension. However, since propositions entail themselves, they are included, on his definition, in the intension. And for the sake of simplicity I have treated the intension here as belonging to the sentence (type). Thus, a sentence "possesses" an intension (a proposition and its entailed propositions) in the precise sense that it expresses a proposition that, in stricter idiom, actually possesses the intension.

Two other points bear mention here: (1) Lewis' notion of "connotation" is different from ordinary usage in that it means intension rather than emotive connotations, etc. (2) Lewis' notion of a "concept," as the intension of a predicate, is typical of theories of meaning but different from Frege's use of the term, which corresponds more to Lewis' signification.

20. Ibid., 43–44; cf. pp. 133ff.

21. Ibid., 171.

22. Ibid., 134. Again, intensions are linguistic entities and not "mental pictures" of attributes, nor are they the attributes themselves. (This holds both for linguistic meaning and sense meaning.)

23. Ibid., 72.

24. Ibid., 133.

25. Ibid., 138.

26. Ibid., 171. As before, I am not attending to distinctions typically drawn between statements and propositions. Indeed, even the sentence-proposition distinction is not of great importance here, as Quine regards propositions as nothing more than sentences.

27. Carnap, "Meaning and Synonymy in Natural Languages," *Meaning and Necessity: A Study in Semantics and Modal Logic*, 2d ed. (Chicago: University of Chicago Press, 1956), pp. 233–44.

28. See, for example, J. J. Katz, *The Underlying Reality of Language and Its Philosophic Import* (New York: Harper & Row, 1971), p. 101.

29. Ibid., chap. 5; cf. Jerrold Katz and Jerry Fodor, "The Structure of Semantic Theory," *The Structure of Language: Readings in the Philosophy of Language* (Englewood Cliffs, N.J.: Prentice-Hall, 1964), pp. 479–518. Also, see Katz's recent discussion of various points in the controversy over linguistic platonism in *Language and Other Abstract Objects* (Totowa, N.J.: Rowan and Littlefield, 1979).

30. Katz and Fodor, "The Structure of Semantic Theory," pp. 172ff.

31. A clear summary of major ideational approaches currently in use in philosophy of language, linguistics, and psycholinguistics may be found in Clark and Clark, *Psychology and Language*, chaps. 1, 11–12. These incorporate elements of Lewis and Goodenough's theories along with those of generative approaches. Also, the book gives a good overview of some of the more recent advances on the epistemic and psycholinguistic concerns of Lewis, Chomsky, et al.

32. Ludwig Wittgenstein, *Philosophical Investigations* (Oxford: Basil Blackwell, 1953); Gilbert Ryle, *The Concept of Mind* (London: Hutchinson, 1966).

33. Michael Bloomfield, *Language* (New York: Holt, 1948), p. 139.

34. *Verbal Behavior* (New York: Appleton Century Crofts, 1957), chap. 6 passim.

35. N. Chomsky, "Review of B. F. Skinner's *Verbal Behavior*," *Language* vol. 35, no. 1 (1959), p. 32.

36. Charles Morris, *Signs, Language, and Behavior* (New York: Prentice-Hall, 1946).

37. Ibid., 347, 349, 354. Certain of Morris' remarks (see ibid., 17–20) suggest a reading of 'signification' more akin to Lewis' comprehension. 'Designation' figures in his tripartite distinction of sign into designative, appraisive, and prescriptive (ibid., 76ff., 98, 347). Compare C. K. Ogden, and I. A. Richards, *The Meaning of Meaning*, 5th ed. (New York: Harcourt, Brace, and World, 1938 [1923]), pp. 223–24.

38. *Signification and Significance: A Study of the Relation of Signs and Values* (Cambridge, Mass.: M.I.T. Press, 1964).

39. Ibid., 3–4.

40. Ibid., 9–10. Morris remarks here that a sign is designative "insofar as it signifies *observable* properties of the environment or of the actor."

41. Morris follows Carnap here in viewing the commitment to attributes as reflecting harmless, pragmatic choices of framework concepts.

42. Wittgenstein, *Philosophical Investigations*, pp. 126e, 49e, 88e, 14e–15e; The *Blue and Brown Books* (Oxford: Basil Blackwell, 1958), p. 98.

43. J. L. Austin, *How to Do Things With Words*, 2d ed. (Cambridge, Mass.: Harvard University Press, 1975 [1962]), chaps. 9–10 (lectures originally delivered in 1955); Alston, *Philosophy of Language*, chap. 2; John Searle, *Speech Acts* (Cambridge: Cambridge University Press, 1969), chaps. 2–3.

44. Searle, *Speech Acts*, p. 29.

45. Ibid.

46. J. R. Ross, "On Declarative Sentences," *Readings in English Transformational Grammar*, ed. R. S. Jacobs and P. Rosenbaum (Waltham, Mass.: Ginn and Co., 1970), pp. 271–72; Searle, *Speech Acts*, pp. 30, 95

47. Ibid., 44ff. Compare H. Paul Grice, "Meaning," *The Philosophical Review*, vol. 66, no. 3 (July 1957), pp. 377–88.

48. Ibid., 48.

49. Compare White, *Toward Reunion in Philosophy*, pp. 54f. and passim. See also Morton White, "The Analytic and Synthetic: An Untenable Dualism," *Semantics and the Philosophy of Language*, ed. L. Linsky (Urbana, Ill.: University of Illinois Press, 1952), pp. 272–86. Compare the related skeptical theses of N. Goodman in *Problems and Projects*

(Indianapolis, Ind.: Bobbs-Merrill, 1972), chap. 5; *The Structure of Appearance*, 3d ed. (Dordrecht: Reidel, 1977), chap. 1. (Goodman's remarks in the latter are interesting when compared to Sapir's regarding the similarities of languages and geometrical systems of reference; see below.) Compare also Donald Davidson, "Truth and Meaning,"*Synthese* 17 (1967): 304–23; "On the Very Idea of a Conceptual Scheme," *Proceedings and Addresses of the American Philosophical Association* 67 (1973–1974): 5–20; Hilary Putnam, "The Analytic and the Synthetic," "How Not to Talk About Meaning," "Is Semantics Possible?," and "The Meaning of 'Meaning'" in *Mind, Language, and Reality* 2 *Philosophical Papers Volume 2* (Cambridge: Cambridge University Press, 1975).

50. Quine emphasizes that ontological simplicity is not his main motivation in "Facts of the Matter," *Essays on the Philosophy of W. V. Quine*, ed. Robert W. Shahan and Chris Swoyer (Norman: University of Oklahoma Press, 1979), pp. 166–67. For comments on Brentano and related views, see *Word and Object*, pp. 216ff.

51. W. Quine, "Two Dogmas of Empiricism," *From a Logical Point of View*, 2d ed. (New York: Harper Torchbooks, 1963 [1953]), 20–46, 27–32. For some rejoinders to Quine on these points, see H. P. Grice and P. F. Strawson, "In Defense of a Dogma," *Philosophical Review* 65 (1956): 151; Searle, *Speech Acts*, p. 8; A. Church, "The Need For Abstract Entities in Semantic Analysis," *Proceedings of the American Academy of Arts and Sciences*, vol. 80, no. 1 (1951), p. 104.

52. W. Quine, *Word and Object*. pp. 157ff.

53. Goodman, N., *The Structure of Appearance*, pp. 99–104, 112–13, 124–25. See its application by psychologists George A. Miller and Phillip N. Johnson-Laird in *Language and Perception* (Cambridge: Harvard University Press, 1976), pp. 12–14. Compare Goodman, "The Revision of Philosophy," *Problems and Projects*, pp. 1–23; "The Way the World Is," ibid., pp. 24–32.

54. W. Quine, "Two Dogmas," pp. 41–42. Compare Pierre Duhem, *The Aim and Structure of Physical Theory* (New York: Atheneum, 1962 [1914]).

55. Quine, *Word and Object*, pp. 8, 13.

56. See, for example, *Philosophical Investigations*, pp. 33–35e.

57. W. Quine, "The Problem of Meaning in Linguistics," *From A Logical Point of View*, pp. 47–64; *Word and Object*, chap. Two. Quine tends in these discussions to equate the receptor language with the *linguist's metalanguage*, which latter *mentions* the receptor- and source-language strings in its translational hypotheses. What Quine has in mind here is a case in which receptor language and metalanguage are derived from the

same natural language. Here and elsewhere I shall endeavor to keep the linguistic levels clear.

58. Quine, "The Problem of Meaning in Linguistics," p. 60.

59. Ibid., 61. Compare Sapir's remark (noted below) that the significant
unconscious processes of language "are to be explained, if explained at all,
as due to the more minute action of psychological factors beyond the control
of will or reason."

60. Ibid., 61.

61. Ibid., 63.

62. Ibid., 63. The empirical scientist has something for his hypotheses to
be about, even where they contain predicates whose extensions comprise
things—theoretical entities—that are unobservable in principle. However,
the linguist has nothing for his hypotheses to be about when he relates expressions that refer to (or express) the unobservable. Again, in saying that
the linguist is projecting his *own* world-view onto the native, Quine is viewing the linguist's natural language as identical to the receptor language.
However, it is important to keep clear that the metalanguage he employs
qua linguist is distinct from the receptor language.

63. Quine, *Word and Object*, p. 8.

64. Carnap, "Meaning and Synonymy in Natural Languages," pp.
233–44.

65. Ibid., 235.

66. Ibid., 237.

67. Ibid., 238, 240.

68. Arne Naess, *Interpretation and Preciseness: A Contribution to the
Theory of Communication* (Oslo: I Kommisjon Hos Jacob Dybwad, 1953).
Compare A. Naess, "Toward a Theory of Interpretation and Preciseness,"
Semantics and the Philosophy of Language, pp. 248–69.

69. Quine, *Word and Object*, Secs. 9–16.

70. Ibid., 23.

71. Ibid., 26.

72. Ibid., 27.

73. Ibid.

74. Ibid., 31–32. For example, the linguist must not count glimpses of
rabbits that are so fleeting that the native misses them and gives negative
responses to 'Gavagai?' where the linguist would affirm 'Rabbit?'. Nor may

the modulus be so long that the native is believed to be denying that he saw a rabbit presented earlier when actually he is noting the present absence of rabbits.

75. Ibid., 34. As Quine's definition collects into classes those stimulations that would prompt assent or dissent, he argues that coherence demands that the members must be forms, or universals, rather than realized and unrealized particulars.

76. Ibid., 34–35. In this connection see Paul Roth, "Paradox and Indeterminacy," *The Journal of Philosophy* 75 (1978): 347–67.

77. Ibid., 35–36.

78. Ibid., 42.

79. Ibid., 40–46, 193–94. W. Quine, "On Empirically Equivalent Systems of the World," *Erkenntnis* 9 (1975): 320. Quine, "Empirical Content," *Theories and Things* (Cambridge: Harvard University Press, 1981), p. 27. Quine endeavors to define 'observation sentence' intersubjectively in *Word and Object*. However, his later "Empirical Content" (p. 25) eschews this in favor of the intrasubjective notion I emphasize here.

80. Quine, *Word and Object*, p. 45.

81. Ibid., 47ff., 68.

82. That is, '(x) (Fx iff Gx)' equates the predicates 'F' and 'G'.

83. Ibid., 54–55.

84. Ibid., 51ff.

85. Ibid., 51–52.

86. Ibid., 52–53.

87. Ibid., 53. Compare 72.

88. Counting those appearing in nonliterary Japanese only: Compare M. Sanches "Language Acquisition and Language Change: Japanese and Numerical Classifiers," *Language, Thought, and Culture*, eds. B. G. Blount and M. Sanches (New York: Academic Press, 1977), pp. 51–62.

89. W. Quine, "Ontological Relativity," *Ontological Relativity and Other Essays* (New York: Columbia University Press, 1969), pp. 35–38. Compare Quine's arguments in this essay (pp. 55–62) that generate ontological relativity from the multiplicity of "proxy functions" adequate to the statement of theoretical ontologies. Quine has recently expressed favor toward this formulation for its clarity and independence from the indeterminacy thesis ("Reply to Paul A. Roth," *The Philosophy of W.V. Quine*,

ed. Lewis E. Hahn [LaSalle, IL: Open Court Press, 1987], p. 460). However, given my anthropological emphasis, I have chosen not to explicate it here.

90. Quine, *Word and Object*, p. 59.

91. Ibid., 60. Quine has modified his *Word and Object* position on the translation of truth-functional logic to allow for partial indeterminacy in the translation of conjunctions and disjunctions. "Philosophical Progress in Language Theory," *Metaphilosophy* 1 (1970): 12–13.

92. Nor will stimulus meaning or its derivatives (stimulus analyticity, etc.) do the work expected of broader analogs in the semantics of Carnap et al. (see below). Strictly speaking, analytic hypotheses are the linguist's dictionary entries correlating source-language terms and phrases in the receptor-language expressions (Ibid., 68). These entries will dictate translations of sentences (and should dictate those translations that may be determined on the basis of stimulus synonymy) and will reflect the grammatical structures, constructions, and rules that the linguist has imputed to the source languge. Also, compare their incorporation in actual field notes and ethnography in the works cited in chap. 1, n.6.

93. Of course empirically *in*adequate manuals are *in*correct. Quine's point concerns our ability to discriminate among manuals that measure up empirically.

94. Ibid., 71.

95. Quine, "The Problem of Meaning in Linguistics," pp. 53–56; "Indeterminacy of Translation Again," *The Journal of Philosophy* 84 (1987): 8–10.

96. Ibid., 72. By 'speech behavior' Quine means the subject's dispositions to accept sentences. Compare Harman, G., "An Introduction to 'Translation and Meaning': Chapter Two of *Word and Object*," and Quine's reply in J. Hintikka and D. Davidson, eds., *Words and Objections* (Dordrecht: Reidel, 1968), pp. 21ff., 205ff.

97. Quine, *Word and Object*, p. 72.

98. Ibid., 73–74. That is, assent or dissent on the part of the linguist: the stimulations that would encourage his assent or dissent would be discernible differences in native response to promptings that would give empirical support to one proposed translation over another.

99. Ibid., 72.

100. Quine, "On the Reasons for Indeterminacy of Translation," *The Journal of Philosophy* 67 (July 1970): 181–82.

101. Ibid., 179–80.

102. Quine, "On Empirically Equivalent Systems," p. 313.

103. Quine, "Epistemology Naturalized," *Ontological Relativity*, p. 80. See Paul Roth's concise summary of this line of argument in "Semantics Without Foundations," *The Philosophy of W. V. Quine*, ed. L. Hahn (LaSalle, Ill.: Open Court Press, 1987), pp. 440–41; compare Roth's earlier "Paradox and Indeterminacy," pp. 335–67. Quine expresses his preference for the holism over the underdetermination line in his reply to Roth in Hahn, *The Philosophy of W. V. Quine*, pp. 459–60.

104. Ibid., 80–81. It is worth noting that being a "theoretical sentence" for Quine does not hinge on the presence of so-called "theoretical terms." Instead, it depends on the sentence not being stimulus-meaning determinate.

105. However, see Dagfinn Follesdal's efforts to distinguish translation from physics in terms of the differing roles that simplicity plays in each: "Indeterminacy of Translation and Under-Determination of the Theory of Nature," *Dialectica* 27 (1973): 289–301.

106. Quine, "Facts of the Matter," pp. 166–67.

Chapter 2

1. F. Boas, "Linguistics and Ethnology," *Language in Culture and Society*, ed. D. Hymes (New York: Harper & Row, 1964), pp. 15–17. Originally in *Handbook of American Indian Languages*, BAE–B40, pt. I (Washington, D.C.: Smithsonian Institution, 1911), pp 59–73.

2. Boas, "Linguistics and Ethnology," p. 17. Indeed, Boas claimed to have mastered the Kwakiutl language (of Vancouver Island) to the point of being able to "develop the idea of the abstract term in the mind of the Indian" through discussion in the native tongue. (Ibid., 18.)

3. D. Hymes, "Linguistic Method in Ethnography: Its Development in the United States," *Method and Theory in Linguistics*, ed. P. Garvin (The Hague and Paris: Mouton, 1970), p. 251. Boas' at least partial awareness of the implications of his work is manifest in his remark that "the study of language must be considered as one of the most important branches of ethnological study, because, on the one hand, a thorough insight into ethnology cannot be gained without practical knowledge of language, and, on the other hand, the fundamental concepts illustrated by human languages are not distinct in kind from ethnological phenomena." (Boas, "Linguistics and Ethnology," p. 22.)

4. Boas, "Linguistics and Ethnology," p. 17.

5. Hymes, "Linguistic Method in Ethnography," p. 253. I shall not be

closely attentive to the differences between the problem areas of *ethnography* (studies of single cultures) and *ethnology* (comparative cross-cultural studies), as I do not believe the important differences between these two affect the present thesis. My main focus is on field translation upon which depends (in the view of many anthropologists) a good deal of *ethnographic* data, and upon problems of objectivity of translation that carry over to both ethnography and ethnology. Hence, I shall usually only refer to these problems as 'translational' or 'ethnographic'.

6. Ibid., 252. As it is employed in the literature, the expression 'linguistic method' comprises both discovery and validation procedures. The philosophical difficulties I shall isolate concern mainly the validational context, although relevant aspects of the context of discovery will be covered as well.

7. Hymes, *Language in Culture and Society*, p. 115.

8. Hymes, "Linguistic Method in Ethnography," p. 259.

9. E. Sapir, *Language* (New York: Harcourt Brace and World 1921), p. 233.

10. Sapir, "Language and Environment," *Selected Writings of Edward Sapir in Language, Culture, and Personality*, ed. D.G. Mandelbaum (Berkeley and Los Angeles: University of California Press, 1949), p. 100. Originally appeared in *American Anthropologist*, vol. 14, no. 2 (January-March, 1912), pp. 226-42.

11. Sapir, "The Status of Linguistics as a Science," *Selected Writings of Edward Sapir*, ed. D.G. Mandelbaum, p. 162. Originally appeared in *Language* 5 (1929): pp. 160-66.

12. See, for example, Whorf and his influential student Harry Hoijer, who place heavy stress on grammar as the key indicator of world-view. Lexicon, on the other hand, is not viewed by them, or by present-day anthropologists generally, as of significance in this regard (although Oswald Werner takes significant exception to this). See H. Hoijer, "Cultural Implications of Some Navajo Linguistic Categories," *Language*, vol. 27, no. 2 (April-June, 1951), pp. 111-20; M. Kearney, "World View Theory and Study," *Annual Reviews in Anthropology*, ed. B.J. Siegel, et al., 10 vols. (Palo Alto, Calif.: Annual Reviews, Inc., 1972-1981), 4 (1975): 247-70; O. Werner, "Cultural Knowledge, Language, and World View," *Cognition: A Multiple View*, ed. P. Garvin (New York: Macmillan, 1968), pp. 153-76.

13. Hymes, "Linguistic Method in Ethnography," p. 262.

14. Sapir, "The Grammarian and His Language," *Selected Writings of Edward Sapir*, p. 159. Originally in *American Mercury*, vol. 1, no. 2 (February 1924), pp. 149-55.

15. Ibid., 153.

16. Sapir, "Conceptual Categories in Primitive Languages," *Language in Culture and Society*, ed. D. Hymes (New York: Harper & Row, 1964), p. 128. Originally in *Science* 74 (1931): 578.

17. Ibid.

18. W. Bright, "Language," *International Encyclopedia of the Social Sciences*, ed. L. Sills, Vol. 9 (New York: Macmillan, 1968), p. 22.

19. F. De Saussure, *Course in General Linguistics*, trans. W. Baskin (New York: Philosophical Library, 1958). E. Cassirer, *The Philosophy of Symbolic Forms*, trans. R. Mannheim, Vol. 1 of *Language* (New Haven: Yale University Press, 1953).

20. Hymes, "Linguistic Method in Ethnography," p. 286. Compare D. Kronenfeld and H. W. Decker, "Structuralism," *Annual Reviews* 8 (1979): 503–41. De Saussure's influence is also felt via his influence on transformational linguistics.

21. F. Lounsbury, "A Semantic Analysis of the Pawnee Kinship Usage," *Language*, vol. 32, no. 1 (January-February 1956), pp. 158–94; J. Greenberg, "Linguistics and Ethnology," *Language in Culture and Society*, ed. D. Hymes, pp. 27–31.

22. Greenberg, "Linguistics and Ethnology," p. 28. Morris treats all morphemes as designating; however, a number of philosophers, including Quine, have found it useful to distinguish designating or *categorematic* expressions, from nondesignating, or *syncategorematic* ones (the latter serve a designative function only when combined with larger expressions). For example, connectives such as 'and' are syncategorematic for Quine and categorematic for Morris. Compare Morris, *Signs, Language, Behavior*, pp. 159ff., and Quine, *Philosophy of Logic* (Englewood Cliffs, N.J.: Prentice-Hall, 1970), pp. 27f.

23. See the discussions of componential analysis and symbolic anthropology below. Morris' influence, though perhaps not as strong, persists in fairly recent literature. See, for example, H. W. Scheffler and F. G. Lounsbury, *A Study in Structural Semantics: The Siriono Kinship System* (Englewood Cliffs, N.J.: Prentice-Hall, 1971), pp. 3–12; H. W. Scheffler, "Kinship Semantics," *Annual Reviews* 1 (1972): 309–28, wherein Morris' terms 'denote', 'designate', and 'signify' (from *Signs, Language, and Behavior*) are explicitly employed. Lounsbury's "A Semantic Analysis of Pawnee Kinship Usage" (1956) also employs these notions. Note also Morris' influence on contemporary sociolinguists and symbolic anthropologists discussed below (stemming from his later *Foundations of the Theory of Signs* [Chicago: University of Chicago Press, 1933]).

24. W. Goodenough, "Cultural Anthropology and Linguistics,"

Language in Culture and Society, ed. D. Hymes, pp. 36ff. Originally appeared in *Report of the Seventh Annual Round Table Meeting on Linguistics and Language Study*, ed., P. L. Garvin. Monograph Series on Languages and Linguistics, No. 9, (Washington, D.C.: Georgetown University Press, 1957), pp. 167–73.

25. Ibid., 36,37.

26. Ibid., 36.

27. Ibid., 39.

28. Ibid., 39.

29. Ibid., 37. As Morris puts it, "a sign is *iconic* to the extent to which it itself has the properties of its denotata; otherwise it is *non-iconic*." (*Signs, Language, and Behavior*, p. 23.) Roughly, the properties involved in iconic signification are those the possession of which is determinable by reference to physical theory, and the sharing of which by objects is taken to be indicative of a significant similarity between them relative to the framework of the theory. (Thus, they approximate what are termed "etic" properties—see below.) Morris' distinction, which is suitable as it stands for my present purposes, is inadequate in a number of important respects: see Richard Rudner, "On Semiotic Aesthetics," *The Journal of Aesthetics and Art Criticism*, vol. 10, no. 1 (1951), p. 70.

30. Ibid., 36.

31. Following the terminology of a recent review article, I am construing the "model" here as the linguistic theory from which an ethnographic theory is developed by analogical extension. It is not always clear when it is a linguistic theory or a modeled ethnographic theory that is being discussed or employed, and some methodologists purposefully resist the distinction; hence, I shall often use the looser term 'approach' to cover both. The article I cite is Mridula Durbin's "Linguistic Models in Anthropology," *Annual Reviews* 1 (1972): pp. 384ff.

32. K. Pike, *Language in Relation to a Unified Theory of the Structure of Human Behavior: Pt. 1* (Glendale, Calif.: Summer Institute of Linguistics, 1954). Pike credits Sapir as having a major influence on his conception of emics (chap. 1 passim., esp. p. 16).

33. Charles O. Frake, "The Ethnographic Study of Cognitive Systems," *Anthropology and Human Behavior*, ed. T. H. Gladwin and W. C. Sturtevant (Washington D.C.: Anthropological Society of Washington, 1962), p. 84; Paul Kay, "Some Theoretical Implications of Ethnographic Semantics," *American Anthropological Association Bulletin*, vol. 3, no. 3, pt. 2 (1970), p. 23.

34. See Goodenough, "Cultural Anthropology and linguistics," p. 37.

35. Durbin, "Linguistic Models in Anthropology," p. 386. The mentalistic character of components has also been stressed by general linguists such as M. Bierwisch ("Semantics," *New Horizons in Linguistics*, ed. J. Lyons [Baltimore: Penguin Books, 1970], pp. 161–85) as well as by generative grammarians who incorporate componential analysis into their broader theory (see below). See Clark and Clark, *Psychology and Language*, chap. 11.

36. Durbin, "Linguistics Models in Anthropology." Indeed, componential analysis was first applied to kinship study by Goodenough and Lounsbury in 1947–1949, during which time both were influenced by Morris (W. Sturtevant, "Studies in Ethnoscience," *Transcultural Studies in Cognition*, ed. A. K. Romney and R. G. D'Andrade, *American Anthropologist*, vol. 66, no. 3, pt. 2 (June 1964), pp. 112–13. It is perhaps because of the early application of this approach to kinship studies that Hymes diverges from Durbin in treating it as an anthropologically, rather than a linguistically, based approach ("Linguistic Method in Ethnography," pp. 291ff.)

37. Goodenough, *Description and Comparison in Cultural Anthropology* (Chicago: Aldine, 1970), pp. 72–97. See also Sturtevant, "Studies in Ethnoscience," pp. 99–131. Compare A. Kroeber, "Classificatory Systems of Relationship," *The Journal of the Royal Anthropological Institute of Great Britain* 39 (1909): 77–84; G. P. Murdock, *Social Structure* (New York: Macmillan, 1949). See also C. H. Brown, "Semantic Components, Meaning, and Use in Ethnosemantics," *Philosophy of Science*, vol. 43, no. 3 (September 1976), pp. 379–80.

38. See, for example, Goodenough, "Componential Analysis and the Study of Meaning," *Language*, vol. 33, no. 1 (1956), p. 195. This discussion of kinship has a particularly mentalistic ring to it.

39. Ibid., 195n.

40. Ibid., 195. He used 'connotation' and 'connotata' here in their typical senses—which, as I noted earlier, differ from Lewis' usage of these terms (for him connotation is intension).

41. Goodenough, "Cultural Anthropology and Linguistics," pp. 37–38; H. W. Scheffler, "Kinship Semantics," p. 317.

42. Goodenough, *Description and Comparison*, p. 72.

43. Scheffler, "Kinship Semantics." Both Scheffler and Goodenough seem to equate *defining* characteristics (the necessary and sufficient conditions) of class membership with *essential* characteristics (those necessary for class membership. However, not all defining characteristics are necessary, in that a *disjunction* of characteristics may be necessary for class membership, no one of which is necessary or essential (while the

conjunction of these characteristics may constitute sufficient conditions for membership). This problem is exemplified in Wittgenstein's famous example of a *game*.

44. Ibid., 322; compare Morris, *Signs, Language, and Behavior*, p. 19.

45. Goodenough, *Description and Comparison*, pp. 108–12; compare pp. 70–72.

46. Ibid. Compare *Property, Kin, and Community on Truk* and D. Oliver, *A Solomon Island Society* (Cambridge: Harvard University Press, 1955).

47. Goodenough, *Description and Comparison*, p. 79.

48. Frake, "Ethnographic Study," p. 83.

49. Ibid., 74n.

50. Ibid., 84.

51. Ibid. Compare Frake's "Plying Frames Can be Dangerous: Some Reflections on Methodology in Cognitive Anthropology," *Quarterly Newsletter of the Institute for Comparative Human Development*, Rockefeller University, Vol. 1, No. 3 (1977), pp. 1–7.

52. R. Burling, "Cognition and Componential Analysis: God's Truth or Hocus-Pocus?" *American Anthropologist*, vol. 66, no. 1 (1964), p. 24; this source *mentions* the target and source-language strings in its translational hypotheses. What Quine has in mind here is a case in which target and metalanguage are derived from the same natural language. Here and elsewhere I shall endeavor to keep the linguistic levels clear.

53. H. C. Conklin, "Lexicographical Treatment of Folk Taxonomies," *International Journal of American Linguistics*, vol. 28, no. 2, pt. 4 (1962) pp. 119–41.

54. Burling, "Cognition and Componential Analysis," pp. 25–26.

55. C. O. Frake, "The Diagnosis of Disease Among the Subanun of Mindanao" *American Anthropologist*, vol. 63, no. 1 (February 1961), pp. 112–32.

56. Burling, "Cognition and Componential Analysis," p. 26.

57. Ibid.

58. Ibid.

59. A. K. Romney, and R. G. D'Andrade, "Cognitive Aspects of English Kin Terms," *Transcultural Studies in Cognition*, p. 168. Compare A. F. C. Wallace, "The Problem of Psychological Validity of Componential Analyses," *Formal Semantic Analysis*, ed. E. A. Hammel, *American Anthropologist*, vol. 67, no. 5 (1965), supplement, pp. 229–48.

60. The *semantic differential* technique developed by Charles Osgood is adapted by Romney and D'Andrade in the determination of psychologically valid results ("Semantic Differential Technique in the Comparative Study of Cultures," *Transcultural Studies in Cognition*, pp. 171–200) and Gary Triandis, "Approaches Toward Minimizing Translation," *Translation*, ed. R. W. Brislin (New York: John Wiley & Sons, 1976), pp. 229–45). Osgood's method seeks to determine native connotation (in a broad sense, comprising emotive meaning, as well as nonessential intension) through eliciting responses to questionnaires in which scaled values are assigned to contrasting word-pairings (e.g., 'hot-cold') associated with certain key terms (e.g., 'mother'). See also Goodenough's earlier application of Guttman's Scale Analysis to Ethnography in Culture Theory," *Southwestern Journal of Anthropology*, vol. 19, no. 3 (Fall 1963), pp. 235–50.

61. Romney and D'Andrade, "Cognitive Aspects of English Kin Terms."

62. Cecil H. Brown, "Semantic Components, Meaning, and Use in Ethnosemantics," p. 382.

63. Ibid. Compare Wittgenstein, *Philosophical Investigations*, p. 49e; and C. H. Brown, *Wittgensteinian Linguistics* (The Hague: Mouton, 1974).

64. R. G. D'Andrade, "Structure and Syntax in the Semantic Analysis of Kinship Terminologies," *Cognition: A Multiple View*, ed. P. Garvin, p. 131.

65. Quine, "On the Reasons for Indeterminacy," pp. 180–81. See also Michael Friedman's critique of Quine on this point, "Physicalism and the Indeterminacy of Translation," *Nous* 9 (1975): 353–73.

66. See, for example, Lawrence Fisher and Oswald Werner, "Explaining Explanation: Tension in American Anthropology," *Journal of Anthropological Research* 34 (1978): 200. Compare Sapir, "The Psychological Reality of Phonemes," *Selected Writings of Edward Sapir*, p. 47. Indeed, Roger Keesing, unlike commentators such as Durbin, Werner, and Hymes, seems to treat "cognitive anthropology" as distinct from "ethnoscience" and "the new ethnography," particularly insofar as it has adapted elements from the "newer transformational paradigm." Keesing, "Paradigms Lost: The New Ethnography and the New Linguistics, " *The Southwestern Journal of Anthropology* 28 (Winter 1972): 299–300. (However, I shall use these labels interchangeably nonetheless.)

67. Hymes, "Linguistic Method in Ethnography," pp. 296–310; D. Hymes, "Directions in (Ethno-) Linguistic Theory," *Transcultural Studies in Cognition*, pp. 29ff.; Durbin "Linguistic Models in Anthropology," p. 394) cites over a dozen studies that have derived a transformational model for kinship. Compare also Kenneth Hale, "Gaps in Grammar and Culture," *Linguistics and Anthropology*, ed. M. D. Kinkade,

et al. (Lisse: DeRidder, 1975), pp. 295–315; J. Lyons, *Introdution to Theoretical Linguistics* (Cambridge: Cambridge University Press, 1968), p. 247; C. F. Hockett, *A Course in Modern Linguistics* (New York: Macmillan, 1958); and Hymes, "Linguistic Method in Ethnography," pp. 296–97.

68. N. W. Schutz, Jr., "On the Autonomy and Comparability of Linguistic and Ethnographic Decription: Toward a Generative Theory of Ethnography," *Linguistics and Anthropology* ed. M. D. Kinkade, pp. 536–37. Schutz explicitly cites J. J. Katz and J. H. Fodor's "The Structure of a Semantic Theory," *The Structure of Language*.

69. Katz, *The Underlying Reality of Language and Its Philosophical Import* (New York: Harper & Row, 1971), pp. 44ff. Katz and Fodor, "The Structure of a Semantic Theory," pp. 172–76. Compare N. Chomsky, *Aspects of the Theory of Syntax* (Cambridge, Mass.: M.I.T. Press, 1965), chaps. 1 and 3. I give Katz and Fodor's account of the semantic component here (see "The Structure of a Semantic Theory," pp. 183ff.), which is somewhat at variance with Chomsky's. (Briefly, Chomsky attributes less generative power to the semantic component.) Given that the imposition problem cuts across grammar and semantics, I shall not attend to the differences here.

70. Hymes, "Linguistic Method in Ethnography," pp. 297–98. He cites Sapir's "Sound Patterns in Language," *Language* 1 (1925): 37–51.

71. Hymes, "Linguistic Method in Ethnography," p. 298.

72. Ibid. Compare also H. C. Conklin, "Lexicographical Treatment of Folk Taxonomies," *International Journal of American Linguistics*, ed. L. Sills, vol. 28. no. 2, pt. 4, pp. 119–41; Frake, "The Ethnographic Study of Cognitive Systems," pp. 72–93. Sturtevant, "Studies in Ethnoscience," pp. 99–131.

73. Schutz, "Autonomy and Comparability," pp. 536–37.

74. Durbin, "Linguistic Models in Anthropology," p. 394; Hymes, "Linguistic Method in Ethnography," p. 299. Compare F. G. Lounsbury, "A Formal Account of the Crow and Omaha-Type Kinship Terminologies," *Explorations in Cultural Anthropology*, ed. W. H. Goodenough (New York: McGraw-Hill, 1964), pp. 351–94. See also E. A. Hammel, "A Transformational Analysis of Comanche Kinship Terminology," *Formal Semantic Analysis*, pp. 65–105.

75. Durbin, "Linguistic Models in Anthropology," p. 394.

76. Ibid., 395. Durbin seems willing to demand only descriptive adequacy of deep structures in kinship analysis and other applications of the transformational *model*: "The only formal contingency of deep structures in a T-model, in its most abstract form, is logical consistency, i.e., noncontradiction and freedom from ambiguity. Such a model is considered descrip-

tively adequate, and . . .there can be no more than one descriptively adequate model," (Ibid.) (Compare below.)

77. O. Werner and J. Fenton, "Method and Theory in Ethnoscience or Ethno-Epistemology," *A Handbook of Method in Cultural Anthropology*, ed. R. Naroll and R. Cohen (Garden City, N.J.: American Museum of Natural History Press, 1970), pp. 537–78: pp. 537–39. Compare Michael Polanyi, *Personal Knowledge: Towards a Post-Critical Philosophy* (Chicago: University of Chicago Press, 1962), p. 4. His maps are "impersonal," though subject to erroneous individual interpretation, and have a "rigid formal structure." (Ibid.)

78. Katz, *The Underlying Reality of Language*, pp. 140–41.

79. Ibid., 142. Compare N. Chomsky and Morris Halle, "Some Controversial Issues in Phonological Theory," *The Journal of Linguistics* 1 (1965): 97–135, esp. p. 100; and N. Chomsky, *Topics in the Theory of Generative Grammar* (The Hague: Mouton, 1966), p. 22.

80. Chomsky's commitments to psychological reality remain firm. See his *Rules and Representations* (New York: Columbia University Press, 1980).

81. I. F. H. Wong, "Field Procedures in Generative Grammar," *Anthropological Linguistics*, vol. 17, no. 2 (February 1975), pp. 49–50. Wong evidently means that the native is taught translated equivalents, in his own language, of linguistic terminology. Compare K. Hale, "On the Use of Informants in Field Work," *Canadian Journal of Linguistics* 10 (1965): 108–19.

82. I shall omit detailed discussion of the *distinctive-feature* model, which supplements the transformational approach with methods of determining surface (e.g., kin) categories through contrast and complementarity of certain binarily opposed features (e.g., 'father' as +masculine, +generational removal, −seniority, etc.). The strict binary opposition of elements from which distinctive features are chosen represents the sharpest difference between this approach and the componential. Durbin, "Linguistic Models in Anthropology," pp. 399ff. Otherwise it seems to inherit all the difficulties plaguing the componential and generative approaches.

83. W. J. M. Levelt, "Whatever Became of LAD?" *Ut Videaum: Contributions to An Understanding of Linguistics*, ed. W. Abraham (Atlantic Highlands, N.J.: Humanities, 1975), pp. 171–90.

84. Ibid., 176–77. He here cites Eve Clark's "What Should LAD Look Like? Some Comments on Levelt." Discussion paper for a colloquium on "The Role of Grammar in Interdisciplinary Linguistic Research" (Bielefeld, Germany, December 1973).

85. Levelt, "Whatever Became of LAD?," pp. 177–78.

86. V. J. Cook, "Is Explanatory Adequacy Adequate?" *Linguistics*, no. 133 (1974) pp. 21–31, pp. 23–24.

87. Ibid., 25.

88. Ibid., 26ff. Compare I. M. Schlesinger, "A Note on the Relationship Between Psychological and Linguistic Theories, *Foundations of Language*, no. 4 (1974) pp. 397–402.

89. Hymes, "Linguistic Method in Ethnography," pp. 291, 309. (Also, it shares with generative grammar the strong influence of DeSaussure and Jakobson.) Hymes contends that structuralists give less attention to semantic analysis than transformationalists. However, David Kronenfeld and H. W. Decker dispute this in "Structuralism," *Annual Reviews* 8 (1979), p. 513.

90. P. Maranda, "Structuralism in Cultural Anthropology," *Annual Reviews*, B. J. Siegel, 1 (1972): 330–31. Hymes notes Levi-Strauss's ambition to broadly relate linguistic and ethnographic method in an effort to determine broader cross-cultural relationships—suggesting, for instance, that among the Hopi, Zuni, and Acoma societies, mythology, kinship, and linguistic structures are closely parallel. ("Linguistic Method in Ethnography," p. 292.)

91. Maranda, "Structuralism in Cultural Anthropology," p. 340.

92. Ibid., 333. Compare C. Levi-Strauss, *Tristes Tropiques*, trans. J. and D. Weightman (New York: Atheneum, 1974 [1955]), p. 178. Katz, *The Underlying Reality of Language*, pp. 3, 47, 51.

93. Ibid., 340–42.

94. C. Levi-Strauss, *The Raw and the Cooked: Introduction to a Science of Mythology*, trans. J. and D. Weightman (New York: Harper & Row, 1969 [1964]), p. 2.

95. Ibid., 3.

96. Maranda, "Structuralism in Cultural Anthropology," p. 342.

97. Levi-Strauss, *The Raw and the Cooked*, p. 307.

98. Ibid., 12.

99. Ibid.

100. Levi-Strauss, *Structural Anthropology*, trans. C. Jacobson and B. G. Schoepf (New York: Basic Books, 1963). pp. 59, 92.

101. Nor does the promise that all structures, informants' and ethnographers', are at their deepest point isomorphic to brain structures of much solace here. For a myriad of incompatible, intermediate structures be-

tween surface and neurological core seem possible to posit, and this possibility on Quine's view, as we shall see, seriously undercuts the objectivity of claims about the structural web of culture in its entirety (however, compare Levi-Strauss's adaptation of the cave metaphor just below).

102. The authors cite T. H. Gladwin's "Semantics, Schemata, and Kinship" here. (Presented at the Mathematical Social Science Board of Advanced Research Seminar in Formal Analysis of Kinship, Riverside, Calif., 1972.)

103. D. Kronenfeld and H. W. Decker, "Structuralism," p. 525. They cite Levi-Strauss's *The Raw and the Cooked*, p. 13.

104. Compare Levi-Strauss, *Tristes Tropiques*, p. 59.

105. Levi-Strauss, *The Savage Mind* (Chicago: University of Chicago Press, 1966), p. 117.

106. See, for example, David Kaplan and Robert A. Manners, *Culture Theory* (Englewood Cliffs, N.J.: Prentice-Hall, 1972), p. 177n.

107. Lee Drummond, "Structure and Process in the Interpretation of South American Myth: The Arawak Dog Spirit People," *American Anthropologist*, vol. 79, no. 4 (December 1977), pp. 845–46. Wittgenstein's notion of an *atomic* proposition better fits Drummond's remarks here.

108. Ibid., 846.

109. Ibid.

110. See chap. 2, n. 66.

111. Fisher and Werner, "Explaining Explanation," p. 200. See also Keesing, "Paradigms Lost," pp. 229–332. Werner and Campbell, "Translating and the Problem of Decentering," pp. 398–420, pp. 398–403, esp. p. 402. Compare Eugene Nida's parallel adaptation of Chomsky's earlier *(Syntactic Structures)* theory, which applies many of the same techniques discussed here, in *Toward a Science of Translating* (Leiden: E. J. Brill, 1964).

112. S. Tyler, ed., *Cognitive Anthropology* (New York: Holt, Rinehart & Winston, 1969), pp. 13, 14.

113. Laboratory of Human Cognition (Rockefeller University), "Cognition as a Residual Category in Anthropology," *Annual Reviews* 7 (1978): 61ff. W. H. Geoghegan, *Natural Information Processing Rules: Formal Theory and Applications to Ethnography*, monograph no. 3, Language-Behavior Research Laboratory, University of California, Berkeley, (February 1973), p. 1. Concerns about inquirers' analytic structure exceeding the levels of formal structure in the societies they study are

expressed by the Laboratory of Human Cognition, "Cognition as a Residual Category," pp. 56ff., and by Carol Ember in "Cross-Cultural Cognitive Studies," *Annual Reviews* 6 (1977): 35–56. Some anthropologists are also motivated by concerns that well-ramified formal systems will distort far less codified source-language systems. (Similar concerns are expressed by symbolic anthropologists.) Compare my discussion of the "reproductive fallacy" below.

114. S. Tyler, "Context and Variation in Koya Kinship Terminology," *Cognitive Anthropology*, pp. 487–503, p. 488.

115. S. R. Wittkowski and C. H. Brown, "Lexical Universals," *Annual Reviews* 7 (1978): 427f. Compare Brown, *Wittgensteinian Linguistics*, chap. 1.

116. Brown, *Wittgensteinian Linguistics*, pp. 120–21.

117. J. Fabian, "Taxonomy and Ideology: On the Boundaries of Concept Classification," *Linguistics and Anthropology*, pp. 183–97. In this work Fabian endeavors to show the evolution of certain Swahili grammatical and metaphysical categories in the context of an evolving folk epic and associated historical events.

118. Laboratory of Human Cognition, "Cognition as Residual Category," p. 62.

119. Brent Berlin and Paul Kay, *Basic Color Terms: Their Universality and Evolution* (Berkeley, Calif.: University of California Press, 1969). Compare Fabian, "Taxonomy and Ideology," pp. 184–85.

120. Laboratory of Human Cognition, "Cognition as Residual Category," p. 62.

121. Ibid.

122. See, for example, Wittkowski and Brown, *Lexical Universals*, p. 433. Rosch's "Cognitive Representations of Semantic Categories," *The Journal of Experimental Psychology: General*, vol. 104, no. 3 (1975), pp. 192–233, seems nonetheless committed to an entificational view of "depth meaning—viewed as a better candidate for psychological reality than "Aristotelean" (i.e., Lewis-Carnap) semantic notions. However, she expresses a caveat about the open interpretability of her constructions in spite of the mentalistic leanings she confesses elsewhere in the article. (Ibid., 225f.) This caveat is evidently more in keeping with the remarks the Laboratory cites (see next reference).

123. Laboratory of Human Cognition, "Cognition as Residual Category," p. 63. Compare Eleanor Rosch, "Principles of Categorization," *Cognition and Categorization*, ed. B. Lloyd and E. Rosch (Hillsdale, N.J.: Erlbaum, 1977), pp. 28–48.

124. Context sensitivity is emphasized in Frake's recent work, where it is also tied to a thesis that inquirer questions result from examination of "query-rich settings" in the source society. See his "Plying Frames Can Be Dangerous," pp. 441–68.

125. L. C. Watson, " 'Etic' and 'Emic' Perspectives on Guajiro Urbanization," *Urban Life* 9 (1981): 451–53, 458.

126. Ibid., 448, 465–67.

127. Ibid., 467.

128. C. Gladwin, "A Model of the Supply of Smoked Fish from Cape Coast to Kumasi," *Formal Methods in Economic Anthropology*, ed. S. Plattner Special Publication No. 4 (Washington, D.C.: American Anthropological Association, 1975), pp. 77–127.

129. Naomi Quinn, "Do Mfantse Fish Sellers Estimate Probabilities in Their Heads?" *American Ethnologist*, vol. 5, no. 2 (1978), pp. 206–26.

130. Not to be confused with the philosopher David K. Lewis whose work shall be discussed below.

131. T. Hugh Gladwin, *East is a Big Bird: Navigation and Logic on Puluwat Atoll* (Cambridge, Mass.: Harvard University Press, 1970); D. Lewis, *We the Navigators* (Honolulu: University of Hawaii Press, 1972).

132. Laboratory of Human Cognition, "Cognition of Residual Category," p. 64. Worth passing mention here is a development of componential analysis known as *procedural semantics*. In this method, components (or semantic markers) are replaced by procedures comprised of sets of yes/no questions regarding the applicability of defining characteristics to the object in question. The use of such procedures, or "decision tables," in the characterization of cognitive processes has certain advantages over the simple listing of components: For example, it circumvents the problems with words like 'game' (noted by Wittgenstein) that do not have a fixed set of essential characteristics. These procedures, which form hierarchical relations analogous to those among components in semantic markers, also contain questions that require factual knowledge not contained in the lexicon but rather in what is called the speaker's "encyclopedia"—thus eroding a problematic distinction between semantic and factual knowledge. Also, this approach is favored by some because of the "concreteness" of these operations: "Each procedure is an actual mental operation that links up directly with the primitive mental operations used in perceiving, attending, deciding, and intending." (Clark and Clark, *Psychology of Language*, p. 442.) This approach thus seems to possess pragmatic advantages in its clearer promise of a unified account of cognition; however, despite its seeming coalescence with Quine in the erosion of the analytic-synthetic distinction (as well as with Wittgenstein in replacing intensional entities with procedures—albeit

mental ones), it inherits most of the problems of indeterminacy that arise in connection with componential analysis.

133. Laboratory of Human Cognition, "Cognition as Residual Category," p. 55. See, for example, Bryan R. Wilson's collection of Essays in *Rationality* (New York: Harper & Row, 1970); and the exchange between Peter Winch and I. C. Jarvie in *Understanding and Social Inquiry*, ed. F. R. Dallmayr and T. A. McCarthy (South Bend, Ind.: University of Notre Dame Press, 1977), pp. 159–214.

134. L. Wittgenstein, *Remarks on Frazer's Golden Bough*, ed. Rush Rhees and trans. A. C. Miles (Atlantic Highlands, N.M.: Humanities Press, 1979). Originally appeared in *Synthese*, 17 (1967). A more recent example of work in the intellectualist perspective is Melford Spiro's "Religion: Problems of Definition and Explanation," *Anthropological Approaches to the Study of Religion*, ed. M. Banton (London: Travistock, 1966), esp. pp. 113–14. (Cited in Kaplan and Manners, *Culture Theory* p. 123.)

135. Frake, "Plying Frames Can Be Dangerous," pp. 1–7.

136. Firth, J. R., "On Sociological Linguistics," *Language in Culture and Society*, ed. D. Hymes p. 66.

137. Hymes, "Linguistic Method in Ethnography," pp. 308–10. Compare Mary C. Bateson's critique of Chomsky's overstress of competence to the exclusion of performance in "Linguistic Models in the Study of Joint Performance," *Linguistics and Anthropology*, ed. M. Kinkade, p. 56. Compare also W. J. Samarin, "Theory of Order with Disorderly Data," *Linguistics and Anthropology*, ed. M. Kinkade, pp. 509–19.

138. R. Bauman and J. Sherzer, "The Ethnography of Speaking," *Annual Reviews* 4 (1975): n. 95.

139. Werner, O., "Ethnoscience 1972," *Annual Reviews* 1 (1972): p. 273.

140. Ibid., pp. 288–89. As noted with Frake and others above, the example employed concerns the relatively unproblematic attribute of color, but the method is evidently intended to apply to all sorts of attributes. Given the aforementioned ambiguity of 'defining characteristic' and similar notions, it is not always clear whether objective properties or "internal representations" of them are being spoken of.

141. D. Hymes, "Models of the Interaction of Language and Social Life," *Directions in Sociolinguistics*, ed. J. J. Gumperz and D. Hymes (New York: Holt, Rinehart & Winston, 1970), pp. 35–71.

142. Bauman and Sherzer, "The Ethnography of Speaking," pp. 105–6.

143. M. K. Foster, "When Words Become Deeds," *Explorations in the*

Ethnography of Speaking, ed. R. Bauman and J. Sherzer (Cambridge: Cambridge University Press, 1974), pp. 354–67.

144. Ibid., 355. Searle characterizes the situation and accompanying actions as "preparatory conditions" for the act (*Speech Acts*, pp. 59ff).

145. Foster, "When Words Become Deeds."

146. Ibid., 360, 469 n.

147. Ibid., 355. Quoting Austin, *How To Do Things With Words*, p. 8.

148. Indeed, evident commitments to *action*-identification in these approaches may involve a special indeterminacy beyond those considered in Chapter 1. See Deborah Soles, "On the Indeterminacy of Action," *Philosophy of the Social Sciences* 14 (1984): pp. 457–88.

149. Judith Irvine, "Strategies of Status Manipulation in the Wolof Greeting," *Explorations in the Ethnography of Speaking*, ed. R. Bauman and J. Scherzer, Cambridge: Cambridge University Press, 1974, pp. 167–91. Morris is cited in a number of sociolinguistic studies of folklore symbols. See V. Turner, "Symbolic Studies," *Annual Reviews* 4 (1975): pp. 145–161, esp. p. 150.

150. Irvine, "Strategies in Status Manipulation," pp. 167–68. She here cites Frake's "Notes on Queries in Ethnography," *Transcultural Studies in Cognition*, p. 132.

151. Turner, "Symbolic Studies," p. 146.

152. Ibid., 143, 148. Compare Kiefer, "Psychological Anthropology," *Annual Reviews* 6 (1977): 110–11. Compare Hymes, *Foundations in Sociolinguistics: An Ethnographic Approach* (Philadelphia, Penn.: University of Pennsylvania Press, 1974) p. 41.

153. Kiefer, "Psychological Anthropology," p. 110.

154. See, for example, Turner, "Symbolic Studies."

155. Mary Douglas, *Natural Symbols: Explorations in Cosmology*, 2d ed. (London: Barrie and Jenkins, 1973), p. 11.

156. Ibid., 42.

157. Ibid., chaps. 3–4.

158. Clifford Geertz, *The Interpretation of Cultures* (New York: Basic Books, 1973), p. 17. Compare Turner, "Symbolic Studies," p. 147. Turner characterizes Geertz's approach as a kind of "processual symbology," (Ibid., 149.)

159. Geertz, *The Interpretation of Cultures*, p. 18; Compare Turner, "Symbolic Studies," p. 148.

160. Malcolm Crick, *Explorations in Language and Meaning* (New York: John Wiley & Sons, 1976), pp. 67, 72.

161. Ibid., 69–74.

162. Ibid., chap. 6.

163. Geertz, "From the Native's Point of View," p. 223.

164. Geertz, "From the Native's Point of View," *Meaning in Anthropology*, ed. K. Basso and H. Selby (Albuquerque, N.M.: University of New Mexico Press, 1976) pp. 221–23 and passim.; compare his *The Interpretation of Cultures*, chap. 1, esp. pp. 24ff. This matter of the use of subjects' concepts will be discussed in more detail below. Geertz cites the affinities of his method with Dilthey's "hermeneutic circle" ("From the Native's Point of View," pp. 234–35.

165. Douglas, *Natural Symbols*, esp. chaps. 2, 4. Compare Kiefer, "Psychological Anthropology," pp. 110–11.

166. See, for example, Quine, *Word and Object*, pp. 157–61.

167. Kaplan and Manners, *Culture Theory*, pp. 123–24.

168. Douglas, "Self-Evidence," *Implicit Meanings: Essays in Anthropology* (London: Routledge and Kegan Paul, 1975), pp. 276–318, pp. 276–77.

169. Ibid. 277.

170. Ibid.

171. Ibid.

172. If one narrows rationality to truth functional logic; however, Quine believes both (1) that it must be imposed, and (2) that no indeterminacy results. See my discussions pp. 41, 238ff.

173. Ibid., 278.

174. Ibid., 280.

Chapter 3

1. Frake, "The Ethnographic Study of Cognitive Systems," pp. 74, n. 74. Frake notes Boas' influence, as well as Goodenough's on his thought (p. 74).

2. Triandis, "Approaches Toward Minimizing Translation," pp. 229–30.

3. Kay, "Ethnographic Implications of Ethnographic Semantics," p. 23. For a discussion of some etics / emics controversies, see my "Emics, Etics, and Social Objectivity," *Current Anthropology* 27 (1986): 243–55.

4. See, for example, Marvin Harris, *Cultural Materialism: The Struggle for a Science of Culture* (New York: Random House, 1979), esp. chap. 2. See also Ron Marano, "Windigo Psychosis: The Anatomy of an Emic-Etic Confusion." *Current Anthropology* 23 (1982): 385–412.

5. See, for example, Burling, "Linguistics and Ethnographic Description," *American Anthropologist* 71 (1969): 817–27.

6. Marvin Harris, "History and Significance of the Emic-Etic Distinction," *Annual Reviews* 5 (1976): 335. Compare his *The Rise of Anthropological Theory* (New York: Crowel, 1968), pp. 571, 575.

7. Harris, "History and Significance of the Emic-Etic Distinction," p. 343; Harris, *Cultural Materialism*, pp. 40–41. Glynn Cochrane, "Use of the Concept of the 'Corporation' ": A Choice Between Colloquialism and Distortion," *American Anthropologist* 73 (1971): 1143–50.

8. Harris, "History and Significance of the Emic-Etic Distinction," p. 340.

9. Harris, *Cultural Materialism*, p. 32; cf. p. 41.

10. Ibid., 49. Compare Kay, "Some Theoretical Implications," pp. 28–29; Geoghegan, *Natural Information Processing Rules*.

11. Marano, "Windigo Psychosis," esp. pp. 394–95.

12. Harris, "History and Significance of the Emic-Etic Distinction," p. 343. See also *The Rise of Anthropological Theory*, chaps. 16–18, 20; *Cultural Materialism*, chaps. 1 (esp. pp. 32–45), 7, 9. His view of the emics / etics relationship is intended as a development of the Marxist position that "social consciousness (or unconsciousness) *reflects* social being." ("History and Significance of the Emic-Etic Distinction," p. 331.)

13. Ibid., 343.

14. Harris, "History and Significance of the Emic-Etic Distinction," p. 344.

15. Ibid., 348.

16. Ibid., 347–48.

17. Ibid., 345.

18. Fisher and Werner, "Explaining Explanation," pp. 202 n., 204 n., 204ff. They also criticize Harris for tying idealist emics too closely to atheoretical descriptivism (p. 200; compare Kay, "Some Theoretical

Implications," pp. 23–24). They add that Harris's efforts to oppose etics and emics—by in effect equating the latter with "the confused" (P. 204).

19. Ibid., 201. Quoting D. T. Campbell, "On the Conflicts Between Biological and Social Evolution and Between Psychology and Moral Tradition," *American Psychologist* 30 (1975): 1120.

20. Rudner, Richard, "Some Essays at Objectivity," *Philosophic Exchange* 1 (1973): 126–28. Compare his *Philosophy of Social Science* (Englewood Cliffs, N.J.: Prentice-Hall, 1966), chap. 4. Compare D. C. Dennett, *Brainstorms: Philosophical Essays on Mind and Psychology* (Cambridge: M.I.T. Press, 1978), p. 191; White, *Toward Reunion in Philosophy*, p. 207. For further discussion of the reproductive fallacy see Feleppa, "Reproducing Social Reality: A Reply to Harrison," *Philosophy of the Social Sciences* 16 (1986): 89–99.

21. Christie Kiefer, "Psychological Anthropology," *Annual Reviews* 6 (1977): 107. Carol Ember, "Cross-Cultural Cognitive Studies," p. 35.

22. Peter Caws, "Operational, Representational, and Explanatory Models," *American Anthropologist* 76 (1974): pp. 7–8. Wallace, "The Problem of Psychological Validity of Componential Analysis," p. 152.

23. Cecil H. Brown, "Psychological, Semantic, and Structural Aspects of American English Kinship Terms," *American Ethnologist* 1 (1974): 429.

24. F. A. Hanson, "Models and Social Reality: An Alternative to Caws," *American Anthropologist* 78 (1976): p. 324.

25. Fisher and Werner, "Explaining Explanation," p. 207. Quoting Karl Popper, *The Logic of Scientific Discovery* (New York: Basic Books, 1961), p. 423.

26. Quine, "Philosophical Progress in Language Theory," *Metaphilosophy* 1 (1970): p. 16.

27. Kay, "Some Theoretical Implications," p. 19. Compare Quine, *Word and Object* p. 3.

28. Ibid., 26.

29. Noam Chomsky, "Quine's Empirical Assumptions," *Words and Objections: Essays on the Work of W. V. Quine*, ed. J. Hintikka and D. Davidson (Dordrecht: Reidel, 1968), pp. 53–68. Richard Rorty, "Indeterminacy of Translation and of Truth," *Synthese* 23 (1972): 443–62.

30. See, for example, Davidson's "On the Very Idea of a Conceptual Scheme," pp. 5–20; and his "Belief and the Basis of Meaning," *Synthese* 27 (1974): pp. 309–23.

31. Quine, "On the Reasons for Indeterminacy of Translation," p. 179.

32. Quine, "On Empirically Equivalent Systems," p. 313.

33. Ibid., 316-18.

34. But I include them because they are required if the theory formulation is actually to imply the observational conditionals.

35. Compare Quine, *Philosophy of Logic* (Englewood Cliffs, N.J.: Prentice-Hall, 1970), p. 56.

36. Quine, "On Empirically Equivalent Systems," pp. 319-21. Nor can the incompatibility be produced by simply adding extraneous material to a formulation, as when we add a sentence, *S*, to a theory and say that this new theory conflicts with, but is empirically equivalent to, the theory produced by adding the denial of *S* to the original theory; that is, "we need to show not only that such branching alternatives exist, but that they are inevitable." (Ibid., 322-23).

37. Ibid., 322.

38. Ibid., 324.

39. Quine, "Empirical Content," p. 28.

40. Quine, "On Empirically Equivalent Systems," p. 324. Compare R. B. Braithwaite, *Scientific Explanation: A Study of the Function of Theory, Probability and Law in Science* (Cambridge: Cambridge University Press, 1953), pp. 51-79; C. G. Hempel, "The Theoretician's Dilemma," *Aspects of Scientific Explanation* (New York: The Free Press, 1965), pp. 204ff; R. Carnap, "Testability and Meaning," *Philosophy of Science*, vol. 8, no. 4 (October 1936), pp. 420-68; vol. 4, no. 1 (January 1937), pp. 1-40; I. Scheffler, *The Anatomy of Inquiry* (New York: Afred A. Knopf, 1963), pp. 189ff.

41. That is, a "prenexed" one with all quantifiers occurring at the beginning of the sentence. See Frank P. Ramsey, *The Foundations of Mathematics*, ed. R. B. Braithwaite (New York: Humanities Press, 1931), Chapter 9, "Theories."

42. Quine, "On Empirically Equivalent Systems," p. 320 n. Compare Scheffler, *The Anatomy of Inquiry*, pp. 218ff.

43. Compare W. Craig, "The Replacement of Auxiliary Expressions," *Philosophical Review*, vol. 65, no. 1 (1956), pp. 38-55. Craig's basic idea is this: If we take any given "proof" of an observational conditional that may be constructed using a theory formulation, assign the proof a Gödel number, *n*, and correlate the proof with that observational conditional repeated in self-conjunction *n* times, we thereby generate a Craigian equivalent of the proof that is devoid of theoretical expressions. And it turns out that the Craig-class generatable from any theory, though infinite, is decid-

able: The procedure of "encoding" proofs into repeated self-conjunctions and of "decoding" them back is a mechanical one that allows us, in principle, to determine effectively whether any given sentence belongs to the Craig-class of a theory (i.e., we see if the number of self-conjunctions of a sentence corresponds to the Gödel number of the proof of that sentence in the original theory).

44. Quine, "On Empirically Equivalent Systems," p. 326.

45. Ibid., 327. Quine remarks:

[Although] Craig's result does not refute the thesis of undetermination, since the Craig class, for all its tightness of fit, is not a finite formulation, this technicality is rather a frail reed at which to grasp. After all, one could reasonably extend the notion of theory formulations to apply not just to an expression but to a recursive set of expressions. So the thesis of underdetermination would seem to be demoted to the status, at best, of a thesis affirming a certain contrast between expressions and recursive sets of expressions.

A recursive system is one in which a finite and relatively small set of rules is used to generate a larger, perhaps infinite set of novel expressions.

46. Ibid.

47. Idib., 322.

48. These and other discussions by Quine may seem to blur distinctions between physics and science. However, any apparant slippage reflects only the fact that Quine gives physics priority over the other sciences owing to its status as the only science assigned "full coverage" of reality. To this point, I think there is no trouble in allowing Quine to treat the limits of physics to be the limits of science. However, this will be cause for concern in subsequent discussions.

49. Roger Gibson, "Translation, Physics, and Facts of the Matter," *The Philosophy of W. V. Quine*, ed. L. E. Hahn (LaSalle, Ill.: Open Court Press, 1987), p. 147. Compare Quine, "On the Very Idea of A Third Dogma," *Theories and Things*, p. 39; Quine, "Ontology and Ideology Revisited," *The Journal of Philosophy* 80 (1983): pp. 499–502.

50. Gibson, "Translation, Physics, and Facts," pp. 147–53. Compare Quine, "Epistemology Naturalized," *Ontological Relativity*, pp. 74–75, 83; "On the Nature of Natural Knowledge," *Mind and Language* ed. Samuel Guttenplan, (Oxford: Clarendon, 1975), p. 67; "Five Milestones of Empiricism," *Theories and Things*, p. 72; Quine, *The Roots of Reference* (LaSalle, Ill.: Open Court Press, 1973) pp. 2–3; "Responses," *Theories and Things*, pp. 181–82; "Things and Their Place in Theories," *Theories and Things*, p. 22; "On the Very Idea of a Third Dogma," p. 39.

51. Quine, *Word and Object*, p. 73.

52. Ibid., 72.

53. Quine, "Facts of the Matter," pp. 166–67. The sentence prior to the quoted passage reads: "Readers have supposed that my complaint is ontological; it is not." Yet while this might seem to add support to an epistemological reading of Quine, he is not remarking that the indeterminacy is an epistemological thesis in the sense under consideration here. Instead, he is claiming that his attack on intension is not to be taken as following from his *nominalist* scruples. Indeed, he is quite willing to accept ontic commitment to abstract objects such as sets if he can see no way of dispensing with them.

54. Gibson, "Translation, Physics, and Facts," pp. 151–53; Quine, "Reply to Roger F. Gibson," *The Philosophy of W. V. Quine*, pp. 155–57.

55. Roger Gibson, *The Philosophy of W. V. Quine: An Expository Essay* (Tampa: University Presses of Florida, 1982), p. 69.

56. Quine, *Word and Object*, pp. 20–21. Compare W. Quine and J. Ullian, *The Web of Belief*, 2d ed. (New York: Random House, 1978), chap 6.

57. Quine and Ullian, *The Web of Belief*, p. 67. Charity may also be partly akin to what Quine and Ullian call "modesty" (ibid. pp. 68–69).

58. Ibid., 75–76.

59. Quine, "Replies" (to Chomsky), *Words and Objections*, p. 303.

60. Gibson, "Translation, Physics, and Facts," pp. 151–52.

61. Quine, "Linguistics and Philosophy," *The Ways of Paradox and Other Essays* (Cambridge: Harvard University Press, 1976) p. 57.

62. Alexander George, "Whence and Whither the Debate Between Quine and Chomsky," *The Journal of Philosophy* 83 (1986): pp. 492–94. Compare Chomsky, *Rules and Representations* p. 5.

63. George, "Whence and Whither the Debate," p. 495. Compare Chomsky, *Aspects of the Theory of Syntax*, p. 8.

64. George, "Whence and Whither the Debate," pp. 495–96. Compare W. Quine, "Methodological Reflections on Current Linguistic Theory," *Semantics of Natural Language* (Boston: Reidel, 1972), p. 442.

65. George, "Whence and Whither the Debate," p. 496. Compare Quine, "Methodological Reflections," p. 444.

66. George, "Whence and Whither the Debate." Compare Quine, "Linguistics and Philosophy," p. 58; "Methodological Reflections," pp. 444, 446, 448.

67. George, "Whence and Whither the Debate," p. 497. Compare Quine, "States of Mind," *The Journal of Philosophy* 82 (1985): p. 6.

68. W. Quine, "Sellars on Behaviorism, Language and Meaning," *Pacific Philosophical Quarterly* 61 (1980): p. 26.

69. W. Quine, "Mind and Verbal Dispositions," *Mind and Language*, ed. S. Guttenplan, p. 87.

70. Ibid., 499, 497.

71. Ibid., 489–90 n.

72. Paul Roth argues for this interpretation in "Paradox and Indeterminacy," *The Journal of Philosophy* 75 (1978): pp. 347–67. Compare George, "Whence and Whither the Debate," p. 499; Quine, "The Scope and Language of Science," *The Ways of Paradox*, p. 244.

73. The general validity of the conservativism principle is not at issue here. I do not intend to brook disagreement with those such as Paul Feyerabend who question it. Thus, I word this remark in a way I believe such critics would find agreeable, as they object to adhering to conservatism when doing so threatens theoretical progress.

74. 'Semantic realism' has been used to describe the thesis Quine attacks. It is adequate, provided it is not taken in the sense typically discussed by Michael Dummett—namely, that truth is an epistemically unconstrained property of sentences.

75. Quine, "Facts of the Matter," p. 167. It is important not to equate too easily the observational/behavioral base for translation with Quine's physical basis for ontology. An *inference* must be made from the claim that behavioral evidence does not epistemically determine translation to the claim that physical truth does not ontologically determine translation. The inference can be challenged, but I shall grant it here, as my concerns lie elsewhere.

Michael Friedman gives precise formulation to the distinction between epistemological determination of translation by behavioral evidence and ontological determination of translation by physical truth, and he challenges the ontological critique. He is concerned that Quine's claim that all *physical fact* fails to determine translation does not clearly follow from the failure of all *behavioral fact* to do so (though he does not challenge the claim that only *behavioral evidence* is relevant to translation). He argues that no clear reason is given why no neurophysiological physical fact can figure in ontological determination and, among other things, brings to the fore a significant distinction between reduction of belief states to single physical states and to sets of functionally equivalent ones. ("Physicalism and the Indeterminacy of Translation," pp. 353–73.)

76. Quine, "Things and Their Place in Theories," p. 23. Let me offer some comments to forestall confusions that might arise in readers acquainted with Quine's discussions of "ultimate ontology." There is a somewhat narrower usage of the term 'ontology' in Quine's discussions of such matters. However, Quine's qualified acceptance of elementary particles here ("to make things vivid") hearkens to recent reflections on the matter of what term best characterizes the ontology of science in the most general way. His position for a long time was that this term was 'physical object'. However, because of the impossibility of squaring this with the behavior of certain microparticles, he has shifted to a "hyperpythagoreanism": He now holds that the ultimate ontology of physical theory is in fact the numbers (set-theoretically construed) that are used to designate regions of space-time to which physical properties are ascribed. What concerns him here is the universe of discourse of physical theory under logical regimentation, and his efforts in this regard are directed (for the sake of simplicity) to finding a single concept to characterize the universe of discourse. But this formal concern—as his Pythagoreanism makes evident—is not to be equated fully with the "ontological" matter at issue in physicalism and realism questions or in Quine's reflections on ontology and ideology. The general ontological question of "what there is" embraces also what he terms "ideology," that is, what predicates will be allowed to have variables bound by existential quantifiers:

> if we make the drastic [Pythagorean] ontological move . . . , all physical objects go by the board—atoms, particles, all—leaving only pure sets. The principle of physicalism must thereupon be formulated by reference not to physical objects but to physical vocabulary.

Quine, "Facts of the Matter," pp. 164–65. Compare W. Quine "Whither Physical Objects?" *Essays in Memory of Imre Lakatos*, ed. R. S. Cohen et al. (Dordrecht, Holland: Reidel, 1976), pp. 497–504; Quine, "Ontology and Ideology Revisited," pp. 499–502; and Quine, "The Scope and Language of Science," p. 245. For discussion of the relationships between his and Carnap's views concerning ontology, see W. Quine's "On Carnap's Views on Ontology," *The Ways of Paradox*, pp. 203–11. His well-known remarks in "On What There Is" [*From A Logical Point of View* (New York: Harper Torchbooks, 1963), pp. 1–19], that "what there is is what we say there is" and "to be is to be the value of a variable," can be read as concerning both ontology and ideology. For further discussion of these points see also my "Physicalism, Indeterminacy, and Interpretive Science," *Metaphilosophy* (forthcoming).

77. Quine, "Goodman's Ways of Worldmaking," *Theories and Things* p. 98; compare "Facts of the Matter," p. 162. For Goodman's contrasting "irrealist" pragmatism, see *Languages of Art: An Approach to the Theory of Symbols* (Indianapolis: Bobbs-Merrill, 1968), esp. chap 6; Goodman, *Ways of Worldmaking* (Indianapolis: Hackett, 1978), esp. chaps. I, VI, VII;

Goodman, *Of Mind and Other Matters* (Cambridge, Mass.: Harvard University Press, 1984), esp. preface and chap. II. I shall discuss salient points of Goodman's irrealism in the conclusion of Chapter 5.

78. Quine, "Things and Their Place in Theories," p. 1.

79. Compare Maurice Mandelbaum, "Societal Facts" reprinted in *The Philosophy of Social Explanation*, ed. Alan Ryan (Oxford: Oxford University Press, 1973), pp. 105–18.

80. Richard Rorty, "Method, Social Science, and Social Hope," *Consequences of Pragmatism (Essays: 1972–1980)* (Minneapolis: University of Minnesota Press, 1982), p. 201.

81. Quine, "Things and Their Place in Theories," p. 23. In the following I draw on Roger Gibson's unpublished "An Update on Underdetermination."

82. Quine, *Word and Object*, pp. 73–74; compare "Reply to Harman," *Words and Objections: Essays on the Work of W. V. Quine*, ed. D. Davidson and J. Hintikka (Dordrecht: Reidel, 1969), pp. 296–97.

83. Quine, "Things and Their Place in Theories," pp. 21–22.

84. Quine, "Empirical Content," *Theories and Things*, pp. 24–30, esp. p. 29.

85. Ibid., 29–30.

86. Quine, "Reply to Gibson," *The Philosophy of W. V. Quine*, p. 156.

87. Ibid., 156–57.

88. D. Davidson, "Radical Interpretation" reprinted in *Inquiries into Truth and Interpretation* (Oxford: Clarendon Press, 1984), p. 154; Davidson, "Reality Without Reference," *Inquiries into Truth and Interpretation*, pp. 224–25.

Chapter 4

1. David Lewis, *Convention: A Philosophic Study* (Cambridge, Mass.: Harvard University Press, 1969), p. 4. Compare Quine's "Truth by Convention," *The Ways of Paradox and Other Essays*, rev. and enl. ed. (Cambridge, Mass.: Harvard University Press, 1976), pp. 71–106, in which he argues against the view that analytic or logically true statements are "true by convention." Lewis takes issue with a number of Quine's points here (and elsewhere), while defending the analytic-synthetic distinction that Quine rejects (*Convention*, pp. 2–3 and passim). In my application of Lewis, I shall try to steer clear of this and other points of conflict with

Quine. For a shorter account of my thesis, see my "Translation as Rule-Governed Behaviour," *Philosophy of the Social Sciences* 12 (1982): 1–31.

2. Ibid., 69.

3. Ibid., 14.

4. Compare, for example, Lewis' "Languages and Language," *Minnesota Studies in the Philosophy of Science*, ed. K. Gunderson, vol. 7 (Minneapolis, Minn.: University of Minnesota Press, 1975), pp. 3–35.

5. Lewis, *Convention*, p. 42.

6. Ibid., 63ff.

7. Ibid., 57f., 87f.

8. Ibid., 76.

9. Compare Nelson Goodman's *Fact, Fiction, and Forecast*, 3d ed. (Indianapolis, Ind.: Bobbs-Merrill, 1973), pp. 62ff; Richard Rudner's "Goodman, Nelson," *The Encyclopedia of Philosophy* 3 (1967): 370f.; John Rawls' *A Theory of Justice* Cambridge, Mass.: Harvard University Press, 1971), pp. 20ff., 577ff., and passim. My use of 'theory', restricted as it is to *descriptive* theories comprised entirely of hypotheses (although theorizing incorporates extensive codificational elements), varies somewhat from Rawls's usage. However, although this can lead to some confusion, this difference is not of any great consequence here.

10. Goodman, *Fact, Fiction, and Forecast*, p. 64. For critical discussions of the circularity of reflective equilibrium justification see, for example, Normal Daniels' "Wide Reflective Equilibrium and Theory Acceptance in Ethics," *The Journal of Philosophy* 76 (May 1979): 256–81; Michael Friedman's "Truth and Confirmation," *The Journal of Philosophy* 76 (July 1979): 361–81; and Stephen Stich's and Robert Nisbett's "Justification and the Psychology of Human Reasoning," *Philosophy of Science* 47 (1980): 188–202.)

11. Rawls, *A Theory of Justice*, pp. 20f.

12. This is not to say one may not judge certain linguistic practices in the source-language community immoral, or seek to change them. The point here is that *initial* conformity to linguistic conventions is preferable and, indeed, necessary for the discovery and eventual reform of any linguistically conditioned injustice.

13. However, such a rule would not be part of a typical translation manual, as the latter specifies rules that are applicable only to its *users* and that could only be violated by them. That is, monolingual source-language speakers could violate a rule of the sort considered here in the text, even though they could not know then what the rule was; however, they could

not violate a rule of the form 'Translate S in the source language as T in the receptor language' consciously or unconsciously. This bears out the fact that the full account of rule compliance and reflective equilibrium of translation involves complexities not encountered in the sorts of cases discussed by Goodman, Lewis, or Rawls—insofar as the parties to conventional coordination need not be privy to the conventions with which their behavior complies. The general purpose of coordination of activities of linguistic and related activities of the communities concerned is still achieved, although one might view the translation manual as comprising *several* coordinated codifications. Such complexities certainly merit attention, but they do not affect my general thesis.

14. Lewis himself is unclear on the canonical form he views statements of conventions as having, and this is directly related to his conflation, noted earlier, of issues concerning the description of the genesis of conventions with questions concerning the justification of their adoption.

15. That is, I accommodate to Quine's views regarding ontic commitments to intension, etc., by providing a more commodious prescriptive setting. Expressions in imperative rule statements *can* refer to intensions, of course, but there is less reason now to think that they *must*. (Also, see my remarks concerning Goodman and descriptive convention in footnote 111, Chapter 5.)

16. Quine, *Word and Object*, p. 76.

17. Ibid., 72.

18. J. H. Greenberg, "Some Universals of Grammar with Particular Reference to the Order of Meaningful Elements," *Universals of Language* (Cambridge, Mass.: M.I.T. Press, 1963). The reader may recall that Quine does not regard grammatical analysis as indeterminate. I discuss this point in the next section.

19. As noted earlier, there are debatable issues concerning the principle of methodological conservatism (e.g., those raised by P. K. Feyerabend), which are beyond the scope of this work. Although somewhat different arguments would be needed to justify translational diversity than are applied by Feyerabend to make a case for theoretical diversity, similar heuristic considerations might be cited: that is, diversity may be favored for its stimulation of research, etc.

20. He argues, for instance, that the "native may achieve the same net effects through linguistic structures so different that any eventual construal of our [grammatical] devices in the native language and vice versa can prove unnatural and largely arbitrary." (*Word and Object*, p. 53.)

21. Compare Goodman, *Fact, Fiction, and Forecast*, chap. 4.

22. I should add that on my construal, even highly observational oc-

casion sentences need not be translated by descriptive hypotheses, yet none-theless maintain their epistemic status. Also, I see no harm in treating them as descriptive.

23. Quine, "On Empirically Equivalent Systems," p. 322.

24. The ambiguity of 'mental entity' lurks here—as it has, indeed, in much discussion of deep structures and the like (i.e., are they concrete or abstract or some synthesis of the two?). Given that Quine's and my reflections cut against both sorts of entity, this ambiguity can be overlooked here, however.

25. Joan Bresnan, "A Realistic Transformational Grammar," *Linguistic Theory and Psychological Reality*, ed. Morris Halle, Joan Bresnan, and George Miller (Cambridge, Mass.: M.I.T. Press, 1978), pp. 1–59; esp. pp. 58–59.

26. The Laboratory of Human Cognition, "Cognition as a Residual Category," p. 66.

27. Chomsky, *Rules and Representations*, pp. 12–22.

28. In this connection see Paul Roth's "Paradox and Indeterminacy."

Chapter 5

1. See also Richard Rudner's "On Semiotic Aesthetics," pp. 67–77, esp. pp. 69f.

2. Symbols and labels are themselves construed by Goodman as compound individuals (roughly speaking, and "translating" Goodman's preferred nominalistic idiom into platonese, classes) comprising symbol and label inscriptions that are "replicas" of one another. Compare *Languages of Art*, pp. 131ff. See Catherine Elgin's enlightening explanations and extensions of key themes in this work in *With Reference to Reference* (Indianapolis: Hackett, 1983).

3. Ibid., 50ff., 68ff., 143ff.

4. Compare R. Rudner, "Show or Tell: Incoherence Among Symbol Systems," *Erkenntnis* 12 (1978): pp. 129–51.

5. Goodman, *Languages of Art*, p. 53.

6. Ibid., 54ff.

7. Ibid., 85ff.

8. Ibid., 31ff.

9. Ibid., 59.

10. The ethnographer might well name the gesture by using a mention of the source-language term that applies to it (if there is one)—for example, the '....'-gesture, or by using a metalinguistic homonym of the source term (the ....-gesture) or a mention of a metalinguistic homonym of the receptor-language term applicable to that gesture. Where the source term is thus employed, it is in neither case (in the strict semantical sense) *used*. Such entries in a field manual, *prima facie*, do not have the strict canonical form of *explicit translation rules*, that is, of the form (CT)" '....' in language *S* is to be translated as '-----' in language *T*." Note that in CT no expression of either the source-language *S* or the receptor-language *T* occurs (strictly speaking). What does occur is a mention rather than a use of those terms. The entire sentence CT is couched in the technical language of the linguist-anthropologist—a language that may, but needn't adopt elements of either source or receptor language.

11. Cf. Rudner, "Some Problems of Non-Semiotic Aesthetic Theories," *Journal of Aesthetics and Art Criticism* (March 1957): 289–310, where an alternative treatment of the semantics of 'express' is given (compare Goodman, *Language of Art*, pp. 45ff.).

12. Goodenough, *Description and Comparison in Cultural Anthropology*, p. 72 n.

13. Ibid., 72f.

14. Goodenough is assuming the role of an object-language speaker here.

15. Goodenough, *Description and Comparison in Cultural Anthropology*, p. 73. Compare Goodenough's "Yankee Kinship Terminology: A Problem in Componential Analysis," *Formal Semantic Analysis*, ed. E. A. Hammel pp. 259–87.

16. Ibid., 74.

17. Ibid., 101.

18. Ibid., 110f.

19. See Goodenough, *Property, Kin and Community on Truk*, pp. 29ff. and the first chapter passim.

20. Ibid., 92ff.

21. Compare Goodenough, "Residence Rules," *Southwestern Journal of Anthropology* 12 (1956): 22–37.

22. Goodenough, *Description and Comparison in Cultural Anthropology*, p. 104.

23. Goodenough, *Property, Kin and Community on Truk*, pp. 30–34.

24. Ibid., 108.

25. Although they have turned out not to be peculiar to them.

26. Ibid., 109.

27. Goodenough, *Description and Comparison in Cultural Anthropology*, pp. 110. Douglas Oliver, *A Solomon Island Society* (Cambridge: Harvard University Press, 1955).

28. Ibid.

29. Ibid., 109.

30. Goodenough, *Property, Kin and Community on Truk*, pp. 31, 32.

31. Ibid., 92.

32. Ibid., 66.

33. Indeed, the reason I have been willing to assume that the metalanguage may incorporate so many meaning postulates from the receptor language is because it is mastery of the *metalanguage* that is required if an ethnography or translation manual is to be of any use.

34. Note how this interpretation fits better with Goodenough's claim that the denotata from which componential definitions are derived are the *linguist's* images of things. (I will not, however, comment on other problems that may undermine the cogency of Goodenough's claim.)

35. Indeed, the rules one learns from the translation manual are *not* the rules of the society, but rules that enable an outsider (or a bilingual) to get along. Ideally, these rules, plus ethnographic information will enable one to get on *as well* as if one understood the native's rules. Compare my discussion of Winch, Hanson, and Crick below.

36. Cochrane "Use of the Concept of the 'Corporation,'" pp. 1144–50 esp. p. 1148. Compare Goodenough, *Property, Kin and Community on Truk*, p. 33.

37. Cochrane, "Use of the Concept of the 'Corporation,'" p. 1149.

38. Goodenough, "Reply to Cochrane," *American Anthropologist* 73 (1971): 1150–52.

39. Goodenough, "Cultural Anthropology and Linguistics," p. 64.

40. Burling, "Cognition and Componential Analysis," p. 28.

41. Lounsbury, "A Semantic Analysis of Pawnee Kinship Usage," pp. 158–94 esp. p. 189. Compare David M. Schneider, "Componential Analysis: A State-of-the-Art Review," Symposium on Cognitive Studies and Artificial Intelligence Research, March 2–8, 1969, University of

Chicago Center for Continuing Education; and A. F. C. Wallace, "A Relational Analysis of American Kinship Terminology: An Example of Relations Between Process and Structure in Cognition," *Cognition*, ed. P. Garvin, pp. 145–53.

42. Ember, "Cross-Cultural Cognitive Studies," 35.

43. Ibid., 45–46.

44. Goodman, "The Way the World Is," *Problems and Projects* (Indianapolis: Bobbs-Merrill, 1972), pp. 24–32.

45. Kiefer, "Psychological Anthropology," p. 107.

46. Ibid, 107–8.

47. As before, I here use 'realism' to apply both to the existence of unobservables and to the truth of hypotheses.

48. Peter Caws, "Operational, Representational, and Explanatory Models," *American Anthropologist* 76 (1974): p. 1.

49. Caws also contends that the theoretical models are best construed as mental, or better as brain structures that are embodied in the anthropologist's theory; while I have misgivings about this, they do not affect the issues I am concerned with here.

50. Caws, "Operational, Representational Models," p. 3. However, Caws subsequently concedes that "it is not to be expected . . . that sets of roughly homologous structures will be found distributed among the heads, which will account for the ability of individuals to talk to one another and make their way around similar obstacles, etc." (Ibid.) Given Caws's (and Quine's) vagueness on this point, it is not clear if this is an important point of conflict or not.

51. Ibid., 6–7. Compare P. Caws, *Science and the Theory of Value* (New York: Random House, 1967), p. 66; Harris, *Cultural Materialism*, chap. 2.

52. Ibid., 7.

53. Ibid., 5.

54. See in this connection Hilary Putnam's *Meaning and the Moral Sciences* (London: Routledge and Kegan Paul, 1978), esp. lectures III–VI. Again, I intend my remarks to bear on the legitimacy of even those approaches not regarded as scientific. I am not sure how one is to go about discriminating sciences from other forms of empirical inquiry; Quine's notion of expressing a fact of the matter is, I suppose, intended as a criterion of demarcation, but I have expressed concern about the adequacy of this notion.

55. F. Allan Hanson, "Models and Social Reality," pp. 323–25, esp. p. 324. Compare F. A. Hanson and Rex Martin, "The Problem of Other Cultures," *Philosophy of the Social Sciences* 3 (1973): 191–208, whose solutions to problems of cultural analysis have, I believe, strong affinities with mine.

56. Ibid.

57. Brown, "Psychological, Semantic, and Structural Aspects," p. 429. Compare Wallace, "A Relational Analysis of Kinship Terminology," p. 152; Schneider, "Componential Analysis"; Lounsbury, "A Semantic Analysis of Pawnee Kinship Usage."

58. Caws, "Operational, Representational Models," p. 9.

59. Ibid., 9–10.

60. Caws, "The Ontology of Social Structure," pp. 326–27.

61. Hanson and Martin, "The Problem of Other Cultures." Compare Gilbert Ryle, *The Concept of Mind* (London: Hutchinson, 1949).

62. F. Allan Hanson, *Meaning in Culture* (London: Routledge and Kegan Paul, 1975).

63. Davidson, "On the Very Idea of a Conceptual Scheme," pp. 185–95.

64. Laboratory of Human Cognition, "Cognition as a Residual Category," p. 66.

65. See Peter Winch, *The Idea of a Social Science and Its Relation to Philosophy* (New York: Humanities Press, 1967), esp. chap. 1. Compare Rudner, "Some Essays at Objectivity," pp. 115–35; and *Philosophy of Social Science* (Englewood Cliffs, N.J.: Prentice-Hall, 1966), chap. 4.

66. Cecil Brown, *Wittgensteinian Linguistics*, p. 45; compare p. 47 and Wittgenstein, *Philosophical Investigations*, p. 109e.

67. Brown, "Psychological, Semantic, and Structural Aspects," p. 81.

68. Ibid., 48; also compare p. 88. Compare Wittgenstein, *Philosophical Investigations*, p.12e.

69. Ibid., 87, 88.

70. Ibid., 89.

71. Ibid., 48.

72. Brown, "Psychological and Semantic Aspects," pp. 422, 428ff. Brown regards the kinship analyses that Burling criticizes for their non-uniqueness as nonetheless having a "contingent psychological reality,"

while relational analyses such as Wallace's (loc. cit.), as well as relational logic in general, have a "necessary psychological reality"—meaning, in part, that they are uniquely determinable. "Structural reality" roughly comprises the relations of kinship analyses to broader analyses of fundamental institutions and practices such as marriage, incest, and inheritance. Structural reality—like psychological reality—being "both conventional and grammatical" (the two "are of the same logical, conceptual order"), is similarly necessary and determinate. In light of these characterizations of Brown's, both of these notions seem to run afoul of the inscrutability of reference theses and thus rendered indeterminate on both Quine's and my accounts. However, I am not entirely sure how purportedly *structurally* real hypotheses fair on my account, as these might well be of the sort that I would regard as determinate, once translation has been settled, and part of the descriptive apparatus of an ethnography.

73. Wittgenstein, *Remarks on Frazer's Golden Bough*, p. 5e.

74. Crick, *Explorations in Language and Meaning*, pp. 2–3, 8–10, 60ff.

75. Ibid., 67.

76. Ibid., 110. He cites K. Thomas, "The Relevance of Social Anthropology to the Historical Study of English Witchcraft," *Witchcraft Confessions and Accusations*, ed. M. Douglas (London: Tavistock, 1970), pp. 47–79.

77. Ibid., 111.

78. Ibid., 112.

79. Ibid.

80. Ibid., 112–23. He cites L. Dumont, *Homo Hierarchicus. The Caste System and Its Implications* (St. Albans: Paladin, 1972), p. 261.

81. Ibid., 113–35, 120–24, chap. 6 passim.

82. Ibid., 120–21.

83. Ibid., 145.

84. Compare the Laboratory of Human Cognition's earlier noted concern with psychology's culture-boundedness.

85. Hanson, *Meaning in Culture*, p. 61.

86. Ibid., 62; compare Ryle, *The Concept of Mind*, p. 54; Wittgenstein, *Philosophical Investigations*, I, secs. 269, 421, 559–592.

87. Hanson, *Meaning in Culture*, p. 63; A. F. C. Wallace, "Culture and Cognition," *Science* 135 (1962): 351–57; Wallace, *Culture and Personality*, 2d ed. (New York: Random House, 1970), pp. 29–36;

Goodenough, "Culture, Language, and Society," *McCaleb Module in Anthropology* (New York: Addison Wesley, 1971), p. 15.

88. Hanson, *Meaning in Culture*, pp. 21–22.

89. Ibid., 22–23.

90. Ibid., 51–52.

91. Ibid., 11–13, 19–22. Winch, *The Idea of a Social Science*, chaps. 4 and 5.

92. Crick, *Explorations in Language and Meaning* pp. 129–32.

93. Ibid., 147, chap. 8.

94. Ibid., 165.

95. Ibid.

96. Ibid., 167.

97. See my "Reproducing Social Reality: A Reply to Harrison," *Philosophy of the Social Sciences* 16 (1986): p. 98.

98. Ibid., 165.

99. Ibid., 164. In addition to the "reproductive fallacy" arguments I considered earlier, Rudner's "Essays at Objectivity" also criticizes efforts (not made explicitly by Winch) to apply Quinean indeterminacy to support Winch. Here Rudner emphasizes, as I have in connection with Goodenough, the value of distinguishing object- and metalanguage.

100. In this connection, see also Roth, Paul, "Resolving the *Rationalitätstreit*," *Archives Europeennes d'Sociologie*, vol. 26 (1985), pp. 142–67, which discusses in more detail the position I maintain here. Also, it is worth noting that while my translation thesis incorporates broader, decision-theoretic notions of rationality, these are attributed to manual users, not source-language speakers per se.

101. Indeed, I am not sure even elements of standard truth-functional logic must necessarily be attributed. It seems conceivable that we might find, on the basis of stimulus meaning, that subjects do not ascribe to the law of the excluded middle ("either p or not p"). It might be that though they have a logical particle '#' that yields affirmed sentences out of the pairs of sentences it connects, provided at least one of the paired sentences is affirmed; there are many pairs of sentences and their denials such that they withhold judgement from either. However, Quine does maintain that the law of noncontradiction cannot be violated. He argues that any string '*' that is correctly translated as 'not' must be such as to yield universal denial of conjunctions of P with *P; otherwise we have no business translating it as 'not', since it would evidently be a poor translation of that connective. To

attribute a willingness to self-contradiction, he argues, is simply to commit a flagrant and unacceptable violation of the principle of charity. See, for example, Quine, *Philosophy of Logic*, pp. 82–85; Quine, *Word and Object*, pp. 59–60. (Critics have noted tension between this and his views espoused in "Two Dogmas of Empiricism," that no belief is immune to revision in light of experience.) With respect to noncontradiction, Quine seems to be holding a position much like the intellectualist one of Martin Hollis, who sees the imputation of logic as a necessary "bridgehead" in the interpretation of other cultures—a synthetic *a priori* imposition on any coherently translatable thought system. But while Quine's views of noncontradiction have this flavor, his bridgehead is evidently narrower than Hollis'. See Hollis' "Reason and Ritual," reprinted in *The Philosophy of Social Explanation*, ed. Alan Ryan (Oxford: Oxford University Press, 1973), pp. 15–32. I am not sure where Crick stands on this issue. He notes similarities between Quine's and Hollis' "bridgehead" strategies, but does not comment on the difference in breadth of imposed logic (*Explorations in Language and Meaning*, p. 164).

102. Quine, "Responses," *Theories and Things*, p. 181.

103. Notably in this connection, a recent (1984) American Philosophical Association Presidential Address by Alasdair MacIntyre raises concerns that antirelativists too easily impose a particular conception of rationality that "makes more plausible than they ought to be those theories which identify every form of rationality with some form of contending power." ("Relativism, Power, and Philosophy," *Proceedings and Addresses of the American Philosophical Association*, vol. 59, no. 1 (1985), p. 19.)

104. Rules of scientific practice are not fully specifiable, as Kuhn and others have shown. My notion of codification fully accommodates this point, however, just as it accommodates similar Winchian-Wittgensteinian points to the effect that not all rules governing practices can be made specific or that "unreflective knowledge" underlies the behavior of a skilled practitioner.

105. See his *Languages of Art*, chap. 6; *Ways of Worldmaking*, chap. 7; *Of Mind and Other Matters*, chap. 1.

106. Goodman, *Of Mind and Other Matters*, p. 29.

107. Ibid., 43.

108. Goodman, *Ways of Worldmaking*, pp. 116ff.; *Of Mind and Other Matters*, pp. 39ff. Compare *The Structure of Appearance*, chap. 1; Donald Davidson, "On the Very Idea of a Conceptual Scheme."

109. Goodman, *Ways of Worldmaking*, pp. 4–5, 7, 119. Compare *Of Mind and Other Matters*, pp. 42–44. Earlier statements of his pluralism may be found in "The Way the World Is" and "The Revision of

Philosophy'' in his *Problems and Projects*. It is worth mentioning here that my characterizing translation as prescriptive and derivative hypotheses as descriptive is perfectly in keeping with Goodman's radical conventionalism. I don't say that translations are *really* prescriptive in form, but offer pragmatic philosophical reasons for this canonical form. Similarly, I don't maintain any rigid distinction between what Carnap once termed ''external'' or ''framework'' matters and ''internal'' theoretical matters. See Quine, ''On Carnap's Views on Ontology.'' Compare Goodman, *Ways of Worldmaking*, p. 114–20. Some sort of notion of framework and content is needed, if nothing else to capture the idea that several divergent theories can be stated in the same language, but it needn't involve all of Carnap's conditions (such as that claims about the framework are ''purely pragmatic'' when the framework is being considered for adoption, or analytic once it is in place).

110. Clifford Geertz, *Local Knowledge: Further Essays in Interpretive Anthropology* (New York: Basic Books, 1983), pp. 118–19, 151, 154–55; 180–81.

111. In this connection, compare Paul Roth's ''Pseudo-Problems in Social Science,'' [*Philosophy of the Social Sciences* 16 (1986): 59–82], which argues for methodological pluralism on similar grounds.

To forestall possible confusions, let me add here that readers should *not* take the prescriptive-descriptive contrast I have drawn as entailing that prescriptive interpretation is ''conventional'' and descriptive physics is not. While there may be important differences between the way I reason to cultural irrealism and the way Goodman might, so to argue would be to depart far more radically from Goodman than I intend. I believe that convention has ''constitutive'' import for *both* description and interpretation. My reasons for saying meaning and synonymy are not described have to do with the specific nature of the conventions involved, particularly with the fact that translation coordinates the conventional practices of diverse groups in a way that makes it hard to see how it could be viewed as describing one set of conventions by means of others.

Bibliography

Abraham, W., ed. *Ut Vidaeum: Contributions to An Understanding of Linguistics*. Atlantic Highlands, N.J.: Humanities Press, 1975.

Alston, William P. *Philosophy of Language*. Englewood Cliffs, N.J.: Prentice-Hall, 1964.

Austin, J. L. *How To Do Things With Words*. 2d ed. Cambridge, Mass.: Harvard University Press, 1975 [1962].

Ayer, A. J. *Language, Truth, and Logic*. New York: Dover, 1946.

Banton, Michael P., ed. *Anthropological Approaches to the Study of Religion*. London: Travistock, 1966.

Basso, Keith H. and Henry A. Selby, eds. *Meaning in Anthropology*. Albuquerque, N.M.: University of New Mexico Press, 1976.

Bateson, Mary C. "Linguistic Models in the Study of Joint Performance." *Linguistics and Anthropology*. Edited by M. Kinkade et al., pp. 53–66.

Bauman, Richard and Joel Sherzer. "The Ethnography of Speaking." *Annual Reviews* 4 (1975): pp. 95–119.

Bauman, R. and J. Sherzer, eds. *Explorations in the Ethnography of Speaking*. Cambridge: Cambridge University Press, 1974.

Berlin, Brent and Paul Kay. *Basic Color Terms: Their University and Evolution*. Berkeley: University of California Press, 1969.

Bierwisch, M. "Semantics." *New Horizons in Linguistics*. Edited by J. Lyons, pp. 161–85.

Bloomfield, Michael. *Language*. New York: Holt, Rinehart & Winston, 1948.

Blount, B. G. and M. Sanchez, eds. *Language, Thought, and Culture*. New York: Academic Press, 1977.

Boas, Franz. *Kwakiutl Ethnography*. Edited by Helen Codere. Chicago: University of Chicago Press, 1966.

Boas, F. "Linguistics and Ethnology." *Language in Culture and Society.* Edited by D. Hymes. pp. 15–39.

Brentano, Franz. "The Distinction Between Mental and Physical Phenomena," *Realism and the Background of Phenomenology.* Edited by R. M. Chilsolm. pp. 39–61.

Bresnan, Joan. "A Realistic Transformational Grammar." *Linguistic Theory and Psychological Reality.* Edited by M. Halle et al. pp. 1–59.

Bright, William. "Language." *International Encyclopedia of the Social Sciences.* Edited by L. Sills. pp. 18–24.

Bright, W., ed. *Sociolinguistics.* The Hague: Mouton, 1966.

Brislin, Richard W., ed. *Translation: Application and Research.* New York: John Wiley & Sons, 1976.

Brower, Reuben A. *On Translation.* New York: Oxford University Press, 1966 (1959).

Brown, Cecil H. "Psychological, Semantic, and Structural Aspects of American English Kinship Terms." *American Ethnologist* 1 (1974): pp. 415–36.

Brown, C. H. "Semantic Components, Meaning, and Use in Ethnosemantics." *Philosophy of Science.* 43, No. 3 (1976), pp. 378–95.

Brown, C. H. *Wittgensteinian Linguistics.* The Hague: Mouton, 1974.

Burling, Robbins. "Cognition and Componential Analysis: God's Truth or Hocus-Pocus?" *American Anthropologist.* 66, No. 1 (1964), pp. 20–28.

Burling, R. "Linguistics and Ethnographic Description." *American Anthropologist* 71 (1969): 817–27.

Campbell, D. T. "On the Conflicts Between Biological and Social Evolution and Between Psychology and Moral Tradition," *American Psychologist* 30 (1975): 1103–26.

Carnap, Rudolf. "Testability and Meaning." *Philosophy of Science* 3 (1936), pp. 420–468; 4 (1937), pp. 1–40.

Carnap, R. *Meaning and Necessity: A Study in Semantics and Modal Logic.* 2d ed. Chicago: University of Chicago Press, 1956.

Carnap, R. "Meaning and Synonymy in Natural Languages." *Meaning and Necessity.* 2d ed. app. D, pp. 233–44.

Cassirer, Ernst. *The Philosopy of Symbolic Forms.* Translated by R. Mannheim. Vol. 1 of *Language.* New Haven, Conn.: Yale University Press, 1953.

Caws, Peter. "The Ontology of Social Structure: A Reply to Hanson." *American Anthropologist* 78 (1976): pp. 325–27.

Caws, P. "Operational, Representational, and Explanatory Models." *American Anthropologist* 76 (1974): 1–10.

Caws, P. *Science and the Theory of Value*. New York: Random House, 1967.

Chomsky, Noam. *Aspects of the Theory of Syntax*. Cambridge, Mass: M.I.T. Press, 1965.

Chomsky, N. "Quine's Empirical Assumptions." *Words and Objections*. Edited by J. Hintikka and D. Davidson, pp. 53–68.

Chomsky, N. "Review of Skinner's *Verbal Behavior*." *Language*. 35, No. 1 (1959), pp. 26–58.

Chomsky, N. *Rules and Representations*. New York: Columbia University Press, 1980.

Chomsky, N. *Syntactic Structures*. The Hague: Mouton, 1957.

Chomsky, N. *Topics in the Theory of Generative Grammar*. The Hague: Mouton, 1966.

Chomsky, N. and Morris Halle. "Some Controversial Issues in Phonological Theory." *The Journal of Linguistics* 1 (1965): 97–135.

Church, Alonzo. "The Need for Abstract Entities in Semantic Analysis," *Proceedings of the American Academy of Arts and Sciences*. 80, No. 1 (1951), pp. 11–112.

Clark, Eve V. "What Should LAD Look Like? Some Comments on Levelt." Discussion paper for a colloquium on "The Role of Grammar in Interdisciplinary Linguistic Research." Bielefeld, Germany (December 1973).

Clark, Herbert H. and Eve V. Clark. *Psychology and Language: An Introduction to Psycholinguistics*. New York: Harcourt Brace Jovanovich, 1977.

Cochrane, Glynn. "Use of the Concept of the 'Corporation': A Choice Between Colloquialism and Distortion." *American Anthropologist* 73 (1971): 1144–50.

Cohen, R. S. et al., eds. *Essays in Memory of Imre Lakatos*. Dordrecht, Holland: Reidel, 1976.

Conklin, Harold C. "Hanunoo Color Terms." *Southwestern Journal of Anthropology*. 11, No. 4 (1955), pp. 339–44.

Conklin, H. "Lexicographical Treatment of Folk Taxonomies."

International Journal of American Linguistics. 28, No. 2, pt. 4 (1962), pp. 119–141.

Cook, V. J. "Is Explanatory Adequacy Adequate?" *Linguistics*. No. 133 (1974), pp. 21–31.

Craig, William. "The Replacement of Auxiliary Expressions." *The Philosophical Review*. 65, No. 1 (1956), pp. 38–55.

Crick, Malcolm. *Explorations in Language and Meaning*. New York: John Wiley & Sons, 1976.

Dallmayr, Fred R. and Thomas A. McCarthy, eds. *Understanding and Social Inquiry*. South Bend, Ind.: University of Notre Dame Press, 1977.

D'Andrade, Roy G. "Structure and Syntax in the Semantic Analysis of Kinship Terminologies." *Cognition*. Edited by P. Garvin, pp. 87–143.

Daniels, Norman. "Wide Reflective Equilibrium and Theory Acceptance in Ethics." *The Journal of Philosophy* 76 (May 1979): 256–81.

Davidson, Donald. "Belief and the Basis of Meaning." *Synthese* 27 (1974): pp. 309–23. Reprinted in *Inquiries into Truth and Interpretation*, pp. 141–54.

Davidson, D. *Inquiries into Truth and Interpretation*. Oxford: Clarendon Press, 1984.

Davidson, D. "On the Very Idea of a Conceptual Scheme." *Proceedings and Addresses of the American Philosophical Association* 67 (1973–1974): 5–20. Reprinted in *Inquiries into Truth and Interpretation*, 183–98.

Davidson, D. "Truth and Meaning." *Synthese* 17 (1967): 304–23. Reprinted in *Inquiries into Truth and Interpretation*, 17–36.

Davidson, D. and G. Harman, eds. *The Semantics of Natural Language*. Boston: Reidel, 1972.

Dennett, Daniel C. *Brainstorms: Philosophical Essays on Mind and Psychology*. Cambridge: M.I.T. Press, 1978.

De Saussure, Ferdinand. *Course in General Linguistics*. Translated by W. Baskin. New York: Philosophical Library, 1958 (1916).

Douglas, Mary. *Implicit Meanings: Essays in Anthropology*. London: Routledge and Kegan Paul, 1975.

Douglas, M. *Natural Symbols: Explorations in Cosmology*. 2d ed. London: Barrie and Jenkins, 1973.

Douglas, M. "Self-Evidence," *Implicit Meanings*. pp. 276–318.

Douglas, M. ed. *Witchcraft Confessions and Accusations.* London: Tavistock, 1970.

Drummond, Lee. "Structure and Process in the Interpretation of South American Myth: The Arawak Dog Spirit People." *American Anthropologist.* 79, No. 1 (1977), pp. 842–68.

Duhem, Pierre. *The Aim and Structure of Physical Theory.* New York: Atheneum, 1962 (1914).

Dummett, Michael. "Frege, Gottlob." *The Encyclopedia of Philosophy.* Edited by P. Edwards, 3 (1967) pp. 228–34.

Dumont, L. *Homo Hierarchicus. The Caste System and Its Implications.* St. Albans: Paladin, 1972.

Durbin, Mridula A. "Linguistic Models in Anthropology." *Annual Reviews* 1 (1972): pp. 383–410.

Edwards, Paul, ed. *The Encyclopedia of Philosophy.* 8 vols. New York: Macmillan, 1967.

Elgin, Catherine. *With Reference to Reference.* Indianapolis: Hackett, 1983.

Ember, Carol R. "Cross-Culture Cognitive Studies." *Annual Reviews* 6 (1977): pp. 35–56.

Evans, Gareth. "The Causal Theory of Names." *Proceedings of the Aristotelian Society* 47 (1973): 187–208.

Fabian, Johannes. "Taxonomy and Ideology: On the Boundaries of Concept Classification." *Linguistics and Anthropology.* Edited by M. Kinkade, pp. 183–97.

Feigl, Herbert G. *The "Mental" and the "Physical."* Minneapolis: University of Minnesota Press, 1958.

Feleppa, Robert. "Emics, Etics, and Social Objectivity." *Current Anthropology* 27 (1986): 243–55.

Feleppa, R. "Physicalism, Indeterminacy, and Interpretive Science." *Metaphilosophy* (forthcoming).

Feleppa, R. "Reproducing Social Reality: A Reply to Harrison." *Philosophy of the Social Sciences* 16 (1986): 89–99.

Feleppa, R. "Translation as Rule-Governed Behaviour." *Philosophy of the Social Sciences* 12 (1982): pp. 1–31.

Feyerabend, Paul K. "Consolations for the Specialist." *Criticism and the Growth of Knowledge.* Edited by I. Lakatos and A. Musgrave, pp. 197–230.

Field, Hartry. "Tarski's Theory of Truth." *The Journal of Philosophy* 64 (1972): pp. 347–75.

Firth, J. R. "On Sociological Linguistics." *Language in Culture and Society*. Edited by D. Hymes, pp. 66–70.

Fisher, L. E. and O. Werner. "Explaining Explanation: Tension in American Anthropology." *Journal of Anthropological Research* 34 (1978): 194–218.

Fodor, Jerry A. and Jerrold J. Katz, eds. *The Structure of Language: Readings in the Philosophy of Language*. Englewood Cliffs, N.J.: Prentice-Hall, 1964.

Follesdal, Dagfin. "Indeterminacy of Translation and Underdetermination of the Theory of Nature." *Dialectica* 27 (1973): 289–301.

Foster, Michael K. "When Words Become Deeds." *Explorations in the Ethnography of Speaking*. Edited by R. Bauman and J. Sherzer, pp. 354–67.

Frake, Charles O. "The Diagnosis of Disease Among the Subanun of Mindanao." *American Anthropologist*. 63, No. 1 (1961), pp. 113–32.

Frake, C. O. "The Ethnographic Study of Cognitive Systems." *Anthropology and Human Behavior*. Edited by T. H. Gladwin and W. C. Sturtevant, pp. 72–93.

Frake, C. O. "Plying Frames Can Be Dangerous: Some Reflections on Methodology in Cognitive Anthropology." *Quarterly Newsletter of the Institute for Comparative Human Development*. Rockefeller University. 1, No. 3 (1977) pp. 1–7.

Frege, Gottlob. "*Begriffsschrift*, I. Explanation of the Symbols." *Translations from the Philosophical Writings of Frege*. Edited by P. Geach and M. Black, pp. 1–20.

Frege, G. "On Sense and Reference." *Translations from the Philosophical Writings of Frege*. Edited by P. Geach and M. Black, pp. 56–78.

Friedman, Michael, "Physicalism and the Indeterminacy of Translation," *Nous* 9 (1975): 353–73.

Friedman, M. "Truth and Confirmation," *The Journal of Philosophy* 76 (1979): pp. 361–81.

Garvin, Paul, ed. *Cognition: A Multiple View*. New York: Macmillan, 1970.

Garvin, P. ed. *Method and Theory in Linguistics*. The Hague: Mouton, 1970.

Geach, Peter and Max Black, eds. and trans. *Translations from the Philosophical Writings of Gottlob Frege.* Oxford: Basil Blackwell, 1966.

Geertz, Clifford. "From the Native's Point of View: On the Nature of Anthropological Understanding." *Meaning in Anthropology.* Edited by K. Basso and H. Selby, pp. 221–37. Reprinted in *Local Knowledge*, pp. 55–72.

Geertz, C. *The Interpretation of Cultures.* New York: Basic Books, 1973.

Geertz, C. *Local Knowledge: Further Essays in Interpretive Anthropology.* New York: Basic Books, 1983.

Geoghegan, William H. *Natural Information Processing Rules: Formal Theory and Applications to Ethnography.* Monograph No. 3, Language-Behavior Research Laboratory, University of California, Berkeley, 1973.

George, Alexander. "Whence and Whither the Debate Between Quine and Chomsky?" *The Journal of Philosophy* 83 (1986): 481–99.

Gibson, Roger. *The Philosophy of W. V. Quine: An Expository Essay.* Tampa: University Presses of Florida, 1982.

Gibson, R. "Translation, Physics, and Facts of the Matter." *The Philosophy of W. V. Quine* Edited by L. E. Hahn, pp. 139–154.

Gladwin, Christina. "A Model of the Supply of Smoked Fish from Cape Coast to Kumasi." *Formal Methods in Economic Anthropology.* Edited by S. Plattner, pp. 77–127.

Gladwin, T. Hugh. *East is a Big Bird: Navigation and Logic on Puluwatt Atoll.* Cambridge, Mass.: Harvard University Press, 1970.

Gladwin, T. H. "Semantics, Schemata, and Kinship." Presented at the Mathematical Social Science Board of Advanced Research Seminar in Formal Analysis of Kinship, Riverside, Calif., 1972.

Gladwin, T. H. and W. C. Sturtevant, eds. *Anthropology and Human Behavior.* Washington, D.C.: Anthropological Society of Washington, 1962.

Goodenough, Ward H. "Componential Analysis and the Study of Meaning." *Language.* 33, No. 1 (1956), pp. 195–216.

Goodenough, W. "Cultural Anthropology and Linguistics." *Language in Culture and Society.* Edited by D. Hymes, pp. 36–39.

Goodenough, W. "Culture, Language, and Society." *McCaleb Module in Anthropology.* New York: Addison Wesley, 1971.

Goodenough, W. *Description and Comparison in Cultural Anthropology.* Chicago: Aldine, 1970.

Goodenough, W., ed. *Explorations in Cultural Anthropology.* New York: McGraw-Hill, 1964.

Goodenough, W. *Property, Kin, and Community on Truk.* New Haven, Conn.: Yale University Press, 1951.

Goodenough, W. "Residence Rules." *Southwestern Journal of Anthropology.* 12, No. 1 (1956), pp. 22–37.

Goodenough, W. "Reply to Cochrane." *American Anthropologist* 73 (1971): 1150–52.

Goodenough, W. "Some Applications of Guttman's Scale Analysis in Ethnography in Cultural Theory." *Southwestern Journal of Anthropology.* 19, No. 3 (1963), pp. 235–50.

Goodenough. W. "Yankee Kinship Terminology: A Problem in Componential Analysis." *Formal Semantic Analysis.* Edited by E. A. Hammel, pp. 259–87.

Goodman, Nelson. *Fact, Fiction, and Forecast.* 3d ed. Indianapolis: Bobbs-Merrill, 1973.

Goodman, N. *Languages of Art: An Approach to the Theory of Symbols.* Indianapolis: Bobbs-Merrill, 1968.

Goodman, N. *Of Mind and Other Matters.* Cambridge, Mass.: Harvard University Press, 1984.

Goodman, N. "On Likeness of Meaning." *Problems and Projects*, pp. 221–30.

Goodman, N. *Problems and Projects.* Indianapolis: Bobbs-Merrill, 1972.

Goodman, N. "The Revision of Philosophy." *Problems and Projects*, pp. 5–23.

Goodman, N. *The Structure of Appearance.* 3d. ed. Dordrecht: Reidel, 1977.

Goodman, N. "The Way the World Is." *Problems and Projects*, pp. 24–32.

Goodman, N. *Ways of Worldmaking.* Indianapolis: Hackett, 1978.

Greenberg, Joseph. *Anthropological Linguistics: An Introduction.* New York: Random House, 1968.

Greenberg, J. "Linguistics and Ethnology," *Language in Culture and Society.* Edited by D. Hymes. pp. 27–31.

Greenberg, J. "Some Universals of Grammar with Particular Reference to the Order of Meaningful Elements" *Universals of Language*, pp. 58–90.

Greenberg, J. ed. *Universals of Language*. Cambridge, Mass.: M.I.T. Press, 1963.

Grice, H. Paul. "Meaning." *The Philosophical Review*. 66, No. 3 (1977), pp. 377–88.

Grice, H. P. and P. F. Strawson. "In Defense of a Dogma." *The Philosophical Review* 65 (1956): 141–58.

Gumperz, John J. and D. H. Hymes, eds. *Direction in Sociolinguistics: The Ethnography of Communication*. New York: Holt, Rinehart & Winston, 1972.

Gunderson, Keith, ed. *Minnesota Studies in the Philosophy of Science*. 7. Minneapolis: University of Minnesota Press, 1975.

Guttenplan, Samuel, ed. *Mind and Language*. Oxford: Clarendon Press, 1975.

Hahn, Lewis E., ed. *The Philosophy of W. V. Quine*. LaSalle, Ill.: Open Court Press, 1987.

Hale, Kenneth. "Gaps in Grammar and Culture." *Linguistics and Anthropology*. Edited by M. D. Kinkade, et al., pp. 295–315.

Hale, K. "On the Use of Informants in Field Work." *Canadian Journal of Linguistics* 10 (1965): 108–19.

Halle, Morris, Joan Bresnan, and George A. Miller, eds. *Linguistic Theory and Psychological Reality*. Cambridge, Mass.: M.I.T. Press, 1978.

Hammel, Eugene A., ed. *Formal Semantic Analysis*. *American Anthropologist*. 67, No. 5 (1965).

Hammel, E. A. "A Transformational Analysis of Comanche Kinship Terminology." *Formal Semantic Analysis*, pp. 65–105.

Hanson, F. Allan. *Meaning in Culture*. London: Routledge and Kegan Paul, 1975.

Hanson, F. A. "Models and Social Reality: An Alternative to Caws." *American Anthropologist* 78 (1976): pp. 323–25.

Hanson, F. A. and Rex Martin. "The Problem of Other Cultures." *Philosophy of the Social Sciences* 3 (1973): 191–208.

Harman, Gilbert. "Three Levels of Meaning." *The Journal of Philosophy* 65 (1968): 590–602.

Harman, G. "An Introduction to 'Translation and Meaning': Chapter Two of Word and Object." *Words and Objections.* Edited by J. Hintikka and D. Davidson. pp. 14–26.

Harris, Marvin. *Cultural Materialism: The Struggle for a Science of Culture.* New York: Random House, 1979.

Harris, M. *Culture, People, and Nature.* 2d ed. New York: Crowell, 1975.

Harris, M. "History and Significance of the Emic-Etic Distinction." *Annual Reviews* 5 (1976): pp. 329–50.

Harris, M. *The Rise of Anthropological Theory.* New York: Crowell, 1968.

Hempel, Carl G. *Aspects of Scientific Explanation.* New York: The Free Press, 1965.

Hempel, C. G. "Empiricist Criteria of Cognitive Significance: Problems and Changes," *Aspects of Scientific Explanation,* pp. 99–122.

Hintikka, Jaakko and Donald Davidson, eds. *Words and Objections: Essays on the Work of W. V. Quine.* Dordrecht: Reidel, 1968.

Hockett, Charles F. *A Course in Modern Linguistics.* New York: Macmillan, 1958.

Hoijer, Harry. "Cultural Implications of Some Navajo Linguistic Categories." *Language.* 27, No. 2 (April-June 1951), pp. 111–120.

Hollis, Martin. "Reason and Ritual." *Philosophy of Social Explanation.* Edited by A. Ryan, pp. 33–49.

Hymes, Dell H. "Directions in (Ethno-) Linguistic Theory." *Transcultural Studies in Cognition.* Edited by A. K. Romney and R. G. D'Andrade, pp. 6–56.

Hymes, D. H. "The Ethnography of Speaking." *Anthropology and Human Behavior.* Edited by T. H. Gladwin and W. C. Sturtevant, pp. 13–53.

Hymes, D. H. *Foundations in Sociolinguistics: An Ethnographic Approach.* Philadelphia, Penn., University of Pennsylvania Press, 1974.

Hymes, D. H. *Language in Culture and Society: A Reader in Linguistics and Anthropology.* New York: Harper & Row, 1964.

Hymes, D. H. "Linguistic Method in Ethnography: Its Development in the United States." *Method and Theory in Linguistics.* Edited by P. Garvin. pp. 249–326.

Hymes, D. H. "Models of Interaction of Language and Social Life." *Directions in Sociolinguistics.* Edited by J. J. Gumperz and D. Humes, pp. 35–71.

Irvine, Judith T. "Strategies of Status Manipulation in Wolof Greeting." *Explorations in the Ethnography of Speaking.* Edited by R. Bauman and J. Sherzer, pp. 167–91.

Jacobs, R. S. and P. Rosenbaum, eds. *Readings in English Transformational Grammar.* Waltham, Mass.: Ginn and Co., 1970.

Jakobson, R., C. G. M. Fant, and L. M. Halle. *Preliminaries to Speech Analysis: The Distinctive Features and Their Correlates.* Acoustics Laboratory, M.I.T Technical Report 13. Cambridge, Mass. 1956.

Kaplan, David and Robert A. Manners. *Culture Theory.* Englewood Cliffs, N.J.: Prentice-Hall, 1972.

Katz, Jerrold J. *Language and Other Abstract Objects.* Totowa, N.J.: Rowan and Littlefield, 1979.

Katz, J. J. "Mentalism in Linguistics." *Language* 40 (1964): 124–37.

Katz, J. J. *Semantic Theory.* New York: Harper & Row, 1971.

Katz, J. J. *The Underlying Reality of Language and Its Philosophical Import.* New York: Harper & Row, 1971.

Katz, J. J. and J. A. Fodor. "The Structure of a Semantic Theory." in Fodor and Katz, *The Structure of Language*, pp. 479–518.

Kay, Paul. "Some Theoretical Implications of Ethnographic Semantics." *Current Directions in Anthropology, American Anthropological Association Bulletin.* 3, No. 3, Pt. 2 (1970), pp. 19–31.

Kearney, Michael. "World View Theory and Study." *Annual Reviews.* 4 (1975): 247–70.

Keesing, Roger. "Paradigms Lost: The New Ethnography and the New Linguistics." *Southwest Journal of Anthropology* 28 (Winter 1972): 229–332.

Kiefer, Christie. "Psychological Anthropology." *Annual Reviews* 6 (1977): 103–19.

Kinkade, M. Dale, Kenneth L. Hall, and Oswald Werner, eds. *Linguistics and Anthrpology: In Honor of C. F. Voegelin.* Lisse: DeRidder, 1975.

Krimmerman, Leonard I., ed. *The Nature and Scope of Social Science: A Critical Anthology.* New York: Appleton, 1969.

Kripke, Saul. *Naming and Necessity.* Cambridge, Mass.: Harvard University Press, 1980.

Kroeber, Alfred L. "Classificatory Systems of Relationship." *The Journal of the Royal Anthropological Institute of Great Britain and Ireland* 39 (1909): 77–84.

Kronenfeld, David and H. W. Decker. "Structuralism." *Annual Reviews* 8 (1979): pp. 503–41.

Laboratory of Comparative Human Cognition (Rockefeller University). "Cognition as a Residual Category in Anthropology." *Annual Reviews* 7 (1978): pp. 51–69.

Lakatos, Imre and Alan Musgrave, eds. *Criticism and the Growth of Knowledge*. Cambridge: Cambridge University Press, 1970.

Levelt, W. J. M. "Whatever Became of LAD?" *Ut Vidaeum*. Edited by W. Abraham, pp. 171–90.

Levi-Strauss, Claude. *The Elementary Structures of Kinship*. Revised edition translated by James Harle Bell and John Richard von Sturmer. Edited by Rodney Needham. London: Eyre and Spottiswoode, 1969 (1949).

Levi-Strauss, C. *The Raw and the Cooked: Introduction to a Science of Mythology*. Translated by J. and D. Weightman. New York: Harper & Row, 1969 (1964).

Levi-Strauss, C. *The Savage Mind*. Translator anonymous. Chicago: University of Chicago Press, 1966 (1962).

Levi-Strauss, C. *Structural Anthropology*. Translated by Claire Jacobson and Brook G. Schoepf. New York: Basic Books, 1963 (1958).

Levi-Strauss, C. *Tristes Tropiques*. Translated by J. and D. Weightman. New York: Atheneum, 1974 (1955).

Lewis, Clarence Irving. *An Analysis of Knowledge and Valuation*. LaSalle, Ill.: Open Court Press, 1946.

Lewis, David. *We the Navigators*. Honolulu: University of Hawaii Press, 1972.

Lewis, David K. *Convention: A Philosophic Study*. Cambridge, Mass.: Harvard University Press, 1969.

Lewis, D. K. "Languages and Language." *Minnesota Studies in the Philosophy of Science*. Edited by K. Gunderson. 7 (1975), pp. 3–35.

Linsky, Leonard, ed. *Semantics and the Philosophy of Language*. Urbana, Ill.: University of Illinois Press, 1952.

Lloyd, Barbara B. and Eleanor Rosch, eds. *Cognition and Categorization*. Hillsdale, N.J.: Eribaum, 1977.

Lounsbury, Floyd G. "A Formal Account of the Crow and Omaha-Type Kinship Terminologies." *Explorations in Culture Anthropology*. Edited by W. Goodenough, pp. 351–94.

Lounsbury, F. G. "A Semantic Analysis of Pawnee Kinship Usage." *Language*. 32, No. 1 (1956), pp. 158–94.

Lyons, John. *Introduction to Theoretical Linguistics*. Cambridge: Cambridge University Press, 1968.

Lyons, J., ed. *New Horizons in Linguistics*. Baltimore: Penguin Books, 1970.

MacIntyre, Alasdair. "Relativism, Power, and Philosophy." *Proceedings and Addresses of the American Philosophical Association*. 59, No. 1 (1985). pp. 5–21.

Mandelbaum, David G., ed. *Selected Writings of Edward Sapir in Language, Culture, and Personality*. Berkeley: University of California Press, 1949.

Mandelbaum, Maurice. "Societal Facts." *Philosophy of Social Explanation*. Edited by A. Ryan, pp. 105–18.

Maranda, Pierre. "Structuralism in Cultural Anthropology," *Annual Reviews* 1 (1972): 329–48.

Marano, Ron. "Windigo Psychosis: The Anatomy of an Emic-Etic Confusion." *Current Anthropology* 23 (1982): 385–412.

Miller, George A. and Phillip N. Johnson-Laird. *Language and Perception*. Cambridge: Harvard University Press, 1976.

Morris, Charles W. *Foundations of the Theory of Signs. International Encyclopedia of Unified Science*. 1, No. 2 Chicago: University of Chicago Press, 1938.

Morris, C. W. *Signification and Significance: A Study of the Relations of Signs and Values*. Cambridge, Mass.: M.I.T. Press, 1964.

Morris, C. W. *Signs, Language, and Behavior*. New York: Prentice-Hall, 1946.

Murdock, George P. *Social Structure*. New York: MacMillan 1949.

Naess, Arne. *Interpretation and Preciseness: A Contribution to the Theory of Communication*. Oslo: I Kommisjon Hos Jacob Dybwad, 1953.

Nagel, Ernest. *The Structure of Science*. New York: Harcourt Brace and World, 1961.

Naroll, R. and R. Cohen, eds. *A Handbook of Method in Cultural Anthropology*. Garden City, N.J.: American Museum of Natural History Press, 1970.

Naroll, R. and F. Naroll, eds. *Main Currents in Anthropology*. New York: Appleton Century Crofts, 1973.

Needham, Rodney. *Belief, Language, and Experience*. Oxford: Basil Black-well, 1972.

Nida, Eugene A. "Science of Translation." *Language*. 45, No. 3 (1969), pp. 483-98.

Nida, E. A. *Toward a Science of Translating*. Leiden: E. J. Brill, 1964.

Ogden, C. K. and I. A. Richards. *The Meaning of Meaning*. 5th ed. New York: Harcourt, Brace, and World.

Oliver, D. *A Solomon Island Society*. Cambridge: Harvard University Press, 1955.

Pike, Kenneth. *Language in Relation to a Unified Theory of the Structure of Human Behavior: Part I*. Glendale, Calif.: Summer Institute of Linguistics, 1954.

Pike, K. "Towards a Theory of the Structure of Human Behavior." *Language in Culture and Society*. Edited by D. Hymes, pp. 54-61.

Plattner, S., ed. *Formal Methods in Economic Anthropology*. Special Publication No. 4. Washington, D.C.: American Anthropological Association, 1975.

Platts, Mark, ed. *Reference, Truth and Reality: Essays on the Philosophy of Language*. London: Routledge and Kegan Paul, 1980.

Polanyi, Michael. *Personal Knowledge: Towards a Post-Critical Philosophy*. Chicago: University of Chicago Press, 1962.

Popper, Karl. *The Logic of Scientific Discovery*. New York: Basic Books, 1961.

Putnam, Hilary. "The Analytic and the Synthetic." *Mind, Language and Reality*, pp. 33-69.

Putnam, H. "How Not to Talk About Meaning." *Mind, Language and Reality*, pp. 117-31.

Putnam, H. "Is Semantics Possible?" *Mind, Language and Reallity*, pp. 139-52.

Putnam, H. "Meaning and Reference." *The Journal of Philosophy* 70 (1973): pp. 699-711.

Putnam, H. *Meaning and the Moral Sciences*. London: Routledge and Kegan Paul, 1978.

Putnam, H. "The Meaning of 'Meaning'." *Mind, Language and Reality*, pp. 215-71.

Putnam, H. *Mind, Language and Reality: Philosophical Papers, 2*. Cambridge: Cambridge University Press, 1975.

Putnam, H. "Realism and Reason." *Meaning and the Moral Sciences*, sec. 4, pp. 123–40.

Quine, Willard Van Orman. "Comments on Newton-Smith." *Analysis* 39 (1979): pp. 66–67.

Quine, W. "Empirical Content." *Theories and Things*, pp. 24–30.

Quine, W. "Epistemology Naturalized." *Ontological Relativity.*, pp. 69–90.

Quine, W. "Facts of the Matter." *Essays on the Philosophy of W. V. Quine.* Edited by R. Shahan and C. Swoyer, pp. 155–69.

Quine, W. "Five Milestones of Empiricism." *Theories and Things.* pp. 67–72.

Quine, W. *From a Logical Point of View.* 2d ed. revised. New York: Harper & Row, 1961.

Quine, W. "Goodman's Ways of Worldmaking." *Theories and Things.* pp. 96–99.

Quine, W. "Indeterminacy of Translation Again." *The Journal of Philosophy* 84 (1987): pp. 1–10.

Quine, W. "Linguistics and Philosophy." *The Ways of Paradox*, pp. 56–58.

Quine, W. "Logic and the Reification of Universals." *Logical Point of View*, pp. 122–29.

Quine, W. "Meaning and Translation." *On Translation.* Edited by R. Brower, pp. 148–72.

Quine, W. "Methodological Reflections on Current Linguistic Theory." *Semantics of Natural Language.* Edited by D. Davidson and G. Harman, pp. 442–54.

Quine, W. "Mind and Verbal Dispositions." *Mind and Language.* Edited by S. Guttenplan, pp. 83–96.

Quine, W. "On Carnap's Views on Ontology." *Ways of Paradox*, pp. 203–11.

Quine, W. "On Empirically Equivalent Systems of the World." *Erkenntnis* 9 (1975): 313–28.

Quine, W. "On the Nature of Natural Knowledge." *Mind and Language.* Edited by S. Guttenplan, pp. 67–82.

Quine, W. "On the Reasons for Indeterminacy of Translation." *The Journal of Philosophy* 67 (1970): 179–83.

Quine, W. "On the Very Idea of a Third Dogma." *Theories and Things*, pp. 38–42.

Quine, W. "Ontological Relativity." *Ontological Relativity*, pp. 26–68.

Quine, W. *Ontological Relativity and Other Essays*. New York: Columbia University Press, 1969.

Quine, W. "Ontology and Ideology Revisited." *The Journal of Philosophy* 80 (1983): 499–502.

Quine, W. "Philosophical Progress in Language Theory." *Metaphilosophy* 1 (1970): 2–19.

Quine, W. *Philosophy of Logic*. Englewood Cliffs, N.J. Prentice-Hall, 1970.

Quine, W. "The Problem of Meaning in Linguistics." *From a Logical Point of View*. pp. 47–64.

Quine, W. "Replies." *Words and Objections*. Edited by J. Hintikka and D. Davidson. pp. 292–319.

Quine, W. "Reply to Paul A. Roth." *The Philosophy of W. V. Quine*. Edited by L. Hahn. pp. 459–61.

Quine, W. "Reply to Roger F. Gibson, Jr.." *The Philosophy of W. V. Quine* Edited by L. Hahn. pp. 155–7.

Quine, W. "Responses." *Theories and Things*, pp. 175–86.

Quine, W. *The Roots of Reference*. LaSalle, Ill.: Open Court Press, 1973.

Quine, W. "The Scope and Language of Science." *Ways of Paradox*, pp. 228–45.

Quine, W. "Sellars on Behaviorism, Language, and Meaning." *Pacific Philosophic Quarterly* 8 (1980):

Quine, W. "States of Mind." *The Journal of Philosophy* 82 (1985): 5–8.

Quine, W. *Theories and Things*. Cambridge: Harvard University Press, 1981.

Quine, W. "Things and Their Place in Theories." *Theories and Things*, pp. 1–23.

Quine, W. "Truth by Convention." *Ways of Paradox*, pp. 77–106.

Quine, W. "Two Dogmas of Empiricism." *From a Logical Point of View*, pp. 20–47.

Quine, W. *The Ways of Paradox and Other Essays*. Revised and enlarged ed. Cambridge: Harvard University Press, 1976.

Quine, W. "Whither Physical Objects?" *Essays in Memory of Imre Lakatos*. Edited by R. S. Cohen et al., pp. 497–504.

Quine, W. *Word and Object*. Cambridge, Mass.: M.I.T. Press, 1960.

Quine, W. and J. Ullian. *The Web of Belief*. 2d ed. New York: Random House, 1978.

Quinn, Naomi. "Do Mfantse Fish Sellers Estimate Probabilities in Their Heads?" *American Ethnologist*. 5, No. 2 (1978), pp. 206–26.

Ramsey, Frank P. *The Foundations of Mathematics*. Edited by R. B. Braithwaite. New York: Humanities Press, 1931.

Rawls, John. *A Theory of Justice*. Cambridge, Mass.: Harvard University Press, 1971.

Romney, A. Kimball and R. G. D'Andrade. "Cognitive Aspects of English Kin Terms." *Transcultural Studies in Cognition*, pp. 146–70.

Romney, A. K. and R. G. D'Andrade. *Transcultural Studies in Cognition*. *American Anthropologist*. 66, No. 3, Pt. 2. Special publication (June 1964).

Rorty, Richard. *Consequences of Pragmatism (Essays: 1972–1980)*. Minneapolis: University of Minnesota Press, 1982.

Rorty, R. "Indeterminacy of Translation and of Truth." *Syntheses* 23 (1972): 443–62.

Rorty, R. "Method, Social Science, and Social Hope." *Consequences of Pragmatism*, pp. 191–210.

Rosch, Eleanor. "Cognitive Representations of Semantic Categories." *The Journal of Experimental Psychology: General*. 104, No. 3 (1975), pp. 192–233.

Rosch, E. "Principles of Categorization." *Cognition and Categorization*. Edited by B. Lloyd and E. Rosch, pp. 28–48.

Ross, J. R. "On Declarative Sentences." *Readings in English Transformational Grammar*. Edited by R. S. Jacobs and P. Rosenbaum. pp. 222–72.

Roth, Paul A. "Paradox and Indeterminacy." *The Journal of Philosophy* 75 (1978): 347–67.

Roth, P. "Pseudo-Problems in Social Science." *Philosophy of the Social Sciences*. 16 (1986): 59–82.

Roth, P. "Resolving the *Rationalitätstreit*." *Archives Europeennes d' Sociologie* 26: 142–57.

Roth, P. "Semantics Without Foundations." *The Philosophy of W. V. Quine*. Edited by L. Hahn, pp. 433–58.

Rudner, Richard S. "Goodman, Nelson." *The Encyclopedia of Philosophy*. Edited by P. Edwards. 3, (1967) pp. 370–74.

Rudner, R. *Philosophy of Social Science*. Englewood Cliffs, N.J.: Prentice-Hall, 1966.

Rudner, R. "On Semiotic Aesthetics." *The Journal of Aesthetics and Art Criticism*. 10, No. 1 (September 1951), pp. 67–77.

Rudner, R. "The Scientist *qua* Scientist Makes Value Judgements." *Philosophy of Science*. 20, No. 1 (1953), pp. 1–6.

Rudner, R. "Show or Tell: Incoherence Among Symbol Systems." *Erkenntnis* 12 (1978): pp. 129–51.

Rudner, R. "Some Problems of Non-Semiotic Aesthetic Theories." *The Journal of Aesthetics and Art Criticism* 15 (March 1957): pp. 298–310.

Rudner, R. "Some Essays at Objectivity." *Philosophical Exchange* 1 (1973): 115–35.

Russell, Bertrand. *An Inquiry into Meaning and Truth*. New York: Norton, 1940.

Russell, B. "On Denoting." *Mind* 14 (1950): pp. 479–93.

Russell, B. "The Philosophy of Logical Atomism," *The Monist* 28 (1918): 495–527; 29 (1919): 32–63, 190–220, 345–80.

Ryan, Alan, ed. *The Philosophy of Social Explanation*. Oxford: Oxford University Press, 1973.

Ryle, Gilbert, *The Concept of Mind*. London: Hutchinson, 1949.

Samarin, W. J. "Theory of Order with Disorderly Data." *Linguistics and Anthropology*, Edited by M. Kinkade et al., pp. 509–19.

Sanches, Mary. "Language Acquisition and Language Change: Japanese and Numerical Classifiers." *Language, Thought, and Culture*. Edited by B. G. Blount and M. Sanches. pp. 51–62.

Sapir, Edward. "Conceptual Categories in Primitive Languages." *Language in Culture and Society*. Edited by D. H. Hymes. p. 128.

Sapir, E. "The Grammarian and His Language." *Selected Writings of Edward Sapir*. Edited by D. G. Mandelbaum. pp. 150–59.

Sapir, E. *Language*. New York: Harcourt Brace and World, 1921.

Sapir, E. "Language and Environment." *Selected Writings of Edward Sapir*. Edited by D. G. Mandelbaum. pp. 160–66.

Scheffler, Harold W. "Kinship Semantics." *Annual Reviews* 1 (1972): pp. 309–28.

Scheffler, H. W. and F. G. Lounsbury. *A Study in Structural Semantics: The Siriono Kinship System.* Englewood Cliffs, N.J.: Prentice-Hall, 1971.

Scheffler, Israel. *The Anatomy of Inquiry.* Indianapolis, In.: Bobbs-Merrill, 1963.

Schlesinger, I. M. "A Note on the Relationship Between Psychological and Linguistic Theories." *Foundations of Language.* No. 4 (1967), pp. 397–402.

Schneider, David M. "Componential Analysis: A State-of-the-Art Review." *Symposium on Cognitive Studies and Artificial Intelligence Research.* March 2–8, 1969. University of Chicago Center for Continuing Education.

Schuldenfrei, Richard. "Quine in Perspective." *The Journal of Philosophy* 69 (1972): 5–16.

Schutz, Noel W. "On the Anatomy and Comparability of Linquistic and Ethnographic Description: Toward a Generative Theory of Ethnography." *Linguistics and Anthropology.* Edited by M. Kinkade et al., pp. 531–96.

Schwayder, David S. *The Stratification of Behavior: A System of Definitions Definitions Propounded and Defended.* London: Routledge and Kegan Paul, 1975.

Searle, John. *Speech Acts.* Cambridge: Cambridge University Press, 1969.

Shahan, Robert W. and Chris Swoyer, eds. *Essays on the Philosophy of W. V. Quine.* Norman: University of Oklahoma Press, 1979.

Siegel, B. J., A. R. Beals, and S. A. Tyler, eds. *Annual Review of Anthropology.* 10 vols. Palo Alto, Calif: Annual Reviews, Inc., 1972–1981.

Sills, L. ed. *International Encyclopedia of the Social Sciences.* New York: Macmillan, 1968.

Soles, Deborah. "On the Indeterminacy of Action." *Philosophy of the Social Sciences,* 14 (1984), pp. 457–88.

Spiro, Melford. "Religion: Problems of Definition and Explanation." *Anthropological Approaches to the Study of Religion.* Edited by M. Banton, pp. 85–126.

Spier, L., A. I. Hallowell, and S. S. Newman, eds. *Language, Culture, and Personality: Essays in Memory of Edward Sapir.* Menasha: Banta, 1941.

Skinner, B. F. *Verbal Behavior*. New York: Appleton Century Crofts, 1957.

Stitch, Stephen P. and R. E. Nisbett. "Justification and the Psychology of Human Reassoning." *Philosophy of Science* 47, (1980): 188–202.

Sturtevant, William C. "Studies in Ethnoscience." *Transcultural Studies in Cognition*. Edited by A. K. Romney and R. G. D'Andrade, pp. 99–131.

Tarski, Alfred. "The Semantic Conception of Truth." *Philosophy and Phenomenological Research* 4 (1944): pp. 341–75.

Thomas, K. "The Relevance of Social Anthropology to the Historical Study of English Witchcraft." *Witchcraft Confessions and Accusations*. Edited by M. Douglas, pp. 47–79.

Triandis, Harry C. "Approaches Toward Minimizing Translation." *Translation*. Edited by R. W. Brislin, pp. 229–44.

Turner, Victor. "Symbolic Studies." *Annual Reviews* 4 (1975): pp. 145–61.

Tyler, Stephen, ed. *Cognitive Anthropology*. New York: Holt Rinehart & Winston, 1969.

Wallace, Anthony F. C. "Culture and Cognition." *Science* 135 (1962): 351–57.

Wallace, A. *Culture and Personality*. 2d ed. New York: Random House, 1970.

Wallace, A. "The Problem of the Psychological Validity of Componential Analysis." *Formal Semantic Analysis*. Edited by E. A. Hammel, pp. 229–48.

Wallace, A. "A Relational Analysis of American Kinship Terminology: An Example of Relations Between Process and Structure in Cognition." *Cognition*. Edited by P. Garvin, pp. 145–53.

Watson, L. C. "'Etic' and 'Emic' Perspectives on Guajiro Urbanization." *Urban Life* 9 (1981): pp. 441–68.

Werner, Oswald. "Culture Knowledge, Language, and World View." *Cognition: A Multiple View*. Edited by P. Garvin, pp. 153–76.

Werner, O. "Ethnoscience 1972," *Annual Reviews* 1 (1972): pp. 271–308.

Werner, O. and D. T. Campbell. "Translating, Working Through Interpreters, and the Problem of Decentering." *Handbook of Method in Cultural Anthropology*. Edited by R. Naroll and R. Cohen, pp. 298–420.

Werner, O. and Joan Fenton. "Method and Theory in Ethnoscience or

Ethno–Epistemology." *Handbook of Method in Cultural Anthropology.* Edited by R. Naroll and R. Cohen, pp. 537–78.

White, Morton. "The Analytic and the Synthetic: An Untenable Dualism." *Semantics and the Philosophy of Language.* Edited by L. Linsky, pp. 272–86.

White, M. *Toward Reunion in Philosophy.* New York: Atheneum, 1963.

Whorf, Benjamin Lee. "The Relation of Habitual Thought and Behavior to Language." *Language, Culture, and Personality.* Edited by L. Spier et al., pp. 75–93.

Wilson, Bryan R., ed. *Rationality.* New York: Harper & Row, 1970.

Winch, Peter. *The Idea of a Social Science and Its Relation to Philosophy.* New York: Humanities Press, 1967.

Wittgenstein, Ludwig. *The Blue and Brown Books.* Oxford: Basil Blackwell, 1958.

Wittgenstein, L. *Remarks on Frazer's Golden Bough.* Translated by A. C. Miles and edited by Rush Rhees. Atlantic Highlands, N.J.: Humanities Press. 1979.

Wittgenstein, L. *Philosophical Investigations.* Oxford: Basil Blackwell, 1953.

Wittkowski, S. R. and C. H. Brown. "Lexical Universals." *Annual Reviews* 7 (1978): pp. 427–51.

Wong, I. F. H. "Field Procedures in Generative Grammar." *Anthropological Linguistics.* 17, No. 2 (February 1975), pp. 43–52.

Index

311